T

BIBLE

SELECTIONS FROM THE

Old and New Testaments

EDITED WITH AN INTRODUCTION

BY ALLAN G.

Holt, Rinehart and Winston

NEW YORK • CHICAGO • SAN FRANCISCO
TORONTO • LONDON

Fifteenth Printing, May, 1965

Introduction and Notes
Copyright, 1952, by Allan G. Chester
Typography by Stefan Salter
Printed in the United States of America
Library of Congress Catalog Card Number: 52-5606

21387-0112

Introduction

The primary values of the Bible, it is generally agreed, are spiritual. "In the beginning God created the heaven and the earth"—"For he shall give his angels charge over thee, to keep thee in all thy ways"—"And the Word was made flesh, and dwelt among us." It is for affirmations and insights such as these that the Bible has been read and will always be read by Jew and Christian, and by many others, neither Jew nor Christian, who cherish its truths while declining or rejecting its doctrines. It is significant, however, that many of the books of the Bible are important not only as religious documents but also as works of literature. They may be read and studied for their literary values, just as *The Divine Comedy* and *Hamlet* and *Paradise Lost* are read and studied. They are a part of world literature and, in their English translation, of English literature. In this respect the sacred books of Israel and of Christianity are unique. The writings of no other religion, either in the original tongues or in translation, have a comparable literary distinction.

The present volume of selections has been prepared primarily for those who wish to consider the Bible as literature. For such readers a book of selections has value. At present, when for various reasons familiarity with the Bible among English-speaking peoples is less than it has been at any other time in the past four centuries, the average reader scarcely knows where or how to begin. He is confronted with a volume of more than a thousand pages printed in double columns and bound forbiddingly in black cloth or imitation leather. More often than not he begins with the first page of Genesis and bogs down at Genesis 4: 18, where he reads, "And unto Enoch was born Irad:

and Irad begat Mehujael: and Mehujael begat Methusael: and Methusael begat Lamech." If he persists through the noble account, in Exodus 20, of the giving of the Commandments at Sinai, only dogged determination will take him through the details of the Levitical law which follow. Such an introduction to the reading of the Bible is likely to prove disastrous. A book of selections may help the reader to avoid such pitfalls. It would be an impertinence to call such a book the "best" of the Bible. But it can serve as a kind of guide to those portions which are of universal significance.

In arranging the selections from the Old Testament we have followed the late but convenient classification of the thirty-nine books into four categories—the Law (or, as it is commonly called in Christian tradition, the Pentateuch), the Former Prophets (that is, the books of monarchic history), the Later Prophets, and the Writings. This is not the order of our familiar Bibles, nor is it the order of composition, since some of the books of the "later" prophets were the earliest to assume their present form. It has the merit, however, of retaining, from the conventional arrangement, the narrative continuity which carries the chronology from the legendary materials of the opening chapters of Genesis through the stories of the patriarchs and of Joseph, the sojourn in Egypt, the flight under the brilliant leadership of Moses, the invasion of Canaan under Joshua, the period of the Judges, and the rise, decline, and fall of the monarchy. This arrangement has the additional merit of placing the utterances of the prophets where they logically belong, immediately after the historical books, and of bringing together those "Writings" which in Jewish tradition are regarded as belonging to a category distinctly different from "the Law and the Prophets."

The selections from these books do not represent the uncontrolled whimsy of the editor. His tentative table of contents was submitted to a number of experts whose suggestions and admonitions have been of the greatest value; as far as is possible within the limitations of space, their advice has been followed except in a few cases where it came into conflict with the convictions of the editor, who of course assumes final responsibility.

The selections from the Pentateuch are principally narrative. The stories of the Creation, the Fall, the Flood, of the patriarchs, of Joseph and Moses—that these narratives from Genesis and Exodus should be well represented there could be no doubt. They belong to the literature of the world. To be unfamiliar with them is not only to miss a significant body of story; it is also to miss a wealth of reference and allusion in the literature of the West, and especially in the literature of England. On the other hand, the legal and ritualistic materials of the latter part of Exodus and of Leviticus and Numbers are not represented at all, nor is there any need to justify the omission. Deuteronomy is represented by the last "song" of Moses, which perhaps may serve to illustrate the exalted ethical tone of the whole book, and by the account of the death and burial of Moses, which brings the narrative of the Pentateuch to a beautiful, quiet close.

In the selections from the historical books, Joshua is represented by three narratives from the early part of the book, including the story of the fall of Jericho. The latter part of Joshua, valuable as it is to the historian and the archaeologist, is confusing to the general reader, with its multiplicity of detail and its not always consistent accounts of the conquest of Canaan. Judges, rich in splendid stories of the heroes ("judges") of what has been called the "dark ages" of Israel's history, presents an embarrassment; Gideon, Jephtha, and Jael, that lion-hearted daughter of Israel who drove the tent-stake through the head of the sleeping Sisera, are absent merely because they had to give place to Samson, whose story underlies *Samson Agonistes*. The books of Samuel and the Kings are represented by fairly full selections from the history of Samuel himself, from the masterful biographies of Saul and David, and from the story of Solomon, whom the Bible itself treats with disappointing brevity. The narratives of the kings who succeeded Solomon, important as they are historically, are too complex for inclusion in a short book of selections. But the political, moral, and religious decline which marked the history of the divided kingdom is illustrated by a selection from the Elijah-Elisha narratives, and these may serve also to effect a transition to the selections from the writing prophets.

The decision to limit the selections from the prophetical books to the major prophets (except for Jonah, which is included because it is a good short story) should by no means be taken to mean that the "minor" prophets are minor in any respect except their comparative brevity. But except for a passage here and there (like Micah's fine "and what doth the Lord require of thee, but to do justly, and to love mercy, and to walk humbly with thy God") the minor prophets require considerable explication in terms of local conditions and of political and religious history. So indeed do the major prophets, and the selections from them have been chosen not only with a view to illustrating their leading ideas and the tone of their work, but also with the hope that the passages will be self-sustaining and require a minimum of explication. The inclusion of so many passages of Messianic prophecy from Isaiah and Deutero-Isaiah is intended to illustrate the particular value which attaches to the prophets in the Christian tradition. The hortatory and denunciatory passages from Jeremiah and Ezekiel will perhaps sufficiently indicate the more characteristic function of the prophets as God's spokesmen to His people.

Little need be said of the selections from the "Writings." The selection from the Psalms especially represents the collective judgment of the editor and his consultants. Every lover of the Psalms will miss one or more of his favorites, but it is hoped that those which are included are representative of the collection as a whole. It has been necessary to treat Daniel, the Song of Solomon, Proverbs, and Ecclesiastes somewhat summarily. Enough of Job is given, however, to illustrate the plan of the book and to suggest the principal ideas which it brings to bear upon the problem of suffering. Fortunately, it has been possible to include Ruth, the most charming book of the Bible, in its entirety.

In planning the selections from the New Testament, the editor and the publisher were agreed that it was desirable to include one complete gospel. Here especially the choice was difficult to make. The Gospel according to St. Mark was decided upon for two reasons apart from its brevity. In the first place, all scholars agree that it is the earliest of the Gospels, and most of them agree that it is based upon the firsthand recollection of Peter (for whom, in his latter days, John Mark served as companion, secretary, and interpreter) and that it served as the primary source for the writers of the other two synoptic gospels. Mark thus is entitled to primacy among the Gospels, not only chronologically but also from the nature of the materials upon which it rests. In the second place, it is widely felt by modern authorities that Mark's directness of expression and the dramatic power of his narrative are deserving of more attention than literary critics of the past were inclined to give them. The other gospels, however, are represented with sufficient fullness to include those major narrative details which are not to be found in Mark and to illustrate those matters of tone and emphasis which give them their distinctive place in the fourfold Gospel. Although some repetition is involved, Luke's account of the trial, the crucifixion, and the resurrection of Jesus is given so that a comparison with the corresponding passages in Mark can be made. Luke is also represented by several selections from the Acts of the Apostles, which is generally regarded as volume two of Luke's book.

It also seemed desirable to include the whole of one of Paul's epistles. Here it was important to choose one of the shorter epistles, not only because of the necessarily limited size of the present volume, but also because Paul's style rises and falls as he is being the mystic, the theologian, the preacher, or the autobiographer, and it is difficult for the inexperienced reader to attend to him at all his levels. The First Epistle to the Thessalonians has therefore been chosen because it is short, because it is the earliest of Paul's writings, and because it is characteristic of many of Paul's facets—for example, his use of autobiographical detail, his concern for a struggling church which he had helped to found, his insistence upon the obligations of Christians, his belief in Christ's return. From Romans and 1 Corinthians have been selected a number of passages which amplify Paul's ideas and which represent him at his literary best.

The selections from Hebrews, James, and 1 John were made because of their intrinsic value, and also because they will enable the reader to make some comparison, however slight, with the thought and style of Paul.

Finally, a word about the selections from the Revelation of St. John the Divine. Here, even more than with Old Testament prophecy, the problem of interpretation is important; whether the book be regarded as predictive or historical, it still demands, in most of its parts, a kind of detailed explication which lies beyond the scope and purpose of this volume. Accordingly, the selections have been limited to the messages to the seven churches and to two other passages in which the remarkable imagery and the general symbolism may be comprehended without reference to a multiplicity of footnotes.

The English Versions of the Bible

The need for translations of the Old and New Testaments was felt even before the canons were established. Thus about 300 B.C. a translation of the Pentateuch into a variant form of Hebrew was prepared for the people of Samaria. During the next two centuries the whole of the Old Testament was translated into Greek for the use of the Greek-speaking Jews of the Diaspora. This version, called the Septuagint from the tradition that it was the work of seventy scholars, is invaluable to textual students for purposes of comparison with the Hebrew original. For western Europe in the early centuries of the Christian era, the translations into Latin are the most significant. The Old-Latin versions were followed by the great work of St. Jerome at the end of the fourth century. Under the name of the Vulgate, the Latin version for which Jerome was chiefly responsible became the Bible of the western Church of the Middle Ages; with some revisions, it is the official Bible of the Roman Catholic Church to the present day.

In the task of translating the Bible into the vernaculars of western Europe, England played a conspicuous part. The

Gospels, the Psalter, and the Hexateuch (Pentateuch + Joshua) were all translated into Anglo-Saxon, primarily for the use of the clergy who had small Latin. For a period after the Norman Conquest, no new translations were made, but in the thirteenth and fourteenth centuries translations and paraphrases of the Gospels, the Psalter, and other portions of Scripture occur with increasing frequency. Some of the later of these were the outgrowth of the teachings of John Wyclif, the great fourteenth-century reformer who taught, among other things, that the Scriptures were sufficient in matters of faith, and that both priest and layman should have the opportunity to study them. The culmination of this teaching was the first complete Bible in English—the Wycliffite version of the late fourteenth century. Wyclif's own share in the actual work of making this translation is by no means certain, and the term "Lollard Bible" (from the name applied to Wyclif's followers) is perhaps the safest designation for it. A revision was completed about 1400, and this version maintained its popularity well into the sixteenth century. In 1408, a Provincial Council held at Oxford and presided over by Archbishop Arundel formally denounced the Lollard Bible as heretical and forbade the making of any new translations without the approval of a bishop. Since no bishop was willing to give such approval, the prohibition was virtually a ban upon the English Bible.

The English Bible as most of us know it today is basically a product of the sixteenth century. The Reformation, spreading rapidly from Germany in the 1520's and 1530's, insisted upon the exclusive authority of the Bible in matters of faith and doctrine. The development of the printing press led to a rapid increase in literacy among people in general, which in turn increased the demand for the Bible in English. Meanwhile, the availability of better texts of the Scriptures in the original tongues (Erasmus' edition of the Greek New Testament is the outstanding example) permitted preparation of new translations in keeping with the spirit of the age and in language more familiar than that of the Lollard Bible. The resultant of these forces was the tradition of the English Bible which begins with Tyndale's

New Testament of 1525 and culminates in the Authorized, or King James, Version of 1611.

William Tyndale, more than any other one man, is responsible for the style and tone of the English Bible as it is known to most Protestant Christians. He was born about 1495, and as a student at Oxford and later at Cambridge he was strongly influenced by the Biblical scholarship of Erasmus and the reforming zeal of Luther. He acquired a mastery of Greek; by 1523 he had resolved to dedicate himself to the task of translating the New Testament. Legally, he could not do so in England without the approval of a bishop. Failing to secure such approval, he went in 1524 to Germany, and the first edition of his work was published at Cologne in 1525. No complete copy of this edition survives. However, a new printing was completed at Worms in 1526. Copies were smuggled into England in considerable numbers, despite the efforts of the authorities to suppress the work. During the years which followed, Tyndale made frequent revisions of his New Testament, and courageously embarked upon the work of translating the Old. He had completed the translation of the Pentateuch, Jonah, and some other parts of the Old Testament before his condemnation for heresy and his execution at Vilvorde in 1535.

It is impossible in a short space to do justice to the qualities of Tyndale's prose and its seminal importance to his successors. His translation is vigorous and idiomatic, in many respects unliterary, but at the same time rhythmical and cadenced. It is the very foundation of what is sometimes called "Bible English." A comparison of almost any passage from Tyndale with the corresponding passage from later translations will reveal the extent and the quality of his influence. As to the accuracy of his translation, the Tyndale New Testament was challenged at certain critical points by no less a person than Thomas More, and it is perfectly true that occasionally Tyndale allowed his doctrine to get the better of his scholarship. In general, however, and in view of the limitations of his day, Tyndale's translations fare remarkably well before the court of modern criticism.

Tyndale's spiritual and literary heir was Miles Coverdale.

In 1535, Coverdale published (in Germany, since the Oxford prohibition was still in effect) the first complete *printed* English Bible. In 1537 a folio edition was published in Southwark; this has the distinction of being the first complete English Bible to be printed *in England*. Coverdale's linguistic equipment was inferior to Tyndale's, and on the title page of his first edition he frankly announced that his work was "faithfully and truly translated out of Dutch [German] and Latin into English." Coverdale's prose style is very similar to that of Tyndale; in some respects it is smoother. His translation of the Psalms has achieved a kind of immortality in the Psalter of the Anglican *Book of Common Prayer*.

In 1537 Henry VIII, as Supreme Head of the English Church, was persuaded to assent to publication of an English Bible. The more Protestant of the English bishops had been working toward this end since 1530; their success was the result of Henry VIII's final break with Rome and the temporary triumph of a Protestant spirit in the English Church. In this same year, 1537, was printed the first English Bible to be published with royal approval. This was the so-called Matthew Bible, "Matthew" being the pseudonym of John Rogers, who prepared it for the press. Actually, the Matthew Bible is a composite: it consists of Tyndale's Pentateuch and New Testament, Coverdale's translation of the books from Ezra through Malachi and of the Apocrypha, and a hitherto unprinted translation of the books from Joshua through 2 Chronicles. This latter is now generally regarded as being also the work of Tyndale. In 1539 appeared the Great Bible, which was a revision under the direction of Coverdale of the Matthew Bible. This also was an official Bible; between 1539 and 1541 it went through several editions and was subjected to some revision. In 1539 also an independent revision of the Matthew Bible was made by Thomas Taverner, a layman.

The period from 1540 until the death of Henry VIII in 1547 is often referred to as the period of Catholic reaction; significantly, no new translations of Scripture were made, and there were few reprintings of the older translations. During the reign of Edward VI, printing of Bibles was resumed, but the work of translation remained in abeyance. In the reign of the Catholic Queen Mary, however, came one of the most significant of the English Bibles. At Geneva, under the influence of Calvin and Beza, a group of Protestant English exiles began the preparation of an entirely new translation. This is the version known as the Geneva Bible; the New Testament was published in 1557, the whole Bible in 1560, after the accession of Elizabeth. The Geneva Bible, with its markedly Protestant tone, became the Puritans' Bible; with the spread of Puritanism and the increasing antagonism toward the episcopal establishment, it became the most popular English Bible. In 1568, the bishops under the leadership of Archbishop Matthew Parker attempted to counteract the popularity of the Geneva Bible by publishing the Bishops' Bible, a further revision of the Great Bible. Until the end of the century, the official Bible of the Bishops competed unsuccessfully with the Geneva Bible for popular favor.

The story of Biblical translation within the limits of the sixteenth century comes to an end with the publication at Rheims in 1582 of the Roman Catholic translation of the New Testament. Although this was translated from the Vulgate and is highly Latinical in style, some of its renderings were incorporated into the King James revision. The Roman Catholic translation of the Old Testament, published at Douai in 1610, was not available to the King James translators before their work went to press.

In January, 1604, the recently crowned King James I convened a conference of churchmen at Hampton Court. The king's hope that this conference would resolve the differences between the Puritans and the episcopacy was but one of James' numerous follies. But since the so-called King James Bible was its glorious by-product, the Hampton Court Conference cannot be said to have convened in vain. The suggestion of Dr. John Reynolds that a revision of the Bishops' Bible be made aroused little enthusiasm in the Bishops, who were satisfied with the Bishops' Bible, and even less in the extreme Puritans, who were more than satisfied with the success of the Geneva. But Dr. Reynolds' motion caught the attention of King James, who fancied himself as a scholar and a theologian. Through the king's enthusiasm the project was set in train, six committees or "companies" of nine men each were appointed (two from Oxford, two from Cambridge, and two from Westminster), and to these was entrusted the work of making the revision. Since King James contributed little beyond his initial enthusiasm, it is unfortunate that the completed work is popularly associated with his name.

The task assigned to the six committees was not that of making a new translation, but rather that of revising the Bishops' Bible. We know the names of some fifty of the fifty-four men who were appointed to the project. In general, they were the most learned Biblical scholars in the England of their day. It is not now possible to determine the extent or the quality of the contribution of any single one of them. Their aptitudes varied, as did their zeal and industriousness. Fortunately, the rules set up for their guidance have been preserved, and these, together with the "Address to the Reader" prefixed to the completed work, reveal much of their goal and method. They worked from the best available texts in the original languages; they compared each proposed revision with the other English versions and with the Latin or the German or any other relevant authority; and they conferred constantly together.

The amazing result was what the late Professor John Livingstone Lowes called "the noblest monument of English prose." Few readers would dissent from that verdict. In the last analysis, the nobility of the prose must be attributed to the King James translators. Tyndale first, and then his successors, had set the stylistic pattern. But neither Tyndale nor Coverdale nor any of the others will furnish a sufficient explanation for the felicities of style in the King James Version. If you will trace a group of the best-loved passages backward through the earlier translations, you will find that almost always the ultimate grace has been conferred by the translators of 1611. The wonder is that such a blessed result could have been achieved by a committee.

The King James Version did not immediately displace the Geneva Bible in the affections of the majority of English readers. But for the past two centuries and more the King James Version has had no peer. In spite of long-standing and well-justified depreciations of its accuracy, and in spite of complaints by some readers that its archaic language is difficult to comprehend, the King James Bible remains the most widely read and deeply cherished of the English versions. The Revised Versions are more accurate; the translations of Goodspeed, Moffett, Monsignor Knox, and the new Revised Standard Version are both clearer and more accurate. Yet almost without exception readers prefer "The Lord is my shepherd" to "Jehovah is my shepherd" (American Revised); "Our Father which art in Heaven, hallowed be Thy name" to "Our Father in Heaven, Your name be revered" (Goodspeed); "We spend our years as a tale that is told" to "We bring our years to an end as a sigh" (Moffett); "And there were in the same country shepherds abiding in the field" to "And in that region there were shepherds out in the field" (Revised Standard). No doubt in the case of many oldsters the preference is sometimes nothing more than stubborn sentimentalism. But I like to think also that it has something to do with beauty, and with the holiness of beauty. At any rate, the unanimous opinion of all who have been consulted has left no doubt that the King James Version is entirely appropriate to a volume of selections such as this.

ALLAN G. CHESTER

Narberth, Pennsylvania
April, 1952

ACKNOWLEDGMENTS

I wish to express my gratitude to all those who were consulted during the planning of this book and who made valuable suggestions concerning the choice of selections. My thanks are due especially to my friend Charles Butterworth for much good advice, and to my wife, Florence Koch Chester, both for good advice and practical assistance.

A. G. C.

THE CONTENTS

Introduction   v
A Table of Authors and Dates   xxv

Selections from the Old Testament

From the Pentateuch

THE BEGINNINGS

The Creation (Genesis 1 and 2)   3
The Fall (Genesis 3)   7
Cain and Abel (Genesis 4:1–16)   9
The Flood (Genesis 6:1 to 8:22; 9:12–15)   10
The Tower of Babel (Genesis 11:1–9)   15

THE PATRIARCHS

The Calling of Abraham (Genesis 12:1–9)   16
Abraham and Hagar (Genesis 16:1–15)   17
The Destruction of Sodom and Gomorrah (Genesis 18
    and 19)   18
The Birth of Isaac (Genesis 21:1–21)   24
The Sacrifice of Isaac (Genesis 22:1–19)   25
Jacob and Esau (Genesis 25:19–34)   27
The Stolen Blessing (Genesis 27:1–40)   28
Jacob at Beth-el (Genesis 28:10–22)   31
Jacob, Leah, and Rachel (Genesis 29:1–31)   32

Contents

Jacob Is Called Israel (Genesis 35:9–29)   35

THE STORY OF JOSEPH

Joseph and His Brethren (Genesis 37:1–36)   36
Joseph and the Wife of Potiphar (Genesis 39:1–23)   39
The Interpreter of Dreams (Genesis 40:1 to 41:44)   41
The Administrator (Genesis 41:45–57)   45
The Reunion of Joseph and His Brethren (Genesis 42:1
to 45:28; 46:26 to 50:26)   46

ISRAEL ENSLAVED AND LIBERATED

The Enslavement of the Hebrews (Exodus 1)   65
The Early Life of Moses (Exodus 2:1–15)   67
The Calling of Moses (Exodus 3)   68
The Warning of Aaron's Rod (Exodus 6:28 to 7:13)   71
The Death of the Firstborn. The Institution of the Passover
(Exodus 11:1 to 12:7; 12:21–36)   72
The Crossing of the Red Sea (Exodus 12:37–42; 13:17 to
14:31)   75
The Song of Moses and Miriam (Exodus 15:1–21)   78
The Wanderings in the Wilderness (Exodus 15:22 to 17:7)   80
Israel at Sinai. The Ten Commandments (Exodus 19;
20:1–21)   85
The Song of Moses (Deuteronomy 31:30 to 32:43)   88
The Death of Moses (Deuteronomy 34)   93

From the Historical Books

THE CONQUEST OF CANAAN AND THE PERIOD OF THE JUDGES

Jehovah's Charge to Joshua (Joshua 1:1–9)   94
Rahab and the Spies (Joshua 2:1–24)   95
The Fall of Jericho (Joshua 6:1–27)   97
Samson, Judge of Israel (Judges 13:1 to 16:31)   100
The Birth and Dedication of Samuel (1 Samuel 1:1 to 2:11;
2:19–26)   109
Samuel and Eli (1 Samuel 3:1 to 4:1ᵃ)   113

Contents

The Philistines' Capture of the Ark of the Covenant. The
Death of Eli (1 Samuel 4:1b–18)   115

THE ESTABLISHMENT OF THE MONARCHY

Samuel, the Last of the Judges (1 Samuel 7:15 to 8:22)   117
The Anointing of Saul (1 Samuel 9:1 to 10:12)   119
Saul's Presumptuousness (1 Samuel 13:1–15)   123
God Rejects Saul (1 Samuel 15:10–35)   124

THE CAREER OF DAVID

The Anointing of David. His Summons to Court (1 Samuel
16:1–23)   127
David and Goliath (1 Samuel 17:1–58)   129
David and Jonathan. Saul's Jealousy (1 Samuel 18:1–16)   134
Saul and the Witch of Endor (1 Samuel 28:3–25)   135
The Death of Saul (1 Samuel 31:1–13)   137
David's Lament for Saul and Jonathan (2 Samuel 1:1–27)   139
David, King of All Israel (2 Samuel 5:1–10)   141
David and Bath-sheba (2 Samuel 11:1 to 12:25)   142
Absalom the Usurper (2 Samuel 15:1–6)   147
The Death of Absalom (2 Samuel 18:1–33)   147
The Death of David (1 Kings 2:1–12)   151

THE WISDOM AND SPLENDOR OF SOLOMON

Solomon's Prayer (1 Kings 3:4–15)   152
Solomon's Wisdom (1 Kings 3:16–28; 4:29–34)   153
King Solomon and the Queen of Sheba (1 Kings 10:1–13)   155
Solomon's Splendor and His Apostasy (1 Kings 10:21 to
11:13)   156

NARRATIVES OF ELIJAH AND ELISHA

Elijah and the Widow of Zarephath (1 Kings 17:1–24)   158
Elijah and the Priests of Baal (1 Kings 18:17–40)   160
Ahab and Naboth's Vineyard (1 Kings 21:1–29)   162
The Translation of Elijah (2 Kings 2:1–15)   165
Elisha and Naaman the Syrian (2 Kings 5:1–27)   167

Contents

From the Prophets

FROM ISAIAH

Isaiah's Call (Isaiah 6)   170
The Unfruitful Vineyard (Isaiah 5:1–25)   171
The Reign of Righteousness (Isaiah 11:1–9)   173
The Happy Future of Zion (Isaiah 35)   174
God's Promise (Isaiah 40)   175
Zion Summoned out of Exile (Isaiah 52)   177
The Servant of Jehovah (Isaiah 53)   178
Mercy to All (Isaiah 55)   179
The Glorified Zion (Isaiah 60)   181

FROM JEREMIAH

Jeremiah's Call (Jeremiah 1)   183
Jeremiah's Sermon at the Temple Gate (Jeremiah 7)   184
A Warning against Idolatry (Jeremiah 10:1–16)   187
The Sign of the Girdle (Jeremiah 13:1–11)   188
The Warning to Judah (Jeremiah 17)   189
The Lesson of the Potter's Vessel (Jeremiah 18:1–17)   192
The Happy Restoration (Jeremiah 31:15–34)   193

FROM EZEKIEL

Ezekiel's Vision (Ezekiel 1)   195
The Punishment of the Sinner and the Reward of the Just (Ezekiel 18)   197
The Valley of Dry Bones (Ezekiel 37)   200

JONAH (Complete)   202

From the "Writings"

RUTH (Complete)   206

FROM THE PSALMS

"Blessed is the man that walketh not in the counsel of the ungodly" (Psalm 1)   213

Contents

"Oh Lord our Lord, how excellent is thy name" (Psalm 8)   214

"How long wilt thou forget me, O Lord?" (Psalm 13)   214

"The heavens declare the glory of God" (Psalm 19)   215

"The Lord is my shepherd" (Psalm 23)   216

"The earth is the Lord's, and the fulness thereof" (Psalm 24)   217

"As the hart panteth after the water brooks" (Psalm 42)   218

"Judge me, O God, and plead my cause" (Psalm 43)   219

"God is our refuge and strength" (Psalm 46)   219

"Have mercy upon me, O God, according to thy loving kindness" (Psalm 51)   220

"O God, thou art my God; early will I seek thee" (Psalm 63)   222

"How amiable are thy tabernacles, O Lord of hosts" (Psalm 84)   223

"Lord thou hast been our dwelling place in all generations" (Psalm 90)   224

"He that dwelleth in the secret place of the most High" (Psalm 91)   225

"O sing unto the Lord a new song" (Psalm 98)   226

"Bless the Lord, O my soul" (Psalm 104)   227

"I will lift up mine eyes unto the hills" (Psalm 121)   229

"I was glad when they said unto me, Let us go into the house of the Lord" (Psalm 122)   230

"Out of the depths have I cried unto thee, O Lord" (Psalm 130)   231

"By the rivers of Babylon" (Psalm 137)   231

"O Lord, thou hast searched me, and known me" (Psalm 139)   232

"I will extol thee, my God, O king" (Psalm 145)   234

"Praise ye the Lord. Praise God in his sanctuary" (Psalm 150)   235

FROM THE SONG OF SOLOMON

The Maiden's Description of Her Lover (Song of Solomon 2:3–17)   236

Contents

The King's Description of His Beloved (Song of Solomon 4:1–7)   237

FROM THE PROVERBS

The Rewards of Wisdom (Proverbs 3:13–26)   239
The Call of Wisdom (Proverbs 8)   240
The Strange Woman (Proverbs 7)   242
The Worthy Woman (Proverbs 31:10–31)   244

FROM ECCLESIASTES

The Vanity of Things (Ecclesiastes 1)   246
Of Time and Seasons (Ecclesiastes 3:1–15)   247
"Remember now thy Creator" (Ecclesiastes 12:1–7)   248

FROM JOB

The Prologue (Job 1 and 2)   249
Job's First Lament (Job 3)   252
Bildad and Job (Job 8, 9, and 10)   254
Job on Man's Frailty (Job 14)   259
God Speaks to Job out of the Whirlwind (Job 38, 39, 42:1–6)   260
The Epilogue (Job 42:7–17)   265

FROM DANIEL

The Fiery Furnace (Daniel 3)   266
Belshazzar's Feast (Daniel 5)   269
The Den of Lions (Daniel 6)   272

Selections from the New Testament

From The Gospels

MARK (Complete)   279

FROM MATTHEW

The Wise Men. The Flight into Egypt (Matthew 2)   320

Contents

The Temptation (Matthew 4:1–11)   322
The Sermon on the Mount (Matthew 5 to 7)   323
The Parable of the Unmerciful Servant (Matthew 18:23–35)   329
The Parable of the Laborers in the Vineyard (Matthew 20:1–16)   330
The Parable of the Marriage Feast (Matthew 22:1–14)   331
Parables of the Coming (Matthew 24:44 to 25:46)   332

FROM LUKE

The Birth of John the Baptist. The Nativity and Infancy of Jesus (Luke 1 and 2)   336
The Good Samaritan (Luke 10:25–42)   343
The Prodigal Son (Luke 15:11–32)   344
The Trial, the Crucifixion, and the Resurrection (Luke 23 and 24)   346

FROM JOHN

The Incarnate Word (John 1:1–18)   352
The Story of Nicodemus (John 3:1–21)   353
The Good Shepherd (John 10)   354
The Raising of Lazarus (John 11:1–46)   357
The Last Discourse (John 14 to 17)   359

From the Acts of the Apostles

The Ascension (Acts 1)   367
The Coming of the Holy Spirit (Acts 2)   369
The First Martyr (Acts 6:8–15; 7:51 to 8:2)   372
The Conversion of Paul (Acts 9:1–22)   373
Peter's Vision (Acts 10)   375
Paul at Athens (Acts 17:16–34)   378
Paul and the Silversmiths of Ephesus (Acts 19:22–41)   379

From the Epistles

PAUL'S FIRST EPISTLE TO THE THESSALONIANS (Complete)   382

Contents

SELECTIONS FROM THE OTHER EPISTLES OF PAUL

"There is therefore now no condemnation . . ." (Romans 8)   387

"I beseech you therefore, brethren, by the mercies of God . . ." (Romans 12)   389

"Let every soul be subject unto the higher powers." (Romans 13)   391

"Though I speak with the tongues of men and of angels . . ." (1 Corinthians 13)   392

"Moreover, brethren, I declare unto you the gospel . . ." (1 Corinthians 15)   393

"Children, obey your parents in the Lord . . ." (Ephesians 6:1–20)   396

FROM THE EPISTLE TO THE HEBREWS

"Now faith is the substance of things hoped for . . ." (Hebrews 11:1–16; 12:1–2)   397

FROM THE EPISTLES GENERAL

"My brethren, count it all joy . . ." (James 1)   399

"That which was from the beginning . . ." (1 John 1:1 to 2:17)   401

"Beloved, let us love one another . . ." (1 John 4:7 to 5:12)   402

From the Revelation of St. John the Divine

The Messages to the Seven Churches (Revelation 1 to 3)   405

War in Heaven Renewed on Earth (Revelation 12)   410

A New Heaven and a New Earth (Revelation 21 to 22)   412

A Table of Authors and Dates

The books of the Bible were written over a period of about a thousand years—a period as great as that which lies between Cynewulf and T. S. Eliot. Readers naturally want to know when, and by whom, the separate books were written. To answer these questions in detail would involve us unnecessarily in all the vexed problems of criticism which have engaged the attention of Biblical scholars for the past two centuries, and it would involve us in a tedious balancing of the claims of conservative orthodoxy against those of the "higher criticism." Still, the questions remain—when and by whom? Accordingly, the following summary statement will give tentative answers to these questions for those books which are represented in this volume. Where it seems desirable, both the conservative and the liberal opinions are indicated. The reader should remember that, from either point of view, precise dating is in most cases impossible. Fuller discussion of the problems involved will be found in any modern commentary.

THE OLD TESTAMENT

BOOK	AUTHORSHIP	DATE OF COMPOSITION	DATE OF EVENTS OR BACKGROUND
The Pentateuch			
Genesis	Traditionally ascribed to Moses. Modernistic scholarship sees in the Pentateuch a redaction of several earlier documents—J (Jahwistic), E (Elohistic), D (Deuteronomic School of Writers), P (Priestly School of Writers).	J—9th century B.C. E—8th century B.C. D—7th century B.C. P—5th century B.C. Final revision, c. 400 B.C.	Age of the Patriarchs, c. 2000–1700 B.C.
Exodus			Sojourn of Israel in Egypt, c. 1700–1300 B.C.
[Leviticus]			
[Numbers]			Career of Moses, 13th century B.C.
Deuteronomy			
The Former Prophets			
Joshua	Based on older documents not now extant. Revised first by D, subsequently by P.	Final revision, 6th century B.C.	Invasion of Canaan by Israel, c. 1250 B.C.

Judges	Originally a collection of hero stories. Probably revised by D.	Final revision, 7th century B.C.	c. 1250–1015 B.C.
1 & 2 Samuel	Based on older documents. Revised by D.	Final revision probably 7th century B.C.	Samuel, fl. latter half 11th century B.C.
			Reign of Saul, c. 1020–1004 B.C.
			Reign of David, c. 1004–965 B.C.
1 & 2 Kings	Revision of older documents.	Final revision, 6th century B.C.	From the reign of Solomon, c. 965–926 B.C., to the fall of Jerusalem—586 B.C.
The Later Prophets			
Isaiah	Chapters 1–39 by Isaiah the son of Amoz ("First Isaiah").	1st Isaiah, 8th century B.C.	Life of Isaiah the son of Amoz, c. 740–701 B.C.
	Chapters 40–66 by an anonymous prophet or prophets ("Second Isaiah").	2nd Isaiah, 6th century B.C.	Second Isaiah—after the return from the Exile, 536 B.C.

BOOK	AUTHORSHIP	DATE OF COMPOSITION	DATE OF EVENTS OR BACKGROUND
Jeremiah	Chapters 1–25 dictated by Jeremiah to Baruch.	Chapters 1–45, 6th century B.C.	Life of Jeremiah, c. 650–585 B.C. Fall of Jerusalem, 586 B.C.
	Chapters 26–45, a biography of Jeremiah, probably by Baruch.		
	Chapters 46–51, a collection of later oracles.		
Ezekiel	Conservatively ascribed to Ezekiel, a contemporary of Jeremiah. Some modern critics believe it was written by unknown writers after the return from the Exile.	6th century B.C.	Ezekiel, flourished c. 586 B.C.
Jonah	Anonymous.	5th century B.C.	8th century B.C. But the "events" are unhistorical.

The Writings

Ruth	Anonymous.	Period of the Judges, 12th century B.C.
Psalms	An anthology of poems by David and others.	Collection completed 5th century B.C.
Song of Solomon	Ascribed to Solomon in the text. Probably of composite authorship.	Final form, 3rd century B.C.
Proverbs	Ascribed to Solomon in the text. Actually an anthology.	Final form, 4th century B.C.
Ecclesiastes	Traditionally ascribed to Solomon. Author or authors unknown.	4th century B.C.
Job	Anonymous. The prologue and epilogue may be an adaptation of an older folk tale.	5th century B.C.
Daniel	Anonymous.	2nd century B.C.

THE NEW TESTAMENT

BOOK	AUTHORSHIP	DATE OF COMPOSITION
The Gospels		
Mark	Conservatively ascribed to John Mark. Some scholars believe it is a revision by a later writer of Mark's original.	Conservatively, *c.* A.D. 50. By modernistic critics, *c.* A.D. 75.
Matthew	Conservatively ascribed to Matthew the Apostle. Modernistic scholars regard it as by a later writer who used Mark and another source now lost.	Conservatively, *c.* A.D. 70. By modernistic critics, *c.* A.D. 90.
Luke	Attributed to Luke, the Greek friend and companion of Paul. Based upon Mark and other sources.	Conservatively, *c.* A.D. 70. By modernistic critics, *c.* A.D. 90.
John	Conservatively attributed to John the Apostle. Modernistic critics assign it to John the Elder (of Ephesus) or some other later writer.	Conservatively, *c.* A.D. 90. By modernistic critics, A.D. 100–110.
The Acts of the Apostles	Generally regarded as "volume two" of Luke's Gospel.	As for Luke, above.

The Epistles

1 Thessalonians	Paul.	c. A.D. 50.
1 Corinthians	Paul.	A.D. 53–55.
Romans	Paul.	c. A.D. 56.
Hebrews	Unknown.	A.D. 90–96.
James	Conservatively assigned to James the brother of Jesus. By modernistic scholars, to a Hellenistic Jewish Christian.	Conservatively, c. A.D. 50. By modernistic scholars, A.D. 100–150.
1 John	By the author of the Fourth Gospel. See above.	A.D. 90–100.
Revelation of St. John the Divine	Conservatively ascribed to John the Apostle. By modernistic critics to a later writer, but probably not the author of the Fourth Gospel or 1 John.	c. A.D. 96.

SELECTIONS FROM

THE OLD TESTAMENT

THE BEGINNINGS

The Creation

• GENESIS 1 AND 2 •

In the beginning God created the heaven and the earth. And the earth was without form, and void; and darkness was upon the face of the deep. And the Spirit of God moved upon the face of the waters. And God said, "Let there be light." And there was light. And God saw the light, that it was good: and God divided the light from the darkness. And God called the light Day, and the darkness he called Night. And the evening and the morning were the first day.

And God said, "Let there be a firmament in the midst of the waters, and let it divide the waters from the waters." And God made the firmament, and divided the waters which were under the firmament from the waters which were above the firmament: and it was so. And God called the firmament Heaven. And the evening and the morning were the second day.

And God said, "Let the waters under the heaven be gathered together unto one place, and let the dry land appear." And it was so. And God called the dry land Earth; and the gathering together of the waters called he Seas: and God saw that it was good. And God said, "Let the earth bring forth grass, the herb yielding seed, and the fruit tree yielding fruit after his[1] kind, whose seed is in itself, upon the earth." And it was so. And the earth brought forth grass, and herb yielding seed after his kind, and the tree yielding

[1] Throughout the King James Version, *his* may be neuter as well as masculine.

fruit, whose seed was in itself, after his kind: and God saw that it was good. And the evening and the morning were the third day.

And God said, "Let there be lights in the firmament of the heaven to divide the day from the night; and let them be for signs, and for seasons, and for days, and years: and let them be for lights in the firmament of the heaven to give light upon the earth." And it was so. And God made two great lights; the greater light to rule the day, and the lesser light to rule the night: he made the stars also. And God set them in the firmament of the heaven to give light upon the earth, and to rule over the day and over the night, and to divide the light from the darkness: and God saw that it was good. And the evening and the morning were the fourth day.

And God said, "Let the waters bring forth abundantly the moving creature that hath life, and fowl that may fly above the earth in the open firmament of heaven." And God created great whales, and every living creature that moveth, which the waters brought forth abundantly, after their kind, and every winged fowl after his kind: and God saw that it was good. And God blessed them, saying, "Be fruitful, and multiply, and fill the waters in the seas, and let fowl multiply in the earth." And the evening and the morning were the fifth day.

And God said, "Let the earth bring forth the living creature after his kind, cattle, and creeping thing, and beast of the earth after his kind." And it was so. And God made the beast of the earth after his kind, and cattle after their kind, and every thing that creepeth upon the earth after his kind: and God saw that it was good.

And God said, "Let us make man in our image, after our likeness: and let them have dominion over the fish of the sea, and over the fowl of the air, and over the cattle, and over all the earth, and over every creeping thing that creepeth upon the earth." So God created man in his own image, in the image of God created he him; male and female created he them. And God blessed them, and God said unto them, "Be fruitful, and multiply, and replenish the earth, and subdue it: and have dominion over the fish of the sea, and over the fowl of the air, and over every living thing that moveth upon the earth."

And God said, "Behold, I have given you every herb bearing seed, which is upon the face of all the earth, and every tree, in the which is the fruit of a tree yielding seed; to you it shall be for meat. And to every beast of the earth, and to every fowl of the air, and to everything that creepeth upon the earth, wherein there is life, I have given every green herb for meat." And it was so. And God saw every thing that he had made, and, behold, it was very good. And the evening and the morning were the sixth day.

Thus the heavens and the earth were finished, and all the host of them. And on the seventh day God ended his work which he had made; and he rested on the seventh day from all his work which he had made. And God blessed the seventh day, and sanctified it: because that in it he had rested from all his work which God created and made.

These are the generations of the heavens and of the earth when they were created, in the day that the LORD God made the earth and the heavens, and every plant of the field before it was in the earth, and every herb of the field before it grew: for the LORD God had not caused it to rain upon the earth, and there was not a man to till the ground. But there went up a mist from the earth, and watered the whole face of the ground. And the LORD God formed man of the dust of the ground, and breathed into his nostrils the breath of life; and man became a living soul.

And the LORD God planted a garden eastward in Eden; and there he put the man whom he had formed. And out of the ground made the LORD God to grow every tree that is pleasant to the sight, and good for food; the tree of life also in the midst of the garden, and the tree of knowledge of good and evil. And a river went out of Eden to water the garden; and from thence it was parted, and became into four heads. The name of the first is Pison:[2] that is it which compasseth the whole land of Havilah, where there is gold; and the gold of that land is good: there is bdellium and the onyx stone. And the name of the second river is Gihon: the same is it that compasseth the whole land of Ethiopia. And the name of the third river is Hiddekel: that is it which goeth toward the east of Assyria. And the fourth river is Euphrates. And the LORD God took the man, and put him into the garden of Eden to dress it and to keep it. And the LORD God commanded the man, saying, "Of every tree of the garden thou mayest freely eat: but of the tree of the knowledge of good and evil, thou shalt not eat of it: for in the day that thou eatest thereof thou shalt surely die."

And the LORD God said, "It is not good that the man should be alone; I will make him an help meet for him." And out of the ground the LORD God formed every beast of the field, and every fowl of the air; and brought them unto Adam to see what he would call them: and whatsoever Adam called every living creature, that was the name thereof. And Adam gave names to all cattle, and to the fowl of the air, and to every beast of the field; but for Adam there was not found an help meet for him. And the LORD God caused a deep sleep to fall upon Adam, and he slept: and he took one of his ribs, and closed up the flesh instead thereof; and the rib, which the LORD God had taken from man, made he a woman, and brought her unto the man. And Adam said, "This is now bone of my bones, and flesh of my flesh: she shall be called Woman, because she was taken out of Man." Therefore shall a man leave his father and his mother, and shall cleave unto his wife: and they shall be one flesh. And they were both naked, the man and his wife, and were not ashamed.

[2] There is no general agreement as to the identity of these rivers.

The Fall

Now the serpent was more subtil than any beast of the field which the LORD God had made. And he said unto the woman, "Yea, hath God said, 'Ye shall not eat of every tree of the garden'?"

And the woman said unto the serpent, "We may eat of the fruit of the trees of the garden: but of the fruit of the tree which is in the midst of the garden, God hath said, 'Ye shall not eat of it, neither shall ye touch it, lest ye die.' "

And the serpent said unto the woman, "Ye shall not surely die: for God doth know that in the day ye eat thereof, then your eyes shall be opened, and ye shall be as gods, knowing good and evil."

And when the woman saw that the tree was good for food, and that it was pleasant to the eyes, and a tree to be desired to make one wise, she took of the fruit thereof, and did eat, and gave also unto her husband with her; and he did eat. And the eyes of them both were opened, and they knew that they were naked; and they sewed fig leaves together, and made themselves aprons.

And they heard the voice of the LORD God walking in the garden in the cool of the day: and Adam and his wife hid themselves from the presence of the LORD God amongst the trees of the garden. And the LORD God called unto Adam, and said unto him, "Where art thou?"

And he said, "I heard thy voice in the garden, and I was afraid, because I was naked, and I hid myself."

And he said, "Who told thee that thou wast naked? Hast thou eaten of the tree, whereof I commanded thee that thou shouldest not eat?"

And the man said, "The woman whom thou gavest to be with me, she gave me of the tree, and I did eat."

And the L<small>ORD</small> God said unto the woman, "What is this that thou hast done?"

And the woman said, "The serpent beguiled me, and I did eat."

And the L<small>ORD</small> God said unto the serpent, "Because thou hast done this, thou art cursed above all cattle, and above every beast of the field; upon thy belly shalt thou go, and dust shalt thou eat all the days of thy life: and I will put enmity between thee and the woman, and between thy seed and her seed; it shall bruise thy head, and thou shalt bruise his heel."

Unto the woman he said, "I will greatly multiply thy sorrow and thy conception; in sorrow thou shalt bring forth children; and thy desire shall be to thy husband, and he shall rule over thee."

And unto Adam he said, "Because thou hast hearkened unto the voice of thy wife, and hast eaten of the tree, of which I commanded thee, saying, 'Thou shalt not eat of it': cursed is the ground for thy sake; in sorrow shalt thou eat of it all the days of thy life; thorns also and thistles shall it bring forth to thee; and thou shalt eat the herb of the field; in the sweat of thy face shalt thou eat bread, till thou return unto the ground; for out of it wast thou taken: for dust thou art, and unto dust shalt thou return."

And Adam called his wife's name Eve; because she was the mother of all living. Unto Adam also and to his wife did the L<small>ORD</small> God make coats of skins, and clothed them.

And the L<small>ORD</small> God said, "Behold, the man is become as one of us, to know good and evil: and now, lest he put forth his hand, and take also of the tree of life, and eat, and live for ever." Therefore the L<small>ORD</small> God sent him forth from the garden of Eden, to till the ground from whence he was taken. So he drove out the man; and he placed at the east of the garden of Eden Cherubims, and a flaming sword which turned every way, to keep the way of the tree of life.

Cain and Abel

• GENESIS 4: 1–16 •

And Adam knew Eve his wife; and she conceived, and bare Cain, and said, "I have gotten a man from the LORD." And she again bare his brother Abel.

And Abel was a keeper of sheep, but Cain was a tiller of the ground. And in process of time it came to pass, that Cain brought of the fruit of the ground an offering unto the LORD. And Abel, he also brought of the firstlings of his flock and of the fat thereof. And the LORD had respect unto Abel and to his offering: but unto Cain and to his offering he had not respect. And Cain was very wroth, and his countenance fell.

And the LORD said unto Cain, "Why art thou wroth? and why is thy countenance fallen? If thou doest well, shalt thou not be accepted? and if thou doest not well, sin lieth at the door. And unto thee shall be his desire, and thou shalt rule over him."

And Cain talked with Abel his brother: and it came to pass, when they were in the field, that Cain rose up against Abel his brother, and slew him.

And the LORD said unto Cain, "Where is Abel thy brother?"

And he said, "I know not. Am I my brother's keeper?"

And he said, "What hast thou done? the voice of thy brother's blood crieth unto me from the ground. And now art thou cursed from the earth, which hath opened her mouth to receive thy brother's blood from thy hand; when thou tillest the ground, it shall not henceforth yield unto thee her strength; a fugitive and a vagabond shalt thou be in the earth."

And Cain said unto the LORD, "My punishment is greater than I can bear. Behold, thou hast driven me out this day from the face of the earth; and from thy face shall I be hid; and I shall be a fugitive and a vagabond in the earth; and it shall come to pass, that every one that findeth me shall slay me."

And the LORD said unto him, "Therefore whosoever slayeth Cain, vengeance shall be taken on him sevenfold." And the LORD set a mark upon Cain, lest any finding him should kill him. And Cain went out from the presence of the LORD, and dwelt in the land of Nod,[8] on the east of Eden.

The Flood

• GENESIS 6:1 TO 8:22; 9:12–15 •

And it came to pass, when men began to multiply on the face of the earth, and daughters were born unto them, that the sons of God saw the daughters of men that they were fair; and they took them wives of all which they chose. And the LORD said, "My spirit shall not always strive with man, for that he also is flesh: yet his days shall be an hundred and twenty years." There were giants in the earth in those days; and also after that, when the sons of God came in unto the daughters of men, and they bare children to them, the same became mighty men which were of old, men of renown.

And God saw that the wickedness of man was great in the earth, and that every imagination of the thoughts of his heart was only evil continually. And it repented the LORD that he had made man on the earth, and it grieved him at his heart. And the LORD said, "I will destroy man whom I have created from the face of the earth; both man, and beast, and the creeping thing, and the fowls of the air; for it repenteth me that I have made them." But Noah found grace in the eyes of the LORD.

These are the generations of Noah: Noah was a just man and perfect in his generations, and Noah walked with God. And Noah begat three sons, Shem, Ham, and Japheth. The earth also was corrupt before God, and the earth was filled with violence.

---

[8] The Hebrew word means "wandering" or "exile."

And God looked upon the earth, and, behold, it was corrupt; for all flesh had corrupted his way upon the earth.

And God said unto Noah, "The end of all flesh is come before me; for the earth is filled with violence through them; and, behold, I will destroy them with the earth.

"Make thee an ark of gopher wood;[4] rooms shalt thou make in the ark, and shalt pitch it within and without with pitch. And this is the fashion which thou shalt make it of: the length of the ark shall be three hundred cubits,[5] the breadth of it fifty cubits, and the height of it thirty cubits. A window shalt thou make to the ark, and in a cubit shalt thou finish it above; and the door of the ark shalt thou set in the side thereof; with lower, second, and third stories shalt thou make it. And, behold, I, even I, do bring a flood of waters upon the earth, to destroy all flesh, wherein is the breath of life, from under heaven; and every thing that is in the earth shall die. But with thee will I establish my covenant; and thou shalt come into the ark, thou, and thy sons, and thy wife, and thy sons' wives with thee. And of every living thing of all flesh, two of every sort shalt thou bring into the ark, to keep them alive with thee; they shall be male and female. Of fowls after their kind, and of cattle after their kind, of every creeping thing of the earth after his kind, two of every sort shall come unto thee, to keep them alive. And take thou unto thee of all food that is eaten, and thou shalt gather it to thee; and it shall be for food for thee, and for them."

Thus did Noah; according to all that God commanded him, so did he.

And the LORD said unto Noah, "Come thou and all thy house into the ark; for thee have I seen righteous before me in this generation. Of every clean beast thou shalt take to thee by sevens, the male and his female: and of beasts that are not clean by two, the male and his female. Of fowls also of the air by sevens, the male and the female; to keep seed alive upon the face

---

[4] Probably cypress.
[5] The cubit was about 18 inches.

of all the earth. For yet seven days, and I will cause it to rain upon the earth forty days and forty nights; and every living substance that I have made will I destroy from off the face of the earth."

And Noah did according unto all that the LORD commanded him. And Noah was six hundred years old when the flood of waters was upon the earth. And Noah went in, and his sons, and his wife, and his sons' wives with him, into the ark, because of the waters of the flood. Of clean beasts, and of beasts that are not clean, and of fowls, and of every thing that creepeth upon the earth, there went in two and two unto Noah into the ark, the male and the female, as God had commanded Noah.

And it came to pass after seven days, that the waters of the flood were upon the earth. In the six hundredth year of Noah's life, in the second month, the seventeenth day of the month, the same day were all the fountains of the great deep broken up, and the windows of heaven were opened. And the rain was upon the earth forty days and forty nights. In the selfsame day entered Noah, and Shem, and Ham, and Japheth, the sons of Noah, and Noah's wife, and the three wives of his sons with them, in the ark; they, and every beast after his kind, and all the cattle after their kind, and every creeping thing that creepeth upon the earth after his kind, and every fowl after his kind, every bird of every sort. And they went in unto Noah into the ark, two and two of all flesh, wherein is the breath of life. And they that went in, went in male and female of all flesh, as God had commanded him: and the LORD shut him in.

And the flood was forty days upon the earth; and the waters increased, and bare up the ark, and it was lift up above the earth. And the waters prevailed, and were increased greatly upon the earth; and the ark went upon the face of the waters. And the waters prevailed exceedingly upon the earth; and all the high hills, that were under the whole heaven, were covered. Fifteen cubits upward did the waters prevail; and the mountains were covered. And all flesh died that moved upon the earth, both of fowl, and of cattle, and of beast, and of every creeping thing that creepeth upon the earth, and every man: all in whose nostrils was the breath of life, of all that was in the dry land, died. And every living substance was destroyed which was upon the face of the ground, both man, and cattle, and the creeping things, and the fowl of the heaven; and they were destroyed from the earth: and Noah only remained alive, and they that were with him in the ark. And the waters prevailed upon the earth an hundred and fifty days.

And God remembered Noah, and every living thing, and all the cattle that was with him in the ark: and God made a wind to pass over the earth, and the waters assuaged; the fountains also of the deep and the windows of heaven were stopped, and the rain from heaven was restrained; and the waters returned from off the earth continually: and after the end of the hundred and fifty days the waters were abated. And the ark rested in the seventh month, on the seventeenth day of the month, upon the mountains of Ararat. And the waters decreased continually until the tenth month: in the tenth month, on the first day of the month, were the tops of the mountains seen.

And it came to pass at the end of forty days, that Noah opened the window of the ark which he had made: and he sent forth a raven, which went forth to and fro, until the waters were dried up from off the earth. Also he sent forth a dove from him, to see if the waters were abated from off the face of the ground; but the dove found no rest for the sole of her foot, and she returned unto him into the ark, for the waters were on the face of the whole earth: then he put forth his hand, and took her, and pulled her in unto him into the ark. And he stayed yet other seven days; and again he sent forth the dove out of the ark; and the dove came in to him in the evening; and, lo, in her mouth was an olive leaf plucked off: so Noah knew that the waters were abated from off the earth. And he stayed yet other seven days; and sent forth the dove; which returned not again unto him any more.

And it came to pass in the six hundredth and first year, in the first month, the first day of the month, the waters were dried up from off the earth: and Noah removed the covering of the ark, and looked, and, behold, the face of the ground was dry. And in the second month, on the seven and twentieth day of the month, was the earth dried.

And God spake unto Noah, saying, "Go forth of the ark, thou, and thy wife, and thy sons, and thy sons' wives with thee. Bring forth with thee every living thing that is with thee, of all flesh, both of fowl, and of cattle, and of every creeping thing that creepeth upon the earth; that they may breed abundantly in the earth, and be fruitful, and multiply upon the earth."

And Noah went forth, and his sons, and his wife, and his sons' wives with him: every beast, every creeping thing, and every fowl, and whatsoever creepeth upon the earth, after their kinds, went forth out of the ark. And Noah builded an altar unto the Lord; and took of every clean beast, and of every clean fowl, and offered burnt offerings on the altar.

And the Lord smelled a sweet savour; and the Lord said in his heart, "I will not again curse the ground any more for man's sake; for the imagination of man's heart is evil from his youth; neither will I again smite any more every thing living, as I have done. While the earth remaineth, seedtime and harvest, and cold and heat, and summer and winter, and day and night shall not cease."

And God said, "This is the token of the covenant which I make between me and you and every living creature that is with you, for perpetual generations: I do set my bow in the cloud, and it shall be for a token of a covenant between me and the earth. And it shall come to pass, when I bring a cloud over the earth, that the bow shall be seen in the cloud: and I will remember my covenant, which is between me and you and every living creature of all flesh; and the waters shall no more become a flood to destroy all flesh."

The Tower of Babel

• GENESIS 11: 1–9 •

And the whole earth was of one language, and of one speech. And it came to pass, as they journeyed from the east, that they found a plain in the land of Shinar;⁶ and they dwelt there. And they said one to another, "Go to, let us make brick, and burn them throughly." And they had brick for stone, and slime had they for mortar. And they said, "Go to, let us build us a city and a tower, whose top may reach unto heaven; and let us make us a name, lest we be scattered abroad upon the face of the whole earth."

And the Lord came down to see the city and the tower, which the children of men builded. And the Lord said, "Behold, the people is one, and they have all one language; and this they begin to do: and now nothing will be restrained from them, which they have imagined to do. Go to, let us go down, and there confound their language, that they may not understand one another's speech."

So the Lord scattered them abroad from thence upon the face of all the earth: and they left off to build the city. Therefore is the name of it called Babel; because the Lord did there confound the language of all the earth: and from thence did the Lord scatter them abroad upon the face of all the earth.

⁶ Babylonia.

The Calling of Abraham

• GENESIS 12:1–9 •

Now the LORD had said unto Abram, "Get thee out of thy country, and from thy kindred, and from thy father's house, unto a land that I will shew thee: and I will make of thee a great nation, and I will bless thee, and make thy name great; and thou shalt be a blessing: and I will bless them that bless thee, and curse him that curseth thee: and in thee shall all families of the earth be blessed."

So Abram departed, as the LORD had spoken unto him; and Lot went with him: and Abram was seventy and five years old when he departed out of Haran.[1] And Abram took Sarai his wife, and Lot his brother's son, and all their substance that they had gathered, and the souls that they had gotten in Haran; and they went forth to go into the land of Canaan; and into the land of Canaan they came.

And Abram passed through the land unto the place of Sichem, unto the plain[2] of Moreh. And the Canaanite was then in the land. And the LORD appeared unto Abram, and said, "Unto thy seed will I give this land." And there builded he an altar unto the LORD, who appeared unto him. And he removed from thence unto a mountain on the east of Beth-el, and pitched his tent, having Beth-el on the west, and Hai on the east: and there

[1] Abraham, with his father Terah, had come from Ur of the Chaldees to Haran, in Mesopotamia. Thence he journeyed to Canaan (Palestine). Thus in the course of his migration he followed the line of the "Fertile Crescent."
[2] Or, better, "oak." The place was probably a grove.

he builded an altar unto the LORD, and called upon the name of the LORD. And Abram journeyed, going on still toward the south.

Abraham and Hagar

· GENESIS 16: 1–15 ·

Now Sarai Abram's wife bare him no children: and she had an handmaid, an Egyptian, whose name was Hagar. And Sarai said unto Abram, "Behold now, the LORD hath restrained me from bearing: I pray thee, go in unto my maid; it may be that I may obtain children by her." And Abram hearkened to the voice of Sarai. And Sarai Abram's wife took Hagar her maid the Egyptian, after Abram had dwelt ten years in the land of Canaan, and gave her to her husband Abram to be his wife. And he went in unto Hagar, and she conceived: and when she saw that she had conceived, her mistress was despised in her eyes.

And Sarai said unto Abram, "My wrong be upon thee: I have given my maid into thy bosom; and when she saw that she had conceived, I was despised in her eyes: the LORD judge between me and thee."

But Abram said unto Sarai, "Behold, thy maid is in thy hand; do to her as it pleaseth thee."

And when Sarai dealt hardly with her, she fled from her face. And the angel of the LORD found her by a fountain of water in the wilderness, by the fountain in the way to Shur.³ And he said, "Hagar, Sarai's maid, whence camest thou? and whither wilt thou go?"

And she said, "I flee from the face of my mistress Sarai."

And the angel of the LORD said unto her, "Return to thy mistress, and submit thyself under her hands." And the angel of the LORD said unto her, "I will multiply thy seed exceedingly, that it shall not be numbered for multitude." And the angel of

³ On the Egyptian frontier.

the LORD said unto her, "Behold, thou art with child, and shalt bear a son, and shalt call his name Ishmael; because the LORD hath heard thy affliction. And he will be a wild man; his hand will be against every man, and every man's hand against him; and he shall dwell in the presence of all his brethren."

And she called the name of the LORD that spake unto her, "Thou God seest me." For she said, "Have I also here looked after him that seeth me?" Wherefore the well was called Beer-lahai-roi,[4] behold, it is between Kadesh and Bered. And Hagar bare Abram a son: and Abram called his son's name, which Hagar bare, Ishmael. And Abram was fourscore and six years old, when Hagar bare Ishmael to Abram.

The Destruction of Sodom and Gomorrah

· GENESIS 18 AND 19 ·

And the LORD appeared unto Abraham in the plains of Mamre:[5] and he sat in the tent door in the heat of the day; and he lift up his eyes and looked, and, lo, three men[6] stood by him: and when he saw them, he ran to meet them from the tent door, and bowed himself toward the ground, and said, "My Lord, if now I have found favour in thy sight, pass not away, I pray thee, from thy servant: let a little water, I pray you, be fetched, and wash your feet, and rest yourselves under the tree: and I will fetch a morsel of bread, and comfort ye your hearts; after that ye shall pass on: for therefore are ye come to your servant."

---

[4] "Well of the living one who sees me."
[5] i.e., "oaks of Mamre." Mamre was near Hebron, some 20 miles south of Jerusalem. Abraham finally settled in Hebron.
[6] Heavenly visitants. One of them (see below) speaks with the voice of God.

And they said, "So do, as thou hast said."

And Abraham hastened into the tent unto Sarah, and said, "Make ready quickly three measures of fine meal, knead it, and make cakes upon the hearth." And Abraham ran unto the herd, and fetched a calf tender and good, and gave it unto a young man; and he hasted to dress it. And he took butter, and milk, and the calf which he had dressed, and set it before them; and he stood by them under the tree, and they did eat.

And they said unto him, "Where is Sarah thy wife?"

And he said, "Behold, in the tent."

And he said, "I will certainly return unto thee according to the time of life; and, lo, Sarah thy wife shall have a son."

And Sarah heard it in the tent door, which was behind him. Now Abraham and Sarah were old and well stricken in age; and it ceased to be with Sarah after the manner of women. Therefore Sarah laughed within herself, saying, "After I am waxed old shall I have pleasure, my lord being old also?"

And the LORD said unto Abraham, "Wherefore did Sarah laugh, saying, 'Shall I of a surety bear a child, which am old'? Is any thing too hard for the LORD? At the time appointed I will return unto thee, according to the time of life, and Sarah shall have a son."

Then Sarah denied, saying, "I laughed not"; for she was afraid.

And he said, "Nay; but thou didst laugh."

And the men rose up from thence, and looked toward Sodom: and Abraham went with them to bring them on the way. And the LORD said, "Shall I hide from Abraham that thing which I do; seeing that Abraham shall surely become a great and mighty nation, and all the nations of the earth shall be blessed in him? For I know him, that he will command his children and his household after him, and they shall keep the way of the LORD, to do justice and judgment; that the LORD may bring upon Abraham that which he hath spoken of him." And the

LORD said, "Because the cry[7] of Sodom and Gomorrah[8] is great, and because their sin is very grievous, I will go down now, and see whether they have done altogether according to the cry of it, which is come unto me; and if not, I will know." And the men turned their faces from thence, and went toward Sodom: but Abraham stood yet before the LORD.

And Abraham drew near, and said, "Wilt thou also destroy the righteous with the wicked? Peradventure there be fifty righteous within the city: wilt thou also destroy and not spare the place for the fifty righteous that are therein? That be far from thee to do after this manner, to slay the righteous with the wicked: and that the righteous should be as the wicked, that be far from thee. Shall not the Judge of all the earth do right?"

And the LORD said, "If I find in Sodom fifty righteous within the city, then I will spare all the place for their sakes."

And Abraham answered and said, "Behold now, I have taken upon me to speak unto the Lord, which am but dust and ashes: peradventure there shall lack five of the fifty righteous: wilt thou destroy all the city for lack of five?"

And he said, "If I find there forty and five, I will not destroy it."

And he spake unto him yet again, and said, "Peradventure there shall be forty found there."

And he said, "I will not do it for forty's sake."

And he said unto him, "Oh let not the Lord be angry, and I will speak: peradventure there shall thirty be found there."

And he said, "I will not do it, if I find thirty there."

And he said, "Behold now, I have taken upon me to speak unto the Lord: peradventure there shall be twenty found there."

And he said, "I will not destroy it for twenty's sake."

And he said, "Oh let not the Lord be angry, and I will speak yet but this once: peradventure ten shall be found there."

[7] Evil reputation.
[8] Sodom and Gomorrah, "Cities of the Plain," were in the "Vale of Siddim," which about the time of Abraham was inundated by the Dead Sea.

And he said, "I will not destroy it for ten's sake."

And the LORD went his way, as soon as he had left communing with Abraham: and Abraham returned unto his place.

And there came two angels to Sodom at even; and Lot[9] sat in the gate of Sodom: and Lot seeing them rose up to meet them; and he bowed himself with his face toward the ground; and he said, "Behold now, my lords, turn in, I pray you, into your servant's house, and tarry all night, and wash your feet, and ye shall rise up early, and go on your ways."

And they said, "Nay; but we will abide in the street all night." And he pressed upon them greatly; and they turned in unto him, and entered into his house; and he made them a feast, and did bake unleavened bread, and they did eat.

But before they lay down, the men of the city, even the men of Sodom, compassed the house round, both old and young, all the people from every quarter: and they called unto Lot, and said unto him, "Where are the men which came in to thee this night? bring them out unto us, that we may know them."

And Lot went out at the door unto them, and shut the door after him, and said, "I pray you, brethren, do not so wickedly. Behold now, I have two daughters which have not known man; let me, I pray you, bring them out unto you, and do ye to them as is good in your eyes: only unto these men do nothing; for therefore came they under the shadow of my roof."

And they said, "Stand back." And they said again, "This one fellow came in to sojourn, and he will needs be a judge: now will we deal worse with thee, than with them." And they pressed sore upon the man, even Lot, and came near to break the door. But the men put forth their hand, and pulled Lot into the house to them, and shut to the door. And they smote the men that were at the door of the house with blindness, both small and great: so that they wearied themselves to find the door.

---

[9] Abraham's nephew. He and his family and retainers had separated from Abraham to dwell in the fertile plain.

And the men said unto Lot, "Hast thou here any besides? son in law, and thy sons, and thy daughters, and whatsoever thou hast in the city, bring them out of this place: for we will destroy this place, because the cry of them is waxen great before the face of the Lord; and the Lord hath sent us to destroy it."

And Lot went out, and spake unto his sons in law, which married his daughters, and said, "Up, get you out of this place; for the Lord will destroy this city." But he seemed as one that mocked unto his sons in law.

And when the morning arose, then the angels hastened Lot, saying, "Arise, take thy wife, and thy two daughters, which are here; lest thou be consumed in the iniquity of the city." And while he lingered, the men laid hold upon his hand, and upon the hand of his wife, and upon the hand of his two daughters; the Lord being merciful unto him: and they brought him forth, and set him without the city.

And it came to pass, when they had brought them forth abroad, that he said, "Escape for thy life; look not behind thee, neither stay thou in all the plain; escape to the mountain, lest thou be consumed."

And Lot said unto them, "Oh, not so, my Lord: behold now, thy servant hath found grace in thy sight, and thou hast magnified thy mercy, which thou hast shewed unto me in saving my life; and I cannot escape to the mountain, lest some evil take me, and I die: behold now, this city is near to flee unto, and it is a little one: Oh, let me escape thither, (is it not a little one?) and my soul shall live."

And he said unto him, "See, I have accepted thee concerning this thing also, that I will not overthrow this city, for the which thou hast spoken. Haste thee, escape thither; for I cannot do any thing till thou be come thither." Therefore the name of the city was called Zoar.

The sun was risen upon the earth when Lot entered into Zoar. Then the Lord rained upon Sodom and upon Gomorrah brimstone and fire[10] from the LORD out of heaven; and he over-threw those cities, and all the plain, and all the inhabitants of the cities, and that which grew upon the ground. But his wife looked back from behind him, and she became a pillar of salt.

And Abraham gat up early in the morning to the place where he stood before the LORD: and he looked toward Sodom and Gomorrah, and toward all the land of the plain, and beheld, and, lo, the smoke of the country went up as the smoke of a furnace.

And it came to pass, when God destroyed the cities of the plain, that God remembered Abraham, and sent Lot out of the midst of the overthrow, when he overthrew the cities in the which Lot dwelt. And Lot went up out of Zoar, and dwelt in the mountain, and his two daughters with him; for he feared to dwell in Zoar: and he dwelt in a cave, he and his two daughters.

And the firstborn said unto the younger, "Our father is old, and there is not a man in the earth to come in unto us after the manner of all the earth: come, let us make our father drink wine, and we will lie with him, that we may preserve seed of our father." And they made their father drink wine that night: and the firstborn went in, and lay with her father; and he perceived not when she lay down, nor when she arose.

And it came to pass on the morrow, that the firstborn said unto the younger, "Behold, I lay yesternight with my father: let us make him drink wine this night also; and go thou in, and lie with him, that we may preserve seed of our father." And they made their father drink wine that night also: and the younger arose, and lay with him; and he perceived not when she lay down, nor when she arose.

Thus were both the daughters of Lot with child by their father. And the firstborn bare a son, and called his name Moab: the same is the father of the Moabites unto this day. And the

[10] Probably an earthquake which was followed by the inundation referred to in a previous note.

younger, she also bare a son, and called his name Ben-ammi: the same is the father of the children of Ammon unto this day.[11]

The Birth of Isaac

• GENESIS 21: 1—21 •

And the Lord visited Sarah as he had said, and the Lord did unto Sarah as he had spoken. For Sarah conceived, and bare Abraham a son in his old age, at the set time of which God had spoken to him. And Abraham called the name of his son that was born unto him, whom Sarah bare to him, Isaac. And Abraham circumcised his son Isaac being eight days old, as God had commanded him. And Abraham was an hundred years old, when his son Isaac was born unto him.

And Sarah said, "God hath made me to laugh, so that all that hear will laugh with me." And she said, "Who would have said unto Abraham, that Sarah should have given children suck? for I have born him a son in his old age." And the child grew, and was weaned: and Abraham made a great feast the same day that Isaac was weaned.

And Sarah saw the son of Hagar the Egyptian, which she had born unto Abraham, mocking. Wherefore she said unto Abraham, "Cast out this bondwoman and her son: for the son of this bondwoman shall not be heir with my son, even with Isaac."

And the thing was very grievous in Abraham's sight because of his son. And God said unto Abraham, "Let it not be grievous in thy sight because of the lad, and because of thy bondwoman; in all that Sarah hath said unto thee, hearken unto her voice; for in Isaac shall thy seed be called. And also of the son of the bondwoman will I make a nation, because he is thy seed."

And Abraham rose up early in the morning, and took bread,

[11] At a later period the Moabites and the Ammonites were hostile to the Israelites.

and a bottle of water, and gave it unto Hagar, putting it on her shoulder, and the child, and sent her away: and she departed, and wandered in the wilderness of Beer-sheba. And the water was spent in the bottle, and she cast the child under one of the shrubs. And she went, and sat her down over against him a good way off, as it were a bowshot: for she said, "Let me not see the death of the child." And she sat over against him, and lift up her voice, and wept.

And God heard the voice of the lad; and the angel of God called to Hagar out of heaven, and said unto her, "What aileth thee, Hagar? fear not; for God hath heard the voice of the lad where he is. Arise, lift up the lad, and hold him in thine hand; for I will make him a great nation." [12]

And God opened her eyes, and she saw a well of water; and she went, and filled the bottle with water, and gave the lad drink. And God was with the lad; and he grew, and dwelt in the wilderness, and became an archer. And he dwelt in the wilderness of Paran: and his mother took him a wife out of the land of Egypt.

The Sacrifice of Isaac

• GENESIS 22: 1–19 •

And it came to pass after these things, that God did tempt Abraham, and said unto him, "Abraham."

And he said, "Behold, here I am."

And he said, "Take now thy son, thine only son Isaac, whom thou lovest, and get thee into the land of Moriah; and offer him there for a burnt offering upon one of the mountains which I will tell thee of."

And Abraham rose up early in the morning, and saddled his ass, and took two of his young men with him, and Isaac his

[12] The Bedouin Arabs, who trace their descent from Abraham through Hagar's son Ishmael.

son, and clave the wood for the burnt offering, and rose up, and went unto the place of which God had told him. Then on the third day Abraham lifted up his eyes, and saw the place afar off. And Abraham said unto his young men, "Abide ye here with the ass; and I and the lad will go yonder and worship, and come again to you."

And Abraham took the wood of the burnt offering, and laid it upon Isaac his son; and he took the fire in his hand, and a knife; and they went both of them together. And Isaac spake unto Abraham his father, and said, "My father."

And he said, "Here am I, my son."

And he said, "Behold the fire and the wood: but where is the lamb for a burnt offering?"

And Abraham said, "My son, God will provide himself a lamb for a burnt offering." So they went both of them together. And they came to the place which God had told him of; and Abraham built an altar there, and laid the wood in order, and bound Isaac his son, and laid him on the altar upon the wood. And Abraham stretched forth his hand, and took the knife to slay his son.

And the angel of the LORD called unto him out of heaven, and said, "Abraham, Abraham."

And he said, "Here am I."

And he said, "Lay not thine hand upon the lad, neither do thou any thing unto him: for now I know that thou fearest God, seeing thou hast not withheld thy son, thine only son from me."

And Abraham lifted up his eyes, and looked, and behold behind him a ram caught in a thicket by his horns: and Abraham went and took the ram, and offered him up for a burnt offering in the stead of his son. And Abraham called the name of that place Jehovah-jireh: as it is said to this day, In the mount of the LORD it shall be seen.

And the angel of the LORD called unto Abraham out of heaven the second time, and said, "By myself have I sworn, saith the LORD, for because thou hast done this thing, and hast not withheld thy son, thine only son: that in blessing I will bless thee, and in multiplying I will multiply thy seed as the stars of the heaven, and as the sand which is upon the sea shore; and thy seed shall possess the gate of his enemies; and in thy seed shall all the nations of the earth be blessed; because thou hast obeyed my voice."

So Abraham returned unto his young men, and they rose up and went together to Beer-sheba; and Abraham dwelt at Beer-sheba.

Jacob and Esau

• GENESIS 25:19–34 •

And these are the generations of Isaac, Abraham's son: Abraham begat Isaac: and Isaac was forty years old when he took Rebekah to wife, the daughter of Bethuel the Syrian of Padan-aram, the sister to Laban the Syrian. And Isaac intreated the LORD for his wife, because she was barren: and the LORD was intreated of him, and Rebekah his wife conceived. And the children struggled together within her; and she said, "If it be so, why am I thus?" And she went to enquire of the LORD.

And the LORD said unto her, "Two nations are in thy womb, and two manner of people shall be separated from thy bowels; and the one people shall be stronger than the other people; and the elder shall serve the younger."

And when her days to be delivered were fulfilled, behold, there were twins in her womb. And the first came out red, all over like an hairy garment; and they called his name Esau. And after that came his brother out, and his hand took hold on Esau's heel; and his name was called Jacob: and Isaac was threescore years old when she bare them.

And the boys grew: and Esau was a cunning hunter, a man of the field; and Jacob was a plain man, dwelling in tents. And

Isaac loved Esau, because he did eat of his venison: but Rebekah loved Jacob.

And Jacob sod[13] pottage: and Esau came from the field, and he was faint: and Esau said to Jacob, "Feed me, I pray thee, with that same red pottage; for I am faint." Therefore was his name called Edom.[14]

And Jacob said, "Sell me this day thy birthright." [15]

And Esau said, "Behold, I am at the point to die: and what profit shall this birthright do to me?"

And Jacob said, "Swear to me this day"; and he sware unto him: and he sold his birthright unto Jacob. Then Jacob gave Esau bread and pottage of lentils; and he did eat and drink, and rose up, and went his way: thus Esau despised his birthright.

The Stolen Blessing

• GENESIS 27: 1–40 •

And it came to pass, that when Isaac was old, and his eyes were dim, so that he could not see, he called Esau his eldest son, and said unto him, "My son."

And he said unto him, "Behold, here am I."

And he said, "Behold now, I am old, I know not the day of my death: now therefore take, I pray thee, thy weapons, thy quiver and thy bow, and go out to the field, and take me some venison; and make me savoury meat, such as I love, and bring it to me, that I may eat; that my soul may bless thee before I die."

And Rebekah heard when Isaac spake to Esau his son. And

---

[13] Boiled.

[14] Edom means "red." The reference is to the pottage of red lentils.

[15] The double inheritance of the first-born. The primacy of the family, also the right of the first-born, passes to Jacob as a result of the deception recorded in the next selection.

Esau went to the field to hunt for venison, and to bring it. And Rebekah spake unto Jacob her son, saying, "Behold, I heard thy father speak unto Esau thy brother, saying, 'Bring me venison, and make me savoury meat, that I may eat, and bless thee before the LORD before my death.' Now therefore, my son, obey my voice according to that which I command thee. Go now to the flock, and fetch me from thence two good kids of the goats; and I will make them savoury meat for thy father, such as he loveth: and thou shalt bring it to thy father, that he may eat, and that he may bless thee before his death."

And Jacob said to Rebekah his mother, "Behold, Esau my brother is a hairy man, and I am a smooth man: my father peradventure will feel me, and I shall seem to him as a deceiver; and I shall bring a curse upon me, and not a blessing."

And his mother said unto him, "Upon me be thy curse, my son: only obey my voice, and go fetch me them." And he went, and fetched, and brought them to his mother: and his mother made savoury meat, such as his father loved. And Rebekah took goodly raiment of her eldest son Esau, which were with her in the house, and put them upon Jacob her younger son: and she put the skins of the kids of the goats upon his hands, and upon the smooth of his neck: and she gave the savoury meat and the bread, which she had prepared, into the hand of her son Jacob.

And he came unto his father, and said, "My father."

And he said, "Here am I; who art thou, my son?"

And Jacob said unto his father, "I am Esau thy firstborn; I have done according as thou badest me: arise, I pray thee, sit and eat of my venison, that thy soul may bless me."

And Isaac said unto his son, "How is it that thou hast found it so quickly, my son?"

And he said, "Because the LORD thy God brought it to me."

And Isaac said unto Jacob, "Come near, I pray thee, that I may feel thee, my son, whether thou be my very son Esau or not." And Jacob went near unto Isaac his father; and he felt him, and said, "The voice is Jacob's voice, but the hands are the hands of Esau." And he discerned him not, because his hands were hairy, as his brother Esau's hands: so he blessed him.

And he said, "Art thou my very son Esau?"

And he said, "I am."

And he said, "Bring it near to me, and I will eat of my son's venison, that my soul may bless thee." And he brought it near to him, and he did eat: and he brought him wine, and he drank. And his father Isaac said unto him, "Come near now, and kiss me, my son."

And he came near, and kissed him: and he smelled the smell of his raiment, and blessed him, and said, "See, the smell of my son is as the smell of a field which the LORD hath blessed: therefore God give thee of the dew of heaven, and the fatness of the earth, and plenty of corn and wine: let people serve thee, and nations bow down to thee: be lord over thy brethren, and let thy mother's sons bow down to thee: cursed be every one that curseth thee, and blessed be he that blesseth thee."

And it came to pass, as soon as Isaac had made an end of blessing Jacob, and Jacob was yet scarce gone out from the presence of Isaac his father, that Esau his brother came in from his hunting. And he also had made savoury meat, and brought it unto his father, and said unto his father, "Let my father arise, and eat of his son's venison, that thy soul may bless me."

And Isaac his father said unto him, "Who art thou?"

And he said, "I am thy son, thy firstborn Esau."

And Isaac trembled very exceedingly, and said, "Who? where is he that hath taken venison, and brought it me, and I have eaten of all before thou camest, and have blessed him? yea, and he shall be blessed."

And when Esau heard the words of his father, he cried with a great and exceeding bitter cry, and said unto his father, "Bless me, even me also, O my father."

And he said, "Thy brother came with subtilty, and hath taken away thy blessing."

And he said, "Is not he rightly named Jacob? [16] for he hath supplanted me these two times: he took away my birthright; and, behold, now he hath taken away my blessing." And he said, "Hast thou not reserved a blessing for me?"

And Isaac answered and said unto Esau, "Behold, I have made him thy lord, and all his brethren have I given to him for servants; and with corn and wine have I sustained him: and what shall I do now unto thee, my son?"

And Esau said unto his father, "Hast thou but one blessing, my father? bless me, even me also, O my father." And Esau lifted up his voice, and wept.

And Isaac his father answered and said unto him, "Behold, thy dwelling shall be[17] the fatness of the earth, and of the dew of heaven from above; and by thy sword shalt thou live, and shalt serve thy brother; and it shall come to pass when thou shalt have the dominion, that thou shalt break his yoke from off thy neck."

Jacob at Beth-el

• GENESIS 28: 10–22 •

And Jacob went out from Beer-sheba, and went toward Haran. And he lighted upon a certain place, and tarried there all night, because the sun was set; and he took of the stones of that place, and put them for his pillows, and lay down in that place to sleep. And he dreamed, and behold a ladder set up on the earth, and the top of it reached to heaven: and behold the angels of God ascending and descending on it.

And, behold, the LORD stood above it, and said, "I am the LORD God of Abraham thy father, and the God of Isaac: the

[16] Jacob means "supplanter."
[17] Or rather, "shall be away from."

land whereon thou liest, to thee will I give it, and to thy seed; and thy seed shall be as the dust of the earth, and thou shalt spread abroad to the west, and to the east, and to the north, and to the south: and in thee and in thy seed shall all the families of the earth be blessed. And, behold, I am with thee, and will keep thee in all places whither thou goest, and will bring thee again into this land; for I will not leave thee, until I have done that which I have spoken to thee of."

And Jacob awaked out of his sleep, and he said, "Surely the LORD is in this place; and I knew it not." And he was afraid, and said, "How dreadful is this place! this is none other but the house of God, and this is the gate of heaven."

And Jacob rose up early in the morning, and took the stone that he had put for his pillows, and set it up for a pillar, and poured oil upon the top of it. And he called the name of that place Beth-el: [18] but the name of that city was called Luz at the first. And Jacob vowed a vow, saying, "If God will be with me, and will keep me in this way that I go, and will give me bread to eat, and raiment to put on, so that I come again to my father's house in peace; then shall the LORD be my God: and this stone, which I have set for a pillar, shall be God's house: and of all that thou shalt give me I will surely give the tenth unto thee."

Jacob, Leah, and Rachel

• GENESIS 29: 1–31 •

Then Jacob went on his journey, and came into the land of the people of the east. And he looked, and behold a well in the field, and, lo, there were three flocks of sheep lying by it; for out of that well they watered the flocks: and a great stone was upon the well's mouth. And thither were all the flocks gathered: and they rolled the stone from the well's mouth, and watered

[18] A village about 12 miles north of Jerusalem.

the sheep, and put the stone again upon the well's mouth in his place.

And Jacob said unto them, "My brethren, whence be ye?" And they said, "Of Haran are we."

And he said unto them, "Know ye Laban the son of Nahor?"

And they said, "We know him."

And he said unto them, "Is he well?"

And they said, "He is well: and, behold, Rachel his daughter cometh with the sheep."

And he said, "Lo, it is yet high day, neither is it time that the cattle should be gathered together: water ye the sheep, and go and feed them."

And they said, "We cannot, until all the flocks be gathered together, and till they roll the stone from the well's mouth; then we water the sheep." [19]

And while he yet spake with them, Rachel came with her father's sheep: for she kept them. And it came to pass, when Jacob saw Rachel the daughter of Laban his mother's brother, and the sheep of Laban his mother's brother, that Jacob went near, and rolled the stone from the well's mouth, and watered the flock of Laban his mother's brother. And Jacob kissed Rachel, and lifted up his voice, and wept. And Jacob told Rachel that he was her father's brother,[20] and that he was Rebekah's son: and she ran and told her father.

And it came to pass, when Laban heard the tidings of Jacob his sister's son, that he ran to meet him, and embraced him, and kissed him, and brought him to his house. And he told Laban all these things. And Laban said to him, "Surely thou art my bone and my flesh." And he abode with him the space of a month.

And Laban said unto Jacob, "Because thou art my brother,

[19] When a well belonged to more than one family, it was covered by a heavy stone which could be moved only by the joint efforts of the shepherds of all the groups.

[20] i.e., nephew.

shouldest thou therefore serve me for nought? tell me, what shall thy wages be?"

And Laban had two daughters: the name of the elder was Leah, and the name of the younger was Rachel. Leah was tender eyed; [21] but Rachel was beautiful and well favoured. And Jacob loved Rachel; and said, "I will serve thee seven years for Rachel thy younger daughter."

And Laban said, "It is better that I give her to thee, than that I should give her to another man: abide with me." And Jacob served seven years for Rachel; and they seemed unto him but a few days, for the love he had to her.

And Jacob said unto Laban, "Give me my wife, for my days are fulfilled, that I may go in unto her."

And Laban gathered together all the men of the place, and made a feast. And it came to pass in the evening, that he took Leah his daughter, and brought her to him; and he went in unto her. And Laban gave unto his daughter Leah Zilpah his maid for an handmaid. And it came to pass, that in the morning, behold, it was Leah: and he said to Laban, "What is this thou hast done unto me? did not I serve with thee for Rachel? wherefore then hast thou beguiled me?"

And Laban said, "It must not be so done in our country, to give the younger before the firstborn. Fulfil her week, and we will give thee this also for the service which thou shalt serve with me yet seven other years."

And Jacob did so, and fulfilled her week: and he gave him Rachel his daughter to wife also. And Laban gave to Rachel his daughter Bilhah his handmaid to be her maid. And he went in also unto Rachel, and he loved also Rachel more than Leah, and served with him yet seven other years. And when the Lord saw that Leah was hated, he opened her womb: but Rachel was barren.

[21] Weak eyed.

Jacob Is Called Israel

• GENESIS 35:9–29 •

And God appeared unto Jacob again, when he came out of Padan-aram,[22] and blessed him. And God said unto him, "Thy name is Jacob: thy name shall not be called any more Jacob, but Israel shall be thy name." And he called his name Israel.

And God said unto him, "I am God Almighty: be fruitful and multiply; a nation and a company of nations shall be of thee, and kings shall come out of thy loins; and the land which I gave Abraham and Isaac, to thee I will give it, and to thy seed after thee will I give the land." And God went up from him in the place where he talked with him.

And Jacob set up a pillar in the place where he talked with him, even a pillar of stone: and he poured a drink offering thereon, and he poured oil thereon. And Jacob called the name of the place where God spake with him, Beth-el.

And they journeyed from Beth-el; and there was but a little way to come to Ephrath: and Rachel travailed, and she had hard labour. And it came to pass, when she was in hard labour, that the midwife said unto her, "Fear not; thou shalt have this son also." And it came to pass, as her soul was in departing, (for she died) that she called his name Ben-oni: [23] but his father called him Benjamin.[24] And Rachel died, and was buried in the way to Ephrath, which is Beth-lehem. And Jacob set a pillar upon her grave: that is the pillar of Rachel's grave unto this day.

Now the sons of Jacob were twelve: the sons of Leah; Reuben, Jacob's firstborn, and Simeon, and Levi, and Judah, and Issachar, and Zebulun: the sons of Rachel; Joseph, and Benjamin: and the sons of Bilhah, Rachel's handmaid; Dan, and Naphtali:

[22] Mesopotamia, where he had married Leah and Rachel.
[23] "Son of my sorrow."
[24] "Son of my right hand." Rachel, after her barrenness was removed, had previously given birth to Joseph.

and the sons of Zilpah, Leah's handmaid; Gad, and Asher: these are the sons of Jacob, which were born to him in Padan-aram.

And Jacob came unto Isaac his father unto Mamre, unto the city of Arbah, which is Hebron, where Abraham and Isaac sojourned. And the days of Isaac were an hundred and fourscore years. And Isaac gave up the ghost, and died, and was gathered unto his people, being old and full of days: and his sons Esau and Jacob buried him.

THE STORY OF JOSEPH

Joseph and His Brethren

• GENESIS 37: 1–36 •

And Jacob dwelt in the land wherein his father was a stranger, in the land of Canaan. These are the generations of Jacob. Joseph, being seventeen years old, was feeding the flock with his brethren; and the lad was with the sons of Bilhah, and with the sons of Zilpah, his father's wives: and Joseph brought unto his father their evil report. Now Israel loved Joseph more than all his children, because he was the son of his old age: and he made him a coat of many colours. And when his brethren saw that their father loved him more than all his brethren, they hated him, and could not speak peaceably unto him.

And Joseph dreamed a dream, and he told it his brethren: and they hated him yet the more. And he said unto them, "Hear, I pray you, this dream which I have dreamed: for, behold, we were binding sheaves in the field, and, lo, my sheaf arose, and also stood upright; and, behold, your sheaves stood round about, and made obeisance to my sheaf."

And his brethren said to him, "Shalt thou indeed reign over us? or shalt thou indeed have dominion over us?" And they hated him yet the more for his dreams, and for his words.

And he dreamed yet another dream, and told it his brethren, and said, "Behold, I have dreamed a dream more; and, behold, the sun and the moon and the eleven stars made obeisance to me."

And he told it to his father, and to his brethren: and his father rebuked him, and said unto him, "What is this dream that thou hast dreamed? Shall I and thy mother and thy brethren indeed come to bow down ourselves to thee to the earth?" And his brethren envied him; but his father observed the saying.

And his brethren went to feed their father's flock in Shechem.[1] And Israel said unto Joseph, "Do not thy brethren feed the flock in Shechem? come, and I will send thee unto them."

And he said to him, "Here am I."

And he said to him, "Go, I pray thee, see whether it be well with thy brethren, and well with the flocks; and bring me word again." So he sent him out of the vale of Hebron, and he came to Shechem.

And a certain man found him, and, behold, he was wandering in the field: and the man asked him, saying, "What seekest thou?"

And he said, "I seek my brethren: tell me, I pray thee, where they feed their flocks."

And the man said, "They are departed hence; for I heard them say, 'Let us go to Dothan'."[2]

And Joseph went after his brethren, and found them in Dothan. And when they saw him afar off, even before he came near unto them, they conspired against him to slay him.

---

[1] Jacob had lands at Shechem, about 50 miles north of Hebron, where Jacob dwelt at this time.

[2] 12 miles north of Shechem, on the caravan route between Syria and Egypt.

And they said one to another, "Behold, this dreamer cometh. Come now therefore, and let us slay him, and cast him into some pit, and we will say, 'Some evil beast hath devoured him': and we shall see what will become of his dreams."

And Reuben[3] heard it, and he delivered him out of their hands; and said, "Let us not kill him." And Reuben said unto them, "Shed no blood, but cast him into this pit that is in the wilderness, and lay no hand upon him"; that he might rid him out of their hands, to deliver him to his father again.

And it came to pass, when Joseph was come unto his brethren, that they stripped Joseph out of his coat, his coat of many colours that was on him; and they took him, and cast him into a pit: and the pit was empty, there was no water in it. And they sat down to eat bread: and they lifted up their eyes and looked, and, behold, a company of Ishmaelites came from Gilead with their camels bearing spicery and balm and myrrh, going to carry it down to Egypt.

And Judah said unto his brethren, "What profit is it if we slay our brother, and conceal his blood? Come, and let us sell him to the Ishmaelites, and let not our hand be upon him; for he is our brother and our flesh." And his brethren were content.

Then there passed by Midianites merchantmen; and they drew and lifted up Joseph out of the pit, and sold Joseph to the Ishmaelites for twenty pieces of silver: and they brought Joseph into Egypt.

And Reuben returned unto the pit; and, behold, Joseph was not in the pit; and he rent his clothes. And he returned unto his brethren, and said, "The child is not and I, whither shall I go?"

And they took Joseph's coat, and killed a kid of the goats, and dipped the coat in the blood; and they sent the coat of many colours, and they brought it to their father; and said, "This have we found: know now whether it be thy son's coat or no."

The narrative which follows seems to be based on two different sources. In one, Joseph is sold to the Ishmaelites; in the other, to the Midianites.

And he knew it, and said, "It is my son's coat; an evil beast hath devoured him; Joseph is without doubt rent in pieces." And Jacob rent his clothes, and put sackcloth upon his loins, and mourned for his son many days. And all his sons and all his daughters rose up to comfort him; but he refused to be comforted; and he said, "For I will go down into the grave unto my son mourning." Thus his father wept for him.

And the Midianites sold him into Egypt unto Potiphar, an officer of Pharaoh's,[4] and captain of the guard.

Joseph and the Wife of Potiphar

• GENESIS 39: 1–23 •

And Joseph was brought down to Egypt; and Potiphar, an officer of Pharaoh, captain of the guard, an Egyptian, bought him of the hands of the Ishmaelites, which had brought him down thither. And the LORD was with Joseph, and he was a prosperous man; and he was in the house of his master the Egyptian. And his master saw that the LORD was with him, and that the LORD made all that he did to prosper in his hand. And Joseph found grace in his sight, and he served him: and he made him overseer over his house, and all that he had he put into his hand. And it came to pass from the time that he had made him overseer in his house, and over all that he had, that the LORD blessed the Egyptian's house for Joseph's sake; and the blessing of the LORD was upon all that he had in the house, and in the field. And he left all that he had in Joseph's hand; and he knew not ought he had, save the bread which he did eat. And Joseph was a goodly person, and well favoured.

And it came to pass after these things, that his master's wife cast her eyes upon Joseph; and she said, "Lie with me."

[4] The date of Joseph's enslavement was c.1700 B.C. The Pharaoh of the story was probably one of the Hyksos dynasty.

But he refused, and said unto his master's wife, "Behold, my master wotteth not what is with me in the house, and he hath committed all that he hath to my hand; there is none greater in this house than I; neither hath he kept back any thing from me but thee, because thou art his wife: how then can I do this great wickedness, and sin against God?"

And it came to pass, as she spake to Joseph day by day, that he hearkened not unto her, to lie by her, or to be with her. And it came to pass about this time, that Joseph went into the house to do his business; and there was none of the men of the house there within. And she caught him by his garment, saying, "Lie with me"; and he left his garment in her hand, and fled, and got him out.

And it came to pass, when she saw that he had left his garment in her hand, and was fled forth, that she called unto the men of her house, and spake unto them, saying, "See, he hath brought in an Hebrew unto us to mock us; he came in unto me to lie with me, and I cried with a loud voice: and it came to pass, when he heard that I lifted up my voice and cried, that he left his garment with me, and fled, and got him out." And she laid up his garment by her, until his lord came home.

And she spake unto him according to these words, saying, "The Hebrew servant, which thou hast brought unto us, came in unto me to mock me: and it came to pass, as I lifted up my voice and cried, that he left his garment with me, and fled out."

And it came to pass, when his master heard the words of his wife, which she spake unto him, saying, "After this manner did thy servant to me," that his wrath was kindled. And Joseph's master took him, and put him into the prison, a place where the king's prisoners were bound: and he was there in the prison.

But the LORD was with Joseph, and shewed him mercy, and gave him favour in the sight of the keeper of the prison. And the keeper of the prison committed to Joseph's hand all the prisoners that were in the prison; and whatsoever they did there, he was the doer of it. The keeper of the prisoner looked not to any thing that was under his hand; because the LORD was with him, and that which he did, the LORD made it to prosper.

The Interpreter of Dreams

• GENESIS 40: 1 TO 41:44 •

And it came to pass after these things, that the butler of the king of Egypt and his baker had offended their lord the king of Egypt. And Pharaoh was wroth against two of his officers, against the chief of the butlers, and against the chief of the bakers. And he put them in ward in the house of the captain of the guard, into the prison, the place where Joseph was bound. And the captain of the guard charged Joseph with them, and he served them: and they continued a season in ward.

And they dreamed a dream both of them, each man his dream in one night, each man according to the interpretation of his dream, the butler and the baker of the king of Egypt, which were bound in the prison. And Joseph came in unto them in the morning, and looked upon them, and, behold, they were sad. And he asked Pharaoh's officers that were with him in the ward of his lord's house, saying, "Wherefore look ye so sadly to day?"

And they said unto him, "We have dreamed a dream, and there is no interpreter of it."

And Joseph said unto them, "Do not interpretations belong to God? tell me them, I pray you." [5]

And the chief butler told his dream to Joseph, and said to him, "In my dream, behold, a vine was before me; and in the vine were three branches: and it was as though it budded, and her blossoms shot forth; and the clusters thereof brought forth ripe grapes: and Pharaoh's cup was in my hand: and I took the grapes, and pressed them into Pharaoh's cup, and I gave the cup into Pharaoh's hand."

[5] i.e., perhaps God will enable me to interpret the dream.

And Joseph said unto him, "This is the interpretation of it: the three branches are three days: yet within three days shall Pharaoh lift up thine head, and restore thee unto thy place: and thou shalt deliver Pharaoh's cup into his hand, after the former manner when thou wast his butler. But think on me when it shall be well with thee, and shew kindness, I pray thee, unto me, and make mention of me unto Pharaoh, and bring me out of this house: for indeed I was stolen away out of the land of the Hebrews: and here also have I done nothing that they should put me into the dungeon."

When the chief baker saw that the interpretation was good, he said unto Joseph, "I also was in my dream, and, behold, I had three white baskets on my head: and in the uppermost basket there was of all manner of bakemeats for Pharaoh; and the birds did eat them out of the basket upon my head."

And Joseph answered and said, "This is the interpretation thereof: the three baskets are three days: yet within three days shall Pharaoh lift up thy head from off thee, and shall hang thee on a tree; and the birds shall eat thy flesh from off thee."

And it came to pass the third day, which was Pharaoh's birthday, that he made a feast unto all his servants: and he lifted up the head of the chief butler and of the chief baker among his servants. And he restored the chief butler unto his butlership again; and he gave the cup into Pharaoh's hand: but he hanged the chief baker: as Joseph had interpreted to them. Yet did not the chief butler remember Joseph, but forgat him.

And it came to pass at the end of two full years, that Pharaoh dreamed: and, behold, he stood by the river. And, behold, there came up out of the river seven well favoured kine and fatfleshed; and they fed in a meadow. And, behold, seven other kine came up after them out of the river, ill favoured and leanfleshed; and stood by the other kine upon the brink of the river. And the ill favoured and leanfleshed kine did eat up the seven well favoured and fat kine. So Pharaoh awoke.

And he slept and dreamed the second time: and, behold,

seven ears of corn came up upon one stalk, rank and good. And, behold, seven thin ears and blasted with the east wind sprung up after them. And the seven thin ears devoured the seven rank and full ears. And Pharaoh awoke, and, behold, it was a dream. And it came to pass in the morning that his spirit was troubled; and he sent and called for all the magicians of Egypt, and all the wise men thereof: and Pharaoh told them his dream; but there was none that could interpret them unto Pharaoh.

Then spake the chief butler unto Pharaoh, saying, "I do remember my faults this day: Pharaoh was wroth with his servants, and put me in ward in the captain of the guard's house, both me and the chief baker: and we dreamed a dream in one night, I and he; we dreamed each man according to the interpretation of his dream. And there was there with us a young man, an Hebrew, servant to the captain of the guard; and we told him, and he interpreted to us our dreams; to each man according to his dream he did interpret. And it came to pass, as he interpreted to us, so it was; me he restored unto mine office, and him he hanged."

Then Pharaoh sent and called Joseph, and they brought him hastily out of the dungeon: and he shaved himself, and changed his raiment, and came in unto Pharaoh. And Pharaoh said unto Joseph, "I have dreamed a dream, and there is none that can interpret it: and I have heard say of thee, that thou canst understand a dream to interpret it."

And Joseph answered Pharaoh, saying, "It is not in me: God shall give Pharaoh an answer of peace."

And Pharaoh said unto Joseph, "In my dream, behold, I stood upon the bank of the river: and, behold, there came up out of the river seven kine, fatfleshed and well favoured; and they fed in a meadow: and, behold, seven other kine came up after them, poor and very ill favoured and leanfleshed, such as I never saw in all the land of Egypt for badness: and the lean and the ill favoured kine did eat up the first seven fat kine: and when they had eaten them up, it could not be known that they had eaten them; but they were still ill favoured, as at the beginning. So I awoke. And I saw in my dream, and, behold, seven ears came up in one stalk, full and good: and, behold, seven ears, withered, thin, and blasted with the east wind, sprung up after them: and the thin ears devoured the seven good ears: and I told this unto the magicians; but there was none that could declare it to me."

And Joseph said unto Pharaoh, "The dream of Pharaoh is one: God hath shewed Pharaoh what he is about to do. The seven good kine are seven years; and the seven good ears are seven years: the dream is one. And the seven thin and ill favoured kine that came up after them are seven years; and the seven empty ears blasted with the east wind shall be seven years of famine. This is the thing which I have spoken unto Pharaoh: what God is about to do he sheweth unto Pharaoh. Behold, there come seven years of great plenty throughout all the land of Egypt: and there shall arise after them seven years of famine; and all the plenty shall be forgotten in the land of Egypt; and the famine shall consume the land; and the plenty shall not be known in the land by reason of that famine following; for it shall be very grievous. And for that the dream was doubled unto Pharaoh twice; it is because the thing is established by God, and God will shortly bring it to pass.

"Now therefore let Pharaoh look out a man discreet and wise, and set him over the land of Egypt. Let Pharaoh do this, and let him appoint officers over the land, and take up the fifth part of the land of Egypt in the seven plenteous years. And let them gather all the food of those good years that come, and lay up corn under the hand of Pharaoh, and let them keep food in the cities. And that food shall be for store to the land against the seven years of famine, which shall be in the land of Egypt; that the land perish not through the famine."

And the thing was good in the eyes of Pharaoh, and in the eyes of all his servants. And Pharaoh said unto his servants, "Can we find such a one as this is, a man in whom the Spirit of

God is?" And Pharaoh said unto Joseph, "Forasmuch as God hath shewed thee all this, there is none so discreet and wise as thou art: thou shalt be over my house, and according unto thy word shall all my people be ruled: only in the throne will I be greater than thou." And Pharaoh said unto Joseph, "See, I have set thee over all the land of Egypt."

And Pharaoh took off his ring from his hand, and put it upon Joseph's hand, and arrayed him in vestures of fine linen, and put a gold chain about his neck; and he made him to ride in the second chariot which he had; and they cried before him, "Bow the knee:" and he made him ruler over all the land of Egypt. And Pharaoh said unto Joseph, "I am Pharaoh, and without thee shall no man lift up his hand or foot in all the land of Egypt." [6]

The Administrator

• GENESIS 41:45-57 •

And Pharaoh called Joseph's name Zaphnath-paaneah; and he gave him to wife Asenath the daughter of Poti-pherah priest of On. And Joseph went out over all the land of Egypt. And Joseph was thirty years old when he stood before Pharaoh king of Egypt. And Joseph went out from the presence of Pharaoh, and went throughout all the land of Egypt. And in the seven plenteous years the earth brought forth by handfuls. And he gathered up all the food of the seven years, which were in the land of Egypt, and laid up the food in the cities: the food of the field, which was round about every city, laid he up in the same. And Joseph gathered corn as the sand of the sea, very much, until he left numbering; for it was without number.

[6] Since the Hyksos kings of Egypt were themselves Asiatics, the elevation of Joseph is not so surprising as it would have been if the Pharaoh had been a native Egyptian.

And unto Joseph were born two sons before the years of famine came, which Asenath the daughter of Poti-pherah priest of On bare unto him. And Joseph called the name of the first-born Manasseh: "For God," said he, "hath made me forget all my toil, and all my father's house." And the name of the second ,called he Ephraim: "For God hath caused me to be fruitful in the land of my affliction."

And the seven years of plenteousness, that was in the land of Egypt, were ended. And the seven years of dearth began to come, according as Joseph had said: and the dearth was in all lands; but in all the land of Egypt there was bread. And when all the land of Egypt was famished, the people cried to Pharaoh for bread: and Pharaoh said unto all the Egyptians, "Go unto Joseph; what he saith to you, do."

And the famine was over all the face of the earth: And Joseph opened all the storehouses, and sold unto the Egyptians; and the famine waxed sore in the land of Egypt. And all countries came into Egypt to Joseph for to buy corn; because that the famine was so sore in all lands.

The Reunion of Joseph and His Brethren

• GENESIS 42:1 TO 45:28; 46:26 TO 50:26 •

Now when Jacob saw that there was corn in Egypt, Jacob said unto his sons, "Why do ye look one upon another?" And he said, "Behold, I have heard that there is corn in Egypt: get you down thither, and buy for us from thence; that we may live, and not die."

And Joseph's ten brethren went down to buy corn in Egypt. But Benjamin, Joseph's brother, Jacob sent not with his brethren; for he said, "Lest peradventure mischief befall him." And the sons of Israel came to buy corn among those that came: for the famine was in the land of Canaan.

And Joseph was the governor over the land, and he it was that sold to all the people of the land: and Joseph's brethren came, and bowed down themselves before him with their faces to the earth. And Joseph saw his brethren, and he knew them, but made himself strange unto them, and spake roughly unto them; and he said unto them, "Whence come ye?"

And they said, "From the land of Canaan to buy food."

And Joseph knew his brethren, but they knew not him. And Joseph remembered the dreams which he dreamed of them, and said unto them, "Ye are spies; to see the nakedness of the land ye are come."

And they said unto him, "Nay, my lord, but to buy food are thy servants come. We are all one man's sons; we are true men, thy servants are no spies."

And he said unto them, "Nay, but to see the nakedness of the land ye are come."

And they said, "Thy servants are twelve brethren, the sons of one man in the land of Canaan; and, behold, the youngest is this day with our father, and one is not."

And Joseph said unto them, "That is it that I spake unto you, saying, 'Ye are spies': hereby ye shall be proved: by the life of Pharaoh ye shall not go forth hence, except your youngest brother come hither. Send one of you, and let him fetch your brother, and ye shall be kept in prison, that your words may be proved, whether there be any truth in you: or else by the life of Pharaoh surely ye are spies." And he put them all together into ward three days.

And Joseph said unto them the third day, "This do, and live; for I fear God: if ye be true men, let one of your brethren be bound in the house of your prison: go ye, carry corn for the famine of your houses: but bring your youngest brother unto me; so shall your words be verified, and ye shall not die." And they did so.

And they said one to another, "We are verily guilty concerning our brother, in that we saw the anguish of his soul, when he besought us, and we would not hear; therefore is this distress come upon us."

And Reuben answered them, saying, "Spake I not unto you, saying, 'Do not sin against the child'; and ye would not hear? therefore, behold, also his blood is required." And they knew not that Joseph understood them; for he spake unto them by an interpreter. And he turned himself about from them, and wept; and returned to them again, and communed with them, and took from them Simeon, and bound him before their eyes.

Then Joseph commanded to fill their sacks with corn, and to restore every man's money into his sack, and to give them provision for the way: and thus did he unto them. And they laded their asses with the corn, and departed thence. And as one of them opened his sack to give his ass provender in the inn, he espied his money; for, behold, it was in his sack's mouth. And he said unto his brethren, "My money is restored; and, lo, it is even in my sack." And their heart failed them, and they were afraid, saying one to another, "What is this that God hath done unto us?"

And they came unto Jacob their father unto the land of Canaan, and told him all that befell unto them; saying, "The man, who is the lord of the land, spake roughly to us, and took us for spies of the country. And we said unto him, 'We are true men; we are no spies: we be twelve brethren, sons of our father; one is not, and the youngest is this day with our father in the land of Canaan.' And the man, the lord of the country, said unto us, 'Hereby shall I know that ye are true men; leave one of your brethren here with me, and take food for the famine of your households, and be gone: and bring your youngest brother unto me: then shall I know that ye are no spies, but that ye are true men: so will I deliver you your brother, and ye shall traffick in the land.'"

And it came to pass as they emptied their sacks, that, behold, every man's bundle of money was in his sack: and when both they and their father saw the bundles of money, they were afraid. And Jacob their father said unto them, "Me have ye bereaved of my children: Joseph is not, and Simeon is not, and ye will take Benjamin away: all these things are against me."

And Reuben spake unto his father, saying, "Slay my two sons, if I bring him not to thee: deliver him into my hand, and I will bring him to thee again."

And he said, "My son shall not go down with you; for his brother is dead, and he is left alone: if mischief befall him by the way in the which ye go, then shall ye bring down my gray hairs with sorrow to the grave."

And the famine was sore in the land. And it came to pass, when they had eaten up the corn which they had brought out of Egypt, their father said unto them, "Go again, buy us a little food."

And Judah spake unto him, saying, "The man did solemnly protest unto us, saying, 'Ye shall not see my face, except your brother be with you.' If thou wilt send our brother with us, we will go down and buy thee food: but if thou wilt not send him, we will not go down: for the man said unto us, 'Ye shall not see my face, except your brother be with you.' "

And Israel said, "Wherefore dealt ye so ill with me, as to tell the man whether ye had yet a brother?"

And they said, "The man asked us straitly of our state, and of our kindred, saying, 'Is your father yet alive? have ye another brother?' and we told him according to the tenor of these words: could we certainly know that he would say, 'Bring your brother down'?"

And Judah said unto Israel his father, "Send the lad with me, and we will arise and go; that we may live, and not die, both we, and thou, and also our little ones. I will be surety for him; of my hand shalt thou require him: if I bring him not unto thee, and set him before thee, then let me bear the blame for ever: for except we had lingered, surely now we had returned this second time."

And their father Israel said unto them, "If it must be so

now, do this; take of the best fruits in the land in your vessels, and carry down the man a present, a little balm, and a little honey, spices, and myrrh, nuts, and almonds: and take double money in your hand; and the money that was brought again in the mouth of your sacks, carry it again in your hand; peradventure it was an oversight: take also your brother, and arise, go again unto the man: and God Almighty give you mercy before the man, that he may send away your other brother, and Benjamin. If I be bereaved of my children, I am bereaved."

And the men took that present, and they took double money in their hand, and Benjamin; and rose up, and went down to Egypt, and stood before Joseph. And when Joseph saw Benjamin with them, he said to the ruler of his house, "Bring these men home, and slay, and make ready; for these men shall dine with me at noon." And the man did as Joseph bade; and the man brought the men into Joseph's house.

And the men were afraid, because they were brought into Joseph's house; and they said, "Because of the money that was returned in our sacks at the first time are we brought in; that he may seek occasion against us, and fall upon us, and take us for bondmen, and our asses." And they came near to the steward of Joseph's house, and they communed with him at the door of the house, and said, "O sir, we came indeed down at the first time to buy food: and it came to pass, when we came to the inn, that we opened our sacks, and, behold, every man's money was in the mouth of his sack, our money in full weight: and we have brought it again in our hand. And other money have we brought down in our hands to buy food: we cannot tell who put our money in our sacks."

And he said, "Peace be to you, fear not: your God, and the God of your father, hath given you treasure in your sacks: I had your money." And he brought Simeon out unto them. And the man brought the men into Joseph's house, and gave them water, and they washed their feet; and he gave their asses provender.

And they made ready the present against Joseph came at noon: for they heard that they should eat bread there.

And when Joseph came home, they brought him the present which was in their hand into the house, and bowed themselves to him to the earth. And he asked them of their welfare, and said, "Is your father well, the old man of whom ye spake? Is he yet alive?"

And they answered, "Thy servant our father is in good health, he is yet alive." And they bowed down their heads, and made obeisance.

And he lifted up his eyes, and saw his brother Benjamin, his mother's son, and said, "Is this your younger brother, of whom ye spake unto me?" And he said, "God be gracious unto thee, my son."

And Joseph made haste; for his bowels did yearn upon his brother: and he sought where to weep; and he entered into his chamber, and wept there. And he washed his face, and went out, and refrained himself, and said, "Set on bread."

And they set on for him by himself, and for them by themselves, and for the Egyptians, which did eat with him, by themselves: because the Egyptians might not eat bread with the Hebrews; for that is an abomination unto the Egyptians. And they sat before him, the firstborn according to his birthright, and the youngest according to his youth: and the men marvelled one at another. And he took and sent messes unto them from before him: but Benjamin's mess was five times so much as any of theirs. And they drank, and were merry with him.

And he commanded the steward of his house, saying, "Fill the men's sacks with food, as much as they can carry, and put every man's money in his sack's mouth. And put my cup, the silver cup, in the sack's mouth of the youngest, and his corn money." And he did according to the word that Joseph had spoken.

As soon as the morning was light, the men were sent away,

they and their asses. And when they were gone out of the city, and not yet far off, Joseph said unto his steward, "Up, follow after the men; and when thou dost overtake them, say unto them, 'Wherefore have ye rewarded evil for good? Is not this it in which my lord drinketh, and whereby indeed he divineth? Ye have done evil in so doing.' "

And he overtook them, and he spake unto them these same words. And they said unto him, "Wherefore saith my lord these words? God forbid that thy servants should do according to this thing: behold, the money, which we found in our sacks' mouths, we brought again unto thee out of the land of Canaan: how then should we steal out of thy lord's house silver or gold? With whomsoever of thy servants it be found, both let him die, and we also will be my lord's bondmen."

And he said, "Now also let it be according unto your words: he with whom it is found shall be my servant; and ye shall be blameless." Then they speedily took down every man his sack to the ground, and opened every man his sack. And he searched, and began at the eldest, and left at the youngest: and the cup was found in Benjamin's sack. Then they rent their clothes, and laded every man his ass, and returned to the city.

And Judah and his brethren came to Joseph's house; for he was yet there: and they fell before him on the ground. And Joseph said unto them, "What deed is this that ye have done? wot ye not that such a man as I can certainly divine?"

And Judah said, "What shall we say unto my lord? what shall we speak? or how shall we clear ourselves? God hath found out the iniquity of thy servants: behold, we are my lord's servants, both we, and he also with whom the cup is found."

And he said, "God forbid that I should do so: but the man in whose hand the cup is found, he shall be my servant; and as for you, get you up in peace unto your father."

Then Judah came near unto him, and said, "Oh my lord, let thy servant, I pray thee, speak a word in my lord's ears, and let not thine anger burn against thy servant: for thou art even as

Pharaoh. My lord asked his servants, saying, 'Have ye a father, or a brother?' And we said unto my lord, 'We have a father, an old man, and a child of his old age, a little one; and his brother is dead, and he alone is left of his mother, and his father loveth him.' And thou saidst unto thy servants, 'Bring him down unto me, that I may set mine eyes upon him.' And we said unto my lord, 'The lad cannot leave his father: for if he should leave his father, his father would die.' And thou saidst unto thy servants, 'Except your youngest brother come down with you, ye shall see my face no more.'

"And it came to pass when we came up unto thy servant my father, we told him the words of my lord. And our father said, 'Go again, and buy us a little food.' And we said, 'We cannot go down: if our youngest brother be with us, then will we go down: for we may not see the man's face, except our youngest brother be with us.' And thy servant my father said unto us, 'Ye know that my wife bare me two sons: and the one went out from me, and I said, "Surely he is torn in pieces"; and I saw him not since: and if ye take this also from me, and mischief befall him, ye shall bring down my gray hairs with sorrow to the grave.'

"Now therefore when I come to thy servant my father, and the lad be not with us; seeing that his life is bound up in the lad's life; it shall come to pass, when he seeth that the lad is not with us, that he will die: and thy servants shall bring down the gray hairs of thy servant our father with sorrow to the grave. For thy servant became surety for the lad unto my father, saying, 'If I bring him not unto thee, then I shall bear the blame to my father for ever.' Now therefore, I pray thee, let thy servant abide instead of the lad a bondman to my lord; and let the lad go up with his brethren. For how shall I go up to my father, and the lad be not with me? lest peradventure I see the evil that shall come on my father."

Then Joseph could not refrain himself before all them that stood by him; and he cried, "Cause every man to go out from me."

And there stood no man with him, while Joseph made himself known unto his brethren. And he wept aloud: and the Egyptians and the house of Pharaoh heard.

And Joseph said unto his brethren, "I am Joseph; doth my father yet live?" And his brethren could not answer him; for they were troubled at his presence. And Joseph said unto his brethren, "Come near to me, I pray you." And they came near.

And he said, "I am Joseph your brother, whom ye sold into Egypt. Now therefore be not grieved, nor angry with yourselves, that ye sold me hither: for God did send me before you to preserve life. For these two years hath the famine been in the land: and yet there are five years, in the which there shall neither be earing nor harvest. And God sent me before you to preserve you a posterity in the earth, and to save your lives by a great deliverance. So now it was not you that sent me hither, but God: and he hath made me a father to Pharaoh, and lord of all his house, and a ruler throughout all the land of Egypt.

"Haste ye, and go up to my father, and say unto him, 'Thus saith thy son Joseph, "God hath made me lord of all Egypt: come down unto me, tarry not. And thou shalt dwell in the land of Goshen,[7] and thou shalt be near unto me, thou, and thy children, and thy children's children, and thy flocks, and thy herds, and all that thou hast: and there will I nourish thee; for yet there are five years of famine; lest thou, and thy household, and all that thou hast, come to poverty." ' And, behold, your eyes see, and the eyes of my brother Benjamin, that it is my mouth that speaketh unto you. And ye shall tell my father of all my glory in Egypt, and of all that ye have seen; and ye shall haste and bring down my father hither."

And he fell upon his brother Benjamin's neck, and wept; and Benjamin wept upon his neck. Moreover he kissed all his brethren, and wept upon them: and after that his brethren talked with him.

[7] In the eastern part of the Nile Delta.

And the fame thereof was heard in Pharaoh's house, saying, "Joseph's brethren are come." And it pleased Pharaoh well, and his servants. And Pharaoh said unto Joseph, "Say unto thy brethren, 'This do ye; lade your beasts, and go, get you unto the land of Canaan; and take your father and your households, and come unto me: and I will give you the good of the land of Egypt, and ye shall eat the fat of the land. Now thou art commanded, this do ye; take you wagons out of the land of Egypt for your little ones, and for your wives, and bring your father, and come. Also regard not your stuff; for the good of all the land of Egypt is yours.'"

And the children of Israel did so: and Joseph gave them wagons, according to the commandment of Pharaoh, and gave them provision for the way. To all of them he gave each man changes of raiment; but to Benjamin he gave three hundred pieces of silver, and five changes of raiment. And to his father he sent after this manner; ten asses laden with the good things of Egypt, and ten she asses laden with corn and bread and meat for his father by the way. So he sent his brethren away, and they departed: and he said unto them, "See that ye fall not out by the way."

And they went up out of Egypt, and came into the land of Canaan unto Jacob their father, and told him, saying, "Joseph is yet alive, and he is governor over all the land of Egypt." And Jacob's heart fainted, for he believed them not. And they told him all the words of Joseph, which he had said unto them: and when he saw the wagons which Joseph had sent to carry him, the spirit of Jacob their father revived.

And Israel said, "It is enough; Joseph my son is yet alive: I will go and see him before I die."

All the souls that came with Jacob into Egypt, which came out of his loins, besides Jacob's sons' wives, all the souls were threescore and six; and the sons of Joseph, which were born him in Egypt, were two souls: all the souls of the house of Jacob, which came into Egypt, were threescore and ten.

And he sent Judah before him unto Joseph, to direct his face unto Goshen; and they came into the land of Goshen. And Joseph made ready his chariot, and went up to meet Israel his father, to Goshen, and presented himself unto him; and he fell on his neck, and wept on his neck a good while.

And Israel said unto Joseph, "Now let me die, since I have seen thy face, because thou art yet alive."

And Joseph said unto his brethren, and unto his father's house, "I will go up, and shew Pharaoh, and say unto him, 'My brethren, and my father's house, which were in the land of Canaan, are come unto me; and the men are shepherds, for their trade hath been to feed cattle; and they have brought their flocks, and their herds, and all that they have.' And it shall come to pass, when Pharaoh shall call you, and shall say, 'What is your occupation?' that ye shall say, 'Thy servants' trade hath been about cattle from our youth even until now, both we, and also our fathers,' that ye may dwell in the land of Goshen; for every shepherd is an abomination unto the Egyptians."

Then Joseph came and told Pharaoh, and said, "My father and my brethren, and their flocks, and their herds, and all that they have, are come out of the land of Canaan; and, behold, they are in the land of Goshen." And he took some of his brethren, even five men, and presented them unto Pharaoh.

And Pharaoh said unto his brethren, "What is your occupation?"

And they said unto Pharaoh, "Thy servants are shepherds, both we, and also our fathers." They said moreover unto Pharaoh, "For to sojourn in the land are we come; for thy servants have no pasture for their flocks; for the famine is sore in the land of Canaan: now therefore, we pray thee, let thy servants dwell in the land of Goshen."

And Pharaoh spake unto Joseph, saying, "Thy father and thy brethren are come unto thee: the land of Egypt is before thee; in the best of the land make thy father and brethren to dwell; in the land of Goshen let them dwell: and if thou knowest any men of activity among them, then make them rulers over my cattle."

And Joseph brought in Jacob his father, and set him before Pharaoh: and Jacob blessed Pharaoh. And Pharaoh said unto Jacob, "How old art thou?"

And Jacob said unto Pharaoh, "The days of the years of my pilgrimage are an hundred and thirty years: few and evil have the days of the years of my life been, and have not attained unto the days of the years of the life of my fathers in the days of their pilgrimage." And Jacob blessed Pharaoh, and went out from before Pharaoh.

And Joseph placed his father and his brethren, and gave them a possession in the land of Egypt, in the best of the land, in the land of Rameses,[8] as Pharaoh had commanded. And Joseph nourished his father, and his brethren, and all his father's household, with bread, according to their families.

And there was no bread in all the land; for the famine was very sore, so that the land of Egypt and all the land of Canaan fainted by reason of the famine. And Joseph gathered up all the money that was found in the land of Egypt, and in the land of Canaan, for the corn which they bought: and Joseph brought the money into Pharaoh's house. And when money failed in the land of Egypt, and in the land of Canaan, all the Egyptians came unto Joseph, and said, "Give us bread: for why should we die in thy presence? for the money faileth."

And Joseph said, "Give your cattle; and I will give you for your cattle, if money fail." And they brought their cattle unto Joseph: and Joseph gave them bread in exchange for horses, and for the flocks, and for the cattle of the herds, and for the asses: and he fed them with bread for all their cattle for that year.

When that year was ended, they came unto him the second year, and said unto him, "We will not hide it from my lord, how

---

[8] Identical with Goshen. The name here used looks forward to the reign of Rameses II, the Pharaoh of the oppression, whose capital was in this region.

that our money is spent; my lord also hath our herds of cattle; there is not ought left in the sight of my lord, but our bodies, and our lands: wherefore shall we die before thine eyes, both we and our land? buy us and our land for bread, and we and our land will be servants unto Pharaoh: and give us seed, that we may live, and not die, that the land be not desolate."

And Joseph bought all the land of Egypt for Pharaoh; for the Egyptians sold every man his field, because the famine prevailed over them: so the land became Pharaoh's. And as for the people, he removed them to cities[9] from one end of the borders of Egypt even to the other end thereof. Only the land of the priests bought he not; for the priests had a portion assigned them of Pharaoh, and did eat their portion which Pharaoh gave them: wherefore they sold not their lands.

Then Joseph said unto the people, "Behold, I have bought you this day and your land for Pharaoh: lo, here is seed for you, and ye shall sow the land. And it shall come to pass in the increase, that ye shall give the fifth part unto Pharaoh, and four parts shall be your own, for seed of the field, and for your food, and for them of your households, and for food for your little ones."

And they said, "Thou hast saved our lives: let us find grace in the sight of my lord, and we will be Pharaoh's servants." And Joseph made it a law over the land of Egypt unto this day, that Pharaoh should have the fifth part; except the land of the priests only, which became not Pharaoh's.

And Israel dwelt in the land of Egypt, in the country of Goshen; and they had possessions therein, and grew, and multiplied exceedingly. And Jacob lived in the land of Egypt seventeen years: so the whole age of Jacob was an hundred forty and seven years. And the time drew nigh that Israel must die: and he called his son Joseph, and said unto him, "If now I have found grace in thy sight, put, I pray thee, thy hand under my

---

[9] Or better, "he made bondmen of them"—that is, they became tenants of the crown.

thigh,[10] and deal kindly and truly with me; bury me not, I pray thee, in Egypt: but I will lie with my fathers, and thou shalt carry me out of Egypt, and bury me in their burying-place."

And he said, "I will do as thou hast said."

And he said, "Swear unto me." And he sware unto him. And Israel bowed himself upon the bed's head. [11]

And it came to pass after these things, that one told Joseph, "Behold, thy father is sick." And he took with him his two sons, Manasseh and Ephraim. And one told Jacob, and said, "Behold, thy son Joseph cometh unto thee." And Israel strengthened himself, and sat upon the bed.

And Jacob said unto Joseph, "God Almighty appeared unto me at Luz [12] in the land of Canaan, and blessed me, and said unto me, 'Behold, I will make thee fruitful, and multiply thee, and I will make of thee a multitude of people; and will give this land to thy seed after thee for an everlasting possession.' And now thy two sons, Ephraim and Manasseh, which were born unto thee in the land of Egypt before I came unto thee into Egypt, are mine; as Reuben and Simeon, they shall be mine. And thy issue, which thou begettest after them, shall be thine, and shall be called after the name of their brethren in their inheritance. And as for me, when I came from Padan, Rachel died by me in the land of Canaan in the way, when yet there was but a little way to come unto Ephrath: and I buried her there in the way of Ephrath; the same is Beth-lehem."

And Israel beheld Joseph's sons, and said, "Who are these?"

And Joseph said unto his father, "They are my sons, whom God hath given me in this place."

And he said, "Bring them, I pray thee, unto me, and I will bless them." Now the eyes of Israel were dim for age, so that he could not see. And he brought them near unto him;

---

[10] A form of oath-taking.
[11] Or better, "worshipped leaning upon his staff."
[12] i.e., Beth-el.

and he kissed them, and embraced them. And Israel said unto Joseph, "I had not thought to see thy face: and, lo, God hath shewed me also thy seed."

And Joseph brought them out from between his knees, and he bowed himself with his face to the earth. And Joseph took them both, Ephraim in his right hand toward Israel's left hand, and Manasseh in his left hand toward Israel's right hand, and brought them near unto him. And Israel stretched out his right hand, and laid it upon Ephraim's head, who was the younger, and his left hand upon Manasseh's head, guiding his hands wittingly; for Manasseh was the firstborn.

And he blessed Joseph, and said, "God, before whom my fathers Abraham and Isaac did walk, the God which fed me all my life long unto this day, the Angel which redeemed me from all evil, bless the lads; and let my name be named on them, and the name of my fathers Abraham and Isaac; and let them grow into a multitude in the midst of the earth."

And when Joseph saw that his father laid his right hand upon the head of Ephraim, it displeased him: and he held up his father's hand, to remove it from Ephraim's head unto Manasseh's head. And Joseph said unto his father, "Not so, my father: for this is the firstborn; put thy right hand upon his head."

And his father refused, and said, "I know it, my son, I know it: he also shall become a people, and he also shall be great: but truly his younger brother shall be greater than he, and his seed shall become a multitude of nations." And he blessed them that day, saying, "In thee shall Israel bless, saying, 'God make thee as Ephraim and as Manasseh.'" And he set Ephraim before Manasseh.

And Israel said unto Joseph, "Behold, I die: but God shall be with you, and bring you again unto the land of your fathers. Moreover I have given to thee one portion above thy brethren, which I took out of the hand of the Amorite with my sword and with my bow." [13]

[13] The reference is to Shechem.

And Jacob called unto his sons, and said, "Gather yourselves together, that I may tell you that which shall befall you in the late days.

Gather yourselves together, and hear, ye sons of Jacob;
And hearken unto Israel your father.
Reuben, thou art my firstborn, my might, and the beginning of
    my strength,
The excellency of dignity, and the excellency of power:
Unstable as water, thou shalt not excel;
Because thou wentest up to thy father's bed;
Then defiledst thou it: he went up to my couch.
    Simeon and Levi are brethren;
Instruments of cruelty are in their habitations.
O my soul, come not thou into their secret;
Unto their assembly, mine honour, be not thou united:
For in their anger they slew a man,
And in their selfwill they digged down a wall.
Cursed be their anger, for it was fierce;
And their wrath, for it was cruel:
I will divide them in Jacob, and scatter them in Israel.
    Judah, thou art he whom thy brethren shall praise:
Thy hand shall be in the neck of thine enemies;
Thy father's children shall bow down before thee.
Judah is a lion's whelp:
From the prey, my son, thou art gone up:
He stooped down, he couched as a lion,
And as an old lion; who shall rouse him up?
The sceptre shall not depart from Judah,
Nor a lawgiver from between his feet,
Until Shiloh come;
And unto him shall the gathering of the people be.
Binding his foal unto the vine,
And his ass's colt unto the choice vine;
He washed his garments in wine,

And his clothes in the blood of grapes:
His eyes shall be red with wine,
And his teeth white with milk.

Zebulun shall dwell at the haven of the sea;
And he shall be for an haven of ships;
And his border shall be unto Zidon.

Issachar is a strong ass
Couching down between two burdens:
And he saw that rest was good,
And the land that it was pleasant;
And bowed his shoulder to bear,
And became a servant unto tribute.

Dan shall judge his people,
As one of the tribes of Israel.
Dan shall be a serpent by the way,
An adder in the path,
That biteth the horse heels,
So that his rider shall fall backward.
I have waited for thy salvation, O LORD.

Gad, a troop shall overcome him:
But he shall overcome at the last.

Out of Asher his bread shall be fat,
And he shall yield royal dainties.

Naphtali is a hind let loose:
He giveth goodly words.

Joseph is a fruitful bough,
Even a fruitful bough by a well;
Whose branches run over the wall:
The archers have sorely grieved him,
And shot at him, and hated him:
But his bow abode in strength,
And the arms of his hands were made strong
By the hands of the mighty God of Jacob;
(From thence is the shepherd, the stone of Israel):
Even by the God of thy father, who shall help thee;

And by the Almighty, who shall bless thee
With blessings of heaven above,
Blessings of the deep that lieth under,
Blessings of the breasts, and of the womb:
The blessings of thy father
Have prevailed above the blessings of my progenitors
Unto the utmost bound of the everlasting hills:
They shall be on the head of Joseph,
And on the crown of the head of him that was separate from his
    brethren.
    Benjamin shall ravin as a wolf:
In the morning he shall devour the prey,
And at night he shall divide the spoil."

All these are the twelve tribes of Israel: and this is it that their father spake unto them, and blessed them; every one according to his blessing he blessed them. And he charged them, and said unto them, "I am to be gathered unto my people: bury me with my fathers in the cave that is in the field of Ephron the Hittite, in the cave that is in the field of Machpelah, which is before Mamre, in the land of Canaan, which Abraham bought with the field of Ephron the Hittite for a possession of a buryingplace. There they buried Abraham and Sarah his wife; there they buried Isaac and Rebekah his wife; and there I buried Leah. The purchase of the field and of the cave that is therein was from the children of Heth." And when Jacob had made an end of commanding his sons, he gathered up his feet into the bed, and yielded up the ghost, and was gathered unto his people.

And Joseph fell upon his father's face, and wept upon him, and kissed him. And Joseph commanded his servants the physicians to embalm his father: and the physicians embalmed Israel. And forty days were fulfilled for him; for so are fulfilled the days of those which are embalmed: and the Egyptians mourned for him threescore and ten days.

And when the days of his mourning were past, Joseph spake

unto the house of Pharaoh, saying. "My father made me swear, saying, 'Lo, I die: in my grave which I have digged for me in the land of Canaan, there shalt thou bury me.' Now therefore let me go up, I pray thee, and bury my father, and I will come again."

And Pharaoh said, "Go up, and bury thy father, according as he made thee swear."

And Joseph went up to bury his father: and with him went up all the servants of Pharaoh, the elders of his house, and all the elders of the land of Egypt, and all the house of Joseph, and his brethren, and his father's house: only their little ones, and their flocks, and their herds, they left in the land of Goshen. And there went up with him both chariots and horsemen: and it was a very great company. And they came to the threshingfloor of Atad,[14] which is beyond Jordan, and there they mourned with a great and very sore lamentation: and he made a mourning for his father seven days.

And when the inhabitants of the land, the Canaanites, saw the mourning in the floor of Atad, they said, "This is a grievous mourning to the Egyptians": wherefore the name of it was called Abel-mizraim, which is beyond Jordan. And his sons did unto him according as he commanded them: for his sons carried him into the land of Canaan, and buried him in the cave of the field of Machpelah, which Abraham bought with the field for a possession of a buryingplace of Ephron the Hittite, before Mamre.

And Joseph returned into Egypt, he, and his brethren, and all that went up with him to bury his father, after he had buried his father. And when Joseph's brethren saw that their father was dead, they said, "Joseph will peradventure hate us, and will certainly requite us all the evil which we did unto him." And they sent a messenger unto Joseph, saying, "Thy father did command before he died, saying, 'So shall ye say unto Joseph, "Forgive, I pray thee now, the trespass of thy brethren, and their sin; for they did unto thee evil."' And now, we pray thee, forgive

---

[14] East of the Jordan. The location is otherwise unknown.

the trespass of the servants of the God of thy father." And Joseph wept when they spake unto him. And his brethren also went and fell down before his face; and they said, "Behold, we be thy servants."

And Joseph said unto them, "Fear not: for am I in the place of God? But as for you, ye thought evil against me; but God meant it unto good, to bring to pass, as it is this day, to save much people alive. Now therefore fear ye not: I will nourish you, and your little ones." And he comforted them, and spake kindly unto them.

And Joseph dwelt in Egypt, he, and his father's house: and Joseph lived an hundred and ten years. And Joseph saw Ephraim's children of the third generation: the children also of Machir the son of Manasseh were brought up upon Joseph's knees. And Joseph said unto his brethren, "I die: and God will surely visit you, and bring you out of this land unto the land which he sware to Abraham, to Isaac, and to Jacob." And Joseph took an oath of the children of Israel, saying, "God will surely visit you, and ye shall carry up my bones from hence."

So Joseph died, being an hundred and ten years old: and they embalmed him, and he was put in a coffin in Egypt.

ISRAEL ENSLAVED AND LIBERATED

The Enslavement of the Hebrews

• EXODUS 1 •

Now these are the names of the children of Israel, which came into Egypt; every man and his household came with Jacob. Reuben, Simeon, Levi, and Judah, Issachar, Zebulun, and Benjamin, Dan, and Naphtali, Gad, and Asher. And all the souls that came out of the loins of Jacob were seventy souls: for Joseph was in Egypt already. And Joseph died, and all his brethren, and all that generation.

And the children of Israel were fruitful, and increased abundantly, and multiplied, and waxed exceeding mighty; and the land was filled with them. Now there arose up a new king over Egypt,[1] which knew not Joseph. And he said unto his people, "Behold, the people of the children of Israel are more and mightier than we: come on, let us deal wisely with them; lest they multiply, and it come to pass, that, when there falleth out any war, they join also unto our enemies, and fight against us, and so get them up out of the land." Therefore they did set over them taskmasters to afflict them with their burdens. And they built for Pharaoh treasure cities, Pithom and Raamses. But the more they afflicted them, the more they multiplied and grew. And they were grieved because of the children of Israel. And the Egyptians made the children of Israel to serve with rigour: and they made their lives bitter with hard bondage, in mortar, and in brick, and in all manner of service in the field: all their service, wherein they made them serve, was with rigour.

And the king of Egypt spake to the Hebrew midwives, of which the name of the one was Shiphrah, and the name of the other Puah: and he said, "When ye do the office of a midwife to the Hebrew women, and see them upon the stools;[2] if it be a son, then ye shall kill him: but if it be a daughter, then she shall live." But the midwives feared God, and did not as the king of Egypt commanded them, but saved the men children alive.

And the king of Egypt called for the midwives, and said unto them, "Why have ye done this thing, and have saved the men children alive?"

[1] It is generally thought that Rameses II (*c.*1301–1234 B.C.) was the Pharaoh of the oppression.
[2] Birth-stools.

And the midwives said unto Pharaoh, "Because the Hebrew women are not as the Egyptian women; for they are lively, and are delivered ere the midwives come in unto them." Therefore God dealt well with the midwives: and the people multiplied, and waxed very mighty. And it came to pass, because the midwives feared God, that he made them houses.[3]

And Pharaoh charged all his people, saying, "Every son that is born ye shall cast into the river, and every daughter ye shall save alive."

The Early Life of Moses

• EXODUS 2:1–15 •

And there went a man of the house of Levi, and took to wife a daughter of Levi. And the woman conceived, and bare a son: and when she saw him that he was a goodly child, she hid him three months. And when she could not longer hide him, she took for him an ark of bulrushes, and daubed it with slime and with pitch, and put the child therein; and she laid it in the flags by the river's brink. And his sister stood afar off, to wit what would be done to him.

And the daughter of Pharaoh came down to wash herself at the river; and her maidens walked along by the river's side; and when she saw the ark among the flags, she sent her maid to fetch it. And when she had opened it, she saw the child: and, behold, the babe wept. And she had compassion on him, and said, "This is one of the Hebrews' children."

Then said his sister to Pharaoh's daughter, "Shall I go and call to thee a nurse of the Hebrew women, that she may nurse the child for thee?"

And Pharaoh's daughter said to her, "Go." And the maid went and called the child's mother.

[3] i.e., gave them many descendants.

And Pharaoh's daughter said unto her, "Take this child away, and nurse it for me, and I will give thee thy wages." And the woman took the child, and nursed it. And the child grew, and she brought him unto Pharaoh's daughter, and he became her son. And she called his name Moses: and she said, "Because I drew him out of the water."

And it came to pass in those days, when Moses was grown, that he went out unto his brethren, and looked on their burdens: and he spied an Egyptian smiting an Hebrew, one of his brethren. And he looked this way and that way, and when he saw that there was no man, he slew the Egyptian, and hid him in the sand. And when he went out the second day, behold, two men of the Hebrews strove together: and he said to him that did the wrong, "Wherefore smitest thou thy fellow?"

And he said, "Who made thee a prince and a judge over us? intendest thou to kill me, as thou killedst the Egyptian?"

And Moses feared, and said, "Surely this thing is known." Now when Pharaoh heard this thing, he sought to slay Moses. But Moses fled from the face of Pharaoh, and dwelt in the land of Midian.[4]

The Calling of Moses

• EXODUS 3 •

Now Moses kept the flock of Jethro his father in law, the priest of Midian: and he led the flock to the backside of the desert, and came to the mountain of God, even to Horeb.[5] And the angel of the LORD appeared unto him in a flame of fire out

---

[4] The southeastern part of the Peninsula of Sinai. Or perhaps on the eastern side of the Gulf of Akaba.
[5] Mt. Sinai, about 60 miles north of the southern tip of the Peninsula of Sinai.

of the midst of a bush: and he looked, and, behold, the bush burned with fire, and the bush was not consumed. And Moses said, "I will now turn aside, and see this great sight, why the bush is not burnt."

And when the LORD saw that he turned aside to see, God called unto him out of the midst of the bush, and said, "Moses, Moses."

And he said, "Here am I."

And he said, "Draw not nigh hither: put off thy shoes from off thy feet, for the place whereon thou standest is holy ground." Moreover he said, "I am the God of thy father, the God of Abraham, the God of Isaac, and the God of Jacob." And Moses hid his face; for he was afraid to look upon God.

And the LORD said, "I have surely seen the affliction of my people which are in Egypt, and have heard their cry by reason of their taskmasters; for I know their sorrows; and I am come down to deliver them out of the hand of the Egyptians, and to bring them up out of that land unto a good land and a large, unto a land flowing with milk and honey; unto the place of the Canaanites, and the Hittites, and the Amorites, and the Perizzites, and the Hivites, and the Jebusites. Now therefore, behold, the cry of the children of Israel is come unto me: and I have also seen the oppression wherewith the Egyptians oppress them. Come now therefore, and I will send thee unto Pharaoh, that thou mayest bring forth my people the children of Israel out of Egypt."

And Moses said unto God, "Who am I, that I should go unto Pharaoh, and that I should bring forth the children of Israel out of Egypt?"

And he said, "Certainly I will be with thee; and this shall be a token unto thee, that I have sent thee: when thou hast brought forth the people out of Egypt, ye shall serve God upon this mountain."

And Moses said unto God, "Behold, when I come unto the children of Israel, and shall say unto them, 'The God of your fathers hath sent me unto you,' and they shall say to me, 'What is his name?' what shall I say unto them?"

And God said unto Moses, "I AM THAT I AM:" [6] and he said, "Thus shalt thou say unto the children of Israel, 'I AM hath sent me unto you.'" And God said moreover unto Moses, "Thus shalt thou say unto the children of Israel, 'The Lord God of your fathers, the God of Abraham, the God of Isaac, and the God of Jacob, hath sent me unto you.' This is my name for ever, and this is my memorial unto all generations. Go, and gather the elders of Israel together, and say unto them, 'The Lord God of your fathers, the God of Abraham, of Isaac, and of Jacob, appeared unto me, saying, "I have surely visited you, and seen that which is done to you in Egypt."' And I have said, 'I will bring you up out of the affliction of Egypt unto the land of the Canaanites, and the Hittites, and the Amorites, and the Perizzites, and the Hivites, and the Jebusites, unto a land flowing with milk and honey.'

"And they shall hearken to thy voice: and thou shalt come, thou and the elders of Israel, unto the king of Egypt, and ye shall say unto him, 'The Lord God of the Hebrews hath met with us: and now let us go, we beseech thee, three days' journey into the wilderness, that we may sacrifice to the Lord our God.' And I am sure that the king of Egypt will not let you go, no, not by a mighty hand. And I will stretch out my hand, and smite Egypt with all my wonders which I will do in the midst thereof: and after that he will let you go. And I will give this people favour in the sight of the Egyptians: and it shall come to pass, that, when ye go, ye shall not go empty: but every woman shall borrow of her neighbour, and of her that sojourneth in her house, jewels of silver, and jewels of gold, and raiment: and ye shall put them upon your sons, and upon your daughters; and ye shall spoil the Egyptians."

[6] The name, as here translated, denotes the absolute self-existence of God.

The Warning of Aaron's Rod

And it came to pass on the day when the LORD spake unto Moses in the land of Egypt, that the LORD spake unto Moses, saying, "I am the LORD: speak thou unto Pharaoh king of Egypt all that I say unto thee."

And Moses said before the LORD, "Behold, I am of uncircumcised [7] lips, and how shall Pharaoh hearken unto me?"

And the LORD said unto Moses, "See, I have made thee a god to Pharaoh: and Aaron thy brother shall be thy prophet. Thou shalt speak all that I command thee: and Aaron thy brother shall speak unto Pharaoh, that he sent the children of Israel out of his land. And I will harden Pharaoh's heart, and multiply my signs and my wonders in the land of Egypt. But Pharaoh shall not hearken unto you, that I may lay my hand upon Egypt, and bring forth mine armies, and my people the children of Israel, out of the land of Egypt by great judgments. And the Egyptians shall know that I am the LORD, when I stretch forth mine hand upon Egypt, and bring out the children of Israel from among them."

And Moses and Aaron did as the LORD commanded them, so did they. And Moses was fourscore years old, and Aaron fourscore and three years old, when they spake unto Pharaoh. And the LORD spake unto Moses and unto Aaron, saying, "When Pharaoh shall speak unto you, saying, 'Shew a miracle for you': then thou shalt say unto Aaron, 'Take thy rod, and cast it before Pharaoh,' and it shall become a serpent."

And Moses and Aaron went in unto Pharaoh, and they did so as the LORD had commanded: and Aaron cast down his rod before Pharaoh, and before his servants, and it became a serpent. Then Pharaoh also called the wise men and the sorcerers: now the magicians of Egypt, they also did in like manner with

[7] Here used metaphorically to mean "unconsecrated," "unworthy."

their enchantments. For they cast down every man his rod, and they became serpents: but Aaron's rod swallowed up their rods. And he hardened Pharaoh's heart, that he hearkened not unto them; as the LORD had said.

The Death of the Firstborn. The Institution of the Passover

• EXODUS 11:1 TO 12:7; 12:21–36 •

And the LORD said unto Moses, "Yet will I bring one plague more[8] upon Pharaoh, and upon Egypt; afterwards he will let you go hence: when he shall let you go, he shall surely thrust you out hence altogether. Speak now in the ears of the people, and let every man borrow of his neighbour, and every woman of her neighbour, jewels of silver, and jewels of gold."

And the LORD gave the people favour in the sight of the Egyptians. Moreover the man Moses was very great in the land of Egypt, in the sight of Pharaoh's servants, and in the sight of the people. And Moses said, "Thus saith the LORD, 'About midnight will I go out into the midst of Egypt: and all the firstborn in the land of Egypt shall die, from the firstborn of Pharaoh that sitteth upon his throne, even unto the firstborn of the maidservant that is behind the mill; and all the firstborn of beasts. And there shall be a great cry throughout all the land of Egypt, such as there was none like it, nor shall be like it any more.' But against any of the children of Israel shall not a dog move his tongue, against man or beast: that ye may know how that the LORD doth put a difference between the Egyptians and Israel. And all these thy servants shall come down unto me, and bow down themselves unto me, saying, 'Get thee out, and all the peo-

[8] The death of the first-born was the last of the ten plagues visited upon the Egyptians. The others were as follows: the turning of the waters of the Nile to blood, frogs, lice, flies, murrain of cattle, boils, hail, locusts, and darkness.

ple that follow thee': and after that I will go out." And he went out from Pharaoh in a great anger.

And the LORD said unto Moses, "Pharaoh shall not hearken unto you; that my wonders may be multiplied in the land of Egypt." And Moses and Aaron did all these wonders before Pharaoh: and the LORD hardened Pharaoh's heart, so that he would not let the children of Israel go out of his land.

And the LORD spake unto Moses and Aaron in the land of Egypt, saying, "This month shall be unto you the beginning of months: it shall be the first month of the year to you. Speak ye unto all the congregation of Israel, saying, 'In the tenth day of this month they shall take to them every man a lamb, according to the house of their fathers, a lamb for an house: and if the household be too little for the lamb,[9] let him and his neighbour next unto his house take it according to the number of the souls; every man according to his eating shall make your count for the lamb. Your lamb shall be without blemish, a male of the first year: ye shall take it out from the sheep, or from the goats: and ye shall keep it up until the fourteenth day of the same month: and the whole assembly of the congregation of Israel shall kill it in the evening. And they shall take of the blood, and strike it on the two side posts and on the upper door post of the houses, wherein they shall eat it.' "

Then Moses called for all the elders of Israel, and said unto them, "Draw out and take you a lamb according to your families, and kill the passover. And ye shall take a bunch of hyssop, and dip it in the blood that is in the basin, and strike the lintel and the two side posts with the blood that is in the basin; and none of you shall go out at the door of his house until the morning. For the LORD will pass through to smite the Egyptians; and when he seeth the blood upon the lintel, and on the two side posts, the LORD will pass over the door, and will not

---

[9] i.e., a household of fewer than ten persons should be combined with its neighbor or neighbors, so that not more than one lamb would be sacrificed for each ten persons.

suffer the destroyer to come in unto your houses to smite you. And ye shall observe this thing for an ordinance to thee and to thy sons for ever. And it shall come to pass, when ye be come to the land which the Lord will give you, according as he hath promised, that ye shall keep this service. And it shall come to pass when your children shall say unto you, 'What mean ye by this service?' that ye shall say, 'It is the sacrifice of the Lord's passover, who passed over the houses of the children of Israel in Egypt, when he smote the Egyptians, and delivered our houses.' " And the people bowed the head and worshipped. And the children of Israel went away, and did as the Lord had commanded Moses and Aaron, so did they.

And it came to pass, that at midnight the Lord smote all the firstborn in the land of Egypt, from the firstborn of Pharaoh that sat on his throne unto the firstborn of the captive that was in the dungeon; and all the firstborn of cattle. And Pharaoh rose up in the night, he, and all his servants, and all the Egyptians; and there was a great cry in Egypt; for there was not a house where there was not one dead.

And he called for Moses and Aaron by night, and said, "Rise up, and get you forth from among my people, both ye and the children of Israel; and go, serve the Lord, as ye have said. Also take your flocks and your herds, as ye have said, and be gone; and bless me also."

And the Egyptians were urgent upon the people, that they might send them out of the land in haste; for they said, "We be all dead men." And the people took their dough before it was leavened, their kneadingtroughs being bound up in their clothes upon their shoulders. And the children of Israel did according to the word of Moses; and they borrowed of the Egyptians jewels of silver, and jewels of gold, and raiment: and the Lord gave the people favour in the sight of the Egyptians, so that they lent unto them such things as they required. And they spoiled the Egyptians.

The Crossing of the Red Sea

› EXODUS 12:37–42; 13:17 TO 14:31 ·

And the children of Israel journeyed from Rameses to Succoth,[10] about six hundred thousand on foot that were men, beside children. And a mixed multitude went up also with them; and flocks, and herds, even very much cattle. And they baked unleavened cakes of the dough which they brought forth out of Egypt, for it was not leavened; because they were thrust out of Egypt, and could not tarry, neither had they prepared for themselves any victual.

Now the sojourning of the children of Israel, who dwelt in Egypt, was four hundred and thirty years. And it came to pass at the end of the four hundred and thirty years, even the selfsame day it came to pass, that all the hosts of the LORD went out from the land of Egypt. It is a night to be much observed unto the LORD for bringing them out from the land of Egypt: this is that night of the LORD to be observed of all the children of Israel in their generations.

And it came to pass, when Pharaoh had let the people go, that God led them not through the way of the land of the Philistines, although that was near; for God said, "Lest peradventure the people repent when they see war, and they return to Egypt": but God led the people about, through the way of the wilderness of the Red sea: and the children of Israel went up harnessed out of the land of Egypt. And Moses took the bones of Joseph with him: for he had straitly sworn the children of Israel, saying, "God will surely visit you; and ye shall carry up my bones away hence with you."

And they took their journey from Succoth, and encamped in Etham,[11] in the edge of the wilderness. And the LORD went

---

[10] About 30 miles in a southeasterly direction.
[11] The exact locations of Etham and the other places named below are unknown.

before them by day in a pillar of a cloud, to lead them the way; and by night in a pillar of fire, to give them light; to go by day and night: he took not away the pillar of the cloud by day, nor the pillar of fire by night, from before the people.

And the LORD spake unto Moses, saying, "Speak unto the children of Israel, that they turn and encamp before Pi-hahiroth, between Migdol and the sea, over against Baal-zephon: before it shall ye encamp by the sea.[12] For Pharaoh will say of the children of Israel, 'They are entangled in the land, the wilderness hath shut them in.' And I will harden Pharaoh's heart, that he shall follow after them; and I will be honoured upon Pharaoh, and upon all his host; that the Egyptians may know that I am the LORD." And they did so.

And it was told the king of Egypt that the people fled: and the heart of Pharaoh and of his servants was turned against the people, and they said, "Why have we done this, that we have let Israel go from serving us?" And he made ready his chariot, and took his people with him: and he took six hundred chosen chariots, and all the chariots of Egypt, and captains over every one of them. And the LORD hardened the heart of Pharaoh king of Egypt, and he pursued after the children of Israel: and the children of Israel went out with an high hand. But the Egyptians pursued after them, all the horses and chariots of Pharaoh, and his horsemen, and his army, and overtook them encamping by the sea, beside Pi-hahiroth, before Baal-zephon.

And when Pharaoh drew nigh, the children of Israel lifted up their eyes, and, behold, the Egyptians marched after them; and they were sore afraid: and the children of Israel cried out unto the LORD. And they said unto Moses, "Because there were no graves in Egypt, hast thou taken us away to die in the wilderness? wherefore hast thou dealt thus with us, to carry us forth out of Egypt? Is not this the word that we did tell thee in

[12] Usually spoken of as the "Red Sea," the "sea" here referred to was probably the upper reaches of the Gulf of Suez, perhaps north of the modern limits of the Gulf.

Egypt, saying, 'Let us alone, that we may serve the Egyptians'? For it had been better for us to serve the Egyptians, than that we should die in the wilderness."

And Moses said unto the people, "Fear ye not, stand still, and see the salvation of the LORD, which he will shew to you to day: for the Egyptians whom ye have seen to day, ye shall see them again no more for ever. The LORD shall fight for you, and ye shall hold your peace."

And the LORD said unto Moses, "Wherefore criest thou unto me? speak unto the children of Israel, that they go forward: but lift thou up thy rod, and stretch out thine hand over the sea, and divide it: and the children of Israel shall go on dry ground through the midst of the sea. And I, behold, I will harden the hearts of the Egyptians, and they shall follow them: and I will get me honour upon Pharaoh, and upon all his host, upon his chariots, and upon his horsemen. And the Egyptians shall know that I am the LORD, when I have gotten me honour upon Pharaoh, upon his chariots, and upon his horsemen."

And the angel of God, which went before the camp of Israel, removed and went behind them; and the pillar of the cloud went from before their face, and stood behind them: and it came between the camp of the Egyptians and the camp of Israel; and it was a cloud and darkness to them, but it gave light by night to these: so that the one came not near the other all the night. And Moses stretched out his hand over the sea; and the LORD caused the sea to go back by a strong east wind all that night, and made the sea dry land, and the waters were divided. And the children of Israel went into the midst of the sea upon the dry ground: and the waters were a wall unto them on their right hand, and on their left.

And the Egyptians pursued, and went in after them to the midst of the sea, even all Pharaoh's horses, his chariots, and his horsemen. And it came to pass, that in the morning watch the LORD looked unto the host of the Egyptians through the pillar of fire and of the cloud, and troubled the host of the Egyptians, and took off their chariot wheels, that they drave them heavily: so that the Egyptians said, "Let us flee from the face of Israel; for the LORD fighteth for them against the Egyptians."

And the LORD said unto Moses, "Stretch out thine hand over the sea, that the waters may come again upon the Egyptians, upon their chariots, and upon their horsemen."

And Moses stretched forth his hand over the sea, and the sea returned to his strength when the morning appeared; and the Egyptians fled against it; and the LORD overthrew the Egyptians in the midst of the sea. And the waters returned, and covered the chariots, and the horsemen, and all the host of Pharaoh that came into the sea after them; there remained not so much as one of them. But the children of Israel walked upon dry land in the midst of the sea; and the waters were a wall unto them on their right hand, and on their left.

Thus the LORD saved Israel that day out of the hand of the Egyptians; and Israel saw the Egyptians dead upon the sea shore. And Israel saw that great work which the LORD did upon the Egyptians: and the people feared the LORD, and believed the LORD, and his servant Moses.

The Song of Moses and Miriam

• EXODUS 15: 1–21 •

Then sang Moses and the children of Israel this song unto the LORD, and spake, saying,

I will sing unto the LORD, for he hath triumphed gloriously:
The horse and his rider hath he thrown into the sea.
The LORD is my strength and song,
And he is become my salvation:
He is my God, and I will prepare him an habitation;
My father's God, and I will exalt him.

The LORD is a man of war:
The LORD is his name.
Pharaoh's chariots and his host hath he cast into the sea:
His chosen captains also are drowned in the Red sea.
The depths have covered them:
They sank into the bottom as a stone.
Thy right hand, O LORD, is become glorious in power:
Thy right hand, O LORD, hath dashed in pieces the enemy.
And in the greatness of thine excellency thou hast overthrown
    them that rose up against thee:
Thou sentest forth thy wrath, which consumed them as stubble.
And with the blast of thy nostrils the waters were gathered to-
    gether,
The floods stood upright as an heap,
And the depths were congealed in the heart of the sea.
The enemy said,
I will pursue, I will overtake, I will divide the spoil;
My lust shall be satisfied upon them;
I will draw my sword, my hand shall destroy them.
Thou didst blow with thy wind, the sea covered them:
They sank as lead in the mighty waters.
Who is like unto thee, O LORD, among the gods?
Who is like thee, glorious in holiness,
Fearful in praises, doing wonders?
Thou stretchedst out thy right hand,
The earth swallowed them.
Thou in thy mercy hast led forth the people which thou hast re-
    deemed:
Thou hast guided them in thy strength unto thy holy habitation.
The people shall hear, and be afraid:
Sorrow shall take hold on the inhabitants of Palestina.
Then the dukes of Edom shall be amazed;
The mighty men of Moab, trembling shall take hold upon them;
All the inhabitants of Canaan shall melt away.
Fear and dread shall fall upon them;

By the greatness of thine arm they shall be as still as a stone;
Till thy people pass over, O LORD,
Till the people pass over, which thou hast purchased.
Thou shalt bring them in, and plant them in the mountain of
    thine inheritance,
In the place, O LORD, which thou hast made for thee to dwell in,
In the Sanctuary, O LORD, which thy hands have established.
The LORD shall reign for ever and ever.

For the horse of Pharaoh went in with his chariots and with his horsemen into the sea, and the LORD brought again the waters of the sea upon them; but the children of Israel went on dry land in the midst of the sea. And Miriam the prophetess, the sister of Aaron, took a timbrel in her hand; and all the women went out after her with timbrels and with dances. And Miriam answered them,

Sing ye to the LORD, for he hath triumphed gloriously;
The horse and his rider hath he thrown into the sea.

The Wanderings in the Wilderness

• EXODUS 15:22 TO 17:7 •

So Moses brought Israel from the Red sea, and they went out into the wilderness of Shur;[18] and they went three days in the wilderness, and found no water. And when they came to Marah, they could not drink of the waters of Marah, for they were bitter: therefore the name of it was called Marah.

And the people murmured against Moses, saying, "What shall we drink?"

[18] The northwestern part of the Peninsula of Sinai. From here the Israelites moved south and east until they came to Mt. Sinai.

And he cried unto the LORD; and the LORD shewed him a tree, which when he had cast into the waters, the waters were made sweet: there he made for them a statute and an ordinance, and there he proved them, and said, "If thou wilt diligently hearken to the voice of the LORD thy God, and wilt do that which is right in his sight, and wilt give ear to his commandments, and keep all his statutes, I will put none of these diseases upon thee, which I have brought upon the Egyptians: for I am the LORD that healeth thee."

And they came to Elim, where were twelve wells of water, and threescore and ten palm trees: and they encamped there by the waters. And they took their journey from Elim, and all the congregation of the children of Israel came unto the wilderness of Sin, which is between Elim and Sinai, on the fifteenth day of the second month after their departing out of the land of Egypt. And the whole congregation of the children of Israel murmured against Moses and Aaron in the wilderness: and the children of Israel said unto them, "Would to God we had died by the hand of the LORD in the land of Egypt, when we sat by the flesh pots, and when we did eat bread to the full; for ye have brought us forth into this wilderness, to kill this whole assembly with hunger."

Then said the LORD unto Moses, "Behold, I will rain bread from heaven for you; and the people shall go out and gather a certain rate every day, that I may prove them, whether they will walk in my law, or no. And it shall come to pass, that on the sixth day they shall prepare that which they bring in; and it shall be twice as much as they gather daily."

And Moses and Aaron said unto all the children of Israel, "At even, then ye shall know that the LORD hath brought you out from the land of Egypt: and in the morning, then ye shall see the glory of the LORD; for that he heareth your murmurings against the LORD: and what are we, that ye murmur against us?" And Moses said, "This shall be, when the LORD shall give you in the evening flesh to eat, and in the morning bread to the full; for that the LORD heareth your murmurings which ye murmur against him: and what are we? your murmurings are not against us, but against the LORD."

And Moses spake unto Aaron, "Say unto all the congregation of the children of Israel, 'Come near before the LORD; for he hath heard your murmurings.'" And it came to pass, as Aaron spake unto the whole congregation of the children of Israel, that they looked toward the wilderness, and, behold, the glory of the LORD appeared in the cloud.

And the LORD spake unto Moses, saying, "I have heard the murmurings of the children of Israel: speak unto them, saying, 'At even ye shall eat flesh, and in the morning ye shall be filled with bread;' and ye shall know that I am the LORD your God."

And it came to pass, that at even the quails came up, and covered the camp: and in the morning the dew lay round about the host. And when the dew that lay was gone up, behold, upon the face of the wilderness there lay a small round thing, as small as the hoar frost on the ground. And when the children of Israel saw it, they said one to another, "It is manna":[14] for they wist not what it was. And Moses said unto them, "This is the bread which the LORD hath given you to eat. This is the thing which the LORD hath commanded, 'Gather of it every man according to his eating, an omer[15] for every man, according to the number of your persons; take ye every man for them which are in his tents.'" And the children of Israel did so, and gathered, some more, some less. And when they did mete it with an omer, he that gathered much had nothing over, and he that gathered little had no lack; they gathered every man according to his eating.

And Moses said, "Let no man leave of it till the morning." Notwithstanding they hearkened not unto Moses; but some of them left of it until the morning, and it bred worms, and stank: and Moses was wroth with them. And they gathered it every

[14] Heb. "what is it?"
[15] About seven pints.

morning, every man according to his eating: and when the sun waxed hot, it melted.

And it came to pass, that on the sixth day they gathered twice as much bread, two omers for one man: and all the rulers of the congregation came and told Moses. And he said unto them, "This is that which the LORD hath said, 'To morrow is the rest of the holy sabbath unto the LORD: bake that which ye will bake to day, and seethe that ye will seethe; and that which remaineth over lay up for you to be kept until the morning.' " And they laid it up till the morning, as Moses bade: and it did not stink, neither was there any worm therein. And Moses said, "Eat that to day; for to day is a sabbath unto the LORD: to day ye shall not find it in the field. Six days ye shall gather it; but on the seventh day, which is the sabbath, in it there shall be none."

And it came to pass, that there went out some of the people on the seventh day for to gather, and they found none. And the LORD said unto Moses, "How long refuse ye to keep my commandments and my laws? See, for that the LORD hath given you the sabbath, therefore he giveth you on the sixth day the bread of two days; abide ye every man in his place, let no man go out of his place on the seventh day." So the people rested on the seventh day. And the house of Israel called the name thereof Manna: and it was like coriander seed, white; and the taste of it was like wafers made with honey.

And Moses said, "This is the thing which the LORD commandeth, 'Fill an omer of it to be kept for your generations; that they may see the bread wherewith I have fed you in the wilderness, when I brought you forth from the land of Egypt.' " And Moses said unto Aaron, "Take a pot, and put an omer full of manna therein, and lay it up before the LORD, to be kept for your generations." As the LORD commanded Moses, so Aaron laid it up before the Testimony, to be kept. And the children of Israel did eat manna forty years, until they came to a land inhabited; they did eat manna, until they came unto the borders of the land of Canaan. Now an omer is the tenth part of an ephah.

And all the congregation of the children of Israel journeyed from the wilderness of Sin, after their journeys, according to the commandment of the LORD, and pitched in Rephidim:[16] and there was no water for the people to drink. Wherefore the people did chide with Moses, and said, "Give us water that we may drink."

And Moses said unto them, "Why chide ye with me? wherefore do ye tempt the LORD?"

And the people thirsted there for water; and the people murmured against Moses, and said, "Wherefore is this that thou hast brought us up out of Egypt, to kill us and our children and our cattle with thirst?"

And Moses cried unto the LORD, saying, "What shall I do unto this people? they be almost ready to stone me."

And the LORD said unto Moses, "Go on before the people, and take with thee of the elders of Israel; and thy rod, wherewith thou smotest the river, take in thine hand, and go. Behold, I will stand before thee there upon the rock in Horeb; and thou shalt smite the rock, and there shall come water out of it, that the people may drink." And Moses did so in the sight of the elders of Israel. And he called the name of the place Massah, and Meribah, because of the chiding of the children of Israel, and because they tempted the LORD, saying, "Is the LORD among us, or not?"

[16] A few miles northwest of Sinai.

Israel at Sinai. The Ten Commandments

• EXODUS 19; 20: 1—21 •

In the third month, when the children of Israel were gone forth out of the land of Egypt, the same day came they into the wilderness of Sinai. For they were departed from Rephidim, and were come to the desert of Sinai, and had pitched in the wilderness; and there Israel camped before the mount.

And Moses went up unto God, and the LORD called unto him out of the mountain, saying, "Thus shalt thou say to the house of Jacob, and tell the children of Israel; 'Ye have seen what I did unto the Egyptians, and how I bare you on eagles' wings, and brought you unto myself. Now therefore, if ye will obey my voice indeed, and keep my covenant, then ye shall be a peculiar treasure unto me above all people: for all the earth is mine: and ye shall be unto me a kingdom of priests, and an holy nation.' These are the words which thou shalt speak unto the children of Israel."

And Moses came and called for the elders of the people, and laid before their faces all these words which the LORD commanded him. And all the people answered together, and said, "All that the LORD hath spoken we will do." And Moses returned the words of the people unto the LORD.

And the LORD said unto Moses, "Lo, I come unto thee in a thick cloud, that the people may hear when I speak with thee, and believe thee for ever." And Moses told the words of the people unto the LORD.

And the LORD said unto Moses, "Go unto the people, and sanctify them to day and to morrow, and let them wash their clothes, and be ready against the third day: for the third day the LORD will come down in the sight of all the people upon mount Sinai. And thou shalt set bounds unto the people round about, saying, 'Take heed to yourselves, that ye go not up into the mount, or touch the border of it: whosoever toucheth the mount shall be surely put to death.' There shall not an hand touch it, but he shall surely be stoned, or shot through; whether it be beast or man, it shall not live: when the trumpet soundeth long, they shall come up to the mount."

And Moses went down from the mount unto the people, and sanctified the people; and they washed their clothes. And he said unto the people, "Be ready against the third day: come not at your wives."

And it came to pass on the third day in the morning, that there were thunders and lightnings, and a thick cloud upon the mount, and the voice of the trumpet exceeding loud; so that all the people that was in the camp trembled. And Moses brought forth the people out of the camp to meet with God; and they stood at the nether part of the mount. And mount Sinai was altogether on a smoke, because the LORD descended upon it in fire: and the smoke thereof ascended as the smoke of a furnace, and the whole mount quaked greatly. And when the voice of the trumpet sounded long, and waxed louder and louder, Moses spake, and God answered him by a voice. And the LORD came down upon mount Sinai, on the top of the mount: and the LORD called Moses up to the top of the mount; and Moses went up.

And the LORD said unto Moses, "Go down, charge the people, lest they break through unto the LORD to gaze, and many of them perish. And let the priests also, which come near to the LORD, sanctify themselves, lest the LORD break forth upon them."

And Moses said unto the LORD, "The people cannot come up to mount Sinai: for thou chargedst us, saying, 'Set bounds about the mount, and sanctify it.' "

And the LORD said unto him, "Away, get thee down, and thou shalt come up, thou, and Aaron with thee: but let not the priests and the people break through to come up unto the LORD, lest he break forth upon them." So Moses went down unto the people, and spake unto them.

And God spake all these words, saying, "I am the LORD thy God, which have brought thee out of the land of Egypt, out of the house of bondage.

"Thou shalt have no other gods before me.

"Thou shalt not make unto thee any graven image, or any likeness of any thing that is in heaven above, or that is in the earth beneath, or that is in the water under the earth: thou shalt not bow down thyself to them, nor serve them: for I the LORD thy God am a jealous God, visiting the iniquity of the fathers upon the children unto the third and fourth generation of them that hate me; and shewing mercy unto thousands of them that love me, and keep my commandments.

"Thou shalt not take the name of the LORD thy God in vain; for the LORD will not hold him guiltless that taketh his name in vain.

"Remember the sabbath day, to keep it holy. Six days shalt thou labour, and do all thy work: but the seventh day is the sabbath of the LORD thy God: in it thou shalt not do any work, thou, nor thy son, nor thy daughter, thy manservant, nor thy maidservant, nor thy cattle, nor thy stranger that is within thy gates: for in six days the LORD made heaven and earth, the sea, and all that in them is, and rested the seventh day: wherefore the LORD blessed the sabbath day, and hallowed it.

"Honour thy father and thy mother: that thy days may be long upon the land which the LORD thy God giveth thee.

"Thou shalt not kill.

"Thou shalt not commit adultery.

"Thou shalt not steal.

"Thou shalt not bear false witness against thy neighbour.

"Thou shalt not covet thy neighbour's house, thou shalt not covet thy neighbour's wife, nor his manservant, nor his maidservant, nor his ox, nor his ass, nor any thing that is thy neighbour's."

And all the people saw the thunderings, and the lightnings, and the noise of the trumpet, and the mountain smoking: and when the people saw it, they removed, and stood afar off. And they said unto Moses, "Speak thou with us, and we will hear: but let not God speak with us, lest we die."

And Moses said unto the people, "Fear not: for God is come to prove you, and that his fear may be before your faces, that ye sin not." And the people stood afar off, and Moses drew near unto the thick darkness where God was.[17]

The Song of Moses

• DEUTERONOMY 31:30 TO 32:43 •

And Moses spake in the ears of all the congregation of Israel the words of this song, until they were ended.

Give ear, O ye heavens, and I will speak;
And hear, O earth, the words of my mouth.
My doctrine shall drop as the rain,
My speech shall distil as the dew,
As the small rain upon the tender herb,
And as the showers upon the grass:
Because I will publish the name of the LORD:
Ascribe ye greatness unto our God.
He is the Rock, his work is perfect:
For all his ways are judgment:
A God of truth and without iniquity,
Just and right is he.
They have corrupted themselves, their spot is not the spot of his
    children:
They are a perverse and crooked generation.

---

[17] The narrative elements in the remainder of Exodus and in Leviticus and Numbers are concerned with subsequent events of the forty years' sojourn in the wilderness. The Song of Moses in the next selection relates to the end of that period, when Israel has come within sight of the Promised Land.

Do ye thus requite the LORD,
O foolish people and unwise?
Is not he thy father that hath bought thee?
Hath he not made thee, and established thee?
Remember the days of old,
Consider the years of many generations:
Ask thy father, and he will shew thee;
Thy elders, and they will tell thee.
When the Most High divided to the nations their inheritance,
When he separated the sons of Adam,
He set the bounds of the people
According to the number of the children of Israel.
For the LORD's portion is his people;
Jacob is the lot of his inheritance.
He found him in a desert land,
And in the waste howling wilderness;
He led him about, he instructed him,
He kept him as the apple of his eye.
As an eagle stirreth up her nest.
Fluttereth over her young,
Spreadeth abroad her wings, taketh them,
Beareth them on her wings:
So the LORD alone did lead him,
And there was no strange god with him.
He made him ride on the high places of the earth,
That he might eat the increase of the fields;
And he made him to suck honey out of the rock,
And oil out of the flinty rock;
Butter of kine, and milk of sheep,
With fat of lambs,
And rams of the breed of Bashan, and goats,
With the fat of kidneys of wheat;
And thou didst drink the pure blood of the grape.
But Jeshurun[18] waxed fat, and kicked:

[18] A symbolic name for Israel. The literal meaning is "upright."

Thou are waxen fat, thou art grown thick, thou art covered with
    fatness;
Then he forsook God which made him,
And lightly esteemed the Rock of his salvation.
They provoked him to jealousy with strange gods,
With abominations provoked they him to anger.
They sacrificed unto devils, not to God;
To gods whom they knew not,
To new gods that came newly up,
Whom your fathers feared not.
Of the Rock that begat thee thou art unmindful,
And hast forgotten God that formed thee.
And when the Lord saw it, he abhorred them,
Because of the provoking of his sons, and of his daughters.
And he said, I will hide my face from them,
I will see what their end shall be:
For they are a very froward generation,
Children in whom is no faith.
They have moved me to jealousy with that which is not God;
They have provoked me to anger with their vanities:
And I will move them to jealousy with those which are not a
    people;
I will provoke them to anger with a foolish nation.
For a fire is kindled in mine anger,
And shall burn unto the lowest hell,
And shall consume the earth with her increase,
And set on fire the foundations of the mountains.
I will heap mischiefs upon them;
I will spend mine arrows upon them.
They shall be burnt with hunger, and devoured with burning
    heat,
And with bitter destruction:
I will also send the teeth of beasts upon them,
With the poison of serpents of the dust.
The sword without, and terror within,

Shall destroy both the young man and the virgin,
The suckling also with the man of gray hairs.
I said, I would scatter them into corners,
I would make the remembrance of them to cease from among
    men:
Were it not that I feared the wrath of the enemy,
Lest their adversaries should behave themselves strangely,
And lest they should say, Our hand is high,
And the LORD hath not done all this.
For they are a nation void of counsel,
Neither is there any understanding in them.
O that they were wise, that they understood this,
That they would consider their latter end!
How should one chase a thousand,
And two put ten thousand to flight,
Except their Rock had sold them,
And the LORD had shut them up?
For their rock is not as our Rock,
Even our enemies themselves being judges.
For their vine is of the vine of Sodom,
And of the fields of Gomorrah:
Their grapes are grapes of gall,
Their clusters are bitter:
Their wine is the poison of dragons,
And the cruel venom of asps.
Is not this laid up in store with me,
And sealed up among my treasures?
To me belongeth vengeance, and recompense;
Their foot shall slide in due time:
For the day of their calamity is at hand,
And the things that shall come upon them make haste.
For the LORD shall judge his people,
And repent himself for his servants,
When he seeth that their power is gone,
And there is none shut up, or left.

And he shall say, Where are their gods,
Their rock in whom they trusted,
Which did eat the fat of their sacrifices,
And drank the wine of their drink offerings?
Let them rise up and help you,
And be your protection.
See now that I, even I, am he,
And there is no god with me:
I kill, and I make alive;
I wound, and I heal:
Neither is there any that can deliver out of my hand.
For I lift up my hand to heaven,
And say, I live for ever.
If I whet my glittering sword,
And mine hand take hold on judgment;
I will render vengeance to mine enemies,
And will reward them that hate me.
I will make mine arrows drunk with blood,
And my sword shall devour flesh;
And that with the blood of the slain and of the captives,
From the beginning of revenges upon the enemy.
Rejoice, O ye nations, with his people:
For he will avenge the blood of his servants,
And will render vengeance to his adversaries,
And will be merciful unto his land, and to his people.

The Death of Moses

And Moses went up from the plains of Moab unto the mountain of Nebo,[19] to the top of Pisgah, that is over against Jericho. And the LORD shewed him all the land of Gilead, unto Dan, and all Naphtali, and the land of Ephraim, and Manasseh, and all the land of Judah, unto the utmost sea, and the south, and the plain of the valley of Jericho, the city of palm trees, unto Zoar. And the LORD said unto him, "This is the land which I sware unto Abraham, unto Isaac, and unto Jacob, saying, 'I will give it unto thy seed:' I have caused thee to see it with thine eyes, but thou shalt not go over thither."

So Moses the servant of the LORD died there in the land of Moab, according to the word of the LORD. And he buried him in a valley in the land of Moab, over against Beth-peor: but no man knoweth of his sepulchre unto this day. And Moses was an hundred and twenty years old when he died: his eye was not dim, nor his natural force abated.

And the children of Israel wept for Moses in the plains of Moab thirty days: so the days of weeping and mourning for Moses were ended. And Joshua the son of Nun was full of the spirit of wisdom; for Moses had laid his hands upon him: and the children of Israel hearkened unto him, and did as the LORD commanded Moses. And there arose not a prophet since in Israel like unto Moses, whom the LORD knew face to face, in all the signs and the wonders, which the LORD sent him to do in the land of Egypt to Pharaoh, and to all his servants, and to all his land, and in all that mighty hand, and in all the great terror which Moses shewed in the sight of all Israel.

---

[19] Just to the east of the place where the Jordan flows into the Dead Sea. From the summit (Pisgah), Moses sees the Promised Land which he may not enter because he smote the rock to provide water instead of merely speaking to it as God had commanded (Numbers 20:10-13).

THE CONQUEST OF CANAAN AND THE
PERIOD OF THE JUDGES

Jehovah's Charge to Joshua

• JOSHUA 1:1–9 •

Now after the death of Moses the servant of the LORD it came to pass, that the LORD spake unto Joshua the son of Nun, Moses' minister, saying, "Moses my servant is dead; now therefore arise, go over this Jordan, thou, and all this people, unto the land which I do give to them, even to the children of Israel. Every place that the sole of your foot shall tread upon, that have I given unto you, as I said unto Moses. From the wilderness and this Lebanon even unto the great river, the river Euphrates, all the land of the Hittites, and unto the great sea[1] toward the going down of the sun, shall be your coast.[2]

"There shall not any man be able to stand before thee all the days of thy life: as I was with Moses, so I will be with thee: I will not fail thee, nor forsake thee. Be strong and of a good courage: for unto this people shalt thou divide for an inheritance the land, which I sware unto their fathers to give them. Only be thou strong and very courageous, that thou mayest observe to do according to all the law, which Moses my servant

---

[1] The Mediterranean. Actually Israel achieved these boundaries only for a brief period under David and Solomon.
[2] Territory.

commanded thee: turn not from it to the right hand or to the left, that thou mayest prosper whithersoever thou goest.

"This book of the law[3] shall not depart out of thy mouth; but thou shalt meditate therein day and night, that thou mayest observe to do according to all that is written therein: for then thou shalt make thy way prosperous, and then thou shalt have good success. Have not I commanded thee? Be strong and of a good courage; be not afraid, neither be thou dismayed: for the LORD thy God is with thee whithersoever thou goest."

Rahab and the Spies

• JOSHUA 2 •

And Joshua the son of Nun sent out of Shittim two men to spy secretly, saying, "Go view the land, even Jericho." And they went, and came into an harlot's house, named Rahab, and lodged there. And it was told the king of Jericho, saying, "Behold, there came men in hither to night of the children of Israel to search out the country."

And the king of Jericho sent unto Rahab, saying, "Bring forth the men that are come to thee, which are entered into thine house: for they be come to search out all the country."

And the woman took the two men, and hid them, and said thus, "There came men unto me, but I wist not whence they were: and it came to pass about the time of shutting of the gate, when it was dark, that the men went out: whither the men went I wot not: pursue after them quickly; for ye shall overtake them." But she had brought them up to the roof of the house, and hid them with the stalks of flax, which she had laid in order upon the roof. And the men pursued after them the way to Jordan unto the fords: and as soon as they which pursued after them were gone out, they shut the gate.

[3] The "law" as written by Moses and given to the Levites and elders (Deut. 31:9).

And before they were laid down, she came up unto them upon the roof; and she said unto the men, "I know that the Lord hath given you the land, and that your terror is fallen upon us, and that all the inhabitants of the land faint because of you. For we have heard how the Lord dried up the water of the Red sea for you, when ye came out of Egypt; and what ye did unto the two kings of the Amorites, that were on the other side Jordan, Sihon and Og, whom ye utterly destroyed. And as soon as we had heard these things, our hearts did melt, neither did there remain any more courage in any man, because of you: for the Lord your God, he is God in heaven above and in earth beneath. Now therefore, I pray you, swear unto me by the Lord, since I have shewed you kindness, that ye will also shew kindness unto my father's house, and give me a true token: and that ye will save alive my father, and my mother, and my brethren, and my sisters, and all that they have, and deliver our lives from death."

And the men answered her, "Our life for your's, if ye utter not this our business. And it shall be, when the Lord hath given us the land, that we will deal kindly and truly with thee."

Then she let them down by a cord through the window: for her house was upon the town wall, and she dwelt upon the wall. And she said unto them, "Get you to the mountains, lest the pursuers meet you; and hide yourselves there three days, until the pursuers be returned: and afterward may ye go your way."

And the men said unto her, "We will be blameless of this thine oath which thou hast made us swear. Behold, when we come into the land, thou shalt bind this line of scarlet thread in the window which thou didst let us down by: and thou shalt bring thy father, and thy mother, and thy brethren, and all thy father's household, home unto thee. And it shall be, that whosoever shall go out of the doors of thy house into the street, his blood shall be upon his head, and we will be guiltless: and whosoever shall be with thee in the house, his blood shall be on our head, if any hand be upon him. And if thou utter this our business, then we will be quit of thine oath which thou hast made us to swear."

And she said, "According unto your words, so be it." And she sent them away, and they departed: and she bound the scarlet line in the window.

And they went, and came unto the mountain, and abode there three days, until the pursuers were returned: and the pursuers sought them throughout all the way, but found them not. So the two men returned, and descended from the mountain, and passed over, and came to Joshua the son of Nun, and told him all things that befell them: and they said unto Joshua, "Truly the LORD hath delivered into our hands all the land; for even all the inhabitants of the country do faint because of us."

The Fall of Jericho

• JOSHUA 6 •

Now Jericho[4] was straitly shut up because of the children of Israel: none went out, and none came in. And the LORD said unto Joshua, "See, I have given into thine hand Jericho, and the king thereof, and the mighty men of valour. And ye shall compass the city, all ye men of war, and go round about the city once. Thus shalt thou do six days. And seven priests shall bear before the ark[5] seven trumpets of rams' horns: and the seventh day ye shall compass the city seven times, and the priests shall blow with the trumpets. And it shall come to pass, that when they make a long blast with the ram's horn, and when ye hear the sound of the trumpet, all the people shall shout with a great

---

[4] A glance at a map will reveal the military importance of Jericho. It was the gateway to the passes leading from the east to the interior of Palestine. Also, by taking it Joshua drove a wedge between the northern Canaanites and the southern.
[5] The Ark of the Covenant, symbolically the dwelling place of Jehovah.

shout; and the wall of the city shall fall down flat, and the people shall ascend up every man straight before him."

And Joshua the son of Nun called the priests, and said unto them, "Take up the ark of the covenant, and let seven priests bear seven trumpets of rams' horns before the ark of the LORD." And he said unto the people, "Pass on, and compass the city, and let him that is armed pass on before the ark of the LORD."

And it came to pass, when Joshua had spoken unto the people, that the seven priests bearing the seven trumpets of rams' horns passed on before the LORD, and blew with the trumpets: and the ark of the covenant of the LORD followed them. And the armed men went before the priests that blew with the trumpets, and the rereward came after the ark, the priests going on, and blowing with the trumpets. And Joshua had commanded the people, saying, "Ye shall not shout, nor make any noise with your voice, neither shall any word proceed out of your mouth, until the day I bid you shout; then shall ye shout." So the ark of the LORD compassed the city, going about it once: and they came into the camp, and lodged in the camp.

And Joshua rose early in the morning, and the priests took up the ark of the LORD. And seven priests bearing seven trumpets of rams' horns before the ark of the LORD went on continually, and blew with the trumpets: and the armed men went before them; but the rereward came after the ark of the LORD, the priests going on, and blowing with the trumpets. And the second day they compassed the city once, and returned into the camp: so they did six days.

And it came to pass on the seventh day, that they rose early about the dawning of the day, and compassed the city after the same manner seven times: only on that day they compassed the city seven times. And it came to pass at the seventh time, when the priests blew with the trumpets, Joshua said unto the people, "Shout; for the LORD hath given you the city. And the city shall be accursed, even it, and all that are therein, to the LORD: only Rahab the harlot shall live, she and all that are with her in the house, because she hid the messengers that we sent. And ye, in any wise keep yourselves from the accursed thing, lest ye make yourselves accursed, when ye take of the accursed thing, and make the camp of Israel a curse, and trouble it. But all the silver, and gold, and vessels of brass and iron, are consecrated unto the LORD: they shall come into the treasury of the LORD."

So the people shouted when the priests blew with the trumpets: and it came to pass, when the people heard the sound of the trumpet, and the people shouted with a great shout, that the wall fell down flat, so that the people went up into the city, every man straight before him, and they took the city. And they utterly destroyed all that was in the city, both man and woman, young and old, and ox, and sheep, and ass, with the edge of the sword.

But Joshua had said unto the two men that had spied out the country, "Go into the harlot's house, and bring out thence the woman, and all that she hath, as ye sware unto her." And the young men that were spies went in, and brought out Rahab, and her father, and her mother, and her brethren, and all that she had; and they brought out all her kindred, and left them without the camp of Israel. And they burnt the city with fire, and all that was therein: only the silver, and the gold, and the vessels of brass and of iron, they put into the treasury of the house of the LORD. And Joshua saved Rahab the harlot alive, and her father's household, and all that she had; and she dwelleth in Israel even unto this day; because she hid the messengers, which Joshua sent to spy out Jericho.

And Joshua adjured them at that time, saying, "Cursed be the man before the LORD, that riseth up and buildeth this city Jericho: he shall lay the foundation thereof in his firstborn, and in his youngest son shall be set up the gates of it." So the LORD was with Joshua; and his fame was noised throughout all the country.

Samson, Judge of Israel [6]

• JUDGES 13:1 TO 16:31 •

And the children of Israel did evil again in the sight of the LORD; and the LORD delivered them into the hand of the Philistines forty years.

And there was a certain man of Zorah, of the family of the Danites, whose name was Manoah; and his wife was barren, and bare not. And the angel of the LORD appeared unto the woman, and said unto her, "Behold now, thou art barren, and bearest not: but thou shalt conceive, and bear a son. Now therefore beware, I pray thee, and drink not wine nor strong drink, and eat not any unclean thing: for, lo, thou shalt conceive, and bear a son; and no razor shall come on his head: for the child shall be a Nazarite[7] unto God from the womb: and he shall begin to deliver Israel out of the hand of the Philistines."

Then the woman came and told her husband, saying, "A man of God came unto me, and his countenance was like the countenance of an angel of God, very terrible: but I asked him not whence he was, neither told he me his name: but he said unto me, 'Behold, thou shalt conceive, and bear a son; and now drink no wine nor strong drink, neither eat any unclean thing: for the child shall be a Nazarite to God from the womb to the day of his death.'"

Then Manoah intreated the LORD, and said, "O my LORD, let the man of God which thou didst send come again unto us, and teach us what we shall do unto the child that shall be born."

And God hearkened to the voice of Manoah; and the angel of God came again unto the woman as she sat in the field: but Manoah her husband was not with her. And the woman made

---

[6] The "judges" were the leaders and heroes of Israel in the period between the leadership of Joshua and the establishment of the monarchy. Samson's story is the last (save for an appendix) in the Book of Judges.
[7] A Nazarite (not to be confused with "Nazarene") was a person consecrated to God by special vows.

haste, and ran, and shewed her husband, and said unto him, "Behold, the man hath appeared unto me, that came unto me the other day."

And Manoah arose, and went after his wife, and came to the man, and said unto him, "Art thou the man that spakest unto the woman?" And he said, "I am." And Manoah said, "Now let thy words come to pass. How shall we order the child, and how shall we do unto him?"

And the angel of the LORD said unto Manoah, "Of all that I said unto the woman let her beware. She may not eat of any thing that cometh of the vine, neither let her drink wine or strong drink, nor eat any unclean thing: all that I commanded her let her observe."

And Manoah said unto the angel of the LORD, "I pray thee, let us detain thee, until we shall have made ready a kid for thee."

And the angel of the LORD said unto Manoah, "Though thou detain me, I will not eat of thy bread: and if thou wilt offer a burnt offering, thou must offer it unto the LORD." For Manoah knew not that he was an angel of the LORD.

And Manoah said unto the angel of the LORD, "What is thy name, that when thy sayings come to pass we may do thee honour?"

And the angel of the LORD said unto him, "Why askest thou thus after my name, seeing it is secret?"

So Manoah took a kid with a meat offering, and offered it upon a rock unto the LORD: and the angel did wonderously; and Manoah and his wife looked on. For it came to pass, when the flame went up toward heaven from off the altar, that the angel of the LORD ascended in the flame of the altar. And Manoah and his wife looked on it, and fell on their faces to the ground. But the angel of the LORD did no more appear to Manoah and to his wife. Then Manoah knew that he was an angel of the LORD.

And Manoah said unto his wife, "We shall surely die, because we have seen God."

But his wife said unto him, "If the LORD were pleased to kill us, he would not have received a burnt offering and a meat offering at our hands, neither would he have shewed us all these things, nor would as at this time have told us such things as these." And the woman bare a son, and called his name Samson: and the child grew, and the LORD blessed him. And the Spirit of the LORD began to move him at times in the camp of Dan between Zorah and Eshtaol.

And Samson went down to Timnath, and saw a woman in Timnath of the daughters of the Philistines. And he came up, and told his father and his mother, and said, "I have seen a woman in Timnath of the daughters of the Philistines: now therefore get her for me to wife."

Then his father and his mother said unto him, "Is there never a woman among the daughters of thy brethren, or among all my people, that thou goest to take a wife of the uncircumcised Philistines?"

And Samson said unto his father, "Get her for me; for she pleaseth me well." But his father and his mother knew not that it was of the LORD, that he sought an occasion against the Philistines: for at that time the Philistines had dominion over Israel.

Then went Samson down, and his father and his mother, to Timnath, and came to the vineyards of Timnath: and, behold, a young lion roared against him. And the Spirit of the LORD came mightily upon him, and he rent him as he would have rent a kid, and he had nothing in his hand: but he told not his father or his mother what he had done. And he went down, and talked with the woman; and she pleased Samson well. And after a time he returned to take her, and he turned aside to see the carcase of the lion: and, behold, there was a swarm of bees and honey in the carcase of the lion. And he took thereof in his hands, and went on eating, and came to his father and mother, and he gave them, and they did eat: but he told not them that he had taken the honey out of the carcase of the lion.

So his father went down unto the woman: and Samson

made there a feast; for so used the young men to do. And it came to pass, when they saw him, that they brought thirty companions to be with him. And Samson said unto them, "I will now put forth a riddle unto you: if ye can certainly declare it me within the seven days of the feast, and find it out, then I will give you thirty sheets and thirty change of garments: but if ye cannot declare it me, then shall ye give me thirty sheets and thirty change of garments."

And they said unto him, "Put forth thy riddle, that we may hear it."

And he said unto them, "Out of the eater came forth meat, and out of the strong came forth sweetness." And they could not in three days expound the riddle.

And it came to pass on the seventh day, that they said unto Samson's wife, "Entice thy husband, that he may declare unto us the riddle, lest we burn thee and thy father's house with fire: have ye called us to take that we have? [8] is it not so?"

And Samson's wife wept before him, and said, "Thou dost but hate me, and lovest me not: thou hast put forth a riddle unto the children of my people, and hast not told it me."

And he said unto her, "Behold, I have not told it my father nor my mother, and shall I tell it thee?" And she wept before him the seven days, while their feast lasted: and it came to pass on the seventh day, that he told her, because she lay sore upon him: and she told the riddle to the children of her people.

And the men of the city said unto him on the seventh day before the sun went down, "What is sweeter than honey? and what is stronger than a lion?"

And he said unto them, "If ye had not plowed with my heifer, ye had not found out my riddle."

And the Spirit of the LORD came upon him, and he went down to Ashkelon, and slew thirty men of them, and took their spoil, and gave change of garments unto them which expounded the riddle. And his anger was kindled, and he went up to his fa-

[8] i.e., have you invited us here in order to impoverish us?

ther's house. But Samson's wife was given to his companion, whom he had used as his friend.[9]

But it came to pass within a while after, in the time of wheat harvest, that Samson visited his wife with a kid; and he said, "I will go in to my wife into the chamber."

But her father would not suffer him to go in. And her father said, "I verily thought that thou hadst utterly hated her; therefore I gave her to thy companion: is not her younger sister fairer than she? take her, I pray thee, instead of her."

And Samson said concerning them, "Now shall I be more blameless than the Philistines, though I do them a displeasure." [10] And Samson went and caught three hundred foxes, and took firebrands, and turned tail to tail, and put a firebrand in the midst between two tails. And when he had set the brands on fire, he let them go into the standing corn of the Philistines, and burnt up both the shocks, and also the standing corn, with the vineyards and olives.

Then the Philistines said, "Who hath done this?"

And they answered, "Samson, the son in law of the Timnite, because he had taken his wife, and given her to his companion." And the Philistines came up, and burnt her and her father with fire.

And Samson said unto them, "Though ye have done this, yet will I be avenged of you, and after that I will cease." And he smote them hip and thigh with a great slaughter: and he went down and dwelt in the top of the rock Etam.[11]

Then the Philistines went up, and pitched in Judah, and spread themselves in Lehi. And the men of Judah said, "Why are ye come up against us?"

And they answered, "To bind Samson are we come up, to do to him as he hath done to us."

---

[9] Samson's hasty departure was an insult to the bride. She was therefore given to Samson's "best-man."
[10] i.e., the Philistines are more at fault than I.
[11] In the neighboring territory of Judah.

Then three thousand men of Judah went to the top of the rock Etam, and said to Samson, "Knowest thou not that the Philistines are rulers over us? what is this that thou hast done unto us?"

And he said unto them, "As they did unto me, so have I done unto them."

And they said unto him, "We are come down to bind thee, that we may deliver thee into the hand of the Philistines."

And Samson said unto them, "Swear unto me, that ye will not fall upon me yourselves."

And they spake unto him, saying, "No; but we will bind thee fast, and deliver thee into their hand: but surely we will not kill thee."

And they bound him with two new cords, and brought him up from the rock. And when he came unto Lehi, the Philistines shouted against him: and the Spirit of the LORD came mightily upon him, and the cords that were upon his arms became as flax that was burnt with fire, and his bands loosed from off his hands. And he found a new jawbone of an ass, and put forth his hand, and took it, and slew a thousand men therewith. And Samson said, "With the jawbone of an ass, heaps upon heaps, with the jaw of an ass have I slain a thousand men." And it came to pass, when he had made an end of speaking, that he cast away the jawbone out of his hand, and called that place Ramath-lehi.[12]

And he was sore athirst and called on the LORD, and said, "Thou hast given this great deliverance into the hand of thy servant: and now shall I die for thirst, and fall into the hand of the uncircumcised?" But God clave an hollow place that was in the jaw, and there came water thereout; and when he had drunk, his spirit came again, and he revived: wherefore he called the name thereof En-hakkore, which is in Lehi unto this day. And he judged Israel in the days of the Philistines twenty years.

[12] "Jawbone height."

Then went Samson to Gaza,[13] and saw there an harlot, and went in unto her. And it was told the Gazites, saying, "Samson is come hither." And they compassed him in, and laid wait for him all night in the gate of the city, and were quiet all the night saying, "In the morning, when it is day, we shall kill him." And Samson lay till midnight, and rose at midnight, and took the doors of the gate of the city, and the two posts, and went away with them, bar and all, and put them upon his shoulders, and carried them up to the top of an hill that is before Hebron.[14]

And it came to pass afterward, that he loved a woman in the valley of Sorek,[15] whose name was Delilah. And the lords of the Philistines came up unto her, and said unto her, "Entice him, and see wherein his great strength lieth, and by what means we may prevail against him, that we may bind him to afflict him: and we will give thee every one of us eleven hundred pieces of silver."

And Delilah said to Samson, "Tell me, I pray thee, wherein thy great strength lieth, and wherewith thou mightest be bound to afflict thee."

And Samson said unto her, "If they bind me with seven green withs[16] that were never dried, then shall I be weak, and be as another man."

Then the lords of the Philistines brought up to her seven green withs which had not been dried, and she bound him with them. Now there were men lying in wait, abiding with her in the chamber. And she said unto him, "The Philistines be upon thee, Samson." And he brake the withs, as a thread of tow is broken when it toucheth the fire. So his strength was not known.

And Delilah said unto Samson, "Behold, thou hast mocked

[13] A city of the Philistines near the coast of the Mediterranean.
[14] The distance from Gaza to Hebron was about 40 miles.
[15] West of Jerusalem.
[16] Bowstrings.

me, and told me lies: now tell me, I pray thee, wherewith thou mightest be bound."

And he said unto her, "If they bind me fast with new ropes that never were occupied, then shall I be weak, and be as another man."

Delilah therefore took new ropes, and bound him therewith, and said unto him, "The Philistines be upon thee, Samson." And there were liers in wait abiding in the chamber. And he brake them from off his arms like a thread.

And Delilah said unto Samson, "Hitherto thou has mocked me, and told me lies: tell me wherewith thou mightest be bound."

And he said unto her, "If thou weavest the seven locks of my head with the web."

And she fastened it with the pin, and said unto him, "The Philistines be upon thee, Samson." And he awaked out of his sleep, and went away with the pin of the beam, and with the web.[17]

And she said unto him, "How canst thou say, I love thee, when thine heart is not with me? thou hast mocked me these three times, and hast not told me wherein thy great strength lieth."

And it came to pass, when she pressed him daily with her words, and urged him, so that his soul was vexed unto death; that he told her all his heart, and said unto her, "There hath not come a razor upon mine head; for I have been a Nazarite unto God from my mother's womb: if I be shaven, then my strength will go from me, and I shall become weak, and be like any other man."

And when Delilah saw that he had told her all his heart, she sent and called for the lords of the Philistines, saying, "Come up this once, for he hath shewed me all his heart."

[17] The sense of the passage is that Delilah wove Samson's hair on a loom to which she left it "pinned." Samson carried away the whole loom.

Then the lords of the Philistines came up unto her, and brought money in their hand.

And she made him sleep upon her knees; and she called for a man, and she caused him to shave off the seven locks of his head; and she began to afflict him, and his strength went from him. And she said, "The Philistines be upon thee, Samson."

And he awoke out of his sleep, and said, "I will go out as at other times before, and shake myself." And he wist not that the LORD was departed from him.

But the Philistines took him, and put out his eyes, and brought him down to Gaza, and bound him with fetters of brass; and he did grind in the prison house. Howbeit the hair of his head began to grow again after he was shaven.

Then the lords of the Philistines gathered them together for to offer a great sacrifice unto Dagon their god, and to rejoice: for they said, "Our god hath delivered Samson our enemy into our hand." And when the people saw him, they praised their god: for they said, "Our god hath delivered into our hands our enemy, and the destroyer of our country, which slew many of us."

And it came to pass, when their hearts were merry, that they said, "Call for Samson, that he may make us sport." And they called for Samson out of the prison house; and he made them sport: and they set him between the pillars.

And Samson said unto the lad that held him by the hand, "Suffer me that I may feel the pillars whereupon the house standeth, that I may lean upon them."

Now the house was full of men and women; and all the lords of the Philistines were there; and there were upon the roof about three thousand men and women, that beheld while Samson made sport. And Samson called unto the LORD, and said, "O LORD God, remember me, I pray thee, and strengthen me, I pray thee, only this once, O God, that I may be at once avenged of the Philistines for my two eyes." And Samson took hold of the two middle pillars upon which the house stood, and on which it was borne up, of the one with his right hand, and of the other with his left. And Samson said, "Let me die with the Philistines." And he bowed himself with all his might; and the house fell upon the lords, and upon all the people that were therein. So the dead which he slew at his death were more than they which he slew in his life.

Then his brethren and all the house of his father came down, and took him, and brought him up, and buried him between Zorah and Eshtaol in the buryingplace of Manoah his father. And he judged Israel twenty years.

The Birth and Dedication of Samuel

• 1 SAMUEL 1:1 TO 2:11; 2:19–26 •

Now there was a certain man of Ramathaim-zophim, of mount Ephraim,[18] and his name was Elkanah, the son of Jeroham, the son of Elihu, the son of Tohu, the son of Zuph, an Ephrathite: and he had two wives; the name of the one was Hannah, and the name of the other Peninnah: and Peninnah had children, but Hannah had no children. And this man went up out of his city yearly to worship and to sacrifice unto the LORD of hosts in Shiloh.[19] And the two sons of Eli, Hophni and Phinehas, the priests of the LORD, were there.

And when the time was that Elkanah offered, he gave to Peninnah his wife, and to all her sons and her daughters, portions: but unto Hannah he gave a worthy portion; for he loved Hannah: but the LORD had shut up her womb. And her adversary[20] also provoked her sore, for to make her fret, because

---

[18] The hill country of Ephraim in central Palestine.
[19] Where the Ark of the Covenant was kept and therefore an important religious center.
[20] Peninnah.

the LORD had shut up her womb. And as he did so year by year, when she went up to the house of the LORD, so she provoked her; therefore she wept, and did not eat. Then said Elkanah her husband to her, "Hannah, why weepest thou? and why eatest thou not? and why is thy heart grieved? am not I better to thee than ten sons?"

So Hannah rose up after they had eaten in Shiloh, and after they had drunk. Now Eli the priest sat upon a seat by a post of the temple of the LORD. And she was in bitterness of soul, and prayed unto the LORD, and wept sore. And she vowed a vow, and said, "O LORD of hosts, if thou wilt indeed look on the affliction of thine handmaid, and remember me, and not forget thine handmaid, but wilt give unto thine handmaid a man child, then I will give him unto the LORD all the days of his life, and there shall no razor come upon his head."

And it came to pass, as she continued praying before the LORD, that Eli marked her mouth. Now Hannah, she spake in her heart; only her lips moved, but her voice was not heard: therefore Eli thought she had been drunken. And Eli said unto her, "How long wilt thou be drunken? put away thy wine from thee."

And Hannah answered and said, "No, my lord, I am a woman of a sorrowful spirit: I have drunk neither wine nor strong drink, but have poured out my soul before the LORD. Count not thine handmaid for a daughter of Belial:[21] for out of the abundance of my complaint and grief have I spoken hitherto."

Then Eli answered and said, "Go in peace: and the God of Israel grant thee thy petition that thou hast asked of him."

And she said, "Let thine handmaid find grace in thy sight." So the woman went her way, and did eat, and her countenance was no more sad.

And they rose up in the morning early, and worshipped before the LORD, and returned, and came to their house to Ramah: and Elkanah knew Hannah his wife; and the LORD remembered

[21] A daughter of wickedness.

her. Wherefore it came to pass, when the time was come about after Hannah had conceived, that she bare a son, and called his name Samuel, saying, "Because I have asked him of the LORD."

And the man Elkanah, and all his house, went up to offer unto the LORD the yearly sacrifice, and his vow. But Hannah went not up; for she said unto her husband, "I will not go up until the child be weaned, and then I will bring him, that he may appear before the LORD, and there abide for ever."

And Elkanah her husband said unto her, "Do what seemeth thee good; tarry until thou have weaned him; only the LORD establish his word." So the woman abode, and gave her son suck until she weaned him.

And when she had weaned him, she took him up with her, with three bullocks, and one ephah of flour, and a bottle of wine, and brought him unto the house of the LORD in Shiloh: and the child was young. And they slew a bullock, and brought the child to Eli. And she said, "Oh my lord, as thy soul liveth, my lord, I am the woman that stood by thee here, praying unto the LORD. For this child I prayed; and the LORD hath given me my petition which I asked of him: therefore also I have lent him to the LORD; as long as he liveth he shall be lent to the LORD."

And Hannah prayed, and said,

My heart rejoiceth in the LORD,
Mine horn is exalted in the LORD:
My mouth is enlarged over mine enemies;
Because I rejoice in thy salvation.
There is none holy as the LORD:
For there is none beside thee:
Neither is there any rock like our God.
Talk no more so exceeding proudly;
Let not arrogancy come out of your mouth:
For the LORD is a God of knowledge,
And by him actions are weighed.
The bows of the mighty men are broken,

And they that stumble are girded with strength.
They that were full have hired out themselves for bread;
And they that were hungry ceased:
So that the barren hath born seven;
And she that hath many children is waxed feeble.
The LORD killeth, and maketh alive:
He bringeth down to the grave, and bringeth up.
The LORD maketh poor, and maketh rich:
He bringeth low, and lifteth up.
He raiseth up the poor out of the dust,
And lifteth up the beggar from the dunghill,
To set them among princes,
And to make them inherit the throne of glory:
For the pillars of the earth are the LORD's,
And he hath set the world upon them.
He will keep the feet of his saints,
And the wicked shall be silent in darkness;
For by strength shall no man prevail.
The adversaries of the LORD shall be broken to pieces;
But of heaven shall he thunder upon them:
The LORD shall judge the ends of the earth;
And he shall give strength unto his king,
And exalt the horn of his anointed.

And Elkanah went to Ramah to his house. And the child did minister unto the LORD before Eli the priest. Moreover his mother made him a little coat, and brought it to him from year to year, when she came up with her husband to offer the yearly sacrifice. And Eli blessed Elkanah and his wife, and said, "The LORD give thee seed of this woman for the loan which is lent to the LORD." And they went unto their own home. And the LORD visited Hannah, so that she conceived, and bare three sons and two daughters. And the child Samuel grew before the LORD.

Now Eli was very old, and heard all that his sons did unto all Israel; and how they lay with the women that assembled at the door of the tabernacle of the congregation.[22] And he said unto them, "Why do ye such things? for I hear of your evil dealings by all this people. Nay, my sons; for it is no good report that I hear: ye make the LORD's people to transgress. If one man sin against another, the judge shall judge him: but if a man sin against the LORD, who shall intreat for him?" Notwithstanding they hearkened not unto the voice of their father, because the LORD would slay them.

And the child Samuel grew on, and was in favour both with the LORD, and also with men.

Samuel and Eli

• 1 SAMUEL 3: 1 TO 4: 1ᵃ •

And the child Samuel ministered unto the LORD before Eli. And the word of the LORD was precious in those days; there was no open vision.[23]

And it came to pass at that time, when Eli was laid down in his place, and his eyes began to wax dim, that he could not see; and ere the lamp of God went out[24] in the temple of the LORD, where the ark of God was, and Samuel was laid down to sleep; that the LORD called Samuel: and he answered, "Here am I." And he ran unto Eli, and said, "Here am I; for thou calledst me."

And he said, "I called not; lie down again."

And he went and lay down. And the LORD called yet again, "Samuel." And Samuel arose and went to Eli, and said, "Here am I; for thou didst call me."

---

[22] They were also guilty of taking for themselves some of the parts of the sacrificial animal ordinarily reserved for the sacrifice itself or for the offerer.
[23] i.e., there were few prophets. "Open" here means "published."
[24] In the early morning, before the candles which burned all night in the sanctuary were extinguished.

And he answered, "I called not, my son; lie down again."

Now Samuel did not yet know the LORD, neither was the word of the LORD yet revealed unto him. And the LORD called Samuel again the third time. And he arose and went to Eli, and said, "Here am I; for thou didst call me."

And Eli perceived that the LORD had called the child. Therefore Eli said unto Samuel, "Go, lie down: and it shall be, if he call thee, that thou shalt say, 'Speak, LORD; for thy servant heareth.'"

So Samuel went and lay down in his place. And the LORD came and stood, and called as at other times, "Samuel, Samuel." Then Samuel answered, "Speak; for thy servant heareth."

And the LORD said to Samuel, "Behold, I will do a thing in Israel, at which both the ears of every one that heareth it shall tingle. In that day I will perform against Eli all things which I have spoken concerning his house: when I begin, I will also make an end. For I have told him that I will judge his house for ever for the iniquity which he knoweth; because his sons made themselves vile, and he restrained them not. And therefore I have sworn unto the house of Eli, that the iniquity of Eli's house shall not be purged with sacrifice nor offering for ever."

And Samuel lay until the morning, and opened the doors of the house of the LORD. And Samuel feared to shew Eli the vision. Then Eli called Samuel, and said, "Samuel, my son."

And he answered, "Here am I."

And he said, "What is the thing that the LORD hath said unto thee? I pray thee hide it not from me: God do so to thee, and more also, if thou hide any thing from me of all the things that he said unto thee." And Samuel told him every whit, and hid nothing from him. And he said, "It is the LORD: let him do what seemeth him good."

And Samuel grew, and the LORD was with him, and did let none of his words fall to the ground. And all Israel from Dan even to Beer-sheba knew that Samuel was established to be a prophet of the LORD. And the LORD appeared again in Shiloh: for the LORD revealed himself to Samuel in Shiloh by the word of the LORD. And the word of Samuel came to all Israel.

The Philistines Capture the Ark of the Covenant. The Death of Eli

· 1 SAMUEL 4: 1^b–18 ·

Now Israel went out against the Philistines to battle, and pitched beside Eben-ezer: and the Philistines pitched in Aphek. And the Philistines put themselves in array against Israel: and when they joined battle, Israel was smitten before the Philistines: and they slew of the army in the field about four thousand men. And when the people were come into the camp, the elders of Israel said, "Wherefore hath the LORD smitten us to day before the Philistines? Let us fetch the ark of the covenant of the LORD out of Shiloh unto us, that, when it cometh among us, it may save us out of the hand of our enemies."

So the people sent to Shiloh, that they might bring from thence the ark of the covenant of the LORD of hosts, which dwelleth between the cherubims: and the two sons of Eli, Hophni and Phinehas, were there with the ark of the covenant of God. And when the ark of the covenant of the LORD came into the camp, all Israel shouted with a great shout, so that the earth rang again.

And when the Philistines heard the noise of the shout, they said, "What meaneth the noise of this great shout in the camp of the Hebrews?" And they understood that the ark of the LORD was come into the camp. And the Philistines were afraid, for they said, "God is come into the camp." And they said, "Woe unto us! for there hath not been such a thing heretofore. Woe unto us! who shall deliver us out of the hand of these mighty

Gods? these are the Gods that smote the Egyptians with all the plagues in the wilderness. Be strong, and quit yourselves like men, O ye Philistines, that ye be not servants unto the Hebrews, as they have been to you: quit yourselves like men, and fight."

And the Philistines fought, and Israel was smitten, and they fled every man into his tent: and there was a very great slaughter; for there fell of Israel thirty thousand footmen. And the ark of God was taken; and the two sons of Eli, Hophni and Phinehas, were slain.

And there ran a man of Benjamin out of the army, and came to Shiloh the same day with his clothes rent, and with earth upon his head. And when he came, lo, Eli sat upon a seat by the wayside watching: for his heart trembled for the ark of God. And when the man came into the city, and told it, all the city cried out. And when Eli heard the noise of the crying, he said, "What meaneth the noise of this tumult?" And the man came in hastily, and told Eli.

Now Eli was ninety and eight years old; and his eyes were dim, that he could not see. And the man said unto Eli, "I am he that came out of the army, and I fled to day out of the army."

And he said, "What is there done, my son?"

And the messenger answered and said, "Israel is fled before the Philistines, and there hath been also a great slaughter among the people, and thy two sons also, Hophni and Phinehas, are dead, and the ark of God is taken."

And it came to pass, when he made mention of the ark of God, that he fell from off the seat backward by the side of the gate, and his neck brake, and he died: for he was an old man, and heavy. And he had judged Israel forty years.

Samuel, the Last of the Judges

• 1 SAMUEL 7:15 TO 8:22 •

And Samuel judged Israel all the days of his life. And he went from year to year in circuit to Beth-el, and Gilgal, and Mizpeh, and judged Israel in all those places. And his return was to Ramah; for there was his house; and there he judged Israel; and there he built an altar unto the LORD.

And it came to pass, when Samuel was old, that he made his sons judges over Israel. Now the name of his first born was Joel; and the name of his second, Abiah: they were judges in Beer-sheba. And his sons walked not in his ways, but turned aside after lucre, and took bribes, and perverted judgment.

Then all the elders of Israel gathered themselves together, and came to Samuel unto Ramah, and said unto him, "Behold, thou art old, and thy sons walk not in thy ways: now make us a king to judge us like all the nations." But the thing displeased Samuel, when they said, "Give us a king to judge us."

And Samuel prayed unto the LORD. And the LORD said unto Samuel, "Hearken unto the voice of the people in all that they say unto thee: for they have not rejected thee, but they have rejected me, that I should not reign over them. According to all the works which they have done since the day that I brought them up out of Egypt even unto this day, wherewith they have forsaken me, and served other gods, so do they also unto thee. Now therefore hearken unto their voice: howbeit yet protest solemnly unto them, and shew them the manner of the king that shall reign over them."

And Samuel told all the words of the LORD unto the people that asked of him a king. And he said, "This will be the manner of the king that shall reign over you: he will take your sons, and appoint them for himself, for his chariots, and to be his horsemen; and some shall run before his chariots. And he will appoint him captains over thousands, and captains over fifties; and will set them to ear his ground, and to reap his harvest, and to make his instruments of war, and instruments of his chariots. And he will take your daughters to be confectionaries, and to be cooks, and to be bakers. And he will take your fields, and your vineyards, and your oliveyards, even the best of them, and give them to his servants. And he will take the tenth of your seed, and of your vineyards, and give to his officers, and to his servants. And he will take your menservants, and your maidservants, and your goodliest young men, and your asses, and put them to his work. He will take the tenth of your sheep: and ye shall be his servants. And ye shall cry out in that day because of your king which ye shall have chosen you; and the LORD will not hear you in that day."

Nevertheless the people refused to obey the voice of Samuel; and they said, "Nay; but we will have a king over us; that we also may be like all the nations; and that our king may judge us, and go out before us, and fight our battles."

And Samuel heard all the words of the people, and he rehearsed them in the ears of the LORD. And the LORD said to Samuel, "Hearken unto their voice, and make them a king." And Samuel said unto the men of Israel, "Go ye every man unto his city."

The Anointing of Saul

Now there was a man of Benjamin, whose name was Kish, the son of Abiel, the son of Zeror, the son of Bechorath, the son of Aphiah, a Benjamite, a mighty man of power. And he had a son, whose name was Saul, a choice young man, and a goodly: and there was not among the children of Israel a goodlier person than he: from his shoulders and upward he was higher than any of the people. And the asses of Kish Saul's father were lost. And Kish said to Saul his son, "Take now one of the servants with thee, and arise, go seek the asses." And he passed through mount Ephraim, and passed through the land of Shalisha, but they found them not: then they passed through the land of Shalim, and there they were not: and he passed through the land of the Benjamites, but they found them not.

And when they were come to the land of Zuph, Saul said to his servant that was with him, "Come, and let us return; lest my father leave caring for the asses, and take thought for us."

And he said unto him, "Behold now, there is in this city a man of God, and he is an honourable man; all that he saith cometh surely to pass: now let us go thither; peradventure he can shew us our way that we should go."

Then said Saul to his servant, "But, behold, if we go, what shall we bring the man? for the bread is spent in our vessels, and there is not a present to bring to the man of God: what have we?"

And the servant answered Saul again, and said, "Behold, I have here at hand the fourth part of a shekel of silver: that will I give to the man of God, to tell us our way." (Beforetime in Israel, when a man went to enquire of God, thus he spake, "Come, and let us go to the seer:" for he that is now called a Prophet was beforetime called a Seer.)

Then said Saul to his servant, "Well said; come, let us go."

So they went unto the city where the man of God was. And as they went up the hill to the city, they found young maidens going out to draw water, and said unto them, "Is the seer here?"

And they answered them, and said, "He is; behold, he is before you: make haste now, for he came to day to the city; for there is a sacrifice of the people to day in the high place: as soon as ye be come into the city, ye shall straightway find him, before he go up to the high place to eat: for the people will not eat until he come, because he doth bless the sacrifice; and afterwards they eat that be bidden. Now therefore get you up; for about this time ye shall find him." And they went up into the city: and when they were come into the city, behold, Samuel came out against them, for to go up to the high place.

Now the LORD had told Samuel in his ear a day before Saul came, saying, "To morrow about this time I will send thee a man out of the land of Benjamin, and thou shalt anoint him to be captain over my people Israel, that he may save my people out of the hand of the Philistines: for I have looked upon my people, because their cry is come unto me." And when Samuel saw Saul, the LORD said unto him, "Behold the man whom I spake to thee of! this same shall reign over my people."

Then Saul drew near to Samuel in the gate, and said, "Tell me, I pray thee, where the seer's house is."

And Samuel answered Saul, and said, "I am the seer: go up before me unto the high place; for ye shall eat with me to day, and to morrow I will let thee go, and will tell thee all that is in thine heart. And as for thine asses that were lost three days ago, set not thy mind on them; for they are found. And on whom is all the desire of Israel? Is it not on thee, and on all thy father's house?"

And Saul answered and said, "Am not I a Benjamite, of the smallest of the tribes of Israel? and my family the least of all the families of the tribe of Benjamin? wherefore then speakest thou so to me?"

And Samuel took Saul and his servant, and brought them

into the parlour, and made them sit in the chiefest place among them that were bidden, which were about thirty persons. And Samuel said unto the cook, "Bring the portion which I gave thee, of which I said unto thee, 'Set it by thee.'" And the cook took up the shoulder, and that which was upon it, and set it before Saul. And Samuel said, "Behold that which is left! set it before thee, and eat: for unto this time hath it been kept for thee since I said, I have invited the people." So Saul did eat with Samuel that day.

And when they were come down from the high place into the city, Samuel communed with Saul upon the top of the house. And they arose early: and it came to pass about the spring of the day, that Samuel called Saul to the top of the house,[1] saying, "Up, that I may send thee away." And Saul arose, and they went out both of them, he and Samuel, abroad. And as they were going down to the end of the city, Samuel said to Saul, "Bid the servant pass on before us," (and he passed on,) "but stand thou still a while, that I may shew thee the word of God."

Then Samuel took a vial of oil, and poured it upon his head, and kissed him, and said, "Is it not because the LORD hath anointed thee to be captain over his inheritance? When thou art departed from me to day, then thou shalt find two men by Rachel's sepulchre[2] in the border of Benjamin at Zelzah; and they will say unto thee, 'The asses which thou wentest to seek are found: and, lo, thy father hath left the care of the asses, and sorroweth for you, saying, What shall I do for my son?' Then shalt thou go on forward from thence, and thou shalt come to the plain of Tabor, and there shall meet thee three men going up to God to Beth-el, one carrying three kids, and another carrying three loaves of bread, and another carrying a bottle of wine: and they will salute thee, and give thee two loaves of bread; which thou shalt receive of their hands.

[a] Saul had been sleeping on the roof, as is the custom in the East.
[b] Near Bethlehem.

"After that thou shalt come to the hill of God,[3] where is the garrison of the Philistines: and it shall come to pass, when thou art come thither to the city, that thou shalt meet a company of prophets coming down from the high place with a psaltery, and a tabret, and a pipe, and a harp, before them; and they shall prophesy: and the Spirit of the LORD will come upon thee, and thou shalt prophesy with them, and shalt be turned into another man. And let it be, when these signs are come unto thee, that thou do as occasion serve thee; for God is with thee. And thou shalt go down before me to Gilgal; and, behold, I will come down unto thee, to offer burnt offerings, and to sacrifice sacrifices of peace offerings: seven days shalt thou tarry, till I come to thee, and shew thee what thou shalt do."

And it was so, that when he had turned his back to go from Samuel, God gave him another heart: and all those signs came to pass that day. And when they came thither to the hill, behold, a company of prophets met him; and the Spirit of God came upon him, and he prophesied among them. And it came to pass, when all that knew him beforetime saw that, behold, he prophesied among the prophets, then the people said one to another, "What is this that is come unto the son of Kish? Is Saul also among the prophets?" And one of the same place answered and said, "But who is their father?" Therefore it became a proverb, "Is Saul also among the prophets?"[4]

[3] Gibeah, near Saul's home, where there was a school of the prophets.
[4] A short time later, Saul was chosen king by lot at Mizpah.

Saul's Presumptuousness

Saul reigned one year; and when he had reigned two years over Israel, Saul chose him three thousand men of Israel; whereof two thousand were with Saul in Michmash and in mount Beth-el, and a thousand were with Jonathan[5] in Gibeah of Benjamin: and the rest of the people he sent every man to his tent. And Jonathan smote the garrison of the Philistines that was in Geba, and the Philistines heard of it. And Saul blew the trumpet throughout all the land, saying, "Let the Hebrews hear." And all Israel heard say that Saul had smitten a garrison of the Philistines, and that Israel also was had in abomination with the Philistines. And the people were called together after Saul to Gilgal.[6]

And the Philistines gathered themselves together to fight with Israel, thirty thousand chariots, and six thousand horsemen, and people as the sand which is on the sea shore in multitude: and they came up, and pitched in Michmash, eastward from Beth-aven. When the men of Israel saw that they were in a strait, (for the people were distressed,) then the people did hide themselves in caves, and in thickets, and in rocks, and in high places, and in pits. And some of the Hebrews went over Jordan to the land of Gad and Gilead. As for Saul, he was yet in Gilgal, and all the people followed him trembling.

And he tarried seven days, according to the set time that Samuel had appointed: but Samuel came not to Gilgal; and the people were scattered from him. And Saul said, "Bring hither a burnt offering to me, and peace offerings." And he offered the burnt offering.

And it came to pass, that as soon as he had made an end of

[5] Saul's eldest son.
[6] Near Jericho.

offering the burnt offering, behold, Samuel came; and Saul went out to meet him, that he might salute him. And Samuel said, "What hast thou done?"

And Saul said, "Because I saw that the people were scattered from me, and that thou camest not within the days appointed, and that the Philistines gathered themselves together at Michmash; therefore said I, 'The Philistines will come down now upon me to Gilgal, and I have not made supplication unto the LORD': I forced myself therefore, and offered a burnt offering."

And Samuel said to Saul, "Thou hast done foolishly: thou hast not kept the commandment of the LORD thy God, which he commanded thee: for now would the LORD have established thy kingdom upon Israel for ever. But now thy kingdom shall not continue: the LORD hath sought him a man after his own heart, and the LORD hath commanded him to be captain over his people, because thou hast not kept that which the LORD commanded thee."

And Samuel arose, and gat him up from Gilgal unto Gibeah of Benjamin. And Saul numbered the people that were present with him, about six hundred men.

God Rejects Saul

• 1 SAMUEL 15: 10–35 •

Then came the word of the LORD unto Samuel, saying, "It repenteth me that I have set up Saul to be king: for he is turned back from following me, and hath not performed my commandments." And it grieved Samuel; and he cried unto the LORD all night. And when Samuel rose early to meet Saul in the morning, it was told Samuel, saying, "Saul came to Carmel, and, behold, he set him up a place, and is gone about, and passed on, and gone down to Gilgal."

And Samuel came to Saul: and Saul said unto him, "Blessed be thou of the Lord: I have performed the commandment of the Lord."

And Samuel said, "What meaneth then this bleating of the sheep in mine ears, and the lowing of the oxen which I hear?"

And Saul said, "They have brought them from the Amalekites:[7] for the people spared the best of the sheep and of the oxen, to sacrifice unto the Lord thy God; and the rest we have utterly destroyed."

Then Samuel said unto Saul, "Stay, and I will tell thee what the Lord hath said to me this night."

And he said unto him, "Say on."

And Samuel said, "When thou wast little in thine own sight, wast thou not made the head of the tribes of Israel, and the Lord anointed thee king over Israel? And the Lord sent thee on a journey, and said, 'Go and utterly destroy the sinners the Amalekites, and fight against them until they be consumed.' Wherefore then didst thou not obey the voice of the Lord, but didst fly upon the spoil, and didst evil in the sight of the Lord?"

And Saul said unto Samuel, "Yea, I have obeyed the voice of the Lord, and have gone the way which the Lord sent me, and have brought Agag the king of Amalek, and have utterly destroyed the Amalekites. But the people took of the spoil, sheep and oxen, the chief of the things which should have been utterly destroyed, to sacrifice unto the Lord thy God in Gilgal."

And Samuel said, "Hath the Lord as great delight in burnt offerings and sacrifices, as in obeying the voice of the Lord? Behold, to obey is better than sacrifice, and to hearken than the fat of rams. For rebellion is as the sin of witchcraft, and stubbornness is as iniquity and idolatry. Because thou hast rejected the word of the Lord, he hath also rejected thee from being king."

And Saul said unto Samuel, "I have sinned: for I have transgressed the commandment of the Lord, and thy words: because I feared the people, and obeyed their voice. Now there-

[7] A tribe of Southern Canaan.

fore, I pray thee, pardon my sin, and turn again with me, that I may worship the LORD."

And Samuel said unto Saul, "I will not return with thee: for thou hast rejected the word of the LORD, and the LORD hath rejected thee from being king over Israel."

And as Samuel turned about to go away, he laid hold upon the skirt of his mantle, and it rent. And Samuel said unto him, "The LORD hath rent the kingdom of Israel from thee this day, and hath given it to a neighbour of thine, that is better than thou. And also the Strength of Israel will not lie nor repent: for he is not a man, that he should repent."

Then he said, "I have sinned: yet honour me now, I pray thee, before the elders of my people, and before Israel, and turn again with me, that I may worship the LORD thy God." So Samuel turned again after Saul; and Saul worshipped the LORD.

Then said Samuel, "Bring ye hither to me Agag the king of the Amalekites."

And Agag came unto him delicately.[8] And Agag said, "Surely the bitterness of death is past."

And Samuel said, "As thy sword hath made women childless, so shall thy mother be childless among women." And Samuel hewed Agag in pieces before the LORD in Gilgal.

Then Samuel went to Ramah; and Saul went up to his house to Gibeah of Saul. And Samuel came no more to see Saul until the day of his death: nevertheless Samuel mourned for Saul: and the LORD repented that he had made Saul king over Israel.

[8] "Cheerfully"—because he thought his life would be spared.

The Anointing of David. His Summons to Court

• 1 SAMUEL 16 •

And the LORD said unto Samuel, "How long wilt thou mourn for Saul, seeing I have rejected him from reigning over Israel? fill thine horn with oil, and go, I will send thee to Jesse the Beth-lehemite: for I have provided me a king among his sons."

And Samuel said, "How can I go? if Saul hear it, he will kill me."

And the LORD said, "Take an heifer with thee, and say, 'I am come to sacrifice to the LORD.' And call Jesse to the sacrifice, and I will shew thee what thou shalt do: and thou shalt anoint unto me him whom I name unto thee."

And Samuel did that which the LORD spake, and came to Beth-lehem. And the elders of the town trembled at his coming, and said, "Comest thou peaceably?"

And he said, "Peaceably: I am come to sacrifice unto the LORD sanctify yourselves, and come with me to the sacrifice." And he sanctified Jesse and his sons, and called them to the sacrifice.

And it came to pass, when they were come, that he looked on Eliab, and said, "Surely the LORD's anointed is before him." But the LORD said unto Samuel, "Look not on his countenance, or on the height of his stature; because I have refused him": for the LORD seeth not as man seeth; for man looketh on the outward appearance, but the LORD looketh on the heart. Then Jesse called Abinadab, and made him pass before Samuel. And he said, "Neither hath the LORD chosen this." Then Jesse made Shammah to pass by. And he said, "Neither hath the LORD chosen this." Again, Jesse made seven of his sons to pass before Samuel. And Samuel said unto Jesse, "The LORD hath not chosen these."

And Samuel said unto Jesse, "Are here all thy children?"

And he said, "There remaineth yet the youngest, and, behold, he keepeth the sheep."

And Samuel said unto Jesse, "Send and fetch him: for we will not sit down till he come hither."

And he sent, and brought him in. Now he was ruddy, and withal of a beautiful countenance, and goodly to look to. And the LORD said, "Arise, anoint him: for this is he."

Then Samuel took the horn of oil, and anointed him in the midst of his brethren: and the Spirit of the LORD came upon David from that day forward. So Samuel rose up, and went to Ramah.

But the Spirit of the LORD departed from Saul, and an evil spirit from the LORD troubled him. And Saul's servants said unto him, "Behold now, an evil spirit from God troubleth thee. Let our lord now command thy servants, which are before thee, to seek out a man, who is a cunning player on an harp: and it shall come to pass, when the evil spirit from God is upon thee, that he shall play with his hand, and thou shalt be well."

And Saul said unto his servants, "Provide me now a man that can play well, and bring him to me."

Then answered one of the servants, and said, "Behold, I have seen a son of Jesse the Beth-lehemite, that is cunning in playing, and a mighty valiant man, and a man of war, and prudent in matters, and a comely person, and the LORD is with him."

Wherefore Saul sent messengers unto Jesse, and said, "Send me David thy son, which is with the sheep." And Jesse took an ass laden with bread, and a bottle of wine, and a kid, and sent them by David his son unto Saul. And David came to Saul, and stood before him: and he loved him greatly; and he became his armourbearer. And Saul sent to Jesse, saying, "Let David, I pray thee, stand before me; for he hath found favour in my sight." And it came to pass, when the evil spirit from God was upon Saul, that David took an harp, and played with his hand: so Saul was refreshed, and was well, and the evil spirit departed from him.

David and Goliath

• 1 SAMUEL 17 •

Now the Philistines gathered together their armies to battle, and were gathered together at Shochoh, which belongeth to Judah, and pitched between Shochoh and Azekah, in Ephes-dammim. And Saul and the men of Israel were gathered together, and pitched by the valley of Elah, and set the battle in array against the Philistines. And the Philistines stood on a mountain on the one side, and Israel stood on a mountain on the other side: and there was a valley between them.

And there went out a champion out of the camp of the Philistines, named Goliath, of Gath, whose height was six cubits and a span.[1] And he had an helmet of brass upon his head, and he was armed with a coat of mail; and the weight of the coat was five thousand shekels[2] of brass. And he had greaves of brass upon his legs, and a target of brass between his shoulders. And the staff of his spear was like a weaver's beam; and his spear's head weighed six hundred shekels of iron: and one bearing a shield went before him. And he stood and cried unto the armies of Israel, and said unto them, "Why are ye come out to set your battle in array? am not I a Philistine, and ye serv-

[1] About nine feet six inches.
[2] The weight of the shekel at this time is unknown.

ants to Saul? choose you a man for you, and let him come down to me. If he be able to fight with me, and to kill me, then will we be your servants: but if I prevail against him, and kill him, then shall ye be our servants, and serve us." And the Philistine said, "I defy the armies of Israel this day; give me a man, that we may fight together." When Saul and all Israel heard those words of the Philistine, they were dismayed, and greatly afraid.

Now David was the son of that Ephrathite of Beth-lehem-judah, whose name was Jesse; and he had eight sons: and the man went among men for an old man in the days of Saul. And the three eldest sons of Jesse went and followed Saul to the battle: and the names of his three sons that went to the battle were Eliab the firstborn, and next unto him Abinadab, and the third Shammah. And David was the youngest: and the three eldest followed Saul. But David went and returned from Saul to feed his father's sheep at Beth-lehem. And the Philistine drew near morning and evening, and presented himself forty days. And Jesse said unto David his son, "Take now for thy brethren an ephah of this parched corn, and these ten loaves, and run to the camp to thy brethren; and carry these ten cheeses unto the captain of their thousand, and look how thy brethren fare, and take their pledge." [3]

Now Saul, and they, and all the men of Israel, were in the valley of Elah, fighting with the Philistines. And David rose up early in the morning, and left the sheep with a keeper, and took, and went, as Jesse had commanded him; and he came to the trench, as the host was going forth to the fight, and shouted for the battle. For Israel and the Philistines had put the battle in array, army against army. And David left his carriage in the hand of the keeper of the carriage, and ran into the army, and came and saluted his brethren. And as he talked with them, behold, there came up the champion, the Philistine of Gath, Goliath by name, out of the armies of the Philistines, and spake according to the same words: and David heard them. And all the men of

[3] "Bring back proof that you have carried out your instructions."

Israel, when they saw the man, fled from him, and were sore afraid.

And the men of Israel said, "Have ye seen this man that is come up? surely to defy Israel is he come up: and it shall be, that the man who killeth him, the king will enrich him with great riches, and will give him his daughter, and make his father's house free in Israel."

And David spake to the men that stood by him, saying, "What shall be done to the man that killeth this Philistine, and taketh away the reproach from Israel? for who is this uncircumcised Philistine, that he should defy the armies of the living God?"

And the people answered him after this manner, saying, "So shall it be done to the man that killeth him."

And Eliab his eldest brother heard when he spake unto the men; and Eliab's anger was kindled against David, and he said, "Why camest thou down hither? and with whom hast thou left those few sheep in the wilderness? I know thy pride, and the naughtiness of thine heart; for thou art come down that thou mightest see the battle."

And David said, "What have I now done? Is there not a cause?" And he turned from him toward another, and spake after the same manner: and the people answered him again after the former manner. And when the words were heard which David spake, they rehearsed them before Saul: and he sent for him.

And David said to Saul, "Let no man's heart fail because of him; thy servant will go and fight with this Philistine."

And Saul said to David, "Thou art not able to go against this Philistine to fight with him: for thou art but a youth, and he a man of war from his youth."

And David said unto Saul, "Thy servant kept his father's sheep, and there came a lion, and a bear, and took a lamb out of the flock: and I went out after him, and smote him, and delivered it out of his mouth: and when he arose against me, I caught him by his beard, and smote him, and slew him. Thy servant slew both the lion and the bear: and this uncircumcised Philistine shall be as one of them, seeing he hath defied the armies of the living God." David said moreover, "The LORD that delivered me out of the paw of the lion, and out of the paw of the bear, he will deliver me out of the hand of this Philistine."

And Saul said unto David, "Go, and the LORD be with thee." And Saul armed David with his armour, and he put an helmet of brass upon his head; also he armed him with a coat of mail. And David girded his sword upon his armour, and he assayed to go; for he had not proved it.[4] And David said unto Saul, "I cannot go with these; for I have not proved them." And David put them off him. And he took his staff in his hand, and chose him five smooth stones out of the brook, and put them in a shepherd's bag which he had, even in a scrip; and his sling was in his hand: and he drew near to the Philistine.

And the Philistine came on and drew near unto David; and the man that bare the shield went before him. And when the Philistine looked about, and saw David, he disdained him: for he was but a youth, and ruddy, and of a fair countenance. And the Philistine said unto David, "Am I a dog, that thou comest to me with staves?" And the Philistine cursed David by his gods. And the Philistine said to David, "Come to me, and I will give thy flesh unto the fowls of the air, and to the beasts of the field."

Then said David to the Philistine, "Thou comest to me with a sword, and with a spear, and with a shield: but I come to thee in the name of the LORD of hosts, the God of the armies of Israel, whom thou hast defied. This day will the LORD deliver thee into mine hand; and I will smite thee, and take thine head from thee; and I will give the carcases of the host of the Philistines this day unto the fowls of the air, and to the wild beasts of the earth; that all the earth may know that there is a God in Israel. And all this assembly shall know that the LORD saveth not

[4] i.e., the armor was too heavy for him.

with sword and spear: for the battle is the LORD's, and he will give you into our hands."

And it came to pass, when the Philistine arose, and came and drew nigh to meet David, that David hasted, and ran toward the army to meet the Philistine. And David put his hand in his bag, and took thence a stone, and slang it, and smote the Philistine in his forehead, that the stone sunk into his forehead; and he fell upon his face to the earth. So David prevailed over the Philistine with a sling and with a stone, and smote the Philistine, and slew him; but there was no sword in the hand of David. Therefore David ran, and stood upon the Philistine, and took his sword, and drew it out of the sheath thereof, and slew him, and cut off his head therewith. And when the Philistines saw their champion was dead, they fled.

And the men of Israel and of Judah arose, and shouted, and pursued the Philistines, until thou come to the valley, and to the gates of Ekron. And the wounded of the Philistines fell down by the way to Shaaraim, even unto Gath, and unto Ekron. And the children of Israel returned from chasing after the Philistines, and they spoiled their tents. And David took the head of the Philistine, and brought it to Jerusalem; but he put his armour in his tent.

And when Saul saw David go forth against the Philistine, he said unto Abner, the captain of the host, "Abner, whose son is this youth?"

And Abner said, "As thy soul liveth, O king, I cannot tell."

And the king said, "Enquire thou whose son the stripling is."

And as David returned from the slaughter of the Philistine, Abner took him, and brought him before Saul with the head of the Philistine in his hand. And Saul said to him, "Whose son art thou, thou young man?"

And David answered, "I am the son of thy servant Jesse the Beth-lehemite."

David and Jonathan. Saul's Jealousy

And it came to pass, when he had made an end of speaking unto Saul, that the soul of Jonathan was knit with the soul of David, and Jonathan loved him as his own soul. And Saul took him that day, and would let him go no more home to his father's house. Then Jonathan and David made a covenant, because he loved him as his own soul. And Jonathan stripped himself of the robe that was upon him, and gave it to David, and his garments, even to his sword, and to his bow, and to his girdle.

And David went out whithersoever Saul sent him, and behaved himself wisely: and Saul set him over the men of war, and he was accepted in the sight of all the people, and also in the sight of Saul's servants. And it came to pass as they came, when David was returned from the slaughter of the Philistine, that the women came out of all cities of Israel, singing and dancing, to meet king Saul, with tabrets,[5] with joy, and with instruments of music. And the women answered one another as they played, and said, "Saul hath slain his thousands, and David his ten thousands." And Saul was very wroth, and the saying displeased him; and he said, "They have ascribed unto David ten thousands, and to me they have ascribed but thousands: and what can he have more but the kingdom?" And Saul eyed David from that day and forward.

And it came to pass on the morrow, that the evil spirit from God came upon Saul, and he prophesied [6] in the midst of the house: and David played with his hand, as at other times: and there was a javelin in Saul's hand. And Saul cast the javelin; for he said, "I will smite David even to the wall with it." And David avoided out of his presence twice. And Saul was afraid of David, because the LORD was with him, and was de-

[5] Drums.
[6] The word here signifies "spoke in a frenzy."

parted from Saul. Therefore Saul removed him from him, and made him his captain over a thousand: and he went out and came in before the people. And David behaved himself wisely in all his ways; and the LORD was with him. Wherefore when Saul saw that he behaved himself very wisely, he was afraid of him. But all Israel and Judah loved David, because he went out and came in before them.

Saul and the Witch of Endor

• 1 SAMUEL 28: 3–25 •

Now Samuel was dead, and all Israel had lamented him, and buried him in Ramah, even in his own city. And Saul had put away those that had familiar spirits, and the wizards, out of the land. And the Philistines gathered themselves together, and came and pitched in Shunem: and Saul gathered all Israel together, and they pitched in Gilboa. And when Saul saw the host of the Philistines, he was afraid, and his heart greatly trembled. And when Saul enquired of the LORD, the LORD answered him not, neither by dreams, nor by Urim,[7] nor by prophets.

Then said Saul unto his servants, "Seek me a woman that hath a familiar spirit, that I may go to her, and enquire of her."

And his servants said to him, "Behold, there is a woman that hath a familiar spirit at En-dor." [8]

And Saul disguised himself, and put on other raiment, and he went, and two men with him, and they came to the woman by night: and he said, "I pray thee, divine unto me by the familiar spirit, and bring me him up, whom I shall name unto thee."

And the woman said unto him, "Behold, thou knowest what

[7] An object, probably a jewel, in the high priest's breastplate, used in divination.
[8] In northern Palestine, about 12 miles southwest of the Sea of Galilee.

Saul hath done, how he hath cut off those that have familiar spirits, and the wizards, out of the land: wherefore then layest thou a snare for my life, to cause me to die?"

And Saul sware to her by the LORD, saying, "As the LORD liveth, there shall no punishment happen to thee for this thing."

Then said the woman, "Whom shall I bring up unto thee?"

And he said, "Bring me up Samuel."

And when the woman saw Samuel, she cried with a loud voice: and the woman spake to Saul, saying, "Why hast thou deceived me? for thou art Saul."

And the king said unto her, "Be not afraid: for what sawest thou?"

And the woman said unto Saul, "I saw gods ascending out of the earth."

And he said unto her, "What form is he of?"

And she said, "An old man cometh up; and he is covered with a mantle."

And Saul perceived that it was Samuel, and he stooped with his face to the ground, and bowed himself. And Samuel said to Saul, "Why hast thou disquieted me, to bring me up?"

And Saul answered, "I am sore distressed; for the Philistines make war against me, and God is departed from me, and answereth me no more, neither by prophets, nor by dreams: therefore I have called thee, that thou mayest make known unto me what I shall do."

Then said Samuel, "Wherefore then dost thou ask of me, seeing the LORD is departed from thee, and is become thine enemy? And the LORD hath done to thee as he spake by me: for the LORD hath rent the kingdom out of thine hand, and given it to thy neighbour, even to David: because thou obeyedst not the voice of the LORD, nor executedst his fierce wrath upon Amalek, therefore hath the LORD done this thing unto thee this day. Moreover the LORD will also deliver Israel with thee into the hand of the Philistines: and to morrow shalt thou and thy sons be with me: the LORD also shall deliver the host of Israel into the hand of the Philistines."

Then Saul fell straightway all along on the earth, and was sore afraid, because of the words of Samuel: and there was no strength in him; for he had eaten no bread all the day, nor all the night. And the woman came unto Saul, and saw that he was sore troubled, and said unto him, "Behold, thine handmaid hath obeyed thy voice, and I have put my life in my hand, and have hearkened unto thy words which thou spakest unto me. Now therefore, I pray thee, hearken thou also unto the voice of thine handmaid, and let me set a morsel of bread before thee; and eat, that thou mayest have strength, when thou goest on thy way."

But he refused, and said, "I will not eat." But his servants, together with the woman, compelled him; and he hearkened unto their voice. So he arose from the earth, and sat upon the bed. And the woman had a fat calf in the house; and she hasted, and killed it, and took flour, and kneaded it, and did bake unleavened bread thereof: and she brought it before Saul, and before his servants; and they did eat. Then they rose up and went away that night.

The Death of Saul

• 1 SAMUEL 31: 1–13 •

Now the Philistines fought against Israel: and the men of Israel fled from before the Philistines, and fell down slain in mount Gilboa. And the Philistines followed hard upon Saul and upon his sons; and the Philistines slew Jonathan, and Abinadab, and Melchi-shua, Saul's sons. And the battle went sore against Saul, and the archers hit him; and he was sore wounded of the archers.

Then said Saul unto his armourbearer, "Draw thy sword,

and thrust me through therewith; lest these uncircumcised come and thrust me through, and abuse me." But his armourbearer would not; for he was sore afraid. Therefore Saul took a sword, and fell upon it. And when his armourbearer saw that Saul was dead, he fell likewise upon his sword, and died with him. So Saul died, and his three sons, and his armourbearer, and all his men, that same day together.

And when the men of Israel that were on the other side of the valley, and they that were on the other side Jordan, saw that the men of Israel fled, and that Saul and his sons were dead, they forsook the cities, and fled; and the Philistines came and dwelt in them. And it came to pass on the morrow, when the Philistines came to strip the slain, that they found Saul and his three sons fallen in mount Gilboa. And they cut off his head, and stripped off his armour, and sent into the land of the Philistines round about, to publish it in the house of their idols, and among the people. And they put his armour in the house of Ashtaroth:[9] and they fastened his body to the wall of Beth-shan.[10]

And when the inhabitants of Jabesh-gilead [11] heard of that which the Philistines had done to Saul, all the valiant men arose, and went all night, and took the body of Saul and the bodies of his sons from the wall of Beth-shan, and came to Jabesh, and burnt them there. And they took their bones, and buried them under a tree at Jabesh, and fasted seven days.

[9] In Ashkelon, a city of the Philistines between Joppa and Gaza.
[10] A town of Manasseh, near Mt. Gilboah.
[11] A city of Gilead which had been saved by Saul from the Ammonites. It was about 10 miles from Beth-Shan.

David's Lament for Saul and Jonathan

Now it came to pass after the death of Saul, when David was returned from the slaughter of the Amalekites, and David had abode two days in Ziklag; it came even to pass on the third day, that, behold, a man came out of the camp from Saul with his clothes rent, and earth upon his head: and so it was, when he came to David, that he fell to the earth, and did obeisance.

And David said unto him, "From whence comest thou?"

And he said unto him, "Out of the camp of Israel am I escaped."

And David said unto him, "How went the matter? I pray thee, tell me."

And he answered, "That the people are fled from the battle, and many of the people also are fallen and dead; and Saul and Jonathan his son are dead also."

And David said unto the young man that told him, "How knowest thou that Saul and Jonathan his son be dead?"

And the young man that told him said, "As I happened by chance upon mount Gilboa, behold, Saul leaned upon his spear; and, lo, the chariots and horsemen followed hard after him. And when he looked behind him, he saw me, and called unto me. And I answered, 'Here am I.' And he said unto me, 'Who art thou?' And I answered him, 'I am an Amalekite.' He said unto me again, 'Stand, I pray thee, upon me, and slay me: for anguish is come upon me, because my life is yet whole in me.' So I stood upon him, and slew him, because I was sure that he could not live after that he was fallen: and I took the crown that was upon his head, and the bracelet that was on his arm, and have brought them hither unto my lord." [12]

Then David took hold on his clothes, and rent them; and

[12] This contradicts the preceding account of Saul's death. It is sometimes assumed that the young man was lying in order to gain David's favor.

likewise all the men that were with him. And they mourned, and wept, and fasted until even, for Saul, and for Jonathan his son, and for the people of the LORD, and for the house of Israel; because they were fallen by the sword.

And David said unto the young man that told him, "Whence art thou?"

And he answered, "I am the son of a stranger, an Amalekite."

And David said unto him, "How wast thou not afraid to stretch forth thine hand to destroy the LORD's anointed?" And David called one of the young men, and said, "Go near, and fall upon him." And he smote him that he died. And David said unto him, "Thy blood be upon thy head; for thy mouth hath testified against thee, saying, 'I have slain the LORD's anointed.'"

And David lamented with this lamentation over Saul and over Jonathan his son: (Also he bade them teach the children of Judah the use of the bow:[13] behold, it is written in the book of Jasher).[14]

The beauty of Israel is slain upon thy high places:
How are the mighty fallen!
Tell it not in Gath,
Publish it not in the streets of Askelon;
Lest the daughters of the Philistines rejoice,
Lest the daughters of the uncircumcised triumph.
Ye mountains of Gilboa,
Let there be no dew, neither let there be rain, upon you, nor
    fields of offerings:
For there the shield of the mighty is vilely cast away,
The shield of Saul, as though he had not been anointed with oil.
From the blood of the slain, from the fat of the mighty,
The bow of Jonathan turned not back,
And the sword of Saul returned not empty.

[13] i.e., "The Song of the Bow," which is the title of the poem which follows.
[14] Evidently a book of heroic verse.

Saul and Jonathan were lovely and pleasant in their lives,
And in their death they were not divided:
They were swifter than eagles,
They were stronger than lions.
Ye daughters of Israel, weep over Saul,
Who clothed you in scarlet, with other delights,
Who put on ornaments of gold upon your apparel.
How are the mighty fallen in the midst of the battle!
O Jonathan, thou wast slain in thine high places.
I am distressed for thee, my brother Jonathan:
Very pleasant hast thou been unto me:
Thy love to me was wonderful,
Passing the love of women.
How are the mighty fallen,
And the weapons of war perished!

David, King of All Israel

• 2 SAMUEL 5: 1–10 •

Then came all the tribes of Israel to David unto Hebron,[15]
and spake, saying, "Behold, we are thy bone and thy flesh. Also
in time past, when Saul was king over us, thou wast he that led-
dest out and broughtest in Israel: and the LORD said to thee,
'Thou shalt feed my people Israel, and thou shalt be a captain
over Israel.'" So all the elders of Israel came to the king to
Hebron; and king David made a league with them in Hebron
before the LORD: and they anointed David king over Israel.[16]
David was thirty years old when he began to reign, and he
reigned forty years. In Hebron he reigned over Judah seven

[15] David's capital until the capture of Jerusalem, about 20 miles to the north.
[16] David reigned from *c.* 1004 to 965 B.C. At first, after the death of Saul,
he was recognized only by the southern tribes (Judah). After the death of
Saul's son Ishbosheth, David was acknowledged as king of all Israel. It is
that acknowledgment which is here recorded.

years and six months: and in Jerusalem he reigned thirty and three years over all Israel and Judah.

And the king and his men went to Jerusalem unto the Jebusites, the inhabitants of the land: which spake unto David, saying, "Except thou take away the blind and the lame, thou shalt not come in hither:" thinking, David cannot come in hither.[17] Nevertheless David took the strong hold of Zion: the same is the city of David. And David said on that day, "Whosoever getteth up to the gutter, and smiteth the Jebusites, and the lame and the blind, that are hated of David's soul, he shall be chief and captain." Wherefore they said, "The blind and the lame shall not come into the house." So David dwelt in the fort, and called it the city of David. And David built round about from Millo[18] and inward. And David went on, and grew great, and the LORD God of hosts was with him.

David and Bath-sheba

• 2 SAMUEL 11:1 TO 12:25 •

And it came to pass, after the year was expired, at the time when kings go forth to battle, that David sent Joab, and his servants with him, and all Israel; and they destroyed the children of Ammon, and besieged Rabbah. But David tarried still at Jerusalem. And it came to pass in an eveningtide, that David arose from off his bed, and walked upon the roof of the king's house: and from the roof he saw a woman washing herself; and the woman was very beautiful to look upon. And David sent and enquired after the woman. And one said, "Is not this Bath-sheba, the daughter of Eliam, the wife of Uriah the Hittite?"

[17] The sense of the passage is that the Jebusites considered Jerusalem so impregnable that it could be defended even by the lame and the blind.
[18] Part of Jerusalem.

And David sent messengers, and took her; and she came in unto him, and he lay with her; for she was purified from her uncleanness: and she returned unto her house. And the woman conceived, and sent and told David, and said, "I am with child."

And David sent to Joab, saying, "Send me Uriah the Hittite." And Joab sent Uriah to David. And when Uriah was come unto him, David demanded of him how Joab did, and how the people did, and how the war prospered. And David said to Uriah, "Go down to thy house, and wash thy feet." And Uriah departed out of the king's house, and there followed him a mess of meat from the king. But Uriah slept at the door of the king's house with all the servants of his lord, and went not down to his house.

And when they had told David, saying, "Uriah went not down unto his house," David said unto Uriah, "Camest thou not from thy journey? why then didst thou not go down unto thine house?"

And Uriah said unto David, "The ark, and Israel, and Judah, abide in tents; and my lord Joab, and the servants of my lord, are encamped in the open fields; shall I then go into mine house, to eat and to drink, and to lie with my wife? as thou livest, and as thy soul liveth, I will not do this thing."

And David said to Uriah, "Tarry here to day also, and to morrow I will let thee depart." So Uriah abode in Jerusalem that day, and the morrow. And when David had called him, he did eat and drink before him; and he made him drunk: and at even he went out to lie on his bed with the servants of his lord, but went not down to his house.

And it came to pass in the morning, that David wrote a letter to Joab, and sent it by the hand of Uriah. And he wrote in the letter, saying, "Set ye Uriah in the forefront of the hottest battle, and retire ye from him, that he may be smitten, and die." And it came to pass, when Joab observed the city, that he assigned Uriah unto a place where he knew that valiant men were. And the men of the city went out, and fought with Joab: and there fell some of the people of the servants of David; and Uriah the Hittite died also.

Then Joab sent and told David all the things concerning the war; and charged the messenger, saying, "When thou hast made an end of telling the matters of the war unto the king, and if so be that the king's wrath arise, and he say unto thee, 'Wherefore approached ye so nigh unto the city when ye did fight? knew ye not that they would shoot from the wall? Who smote Abimelech[19] the son of Jerubbesheth? did not a woman cast a piece of a millstone upon him from the wall, that he died in Thebez? why went ye nigh the wall?' then say thou, 'Thy servant Uriah the Hittite is dead also.' "

So the messenger went, and came and shewed David all that Joab had sent him for. And the messenger said unto David, "Surely the men prevailed against us, and came out unto us into the field, and we were upon them even unto the entering of the gate. And the shooters shot from off the wall upon thy servants; and some of the king's servants be dead, and thy servant Uriah the Hittite is dead also."

Then David said unto the messenger, "Thus shalt thou say unto Joab, 'Let not this thing displease thee, for the sword devoureth one as well as another: make thy battle more strong against the city, and overthrow it': and encourage thou him."

And when the wife of Uriah heard that Uriah her husband was dead, she mourned for her husband. And when the mourning was past, David sent and fetched her to his house, and she became his wife, and bare him a son. But the thing that David had done displeased the LORD.

And the LORD sent Nathan unto David. And he came unto him, and said unto him, "There were two men in one city; the one rich, and the other poor. The rich man had exceeding many flocks and herds: but the poor man had nothing, save one little ewe lamb, which he had bought and nourished up: and it

[19] His story is in Judges 9.

grew up together with him, and with his children; it did eat of his own meat, and drank of his own cup, and lay in his bosom, and was unto him as a daughter. And there came a traveller unto the rich man, and he spared to take of his own flock and of his own herds, to dress for the wayfaring man that was come unto him; but took the poor man's lamb, and dressed it for the man that was come to him.''

And David's anger was greatly kindled against the man; and he said to Nathan, "As the LORD liveth, the man that hath done this thing shall surely die: and he shall restore the lamb fourfold, because he did this thing, and because he had no pity."

And Nathan said to David, "Thou art the man. Thus saith the LORD God of Israel, 'I anointed thee king over Israel, and I delivered thee out of the hand of Saul; and I gave thee thy master's house, and thy master's wives into thy bosom, and gave thee the house of Israel and of Judah; and if that had been too little, I would moreover have given unto thee such and such things. Wherefore hast thou despised the commandment of the LORD, to do evil in his sight? thou hast killed Uriah the Hittite with the sword, and hast taken his wife to be thy wife, and hast slain him with the sword of the children of Ammon. Now therefore the sword shall never depart from thine house; because thou hast despised me, and hast taken the wife of Uriah the Hittite to be thy wife.' Thus saith the LORD, 'Behold, I will raise up evil against thee out of thine own house, and I will take thy wives before thine eyes, and give them unto thy neighbour, and he shall lie with thy wives in the sight of this sun. For thou didst it secretly: but I will do this thing before all Israel, and before the sun.'"

And David said unto Nathan, "I have sinned against the LORD."

And Nathan said unto David, "The LORD also hath put away thy sin; thou shalt not die. Howbeit, because by this deed thou hast given great occasion to the enemies of the LORD to blaspheme, the child also that is born unto thee shall surely die."

And Nathan departed unto his house. And the LORD struck the child that Uriah's wife bare unto David, and it was very sick. David therefore besought God for the child; and David fasted, and went in, and lay all night upon the earth. And the elders of his house arose, and went to him, to raise him up from the earth: but he would not, neither did he eat bread with them. And it came to pass on the seventh day, that the child died. And the servants of David feared to tell him that the child was dead: for they said, "Behold, while the child was yet alive, we spake unto him, and he would not hearken unto our voice: how will he then vex himself, if we tell him that the child is dead?"

But when David saw that his servants whispered, David perceived that the child was dead: therefore David said unto his servants, "Is the child dead?"

And they said, "He is dead."

Then David arose from the earth, and washed, and anointed himself, and changed his apparel, and came into the house of the LORD, and worshipped: then he came to his own house; and when he required, they set bread before him, and he did eat. Then said his servants unto him, "What thing is this that thou hast done? thou didst fast and weep for the child, while it was alive; but when the child was dead, thou didst rise and eat bread."

And he said, "While the child was yet alive, I fasted and wept: for I said, 'Who can tell whether GOD will be gracious to me, that the child may live?' But now he is dead, wherefore should I fast? can I bring him back again? I shall go to him, but he shall not return to me."

And David comforted Bath-sheba his wife, and went in unto her, and lay with her: and she bare a son, and he called his name Solomon: and the LORD loved him. And he sent by the hand of Nathan the prophet; and he called his name Jedidiah,[20] because of the LORD.

---

[20] "Beloved of Jehovah."

Absalom the Usurper

• 2 SAMUEL 15: 1–6 •

And it came to pass after this, that Absalom[21] prepared him chariots and horses, and fifty men to run before him. And Absalom rose up early, and stood beside the way of the gate: and it was so, that when any man that had a controversy came to the king for judgment, then Absalom called unto him, and said, "Of what city art thou?" And he said, "Thy servant is one of the tribes of Israel." And Absalom said unto him, "See, thy matters are good and right; but there is no man deputed of the king to hear thee." Absalom said moreover, "Oh that I were made judge in the land, that every man which hath any suit or cause might come unto me, and I would do him justice!" And it was so, that when any man came nigh to him to do him obeisance, he put forth his hand, and took him, and kissed him. And on this manner did Absalom to all Israel that came to the king for judgment: so Absalom stole the hearts of the men of Israel.

The Death of Absalom

• 2 SAMUEL 18 •

And David numbered the people that were with him, and set captains of thousands and captains of hundreds over them. And David sent forth a third part of the people under the hand of Joab, and a third part under the hand of Abishai the son of Zeruiah, Joab's brother, and a third part under the hand of Ittai the Gittite. And the king said unto the people, "I will surely go forth with you myself also."

---

[21] David's son by Maacah. He had been banished for killing his half-brother Ammon. After a brief reconciliation with his father, he organized a revolt, with Ahitophel as his principal adviser.

But the people answered, "Thou shalt not go forth: for if we flee away, they will not care for us; neither if half of us die, will they care for us: but now thou art worth ten thousand of us: therefore now it is better that thou succour us out of the city."

And the king said unto them, "What seemeth you best I will do." And the king stood by the gate side, and all the people came out by hundreds and by thousands. And the king commanded Joab and Abishai and Ittai, saying, "Deal gently for my sake with the young man, even with Absalom." And all the people heard when the king gave all the captains charge concerning Absalom.

So the people went out into the field against Israel: and the battle was in the wood of Ephraim; where the people of Israel were slain before the servants of David, and there was there a great slaughter that day of twenty thousand men. For the battle was there scattered over the face of all the country: and the wood devoured more people that day than the sword devoured.

And Absalom met the servants of David. And Absalom rode upon a mule, and the mule went under the thick boughs of a great oak, and his head caught hold of the oak, and he was taken up between the heaven and the earth; and the mule that was under him went away.

And a certain man saw it, and told Joab, and said, "Behold, I saw Absalom hanged in an oak."

And Joab said unto the man that told him, "And, behold, thou sawest him, and why didst thou not smite him there to the ground? and I would have given thee ten shekels of silver, and a girdle."

And the man said unto Joab, "Though I should receive a thousand shekels of silver in mine hand, yet would I not put forth mine hand against the king's son: for in our hearing the king charged thee and Abishai and Ittai, saying, 'Beware that none touch the young man Absalom.' Otherwise I should have wrought falsehood against mine own life: for there is no matter hid from the king, and thou thyself wouldest have set thyself against me."

Then said Joab, "I may not tarry thus with thee." And he took three darts in his hand, and thrust them through the heart of Absalom, while he was yet alive in the midst of the oak. And ten young men that bare Joab's armour compassed about and smote Absalom, and slew him. And Joab blew the trumpet, and the people returned from pursuing after Israel: for Joab held back the people. And they took Absalom, and cast him into a great pit in the wood, and laid a very great heap of stones upon him: and all Israel fled every one to his tent. Now Absalom in his lifetime had taken and reared up for himself a pillar, which is in the king's dale: for he said, 'I have no son to keep my name in remembrance': and he called the pillar after his own name: and it is called unto this day, Absalom's place.

Then said Ahimaaz the son of Zadok, "Let me now run, and bear the king tidings, how that the LORD hath avenged him of his enemies."

And Joab said unto him, "Thou shalt not bear tidings this day, but thou shalt bear tidings another day: but this day thou shalt bear no tidings, because the king's son is dead." Then said Joab to Cushi, "Go tell the king what thou hast seen." And Cushi bowed himself unto Joab, and ran.

Then said Ahimaaz the son of Zadok yet again to Joab, "But howsoever, let me, I pray thee, also run after Cuhi."

And Joab said, "Wherefore wilt thou run, my son, seeing that hast no tidings ready?"

"But howsoever," said he, "let me run."

And he said unto him, "Run." Then Ahimaaz ran by the way of the plain, and overran Cushi.

And David sat between the two gates: and the watchman went up to the roof over the gate unto the wall, and lifted up his eyes, and looked, and behold a man running alone. And the watchman cried, and told the king. And the king said, "If he be alone, there is tidings in his mouth." And he came apace, and drew near.

And the watchman saw another man running: and the watchman called unto the porter, and said, "Behold another man running alone."

And the king said, "He also bringeth tidings."

And the watchman said, "Me thinketh the running of the foremost is like the running of Ahimaaz the son of Zadok."

And the king said, "He is a good man, and cometh with good tidings."

And Ahimaaz called, and said unto the king, "All is well." And he fell down to the earth upon his face before the king, and said, "Blessed be the Lord thy God, which hath delivered up the men that lifted up their hand against my lord the king."

And the king said, "Is the young man Absalom safe?"

And Ahimaaz answered, "When Joab sent the king's servant, and me thy servant, I saw a great tumult, but I knew not what it was."

And the king said unto him, "Turn aside, and stand here." And he turned aside, and stood still.

And, behold, Cushi came; and Cushi said, "Tidings, my lord the king: for the Lord hath avenged thee this day of all them that rose up against thee."

And the king said unto Cushi, "Is the young man Absalom safe?"

And Cushi answered, "The enemies of my lord the king, and all that rise against thee to do thee hurt, be as that young man is."

And the king was much moved, and went up to the chamber over the gate, and wept: and as he went, thus he said, "O my son Absalom, my son, my son Absalom! would God I had died for thee, O Absalom, my son, my son!"

The Death of David

Now the days of David drew nigh that he should die; and he charged Solomon his son, saying, "I go the way of all the earth: be thou strong therefore, and shew thyself a man; and keep the charge of the LORD thy God, to walk in his ways, to keep his statutes, and his commandments, and his judgments, and his testimonies, as it is written in the law of Moses, that thou mayest prosper in all that thou doest, and whithersoever thou turnest thyself: that the LORD may continue his word which he spake concerning me, saying, 'If thy children take heed to their way, to walk before me in truth with all their heart and with all their soul, there shall not fail thee (said he) a man on the throne of Israel.'

"Moreover thou knowest also what Joab the son of Zeruiah did to me, and what he did to the two captains of the hosts of Israel, unto Abner the son of Ner, and unto Amasa the son of Jether, whom he slew, and shed the blood of war in peace, and put the blood of war upon his girdle that was about his loins, and in his shoes that were on his feet.[22] Do therefore according to thy wisdom, and let not his hoar head go down to the grave in peace. But shew kindness unto the sons of Barzillai the Gileadite,[23] and let them be of those that eat at thy table: for so they came to me when I fled because of Absalom thy brother. And, behold, thou hast with thee Shimei the son of Gera, a Benjamite of Bahurim, which cursed me with a grievous curse in the day when I went to Mahanaim: but he came down to meet me at Jordan, and I sware to him by the LORD, saying, 'I will not put thee to death with the sword.' Now therefore hold him not guiltless: for thou art a wise man, and knowest what thou ought-

---

[22] Although Joab had been David's principal field general, he had killed Abner and Amasa. The law required that their deaths should be avenged.
[23] He had befriended David.

est to do unto him; but his hoar head bring thou down to the grave with blood."

So David slept with his fathers, and was buried in the city of David. And the days that David reigned over Israel were forty years: seven years reigned he in Hebron, and thirty and three years reigned he in Jerusalem. Then sat Solomon upon the throne of David his father; and his kingdom was established greatly.[24]

THE WISDOM AND SPLENDOR OF SOLOMON

Solomon's Prayer

• 1 KINGS 3:4–15 •

And the king went to Gibeon to sacrifice there;[1] for that was the great high place: a thousand burnt offerings did Solomon offer upon that altar. In Gibeon the LORD appeared to Solomon in a dream by night: and God said, "Ask what I shall give thee."

And Solomon said, "Thou hast shewed unto thy servant David my father great mercy, according as he walked before thee in truth, and in righteousness, and in uprightness of heart with thee; and thou hast kept for him this great kindness, that thou hast given him a son to sit on his throne, as it is this day. And now, O LORD my God, thou hast made thy servant king instead of David my father: and I am but a little child: I know not how

[24] Solomon reigned from c.965 to c.926 B.C.
[1] According to 2 Chronicles 2:1 the "tent of the meeting of God" was at Gibeon, about 7 miles north of Jerusalem.

to go out or come in. And thy servant is in the midst of thy people which thou hast chosen, a great people, that cannot be numbered nor counted for multitude. Give therefore thy servant an understanding heart to judge thy people, that I may discern between good and bad: for who is able to judge this thy so great a people?"

And the speech pleased the Lord, that Solomon had asked this thing. And God said unto him, "Because thou hast asked this thing, and hast not asked for thyself long life; neither hast asked riches for thyself, nor hast asked the life of thine enemies; but hast asked for thyself understanding to discern judgment; behold, I have done according to thy words: lo, I have given thee a wise and an understanding heart; so that there was none like thee before thee, neither after thee shall any arise like unto thee. And I have also given thee that which thou hast not asked, both riches, and honour: so that there shall not be any among the kings like unto thee all thy days. And if thou wilt walk in my ways, to keep my statutes and my commandments, as thy father David did walk, then I will lengthen thy days."

And Solomon awoke; and, behold, it was a dream. And he came to Jerusalem, and stood before the ark of the covenant of the Lord, and offered up burnt offerings, and offered peace offerings, and made a feast to all his servants.

Solomon's Wisdom

• 1 KINGS 3:16–28; 4:29–34 •

Then came there two women, that were harlots, unto the king, and stood before him. And the one woman said, "O my lord, I and this woman dwell in one house; and I was delivered of a child with her in the house. And it came to pass the third day after that I was delivered, that this woman was delivered also: and we were together; there was no stranger with us in the house, save we two in the house. And this woman's child died in the night; because she overlaid it. And she arose at midnight, and took my son from beside me, while thine handmaid slept, and laid it in her bosom, and laid her dead child in my bosom. And when I rose in the morning to give my child suck, behold, it was dead: but when I had considered it in the morning, behold, it was not my son, which I did bear."

And the other woman said, "Nay; but the living is my son, and the dead is thy son. And this said, 'No; but the dead is thy son, and the living is my son.'" Thus they spake before the king.

Then said the king, "The one saith, 'This is my son that liveth, and thy son is the dead:' and the other saith, 'Nay; but thy son is the dead, and my son is the living.'" And the king said, "Bring me a sword." And they brought a sword before the king. And the king said, "Divide the living child in two, and give half to the one, and half to the other."

Then spake the woman whose the living child was unto the king, for her bowels yearned upon her son, and she said, "O my lord, give her the living child, and in no wise slay it."

But the other said, "Let it be neither mine nor thine, but divide it."

Then the king answered and said, "Give her the living child, and in no wise slay it: she is the mother thereof."

And all Israel heard of the judgment which the king had judged; and they feared the king: for they saw that the wisdom of God was in him, to do judgment.

And God gave Solomon wisdom and understanding exceeding much, and largeness of heart, even as the sand that is on the sea shore. And Solomon's wisdom excelled the wisdom of all the children of the east country, and all the wisdom of Egypt. For he was wiser than all men; than Ethan the Ezrahite, and Heman, and Chalcol, and Darda, the son of Mahol:[2] and his fame was in all nations round about. And he spake three thousand proverbs: and his songs were a thousand and five. And he spake of

[2] Sages not otherwise identifiable.

trees, from the cedar tree that is in Lebanon even unto the hyssop that springeth out of the wall: he spake also of beasts, and of fowl, and of creeping things, and of fishes. And there came of all people to hear the wisdom of Solomon, from all kings of the earth, which had heard of his wisdom.

King Solomon and the Queen of Sheba

· 1 KINGS 10: 1–13 ·

And when the queen of Sheba[3] heard of the fame of Solomon concerning the name of the LORD, she came to prove him with hard questions. And she came to Jerusalem with a very great train, with camels that bare spices, and very much gold, and precious stones: and when she was come to Solomon, she communed with him of all that was in her heart. And Solomon told her all her questions: there was not any thing hid from the king, which he told her not. And when the queen of Sheba had seen all Solomon's wisdom, and the house that he had built, and the meat of his table, and the sitting of his servants, and the attendance of his ministers, and their apparel, and his cupbearers, and his ascent by which he went up unto[4] the house of the LORD; there was no more spirit in her.

And she said to the king, "It was a true report that I heard in mine own land of thy acts and of thy wisdom. Howbeit I believed not the words, until I came, and mine eyes had seen it: and, behold, the half was not told me: thy wisdom and prosperity exceedeth the fame which I heard. Happy are thy men, happy are these thy servants, which stand continually before thee, and that hear thy wisdom. Blessed be the LORD thy God, which delighted in thee, to set thee on the throne of Israel: because the

[3] In southwestern Arabia.
[4] Or, "his burnt offering which he offered in the."

LORD loved Israel for ever, therefore made he thee king, to do judgment and justice."

And she gave the king an hundred and twenty talents of gold, and of spices very great store, and precious stones: there came no more such abundance of spices as these which the queen of Sheba gave to king Solomon. And the navy also of Hiram,[5] that brought gold from Ophir,[6] brought in from Ophir great plenty of almug[7] trees, and precious stones. And the king made of the almug trees pillars for the house of the LORD, and for the king's house, harps also and psalteries for singers: there came no such almug trees, nor were seen unto this day. And king Solomon gave unto the queen of Sheba all her desire, whatsoever she asked, beside that which Solomon gave her of his royal bounty. So she turned and went to her own country, she and her servants.

Solomon's Splendor and His Apostasy

• 1 KINGS 10:21 TO 11:13 •

And all king Solomon's drinking vessels were of gold, and all the vessels of the house of the forest of Lebanon were of pure gold; none were of silver: it was nothing accounted of in the days of Solomon. For the king had at sea a navy of Tharshish[8] with the navy of Hiram: once in three years came the navy of Tharshish, bringing gold, and silver, ivory, and apes, and peacocks. So king Solomon exceeded all the kings of the earth for riches and for wisdom. And all the earth sought to Solomon, to hear his wisdom, which God had put in his heart.

[5] King of Tyre.
[6] Adjacent to Sheba.
[7] Probably sandalwood.
[8] Ships of the type used in voyages to the western Mediterranean.

And they brought every man his present, vessels of silver, and vessels of gold, and garments, and armour, and spices, horses, and mules, a rate year by year. And Solomon gathered together chariots and horsemen: and he had a thousand and four hundred chariots, and twelve thousand horsemen, whom he bestowed in the cities for chariots, and with the king at Jerusalem. And the king made silver to be in Jerusalem as stones, and cedars made he to be as the sycamore trees that are in the vale, for abundance. And Solomon had horses brought out of Egypt, and linen yarn: the king's merchants received the linen yarn at a price. And a chariot came up and went out of Egypt for six hundred shekels of silver, and an horse for an hundred and fifty: and so for all the kings of the Hittites, and for the kings of Syria, did they bring them out by their means.

But king Solomon loved many strange women, together with the daughter of Pharaoh, women of the Moabites, Ammonites, Edomites, Zidonians, and Hittites; of the nations concerning which the LORD said unto the children of Israel, "Ye shall not go in to them, neither shall they come in unto you: for surely they will turn away your heart after their gods": Solomon clave unto these in love. And he had seven hundred wives, princesses, and three hundred concubines: and his wives turned away his heart. For it came to pass, when Solomon was old, that his wives turned away his heart after other gods: and his heart was not perfect with the LORD his God, as was the heart of David his father. For Solomon went after Ashtoreth the goddess of the Zidonians, and after Milcom the abomination of the Ammonites. And Solomon did evil in the sight of the LORD, and went not fully after the LORD, as did David his father. Then did Solomon build an high place for Chemosh, the abomination of Moab, in the hill that is before Jerusalem, and for Molech, the abomination of the children of Ammon. And likewise did he for all his strange wives, which burnt incense and sacrificed unto their gods.

And the LORD was angry with Solomon, because his heart was turned from the LORD God of Israel, which had appeared unto him twice, and had commanded him concerning this thing, that he should not go after other gods: but he kept not that which the LORD commanded. Wherefore the LORD said unto Solomon, "Forasmuch as this is done of thee, and thou hast not kept my covenant and my statutes, which I have commanded thee, I will surely rend the kingdom from thee, and will give it to thy servant. Notwithstanding in thy days I will not do it for David thy father's sake: but I will rend it out of the hand of thy son. Howbeit I will not rend away all the kingdom; but will give one tribe to thy son for David my servant's sake, and for Jerusalem's sake which I have chosen." [9]

NARRATIVES OF ELIJAH AND ELISHA

Elijah and the Widow of Zarephath

• 1 KINGS 17 •

And Elijah the Tishbite, who was of the inhabitants of Gilead, said unto Ahab,[1] "As the LORD God of Israel liveth, before whom I stand, there shall not be dew nor rain these years, but according to my word."

And the word of the LORD came unto him, saying, "Get thee

[9] This looks forward to the revolt which occurred during the reign of Solomon's son Rehoboam. The history of the books of Kings becomes thenceforth the account of the divided kingdom—the northern kingdom of Israel, with its capital at Samaria, and the southern kingdom of Judah, with Jerusalem as its capital.

[1] King of the northern kingdom of Israel (871-852 B.C.). Through the influence of his wife Jezebel he instituted the worship of Baal (a generic name for the local deities of the Canaanites).

hence, and turn thee eastward, and hide thyself by the brook Cherith, that is before Jordan. And it shall be, that thou shalt drink of the brook; and I have commanded the ravens to feed thee there."

So he went and did according unto the word of the LORD: for he went and dwelt by the brook Cherith, that is before Jordan. And the ravens brought him bread and flesh in the morning, and bread and flesh in the evening; and he drank of the brook. And it came to pass after a while, that the brook dried up, because there had been no rain in the land.

And the word of the LORD came unto him, saying, "Arise, get thee to Zarephath, which belongeth to Zidon, and dwell there: behold, I have commanded a widow woman there to sustain thee."

So he arose and went to Zarephath. And when he came to the gate of the city, behold, the widow woman was there gathering of sticks: and he called to her, and said, "Fetch me, I pray thee, a little water in a vessel, that I may drink." And as she was going to fetch it, he called to her, and said, "Bring me, I pray thee, a morsel of bread in thine hand."

And she said, "As the LORD thy God liveth, I have not a cake, but an handful of meal in a barrel, and a little oil in a cruse: and, behold, I am gathering two sticks, that I may go in and dress it for me and my son, that we may eat it, and die."

And Elijah said unto her, "Fear not; go and do as thou hast said: but make me thereof a little cake first, and bring it unto me, and after make for thee and for thy son. For thus saith the LORD God of Israel, 'The barrel of meal shall not waste, neither shall the cruse of oil fail, until the day that the LORD sendeth rain upon the earth.'"

And she went and did according to the saying of Elijah: and she, and he, and her house, did eat many days. And the barrel of meal wasted not, neither did the cruse of oil fail, according to the word of the LORD, which he spake by Elijah.

And it came to pass after these things, that the son of the

woman, the mistress of the house, fell sick; and his sickness was so sore, that there was no breath left in him. And she said unto Elijah, "What have I to do with thee, O thou man of God? art thou come unto me to call my sin to remembrance, and to slay my son?"

And he said unto her, "Give me thy son." And he took him out of her bosom, and carried him up into a loft, where he abode, and laid him upon his own bed. And he cried unto the LORD, and said, "O LORD my God, hast thou also brought evil upon the widow with whom I sojourn, by slaying her son?" And he stretched himself upon the child three times, and cried unto the LORD, and said, "O LORD my God, I pray thee, let this child's soul come into him again."

And the LORD heard the voice of Elijah; and the soul of the child came into him again, and he revived. And Elijah took the child, and brought him down out of the chamber into the house, and delivered him unto his mother: and Elijah said, "See, thy son liveth."

And the woman said to Elijah, "Now by this I know that thou art a man of God, and that the word of the LORD in thy mouth is truth."

Elijah and the Priests of Baal

• 1 KINGS 18: 17–40 •

And it came to pass, when Ahab saw Elijah, that Ahab said unto him, "Art thou he that troubleth Israel?"

And he answered, "I have not troubled Israel; but thou, and thy father's house, in that ye have forsaken the commandments of the LORD, and thou hast followed Baalim. Now therefore send, and gather to me all Israel unto mount Carmel, and the prophets of Baal four hundred and fifty, and the prophets of the groves four hundred, which eat at Jezebel's table."

So Ahab sent unto all the children of Israel, and gathered the prophets together unto mount Carmel. And Elijah came unto all the people, and said, "How long halt ye between two opinions? if the LORD be God, follow him: but if Baal, then follow him." And the people answered him not a word. Then said Elijah unto the people, "I, even I only, remain a prophet of the LORD; but Baal's prophets are four hundred and fifty men. Let them therefore give us two bullocks; and let them choose one bullock for themselves, and cut it in pieces, and lay it on wood, and put no fire under: and I will dress the other bullock, and lay it on wood, and put no fire under: and call ye on the name of your gods, and I will call on the name of the LORD: and the God that answereth by fire, let him be God."

And all the people answered and said, "It is well spoken."

And Elijah said unto the prophets of Baal, "Choose you one bullock for yourselves, and dress it first; for ye are many; and call on the name of your gods, but put no fire under."

And they took the bullock which was given them, and they dressed it, and called on the name of Baal from morning even until noon, saying, "O Baal, hear us." But there was no voice, nor any that answered. And they leaped upon the altar which was made.

And it came to pass at noon, that Elijah mocked them, and said, "Cry aloud: for he is a god; either he is talking, or he is pursuing, or he is in a journey, or peradventure he sleepeth, and must be awaked."

And they cried aloud, and cut themselves after their manner with knives and lancets, till the blood gushed out upon them. And it came to pass, when midday was past, and they prophesied until the time of the offering of the evening sacrifice, that there was neither voice, nor any to answer, nor any that regarded.

And Elijah said unto all the people, "Come near unto me." And all the people came near unto him. And he repaired the altar of the LORD that was broken down. And Elijah took twelve stones, according to the number of the tribes of the sons of Jacob, unto whom the word of the LORD came, saying, "Israel shall be thy name": and with the stones he built an altar in the name of the LORD: and he made a trench about the altar, as great as would contain two measures of seed. And he put the wood in order, and cut the bullock in pieces, and laid him on the wood, and said, "Fill four barrels with water, and pour it on the burnt sacrifice, and on the wood." And he said, "Do it the second time." And they did it the second time. And he said, "Do it the third time." And they did it the third time. And the water ran round about the altar; and he filled the trench also with water.

And it came to pass at the time of the offering of the evening sacrifice, that Elijah the prophet came near, and said, "LORD God of Abraham, Isaac, and of Israel, let it be known this day that thou art God in Israel, and that I am thy servant, and that I have done all these things at thy word. Hear me, O LORD, hear me, that this people may know that thou art the LORD God, and that thou hast turned their heart back again."

Then the fire of the LORD fell, and consumed the burnt sacrifice, and the wood, and the stones, and the dust, and licked up the water that was in the trench. And when all the people saw it, they fell on their faces: and they said, "The LORD, he is the God; the LORD, he is the God."

And Elijah said unto them, "Take the prophets of Baal; let not one of them escape." And they took them: and Elijah brought them down to the brook Kishon, and slew them there.

Ahab and Naboth's Vineyard

• 1 KINGS 21 •

And it came to pass after these things, that Naboth the Jezreelite had a vineyard, which was in Jezreel, hard by the palace of Ahab king of Samaria.[2] And Ahab spake unto Naboth, say-

[2] The capital of the northern kingdom.

ing, "Give me thy vineyard, that I may have it for a garden of herbs, because it is near unto my house: and I will give thee for it a better vineyard than it; or, if it seem good to thee, I will give thee the worth of it in money."

And Naboth said to Ahab, "The Lord forbid it me, that I should give the inheritance of my fathers unto thee."

And Ahab came into his house heavy and displeased because of the word which Naboth the Jezreelite had spoken to him: for he had said, "I will not give thee the inheritance of my father." And he laid him down upon his bed, and turned away his face, and would eat no bread.

But Jezebel his wife came to him, and said unto him, "Why is thy spirit so sad, that thou eatest no bread?"

And he said unto her, "Because I spake unto Naboth the Jezreelite, and said unto him, 'Give me thy vineyard for money; or else, if it please thee, I will give thee another vineyard for it': and he answered, 'I will not give thee my vineyard.' "

And Jezebel his wife said unto him, "Dost thou now govern the kingdom of Israel? arise, and eat bread, and let thine heart be merry: I will give thee the vineyard of Naboth the Jezreelite."

So she wrote letters in Ahab's name, and sealed them with his seal, and sent the letters unto the elders and to the nobles that were in his city, dwelling with Naboth. And she wrote in the letters, saying, "Proclaim a fast, and set Naboth on high among the people: and set two men, sons of Belial, before him, to bear witness against him, saying, 'Thou didst blaspheme God and the king.' And then carry him out, and stone him, that he may die."

And the men of his city, even the elders and the nobles who were the inhabitants in his city, did as Jezebel had sent unto them, and as it was written in the letters which she had sent unto them. They proclaimed a fast, and set Naboth on high among the people. And there came in two men, children of Belial, and sat before him: and the men of Belial witnessed against him, even against Naboth, in the presence of the people, saying,

"Naboth did blaspheme God and the king." Then they carried him forth out of the city, and stoned him with stones, that he died. Then they sent to Jezebel, saying, "Naboth is stoned, and is dead."

And it came to pass, when Jezebel heard that Naboth was stoned, and was dead, that Jezebel said to Ahab, "Arise, take possession of the vineyard of Naboth the Jezreelite, which he refused to give thee for money: for Naboth is not alive, but dead." And it came to pass, when Ahab heard that Naboth was dead, that Ahab rose up to go down to the vineyard of Naboth the Jezreelite, to take possession of it.

And the word of the LORD came to Elijah the Tishbite, saying, "Arise, go down to meet Ahab king of Israel, which is in Samaria: behold, he is in the vineyard of Naboth, whither he is gone down to possess it. And thou shalt speak unto him, saying, 'Thus saith the LORD, Hast thou killed, and also taken possession?' And thou shalt speak unto him, saying, 'Thus saith the LORD, In the place where dogs licked the blood of Naboth shall dogs lick thy blood, even thine.' "

And Ahab said to Elijah, "Hast thou found me, O mine enemy?"

And he answered, "I have found thee: because thou hast sold thyself to work evil in the sight of the LORD. Behold, I will bring evil upon thee, and will take away thy posterity, and will cut off from Ahab every man-child and him that is shut up and left in Israel, and will make thine house like the house of Jeroboam the son of Nebat, and like the house of Baasha the son of Ahijah, for the provocation wherewith thou hast provoked me to anger, and made Israel to sin. And of Jezebel also spake the LORD, saying, 'The dogs shall eat Jezebel by the wall of Jezreel.' Him that dieth of Ahab in the city the dogs shall eat; and him that dieth in the field shall the fowls of the air eat."

But there was none like unto Ahab, which did sell himself to work wickedness in the sight of the LORD, whom Jezebel his wife stirred up. And he did very abominably in following idols, according to all things as did the Amorites, whom the LORD cast out before the children of Israel. And it came to pass, when Ahab heard those words, that he rent his clothes, and put sackcloth upon his flesh, and fasted, and lay in sackcloth, and went softly.

And the word of the LORD came to Elijah the Tishbite, saying, "Seest thou how Ahab humbleth himself before me? because he humbleth himself before me, I will not bring the evil in his days: but in his son's days will I bring the evil upon his house."

The Translation of Elijah

• 2 KINGS 2: 1–15 •

And it came to pass, when the LORD would take up Elijah into heaven by a whirlwind, that Elijah went with Elisha from Gilgal. And Elijah said unto Elisha, "Tarry here, I pray thee; for the LORD hath sent me to Beth-el."

And Elisha said unto him, "As the LORD liveth, and as thy soul liveth, I will not leave thee." So they went down to Beth-el.

And the sons of the prophets that were at Beth-el came forth to Elisha, and said unto him, "Knowest thou that the LORD will take away thy master from thy head to day?"

And he said, "Yea, I know it; hold ye your peace."

And Elijah said unto him, "Elisha, tarry here, I pray thee; for the LORD hath sent me to Jericho."

And he said, "As the LORD liveth, and as thy soul liveth, I will not leave thee." So they came to Jericho.

And the sons of the prophets that were at Jericho came to Elisha, and said unto him, "Knowest thou that the LORD will take away thy master from thy head to day?"

And he answered, "Yea, I know it; hold ye your peace."

And Elijah said unto him, "Tarry, I pray thee, here; for the LORD hath sent me to Jordan."

And he said, "As the LORD liveth, and as thy soul liveth, I will not leave thee." And they two went on.

And fifty men of the sons of the prophets went, and stood to view afar off: and they two stood by Jordan. And Elijah took his mantle, and wrapped it together, and smote the waters, and they were divided hither and thither, so that they two went over on dry ground.

And it came to pass, when they were gone over, that Elijah said unto Elisha, "Ask what I shall do for thee, before I be taken away from thee."

And Elisha said, "I pray thee, let a double portion of thy spirit be upon me."

And he said, "Thou hast asked a hard thing: nevertheless, if thou see me when I am taken from thee, it shall be so unto thee; but if not, it shall not be so."

And it came to pass, as they still went on, and talked, that, behold, there appeared a chariot of fire, and horses of fire, and parted them both asunder; and Elijah went up by a whirlwind into heaven. And Elisha saw it, and he cried, "My father, my father, the chariot of Israel, and the horsemen thereof." And he saw him no more: and he took hold of his own clothes, and rent them in two pieces. He took up also the mantle of Elijah that fell from him, and went back, and stood by the bank of Jordan; and he took the mantle of Elijah that fell from him, and smote the waters, and said, "Where is the LORD God of Elijah?" and when he also had smitten the waters, they parted hither and thither: and Elisha went over.

And when the sons of the prophets which were to view at Jericho saw him, they said, "The spirit of Elijah doth rest on Elisha." And they came to meet him, and bowed themselves to the ground before him.

Elisha and Naaman the Syrian

• 2 KINGS 5 •

Now Naaman, captain of the host of the king of Syria, was a great man with his master, and honourable, because by him the LORD had given deliverance unto Syria: he was also a mighty man in valour, but he was a leper. And the Syrians had gone out by companies, and had brought away captive out of the land of Israel a little maid; and she waited on Naaman's wife. And she said unto her mistress, "Would God my lord were with the prophet that is in Samaria! for he would recover him of his leprosy." And one went in, and told his lord, saying, "Thus and thus said the maid that is of the land of Israel."

And the king of Syria said, "Go to, go, and I will send a letter unto the king of Israel." And he departed, and took with him ten talents of silver, and six thousand pieces of gold, and ten changes of raiment. And he brought the letter to the king of Israel, saying, "Now when this letter is come unto thee, behold, I have therewith sent Naaman my servant to thee, that thou mayest recover him of his leprosy."

And it came to pass, when the king of Israel had read the letter, that he rent his clothes, and said, "Am I god, to kill and to make alive, that this man doth send unto me to recover a man of his leprosy? wherefore consider, I pray you, and see how he seeketh a quarrel against me."

And it was so, when Elisha the man of God had heard that the king of Israel had rent his clothes that he sent to the king, saying, "Wherefore hast thou rent thy clothes? let him come now to me, and he shall know that there is a prophet in Israel." So Naaman came with his horses and with his chariot, and stood at the door of the house of Elisha. And Elisha sent a messenger unto him, saying, "Go and wash in Jordan seven times, and thy flesh shall come again to thee, and thou shalt be clean."

But Naaman was wroth, and went away, and said, "Behold,

I thought, 'He will surely come out to me, and stand, and call on the name of the LORD his God, and strike his hand over the place, and recover the leper.' Are not Abana and Pharpar, rivers of Damascus, better than all the waters of Israel? may I not wash in them, and be clean?" So he turned and went away in a rage.

And his servants came near, and spake unto him, and said, "My father, if the prophet had bid thee do some great thing, wouldest thou not have done it? how much rather then, when he saith to thee, 'Wash, and be clean'?"

Then went he down, and dipped himself seven times in Jordan, according to the saying of the man of God: and his flesh came again like unto the flesh of a little child, and he was clean. And he returned to the man of God, he and all his company, and came, and stood before him: and he said, "Behold, now I know that there is no God in all the earth, but in Israel: now therefore, I pray thee, take a blessing of thy servant."

But he said, "As the LORD liveth, before whom I stand, I will receive none." And he urged him to take it; but he refused.

And Naaman said, "Shall there not then, I pray thee, be given to thy servant two mules' burden of earth? for thy servant will henceforth offer neither burnt offering nor sacrifice unto other gods, but unto the LORD. In this thing the LORD pardon thy servant, that when my master goeth into the house of Rimmon[3] to worship there, and he leaneth on my hand, and I bow myself in the house of Rimmon: when I bow down myself in the house of Rimmon, the LORD pardon thy servant in this thing."

And he said unto him, "Go in peace." So he departed from him a little way.

But Gehazi, the servant of Elisha the man of God, said, "Behold, my master hath spared Naaman this Syrian, in not receiving at his hands that which he brought: but, as the LORD liveth, I will run after him, and take somewhat of him."

So Gehazi followed after Naaman. And when Naaman saw

[3] A Syrian deity.

him running after him, he lighted down from the chariot to meet him, and said, "Is all well?"

And he said, "All is well. My master hath sent me, saying, 'Behold, even now there be come to me from mount Ephraim two young men of the sons of the prophets: give them, I pray thee, a talent of silver, and two changes of garments.' "

And Naaman said, "Be content, take two talents." And he urged him, and bound two talents of silver in two bags, with two changes of garments, and laid them upon two of his servants; and they bare them before him. And when he came to the tower, he took them from their hand, and bestowed them in the house: and he let the men go, and they departed.

But he went in, and stood before his master. And Elisha said unto him, "Whence comest thou, Gehazi?"

And he said, "Thy servant went no whither."

And he said unto him, "Went not mine heart with thee, when the man turned again from his chariot to meet thee? Is it a time to receive money, and to receive garments, and oliveyards, and vineyards, and sheep, and oxen, and menservants, and maidservants? The leprosy therefore of Naaman shall cleave unto thee, and unto thy seed for ever." And he went out from his presence a leper as white as snow.

From ISAIAH

Isaiah's Call

• ISAIAH 6 •

In the year that king Uzziah[1] died I saw also the LORD sitting upon a throne, high and lifted up, and his train filled the temple. Above it stood the seraphims: each one had six wings; with twain he covered his face, and with twain he covered his feet, and with twain he did fly. And one cried unto another, and said, Holy, holy, holy, is the LORD of hosts: the whole earth is full of his glory. And the posts of the door moved at the voice of him that cried, and the house was filled with smoke.

Then said I, Woe is me! for I am undone; because I am a man of unclean lips, and I dwell in the midst of a people of unclean lips: for mine eyes have seen the King, the LORD of hosts.

Then flew one of the seraphims unto me, having a live coal in his hand, which he had taken with the tongs from off the altar: and he laid it upon my mouth, and said, Lo, this hath touched thy lips; and thine iniquity is taken away, and thy sin purged.

Also I heard the voice of the Lord, saying, Whom shall I send, and who will go for us?

Then said I, Here am I; send me.

And he said, Go, and tell this people, Hear ye indeed, but understand not; and see ye indeed, but perceive not. Make the

[1] Or Azariah, king of Judah (the southern kingdom), 785–747 B.C.

heart of this people fat, and make their ears heavy, and shut their eyes; lest they see with their eyes, and hear with their ears, and understand with their heart, and convert, and be healed.

Then said I, Lord, how long?

And he answered, Until the cities be wasted without inhabitant, and the houses without man, and the land be utterly desolate, and the LORD have removed men far away, and there be a great forsaking in the midst of the land. But yet in it shall be a tenth, and it shall return, and shall be eaten: as a teil tree,[2] and as an oak, whose substance is in them, when they cast their leaves: so the holy seed shall be the substance thereof.[3]

The Unfruitful Vineyard

• ISAIAH 5:1–25 •

Now will I sing to my wellbeloved a song of my beloved touching his vineyard. My wellbeloved hath a vineyard in a very fruitful hill: and he fenced it, and gathered out the stones thereof, and planted it with the choicest vine, and built a tower in the midst of it, and also made a winepress therein: and he looked that it should bring forth grapes, and it brought forth wild grapes. And now, O inhabitants of Jerusalem, and men of Judah, judge, I pray you, betwixt me and my vineyard. What could have been done more to my vineyard, that I have not done in it? wherefore, when I looked that it should bring forth grapes, brought it forth wild grapes? And now go to; I will tell you what I will do to my vineyard: I will take away the hedge thereof, and it shall be eaten up; and break down the wall thereof, and it shall be trodden down: and I will lay it waste: it shall not be pruned, nor digged; but there shall come up briers

[2] Probably the teberinth, noted for its longevity.
[3] The thought is, there will be a tenth, the "saving remnant," from which the renewal of Israel will spring.

and thorns: I will also command the clouds that they rain no rain upon it. For the vineyard of the LORD of hosts is the house of Israel, and the men of Judah his pleasant plant: and he looked for judgment, but behold oppression; for righteousness, but behold a cry.

Woe unto them that join house to house, that lay field to field,[4] till there be no place, that they may be placed alone in the midst of the earth! In mine ears said the LORD of hosts, Of a truth many houses shall be desolate, even great and fair, without inhabitant. Yea, ten acres of vineyard shall yield one bath,[5] and the seed of an omer shall yield an ephah.[6] Woe unto them that rise up early in the morning, that they may follow strong drink; that continue until night, till wine inflame them! And the harp, and the viol, the tabret, and pipe, and wine, are in their feasts: but they regard not the work of the LORD, neither consider the operation of his hands.

Therefore my people are gone into captivity, because they have no knowledge: and their honourable men are famished, and their multitude dried up with thirst. Therefore hell hath enlarged herself, and opened her mouth without measure: and their glory, and their multitude, and their pomp, and he that rejoiceth, shall descend into it. And the mean man shall be brought down, and the mighty man shall be humbled, and the eyes of the lofty shall be humbled: but the LORD of hosts shall be exalted in judgment, and God that is holy shall be sanctified in righteousness. Then shall the lambs feed after their manner, and the waste places of the fat ones shall strangers eat.

Woe unto them that draw iniquity with cords of vanity, and sin as it were with a cart rope:[7] that say, Let him make speed, and hasten his work, that we may see it: and let the counsel of the Holy One of Israel draw nigh and come, that we may know

---

[4] Seize land unjustly, with resultant barrenness and depopulation.
[5] About 7 gallons.
[6] "An ephah is the tenth part of an omer."
[7] i.e., who are tied to their sins.

it! Woe unto them that call evil good, and good evil; that put darkness for light, and light for darkness; that put bitter for sweet, and sweet for bitter! Woe unto them that are wise in their own eyes, and prudent in their own sight! Woe unto them that are mighty to drink wine, and men of strength to mingle strong drink: which justify the wicked for reward, and take away the righteousness of the righteous from him!

Therefore as the fire devoureth the stubble, and the flame consumeth the chaff, so their root shall be as rottenness, and their blossom shall go up as dust: because they have cast away the law of the LORD of hosts, and despised the word of the Holy One of Israel. Therefore is the anger of the LORD kindled against his people, and he hath stretched forth his hand against them, and hath smitten them: and the hills did tremble, and their carcases were torn in the midst of the streets. For all this his anger is not turned away, but his hand is stretched out still.

The Reign of Righteousness

• ISAIAH 11:1–9 •

And there shall come forth a rod out of the stem of Jesse, and a Branch shall grow out of his roots: and the spirit of the LORD shall rest upon him, the spirit of wisdom and understanding, the spirit of counsel and might, the spirit of knowledge and of the fear of the LORD; and shall make him of quick understanding in the fear of the LORD: and he shall not judge after the sight of his eyes, neither reprove after the hearing of his ears: but with righteousness shall he judge the poor, and reprove with equity for the meek of the earth; and he shall smite the earth with the rod of his mouth, and with the breath of his lips shall he slay the wicked. And righteousness shall be the girdle of his loins, and faithfulness the girdle of his reins.[8]

[8] Kidneys, in Biblical imagery the seat of the affections.

The wolf also shall dwell with the lamb, and the leopard shall lie down with the kid; and the calf and the young lion and the fatling together; and a little child shall lead them. And the cow and the bear shall feed; their young ones shall lie down together: and the lion shall eat straw like the ox. And the sucking child shall play on the hole of the asp, and the weaned child shall put his hand on the cockatrice' [9] den. They shall not hurt nor destroy in all my holy mountain: for the earth shall be full of the knowledge of the Lord, as the waters cover the sea.

The Happy Future of Zion

• ISAIAH 35 •

The wilderness and the solitary place shall be glad for them; and the desert shall rejoice, and blossom as the rose. It shall blossom abundantly, and rejoice even with joy and singing: the glory of Lebanon shall be given unto it, the excellency of Carmel and Sharon, they shall see the glory of the Lord, and the excellency of our God.

Strengthen ye the weak hands, and confirm the feeble knees. Say to them that are of a fearful heart, Be strong, fear not: behold, your God will come with vengeance, even God with a recompense; he will come and save you. Then the eyes of the blind shall be opened, and the ears of the deaf shall be unstopped. Then shall the lame man leap as an hart, and the tongue of the dumb sing: for in the wilderness shall waters break out, and streams in the desert. And the parched ground shall become a pool, and the thirsty land springs of water: in the habitation of dragons, where each lay, shall be grass with reeds and rushes. And an highway shall be there, and a way, and it shall be called the way of holiness; the unclean shall not pass over it; but it shall be for those: the wayfaring men,

[9] A serpent.

though fools, shall not err therein. No lion shall be there, nor any ravenous beast shall go up thereon, it shall not be found there; but the redeemed shall walk there: and the ransomed of the LORD shall return, and come to Zion with songs and everlasting joy upon their heads: they shall obtain joy and gladness, and sorrow and sighing shall flee away.

God's Promise

• ISAIAH 40 •

Comfort ye, comfort ye my people, saith your God. Speak ye comfortably to Jerusalem, and cry unto her, that her warfare is accomplished, that her iniquity is pardoned: for she hath received of the LORD's hand double for all her sins. The voice of him that crieth in the wilderness, Prepare ye the way of the LORD, make straight in the desert a highway for our God. Every valley shall be exalted, and every mountain and hill shall be made low: and the crooked shall be made straight, and the rough places plain: and the glory of the LORD shall be revealed, and all flesh shall see it together: for the mouth of the LORD hath spoken it.

The voice said, Cry. And he said, What shall I cry? All flesh is grass, and all the goodliness thereof is as the flower of the field: the grass withereth, the flower fadeth: because the spirit of the LORD bloweth upon it: surely the people is grass The grass withereth, the flower fadeth: but the word of our God shall stand for ever.

O Zion, that bringest good tidings, get thee up into the high mountain; O Jerusalem, that bringest good tidings, lift up thy voice with strength; lift it up, be not afraid; say unto the cities of Judah, Behold your God! Behold, the Lord God will come with strong hand, and his arm shall rule for him: behold, his reward is with him, and his work before him. He shall feed his flock like a shepherd: he shall gather the lambs with his arm, and carry them in his bosom, and shall gently lead those that are with young. Who hath measured the waters in the hollow of his hand, and meted out heaven with the span, and comprehended the dust of the earth in a measure, and weighed the mountains in scales, and the hills in a balance? Who hath directed the Spirit of the LORD, or being his counsellor hath taught him? With whom took he counsel, and who instructed him, and taught him in the path of judgment, and taught him knowledge, and shewed to him the way of understanding? Behold, the nations are as a drop of a bucket, and are counted as the small dust of the balance: behold, he taketh up the isles as a very little thing. And Lebanon is not sufficient to burn, nor the beasts thereof sufficient for a burnt offering. All nations before him are as nothing; and they are counted to him less than nothing, and vanity.

To whom then will ye liken God? or what likeness will ye compare unto him? The workman melteth a graven image, and the goldsmith spreadeth it over with gold, and casteth silver chains. He that is so impoverished that he hath no oblation chooseth a tree that will not rot; he seeketh unto him a cunning workman to prepare a graven image, that shall not be moved. Have ye not known? have ye not heard? hath it not been told you from the beginning? have ye not understood from the foundations of the earth? It is he that sitteth upon the circle of the earth, and the inhabitants thereof are as grasshoppers; that stretcheth out the heavens as a curtain, and spreadeth them out as a tent to dwell in: that bringeth the princes to nothing; he maketh the judges of the earth as vanity. Yea, they shall not be planted; yea, they shall not be sown: yea, their stock shall not take root in the earth: and he shall also blow upon them, and they shall wither, and the whirlwind shall take them away as stubble.

To whom then will ye liken me, or shall I be equal? saith the Holy One. Lift up your eyes on high, and behold who hath created these things, that bringeth out their host by number: he calleth them all by names by the greatness of his might, for that he is strong in power; not one faileth.

Why sayest thou, O Jacob, and speakest, O Israel, My way is hid from the LORD, and my judgment is passed over from my God? Hast thou not known? hast thou not heard, that the everlasting God, the LORD, the Creator of the ends of the earth, fainteth not, neither is weary? there is no searching of his understanding. He giveth power to the faint; and to them that have no might he increaseth strength. Even the youths shall faint and be weary, and the young men shall utterly fall: but they that wait upon the LORD shall renew their strength; they shall mount up with wings as eagles; they shall run, and not be weary; and they shall walk, and not faint.

Zion Summoned out of Exile

• ISAIAH 52 •

Awake, awake; put on thy strength, O Zion; put on thy beautiful garments, O Jerusalem, the holy city: for henceforth there shall no more come into thee the uncircumcised and the unclean. Shake thyself from the dust; arise, and sit down, O Jerusalem: loose thyself from the bands of thy neck, O captive daughter of Zion. For thus saith the LORD, Ye have sold yourselves for nought; and ye shall be redeemed without money. For thus saith the Lord God, My people went down aforetime into Egypt to sojourn there; and the Assyrian oppressed them without cause. Now therefore, what have I here, saith the LORD, that my people is taken away for nought? they that rule over them make them to howl, saith the LORD; and my name continually every day is blasphemed. Therefore my people shall know my name: therefore they shall know in that day that I am he that doth speak: behold, it is I.

How beautiful upon the mountains are the feet of him that bringeth good tidings, that publisheth peace; that bringeth good tidings of good, that publisheth salvation; that saith unto Zion, Thy God reigneth! Thy watchmen shall lift up the voice; with the voice together shall they sing: for they shall see eye to eye, when the LORD shall bring again Zion. Break forth into joy, sing together, ye waste places of Jerusalem: for the LORD hath comforted his people, he hath redeemed Jerusalem. The LORD hath made bare his holy arm in the eyes of all the nations; and all the ends of the earth shall see the salvation of our God.

Depart ye, depart ye, go ye out from thence, touch no unclean thing; go ye out of the midst of her; be ye clean, that bear the vessels of the LORD. For ye shall not go out with haste, nor go by flight: for the LORD will go before you; and the God of Israel will be your rereward.

Behold, my servant shall deal prudently, he shall be exalted and extolled, and be very high. As many were astonied at thee; his visage was so marred more than any man, and his form more than the sons of men. So shall he sprinkle many nations; the kings shall shut their mouths at him: for that which had not been told them shall they see; and that which they had not heard shall they consider.

The Servant of Jehovah

• ISAIAH 53 •

Who hath believed our report? and to whom is the arm of the LORD revealed? For he shall grow up before him as a tender plant, and as a root out of a dry ground: he hath no form nor comeliness; and when we shall see him, there is no beauty that we should desire him. He is despised and rejected of men; a man of sorrows, and acquainted with grief: and we hid as it were our faces from him; he was despised, and we esteemed him not.

Surely he hath borne our griefs, and carried our sorrows: yet we did esteem him stricken, smitten of God, and afflicted. But he was wounded for our transgressions, he was bruised for our iniquities: the chastisement of our peace was upon him; and with his stripes we are healed. All we like sheep have gone astray; we have turned every one to his own way; and the LORD hath laid on him the iniquity of us all. He was oppressed, and he was afflicted, yet he opened not his mouth: he is brought as a lamb to the slaughter, and as a sheep before her shearers is dumb, so he openeth not his mouth. He was taken from prison and from judgment: and who shall declare his generation? for he was cut off out of the land of the living: for the transgression of my people was he stricken. And he made his grave with the wicked, and with the rich in his death; because he had done no violence, neither was any deceit in his mouth.

Yet it pleased the LORD to bruise him; he hath put him to grief: when thou shalt make his soul an offering for sin, he shall see his seed, he shall prolong his days, and the pleasure of the LORD shall prosper in his hand. He shall see of the travail of his soul, and shall be satisfied: by his knowledge shall my righteous servant justify many; for he shall bear their iniquities. Therefore will I divide him a portion with the great, and he shall divide the spoil with the strong; because he hath poured out his soul unto death: and he was numbered with the transgressors; and he bare the sin of many, and made intercession for the transgressors.

Mercy to All

• ISAIAH 55 •

Ho, every one that thirsteth, come ye to the waters, and he that hath no money; come ye, buy, and eat; yea, come, buy wine and milk without money and without price. Wherefore do ye spend money for that which is not bread? and your labour for that which satisfieth not? hearken diligently unto me, and eat ye that which is good, and let your soul delight itself in fatness. Incline your ear, and come unto me: hear, and your soul shall live; and I will make an everlasting covenant with you, even the sure mercies of David. Behold, I have given him for a witness to the people, a leader and commander to the people. Behold, thou shalt call a nation that thou knowest not, and nations that knew not thee shall run unto thee because of the LORD thy God, and for the Holy One of Israel; for he hath glorified thee.

Seek ye the LORD while he may be found, call ye upon him while he is near: let the wicked forsake his way, and the unrighteous man his thoughts: and let him return unto the LORD, and he will have mercy upon him; and to our God, for he will abundantly pardon. For my thoughts are not your thoughts, neither are your ways my ways, saith the LORD. For as the heavens are higher than the earth, so are my ways higher than your ways, and my thoughts than your thoughts. For as the rain cometh down, and the snow from heaven, and returneth not thither, but watereth the earth, and maketh it bring forth and bud, that it may give seed to the sower, and bread to the eater: so shall my word be that goeth forth out of my mouth: it shall not return unto me void, but it shall accomplish that which I please, and it shall prosper in the thing whereto I sent it. For ye shall go out with joy, and be led forth with peace: the mountains and the hills shall break forth before you into singing, and all the trees of the field shall clap their hands. Instead of the thorn shall come up the fir tree, and instead of the brier shall come up the myrtle tree: and it shall be to the LORD for a name, for an everlasting sign that shall not be cut off.

The Glorified Zion

• ISAIAH 60 •

Arise, shine; for thy light is come, and the glory of the LORD is risen upon thee. For, behold, the darkness shall cover the earth, and gross darkness the people: but the LORD shall arise upon thee, and his glory shall be seen upon thee. And the Gentiles shall come to thy light, and kings to the brightness of thy rising. Lift up thine eyes round about, and see: all they gather themselves together, they come to thee: thy sons shall come from far, and thy daughters shall be nursed at thy side. Then thou shalt see, and flow together, and thine heart shall fear, and be enlarged; because the abundance of the sea shall be converted unto thee, the forces of the Gentiles shall come unto thee. The multitude of camels shall cover thee, the dromedaries of Midian and Ephah; all they from Sheba shall come: they shall bring gold and incense; and they shall shew for the praises of the LORD. All the flocks of Kedar shall be gathered together unto thee, the rams of Nebaioth shall minister unto thee: they shall come up with acceptance on mine altar, and I will glorify the house of my glory. Who are these that fly as a cloud, and as the doves to their windows? Surely the isles shall wait for me, and the ships of Tarshish first, to bring thy sons from far, their silver and their gold with them, unto the name of the LORD thy God, and to the Holy One of Israel, because he hath glorified thee.

And the sons of strangers shall build up thy walls, and their kings shall minister unto thee: for in my wrath I smote thee, but in my favour have I had mercy on thee. Therefore thy gates shall be open continually; they shall not be shut day nor night; that men may bring unto thee the forces of the Gentiles, and that their kings may be brought. For the nation and kingdom that will not serve thee shall perish; yea, those nations shall be

utterly wasted. The glory of Lebanon shall come unto thee, the
r tree, the pine tree, and the box together, to beautify the place
f my sanctuary; and I will make the place of my feet glorious.
The sons also of them that afflicted thee shall come bending unto
thee; and all they that despised thee shall bow themselves down
at the soles of thy feet; and they shall call thee, The city of the
LORD, The Zion of the Holy One of the Israel.

Whereas thou hast been forsaken and hated, so that no man
went through thee, I will make thee an eternal excellency, a joy
of many generations. Thou shalt also suck the milk of the Gentiles, and shalt suck the breast of kings: and thou shalt know
that I the LORD am thy Saviour and thy Redeemer, the mighty
One of Jacob. For brass I will bring gold, and for iron I will
bring silver, and for wood brass, and for stones iron: I will also
make thy officers peace, and thine exactors[10] righteousness. Violence shall no more be heard in thy land, wasting nor destruction
within thy borders; but thou shalt call thy walls Salvation, and
thy gates Praise. The sun shall be no more thy light by day;
neither for brightness shall the moon give light unto thee: but
the LORD shall be unto thee an everlasting light, and thy God
thy glory. Thy sun shall no more go down; neither shall thy moon
withdraw itself: for the LORD shall be thine everlasting light, and
the days of thy mourning shall be ended. Thy people also shall
be all righteous: they shall inherit the land for ever, the branch
of my planting, the work of my hands, that I may be glorified.
A little one shall become a thousand, and a small one a strong
nation: I the LORD will hasten it in his time.

[10] Taskmasters.

Jeremiah's Call

• JEREMIAH 1 •

The words of Jeremiah the son of Hilkiah, of the priests that were in Anathoth in the land of Benjamin: to whom the word of the LORD came in the days of Josiah the son of Amon king of Judah, in the thirteenth year of his reign.[1] It came also in the days of Jehoiakim the son of Josiah king of Judah, unto the end of the eleventh year of Zedekiah the son of Josiah king of Judah, unto the carrying away of Jerusalem captive in the fifth month.

Then the word of the LORD came unto me, saying, Before I formed thee in the belly I knew thee; and before thou camest forth out of the womb I sanctified thee, and I ordained thee a prophet unto the nations.

Then said I, Ah, Lord God! behold, I cannot speak: for I am a child.

But the LORD said unto me, Say not, I am a child: for thou shalt go to all that I shall send thee, and whatsoever I command thee thou shalt speak. Be not afraid of their faces: for I am with thee to deliver thee, saith the LORD. Then the LORD put forth his hand, and touched my mouth. And the LORD said unto me, Behold, I have put my words in thy mouth. See, I have this day set thee over the nations and over the kingdoms, to root out, and to pull down, and to destroy, and to throw down, to build, and to plant.

[1] Josiah reigned from 639 to 609 B.C. Jeremiah's call would therefore be dated 626. He continued his prophetical office until after the fall of Jerusalem to the Babylonians in 587 B.C.

Moreover the word of the Lord came unto me, saying, Jeremiah, what seest thou?

And I said, I see a rod of an almond tree.

Then said the Lord unto me, Thou hast well seen: for I will hasten my word to perform it.

And the word of the Lord came unto me the second time, saying, What seest thou?

And I said, I see a seething pot; and the face thereof is toward the north.

Then the Lord said unto me, Out of the north an evil shall break forth upon all the inhabitants of the land. For, lo, I will call all the families of the kingdoms of the north, saith the Lord; and they shall come, and they shall set every one his throne at the entering of the gates of Jerusalem, and against all the walls thereof round about, and against all the cities of Judah. And I will utter my judgments against them touching all their wickedness, who have forsaken me, and have burned incense unto other gods, and worshipped the works of their own hands. Thou therefore gird up thy loins, and arise, and speak unto them all that I command thee: be not dismayed at their faces, lest I confound thee before them. For, behold, I have made thee this day a defenced city, and an iron pillar, and brasen walls against the whole land, against the kings of Judah, against the princes thereof, against the priests thereof, and against the people of the land. And they shall fight against thee; but they shall not prevail against thee; for I am with thee, saith the Lord, to deliver thee.

Jeremiah's Sermon at the Temple Gate

• JEREMIAH 7 •

The word that came to Jeremiah from the Lord, saying, Stand in the gate of the Lord's house, and proclaim there this word, and say, Hear the word of the Lord, all ye of Judah, that enter in at these gates to worship the LORD. Thus saith the LORD of hosts, the God of Israel, Amend your ways and your doings, and I will cause you to dwell in this place. Trust ye not in lying words, saying, The temple of the LORD, The temple of the LORD, The temple of the LORD, are these. For if ye throughly amend your ways and your doings; if ye throughly execute judgment between a man and his neighbour; if ye oppress not the stranger, the fatherless, and the widow, and shed not innocent blood in this place, neither walk after other gods to your hurt: then will I cause you to dwell in this place, in the land that I gave to your fathers, for ever and ever.

Behold, ye trust in lying words, that cannot profit. Will ye steal, murder, and commit adultery, and swear falsely, and burn incense unto Baal, and walk after other gods whom ye know not; and come and stand before me in this house, which is called by my name, and say, We are delivered to do all these abominations? Is this house, which is called by my name, become a den of robbers in your eyes? Behold, even I have seen it, saith the LORD. But go ye now unto my place which was in Shiloh, where I set my name at the first, and see what I did to it for the wickedness of my people Israel. And now, because ye have done all these works, saith the LORD, and I spake unto you, rising up early and speaking, but ye heard not; and I called you, but ye answered not; therefore will I do unto this house, which is called by my name, wherein ye trust, and unto the place which I gave to you and to your fathers, as I have done to Shiloh. And I will cast you out of my sight, as I have cast out all your brethren, even the whole seed of Ephraim.

Therefore pray not thou for this people, neither lift up cry nor prayer for them, neither make intercession to me: for I will not hear thee. Seest thou not what they do in the cities of Judah and in the streets of Jerusalem? The children gather wood, and the fathers kindle the fire, and the women knead their dough, to make cakes to the queen of heaven, and to pour out drink offerings unto other gods, that they may provoke me to anger. Do they provoke me to anger? saith the LORD: do they not provoke themselves to the confusion of their own faces? Therefore thus saith the Lord God; Behold, mine anger and my fury shall be poured out upon this place, upon man, and upon beast, and upon the trees of the field, and upon the fruit of the ground; and it shall burn, and shall not be quenched.

Thus saith the LORD of hosts, the God of Israel; Put your burnt offerings unto your sacrifices, and eat flesh. For I spake not unto your fathers, nor commanded them in the day that I brought them out of the land of Egypt, concerning burnt offerings or sacrifices: but this thing commanded I them, saying, Obey my voice, and I will be your God, and ye shall be my people: and walk ye in all the ways that I have commanded you, that it may be well unto you. But they hearkened not, nor inclined their ear, but walked in the counsels and in the imagination of their evil heart, and went backward, and not forward. Since the day that your fathers came forth out of the land of Egypt unto this day I have even sent unto you all my servants the prophets, daily rising up early and sending them: yet they hearkened not unto me, nor inclined their ear, but hardened their neck: they did worse than their fathers. Therefore thou shalt speak all these words unto them; but they will not hearken to thee: thou shalt also call unto them; but they will not answer thee. But thou shalt say unto them, This is a nation that obeyeth not the voice of the LORD their God, nor receiveth correction: truth is perished, and is cut off from their mouth.

Cut off thine hair, O Jerusalem, and cast it away, and take up a lamentation on high places; for the LORD hath rejected and forsaken the generation of his wrath. For the children of Judah have done evil in my sight, saith the LORD: they have set their abominations in the house which is called by my name, to pollute it. And they have built the high places of Tophet, which is in the valley of the son of Hinnom,[2] to burn their sons and

---

[2] On the outskirts of Jerusalem. Human sacrifice to Moloch had been practiced there.

their daughters in the fire; which I commanded them not, neither came it into my heart.

Therefore, behold, the days come, saith the Lord, that it shall no more be called Tophet, nor the valley of the son of Hinnom, but the valley of slaughter: for they shall bury in Tophet, till there be no place. And the carcases of this people shall be meat for the fowls of the heaven, and for the beasts of the earth; and none shall fray them away. Then will I cause to cease from the cities of Judah, and from the streets of Jerusalem, the voice of mirth, and the voice of gladness, the voice of the bridegroom, and the voice of the bride: for the land shall be desolate.

A Warning against Idolatry

• JEREMIAH 10: 1–16 •

Hear ye the word which the Lord speaketh unto you, O house of Israel: Thus saith the Lord, Learn not the way of the heathen, and be not dismayed at the signs of heaven; for the heathen are dismayed at them. For the customs of the people are vain: for one cutteth a tree out of the forest, the work of the hands of the workman, with the ax. They deck it with silver and with gold; they fasten it with nails and with hammers, that it move not. They are upright as the palm tree, but speak not: they must needs be borne, because they cannot go. Be not afraid of them; for they cannot do evil, neither also is it in them to do good.

Forasmuch as there is none like unto thee, O Lord; thou art great, and thy name is great in might. Who would not fear thee, O King of nations? for to thee doth it appertain: forasmuch as among all the wise men of the nations, and in all their kingdoms, there is none like unto thee. But they are altogether brutish and foolish: the stock is a doctrine of vanities.

Silver spread into plates is brought from Tarshish, and gold from Uphaz, the work of the workman, and of the hands of the founder: blue and purple is their clothing: they are all the work of cunning men. But the LORD is the true God, he is the living God, and an everlasting king: at his wrath the earth shall tremble, and the nations shall not be able to abide his indignation.

Thus shall ye say unto them, The gods that have not made the heavens and the earth, even they shall perish from the earth, and from under these heavens. He hath made the earth by his power, he hath established the world by his wisdom, and hath stretched out the heavens by his discretion. When he uttereth his voice, there is a multitude of waters in the heavens, and he causeth the vapours to ascend from the ends of the earth; he maketh lightnings with rain, and bringeth forth the wind out of his treasures. Every man is brutish in his knowledge: every founder is confounded by the graven image: for his molten image is falsehood, and there is no breath in them. They are vanity, and the work of errors: in the time of their visitation they shall perish. The portion of Jacob is not like them: for he is the former of all things; and Israel is the rod of his inheritance: The LORD of hosts is his name.

The Sign of the Girdle

· JEREMIAH 13: 1–11 ·

Thus saith the LORD unto me, Go and get thee a linen girdle, and put it upon thy loins, and put it not in water. So I got a girdle according to the word of the LORD, and put it on my loins.

And the word of the LORD came unto me the second time, saying, Take the girdle that thou hast got, which is upon thy loins, and arise, go to Euphrates, and hide it there in a hold of the rock. So I went, and hid it by Euphrates, as the LORD commanded me.

And it came to pass after many days, that the LORD said unto me, Arise, go to Euphrates, and take the girdle from thence, which I commanded thee to hide there. Then I went to Euphrates, and digged, and took the girdle from the place where I had hid it: and, behold, the girdle was marred, it was profitable for nothing.

Then the word of the LORD came unto me, saying, Thus saith the LORD, After this manner will I mar the pride of Judah, and the great pride of Jerusalem. This evil people, which refuse to hear my words, which walk in the imagination of their heart, and walk after other gods, to serve them, and to worship them, shall even be as this girdle, which is good for nothing. For as the girdle cleaveth to the loins of a man, so have I caused to cleave unto me the whole house of Israel and the whole house of Judah saith the LORD, that they might be unto me for a people, and for a name, and for a praise, and for a glory: but they would not hear.

The Warning to Judah

• JEREMIAH 17 •

The sin of Judah is written with a pen of iron, and with the point of a diamond: it is graven upon the table of their heart, and upon the horns of your altars; whilst their children remember their altars and their groves[3] by the green trees upon the high hills. O my mountain in the field, I will give thy substance and all thy treasures to the spoil, and thy high places for sin, throughout all thy borders. And thou, even thyself, shalt discontinue from thine heritage that I gave thee; and I will cause thee

---

[3] Pillars erected in honor of Astoreth (Astarte).

to serve thine enemies in the land which thou knowest not: for ye have kindled a fire in mine anger, which shall burn for ever.

Thus saith the LORD; Cursed be the man that trusteth in man, and maketh flesh his arm, and whose heart departeth from the LORD. For he shall be like the heath in the desert, and shall not see when good cometh; but shall inhabit the parched places in the wilderness, in a salt land and not inhabited. Blessed is the man that trusteth in the LORD, and whose hope the LORD is. For he shall be as a tree planted by the waters, and that spreadeth out her roots by the river, and shall not see when heat cometh, but her leaf shall be green; and shall not be careful in the year of drought, neither shall cease from yielding fruit.

The heart is deceitful above all things, and desperately wicked: who can know it? I the LORD search the heart, I try the reins, even to give every man according to his ways, and according to the fruit of his doings. As the partridge sitteth on eggs, and hatcheth them not; so he that getteth riches, and not by right, shall leave them in the midst of his days, and at his end shall be a fool.

A glorious high throne from the beginning is the place of our sanctuary. O LORD, the hope of Israel, all that forsake thee shall be ashamed, and they that depart from me shall be written in the earth, because they have forsaken the LORD, the fountain of living waters.

Heal me, O LORD, and I shall be healed; save me, and I shall be saved: for thou art my praise. Behold, they say unto me, Where is the word of the LORD? let it come now. As for me, I have not hastened from being a pastor to follow thee: neither have I desired the woeful day; thou knowest: that which came out of my lips was right before thee. Be not a terror unto me: thou art my hope in the day of evil. Let them be confounded that persecute me, but let not me be confounded: let them be dismayed, but let not me be dismayed: bring upon them the day of evil, and destroy them with double destruction.

Thus said the LORD unto me; Go and stand in the gate of the children of the people, whereby the kings of Judah come in, and by the which they go out, and in all the gates of Jerusalem; and say unto them, Hear ye the word of the LORD, ye kings of Judah, and all Judah, and all the inhabitants of Jerusalem, that enter in by these gates. Thus saith the LORD; Take heed to yourselves, and bear no burden on the sabbath day, nor bring it in by the gates of Jerusalem; neither carry forth a burden out of your houses on the sabbath day, neither do ye any work, but hallow ye the sabbath day, as I commanded your fathers. But they obeyed not, neither inclined their ear, but made their neck stiff, that they might not hear, nor receive instruction. And it shall come to pass, if ye diligently hearken unto me, saith the LORD, to bring in no burden through the gates of this city on the sabbath day, but hallow the sabbath day, to do no work therein; then shall there enter into the gates of this city kings and princes sitting upon the throne of David, riding in chariots and on horses, they, and their princes, the men of Judah, and the inhabitants of Jerusalem: and this city shall remain for ever. And they shall come from the cities of Judah, and from the places about Jerusalem, and from the land of Benjamin, and from the plain, and from the mountains, and from the south, bringing burnt offerings, and sacrifices, and meat offerings, and incense, and bringing sacrifices of praise, unto the house of the LORD. But if ye will not hearken unto me to hallow the sabbath day, and not to hear a burden, even entering in at the gates of Jerusalem on the sabbath day; then will I kindle a fire in the gates thereof, and it shall devour the palaces of Jerusalem, and it shall not be quenched.

The Lesson of the Potter's Vessel

• JEREMIAH 18: 1–17 •

The word which came to Jeremiah from the LORD, saying, Arise, and go down to the potter's house, and there I will cause thee to hear my words.

Then I went down to the potter's house, and, behold, he wrought a work on the wheels. And the vessel that he made of clay was marred in the hand of the potter: so he made it again another vessel, as seemed good to the potter to make it.

Then the word of the LORD came to me, saying, O house of Israel, cannot I do with you as this potter? saith the LORD. Behold, as the clay is in the potter's hand, so are ye in mine hand, O house of Israel. At what instant I shall speak concerning a nation, and concerning a kingdom, to pluck up, and to pull down, and to destroy it; if that nation, against whom I have pronounced, turn from their evil, I will repent of the evil that I thought to do unto them. And at what instant I shall speak concerning a nation, and concerning a kingdom, to build and to plant it; if it do evil in my sight, that it obey not my voice, then I will repent of the good, wherewith I said I would benefit them.

Now therefore go to, speak to the men of Judah, and to the inhabitants of Jerusalem, saying, Thus saith the LORD; Behold, I frame evil against you, and devise a device against you: return ye now every one from his evil way, and make your ways and your doings good.

And they said, There is no hope: but we will walk after our own devices, and we will every one do the imagination of his evil heart.

Therefore thus saith the LORD; Ask ye now among the heathen, who hath heard such things: the virgin of Israel hath done a very horrible thing. Will a man leave the snow of Lebanon which cometh from the rock of the field? or shall the cold flowing waters that come from another place be forsaken? Because my people hath forgotten me, they have burned incense to vanity, and they have caused them to stumble in their ways from the ancient paths, to walk in paths, in a way not cast up; to make their land desolate, and a perpetual hissing; every one that passeth thereby shall be astonished, and wag his head. I will scatter them as with an east wind before the enemy; I will shew them the back, and not the face, in the day of their calamity.

The Happy Restoration

• JEREMIAH 31:15–34 •

Thus saith the LORD; A voice was heard in Ramah, lamentation, and bitter weeping; Rachel weeping for her children refused to be comforted for her children, because they were not.

Thus saith the LORD; Refrain thy voice from weeping, and thine eyes from tears: for thy work shall be rewarded, saith the LORD; and they shall come again from the land of the enemy. And there is hope in thine end, saith the LORD, that thy children shall come again to their own border.

I have surely heard Ephraim bemoaning himself thus; Thou hast chastised me, and I was chastised, as a bullock unaccustomed to the yoke: turn thou me, and I shall be turned; for thou art the LORD my God. Surely after that I was turned, I repented; and after that I was instructed, I smote upon my thigh: I was ashamed, yea, even confounded, because I did bear the reproach of my youth. Is Ephraim my dear son? is he a pleasant child? for since I spake against him, I do earnestly remember him still: therefore my bowels are troubled for him; I will surely have mercy upon him, saith the LORD.

Set thee up waymarks, make thee high heaps: set thine heart toward the highway, even the way which thou wentest: turn again, O virgin of Israel, turn again to these thy cities.

How long wilt thou go about, O thou backsliding daughter? for the Lord hath created a new thing in the earth, a woman shall compass a man.

Thus saith the Lord of hosts, the God of Israel; As yet they shall use this speech in the land of Judah and in the cities thereof, when I shall bring again their captivity; the Lord bless thee, O habitation of justice, and mountain of holiness. And there shall dwell in Judah itself, and in all the cities thereof together, husbandmen, and they that go forth with flocks. For I have satiated the weary soul, and I have replenished every sorrowful soul. Upon this I awaked, and beheld; and my sleep was sweet unto me.

Behold, the days come, saith the Lord, that I will sow the house of Israel and the house of Judah with the seed of man, and with the seed of beast. And it shall come to pass, that like as I have watched over them to pluck up, and to break down, and to throw down, and to destroy, and to afflict; so will I watch over them, to build, and to plant, saith the Lord. In those days they shall say no more, The fathers have eaten a sour grape, and the children's teeth are set on edge.[3] But every one shall die for his own iniquity: every man that eateth the sour grape, his teeth shall be set on edge.

Behold, the days come, saith the Lord, that I will make a new covenant with the house of Israel, and with the house of Judah: not according to the covenant that I made with their fathers in the day that I took them by the hand to bring them out of the land of Egypt; which my covenant they brake, although I was an husband unto them, saith the Lord. But this shall be the covenant that I will make with the house of Israel; after those days, saith the Lord, I will put my law in their inward parts, and write it in their hearts; and will be their God, and they shall be my people. And they shall teach no more every man his neighbour, and every man his brother, saying, Know the Lord: for they shall all know me, from the least of them

---

[3] A proverbial expression. It is used also by Ezekiel.

unto the greatest of them, saith the Lord: for I will forgive their
iniquity, and I will remember their sin no more.

From EZEKIEL

Ezekiel's Vision

• EZEKIEL 1 •

Now it came to pass in the thirtieth year, in the fourth
month, in the fifth day of the month, as I was among the captives by the river of Chebar, that the heavens were opened, and I
saw visions of God. In the fifth day of the month, which was the
fifth year of king Jehoiachin's captivity,[1] the word of the Lord
came expressly unto Ezekiel the priest, the son of Buzi, in the
land of the Chaldeans by the river Chebar; and the hand of the
Lord was there upon him.

And I looked, and, behold, a whirlwind came out of the
north, a great cloud, and a fire infolding itself, and a brightness
was about it, and out of the midst thereof as the colour of
amber, out of the midst of the fire. Also out of the midst thereof
came the likeness of four living creatures. And this was their appearance; they had the likeness of a man. And every one had
four faces, and every one had four wings. And their feet were
straight feet; and the sole of their feet was like the sole of a
calf's foot: and they sparkled like the colour of burnished brass.
And they had the hands of a man under their wings on their
four sides; and they four had their faces and their wings. Their
wings were joined one to another; they turned not when they

[1] i.e., 592 B.C.

went; they went every one straight forward. As for the likeness of their faces, they four had the face of a man, and the face of a lion, on the right side: and they four had the face of an ox, on the left side; they four also had the face of an eagle. Thus were their faces: and their wings were stretched upward; two wings of every one were joined one to another, and two covered their bodies. And they went every one straight forward: whither the spirit was to go, they went; and they turned not when they went. As for the likeness of the living creatures, their appearance was like burning coals of fire, and like the appearance of lamps: it went up and down among the living creatures; and the fire was bright, and out of the fire went forth lightning. And the living creatures ran and returned as the appearance of a flash of lightning.

Now as I beheld the living creatures, behold one wheel upon the earth by the living creatures, with his four faces. The appearance of the wheels and their work was like unto the colour of a beryl: and they four had one likeness: and their appearance and their work was as it were a wheel in the middle of a wheel. When they went, they went upon their four sides: and they turned not when they went. As for their rings, they were so high that they were dreadful; and their rings were full of eyes round about them four. And when the living creatures went, the wheels went by them: and when the living creatures were lifted up from the earth, the wheels were lifted up. Whithersoever the spirit was to go, they went, thither was their spirit to go; and the wheels were lifted up over against them: for the spirit of the living creature was in the wheels. When those went, these went, and when those stood, these stood; and when those were lifted up from the earth, the wheels were lifted up over against them: for the spirit of the living creature was in the wheels. And the likeness of the firmament upon the heads of the living creature was as the colour of the terrible crystal, stretched forth over their heads above. And under the firmament were their wings straight, the one toward the other: every one had two, which covered on this side, and every one had two, which covered on that side, their bodies. And when they went, I heard the noise of their wings, like the noise of great waters, as the voice of the Almighty, the voice of speech, as the noise of an host: when they stood, they let down their wings. And there was a voice from the firmament that was over their heads, when they stood, and had let down their wings.

And above the firmament that was over their heads was the likeness of a throne, as the appearance of a sapphire stone: and upon the likeness of the throne was the likeness as the appearance of a man above upon it. And I saw as the colour of amber, as the appearance of fire round about within it, from the appearance of his loins even upward, and from the appearance of his loins even downward, I saw as it were the appearance of fire, and it had brightness round about. As the appearance of the bow that is in the cloud in the day of rain, so was the appearance of the brightness round about. This was the appearance of the likeness of the glory of the LORD. And when I saw it, I fell upon my face, and I heard a voice of one that spake.

The Punishment of the Sinner and the Reward of the Just

· EZEKIEL 18 ·

The word of the LORD came unto me again, saying, What mean ye, that ye use this proverb concerning the land of Israel, saying, The fathers have eaten sour grapes, and the children's teeth are set on edge? As I live, saith the Lord GOD, ye shall not have occasion any more to use this proverb in Israel. Behold, all souls are mine; as the soul of the father, so also the soul of the son is mine: the soul that sinneth, it shall die. But if a man be just, and do that which is lawful and right, and hath not eaten upon the mountains, neither hath lifted up his eyes to the idols of the house of Israel, neither hath defiled his neighbour's wife, neither hath come near to a menstruous woman, and hath not oppressed any, but hath restored to the debtor his pledge, hath spoiled none by violence, hath given his bread to the hungry, and hath covered the naked with a garment; he that hath not given forth upon usury, neither hath taken any increase, that hath withdrawn his hand from iniquity, hath executed true judgment between man and man, hath walked in my statutes, and hath kept my judgments, to deal truly; he is just, he shall surely live, saith the Lord GOD.

If he beget a son that is a robber, a shedder of blood, and that doeth the like to any one of these things, and that doeth not any of those duties, but even hath eaten upon the mountains, and defiled his neighbour's wife, hath oppressed the poor and needy, hath spoiled by violence, hath not restored the pledge, and hath lifted up his eyes to the idols, hath committed abomination, hath given forth upon usury, and hath taken increase: shall he then live? he shall not live: he hath done all these abominations; he shall surely die; his blood shall be upon him.

Now, lo, if he beget a son, that seeth all his father's sins which he hath done, and considereth, and doeth not such like, that hath not eaten upon the mountains, neither hath lifted up his eyes to the idols of the house of Israel, hath not defiled his neighbour's wife, neither hath oppressed any, hath not withholden the pledge, neither hath spoiled by violence, but hath given his bread to the hungry, and hath covered the naked with a garment, that hath taken off his hand from the poor, that hath not received usury nor increase, hath executed my judgments, hath walked in my statutes; he shall not die for the iniquity of his father, he shall surely live. As for his father, because he cruelly oppressed, spoiled his brother by violence, and did that which is not good among his people, lo, even he shall die in his iniquity.

Yet say ye, Why? doth not the son bear the iniquity of the father? When the son hath done that which is lawful and right, and hath kept all my statutes, and hath done them, he shall surely live. The soul that sinneth, it shall die. The son shall not bear the iniquity of the father, neither shall the father beaı the iniquity of the son: the righteousness of the righteous shall be upon him, and the wickedness of the wicked shall be upon him. But if the wicked will turn from all his sins that he hath committed, and keep all my statutes, and do that which is lawful and right, he shall surely live, he shall not die. All his trangressions that he hath committed, they shall not be mentioned unto him: in his righteousness that he hath done he shall live. Have I any pleasure at all that the wicked should die? saith the Lord GOD: and not that he should return from his ways, and live? But when the righteous turneth away from his righteousness, and committeth iniquity, and doeth according to all the abominations that the wicked man doeth, shall he live? All his righteousness that he hath done shall not be mentioned: in his trespass that he hath trespassed, and in his sin that he hath sinned, in them shall he die.

Yet ye say, The way of the Lord is not equal. Hear now, O house of Israel; Is not my way equal? are not your ways unequal? When a righteous man turneth away from his righteousness, and committeth iniquity, and dieth in them; for his iniquity that he hath done shall he die. Again, when the wicked man turneth away from his wickedness that he hath committed, and doeth that which is lawful and right, he shall save his soul alive. Because he considereth, and turneth away from all his transgressions that he hath committed, he shall surely live, he shall not die. Yet saith the house of Israel, The way of the Lord is not equal. O house of Israel, are not my ways equal? are not your ways unequal? Therefore I will judge you, O house of Israel, every one according to his ways, saith the Lord GOD. Repent, and turn yourselves from all your transgressions; so iniquity shall not be your ruin. Cast away from you all your transgressions, whereby ye have transgressed; and make you a new heart and a new spirit: for why will ye die, O house of

Israel? For I have no pleasure in the death of him that dieth, saith the Lord GOD: wherefore turn yourselves, and live ye.

The Valley of Dry Bones

• EZEKIEL 37 •

The hand of the LORD was upon me, and carried me out in the spirit of the LORD, and set me down in the midst of the valley which was full of bones, and caused me to pass by them round about: and, behold, there were very many in the open valley; and, lo, they were very dry. And he said unto me, Son of man, can these bones live? And I answered, O Lord GOD, thou knowest. Again he said unto me, Prophesy upon these bones, and say unto them, O ye dry bones, hear the word of the LORD. Thus saith the Lord GOD unto these bones; Behold, I will cause breath to enter into you, and ye shall live: and I will lay sinews upon you, and will bring up flesh upon you, and cover you with skin, and put breath in you, and ye shall live; and ye shall know that I am the LORD.

So I prophesied as I was commanded: and as I prophesied, there was a noise, and behold a shaking, and the bones came together, bone to his bone. And when I beheld, lo, the sinews and the flesh came up upon them, and the skin covered them above: but there was no breath in them. Then said he unto me, Prophesy unto the wind, prophesy, son of man, and say to the wind, Thus saith the Lord GOD; Come from the four winds, O breath, and breathe upon these slain, that they may live. So I prophesied as he commanded me, and the breath came into them, and they lived, and stood up upon their feet, an exceeding great army.

Then he said unto me, Son of man, these bones are the whole house of Israel: behold, they say, Our bones are dried, and our hope is lost: we are cut off for our parts. Therefore

prophesy and say unto them, Thus saith the Lord GOD; Behold,
O my people, I will open your graves, and cause you to come up
out of your graves, and bring you into the land of Israel. And
ye shall know that I am the LORD, when I have opened your
graves, O my people, and brought you up out of your graves,
and shall put my spirit in you, and ye shall live, and I shall
place you in your own land: then shall ye know that I the LORD
have spoken it, and performed it, saith the LORD.

The word of the LORD came again unto me, saying, Moreover, thou son of man, take thee one stick, and write upon it,
For Judah, and for the children of Israel his companions: then
take another stick, and write upon it, For Joseph, the stick of
Ephraim, and for all the house of Israel his companions: and
join them one to another into one stick; and they shall become
one in thine hand. And when the children of thy people shall
speak unto thee, saying, Wilt thou not shew us what thou meanest by these? say unto them, Thus saith the Lord GOD; Behold,
I will take the stick of Joseph, which is in the hand of Ephraim,
and the tribes of Israel his fellows, and will put them with him,
even with the stick of Judah, and make them one stick, and they
shall be one in mine hand. And the sticks whereon thou writest
shall be in thine hand before their eyes.

And say unto them, Thus saith the Lord GOD; Behold, I
will take the children of Israel from among the heathen, whither
they be gone, and will gather them on every side, and bring
them into their own land: and I will make them one nation in
the land upon the mountains of Israel; and one king shall be
king to them all: and they shall be no more two nations, neither
shall they be divided into two kingdoms any more at all:
neither shall they defile themselves any more with their idols,
nor with their detestable things, nor with any of their transgressions: but I will save them out of all their dwellingplaces,
wherein they have sinned, and will cleanse them: so shall they
be my people, and I will be their God. And David my servant
shall be king over them; and they all shall have one shepherd:

they shall also walk in my judgments, and observe my statutes, and do them. And they shall dwell in the land that I have given unto Jacob my servant, wherein your fathers have dwelt; and they shall dwell therein, even they, and their children, and their children's children for ever: and my servant David shall be their prince for ever. Moreover I will make a covenant of peace with them; it shall be an everlasting covenant with them: and I will place them, and multiply them, and will set my sanctuary in the midst of them for evermore. My tabernacle also shall be with them: yea, I will be their God, and they shall be my people. And the heathen shall know that I the LORD do sanctify Israel, when my sanctuary shall be in the midst of them for evermore.

JONAH

Now the word of the LORD came unto Jonah[1] the son of Amittai, saying, "Arise, go to Nineveh, that great city, and cry against it; for their wickedness is come up before me." But Jonah rose up to flee unto Tarshish from the presence of the LORD, and went down to Joppa; and he found a ship going to Tarshish: so he paid the fare thereof, and went down into it, to go with them unto Tarshish from the presence of the LORD.

But the LORD sent out a great wind into the sea, and there was a mighty tempest in the sea, so that the ship was like to be broken. Then the mariners were afraid, and cried every man unto his god, and cast forth the wares that were in the ship into the sea, to lighten it of them.

But Jonah was gone down into the sides of the ship; and he lay, and was fast asleep. So the shipmaster came to him, and said unto him, "What meanest thou, O sleeper? arise, call upon

[1] The hero of the story belongs to the 8th century B.C. The book was probably written in the 5th century.

thy God, if so be that God will think upon us, that we perish not."

And they said every one to his fellow, "Come, and let us cast lots, that we may know for whose cause this evil is upon us." So they cast lots, and the lot fell upon Jonah.

Then said they unto him, "Tell us, we pray thee, for whose cause this evil is upon us; what is thine occupation? and whence comest thou? what is thy country? and of what people art thou?"

And he said unto them, "I am an Hebrew; and I fear the LORD, the God of heaven, which hath made the sea and the dry land."

Then were the men exceedingly afraid, and said unto him, "Why hast thou done this?" For the men knew that he fled from the presence of the LORD, because he had told them. Then said they unto him, "What shall we do unto thee, that the sea may be calm unto us?" for the sea wrought, and was tempestuous.

And he said unto them, "Take me up, and cast me forth into the sea; so shall the sea be calm unto you: for I know that for my sake this great tempest is upon you."

Nevertheless the men rowed hard to bring it to the land; but they could not: for the sea wrought, and was tempestuous against them. Wherefore they cried unto the LORD, and said, "We beseech thee, O LORD, we beseech thee, let us not perish for this man's life, and lay not upon us innocent blood: for thou, O LORD, hast done as it pleased thee."

So they took up Jonah, and cast him forth into the sea: and the sea ceased from her raging. Then the men feared the LORD exceedingly, and offered a sacrifice unto the LORD, and made vows.

Now the LORD had prepared a great fish to swallow up Jonah. And Jonah was in the belly of the fish three days and three nights.

Then Jonah prayed unto the LORD his God out of the fish's belly, and said, "I cried by reason of mine affliction unto the

LORD, and he heard me; out of the belly of hell cried I, and thou heardest my voice. For thou hadst cast me into the deep, in the midst of the seas; and the floods compassed me about: all thy billows and thy waves passed over me. Then I said, 'I am cast out of thy sight; yet I will look again toward thy holy temple.' The waters compassed me about, even to the soul: the depth closed me round about, the weeds were wrapped about my head. I went down to the bottoms of the mountains; the earth with her bars was about me for ever: yet hast thou brought up my life from corruption, O LORD my God. When my soul fainted within me I remembered the LORD: and my prayer came in unto thee, into thine holy temple. They that observe lying vanities forsake their own mercy. But I will sacrifice unto thee with the voice of thanksgiving; I will pay that that I have vowed. Salvation is of the LORD."

And the LORD spake unto the fish, and it vomited out Jonah upon the dry land.

And the word of the LORD came unto Jonah the second time, saying, "Arise, go unto Nineveh, that great city, and preach unto it the preaching that I bid thee." So Jonah arose, and went unto Nineveh, according to the word of the LORD. Now Nineveh was an exceeding great city of three days' journey. And Jonah began to enter into the city a day's journey, and he cried, and said, "Yet forty days, and Nineveh shall be overthrown."

So the people of Nineveh believed God, and proclaimed a fast, and put on sackcloth, from the greatest of them even to the least of them. For word came unto the king of Nineveh, and he arose from his throne, and he laid his robe from him, and covered him with sackcloth, and sat in ashes. And he caused it to be proclaimed and published through Nineveh by the decree of the king and his nobles saying, "Let neither man nor beast, herd nor flock, taste any thing: let them not feed, nor drink water: but let man and beast be covered with sackcloth, and cry mightily unto God: yea, let them turn every one from his evil way, and from the violence that is in their hands. Who can tell if God will turn and repent, and turn away from his fierce anger, that we perish not?"

And God saw their works, that they turned from their evil way; and God repented of the evil that he had said that he would do unto them; and he did it not.

But it displeased Jonah exceedingly, and he was very angry. And he prayed unto the Lord, and said, "I pray thee, O Lord, was this my saying, when I was yet in my country? Therefore I fled before unto Tarshish: for I knew that thou art a gracious God, and merciful, slow to anger, and of great kindness, and repentest thee of the evil. Therefore now, O Lord, take, I beseech thee, my life from me; for it is better for me to die than to live."

Then said the Lord, "Doest thou well to be angry?"

So Jonah went out of the city, and sat on the east side of the city, and there made him a booth, and sat under it in the shadow, till he might see what would become of the city.

And the Lord God prepared a gourd, and made it to come up over Jonah, that it might be a shadow over his head, to deliver him from his grief. So Jonah was exceeding glad of the gourd. But God prepared a worm when the morning rose the next day, and it smote the gourd that it withered. And it came to pass, when the sun did arise, that God prepared a vehement east wind; and the sun beat upon the head of Jonah, that he fainted, and wished in himself to die, and said, "It is better for me to die than to live."

And God said to Jonah, "Doest thou well to be angry for the gourd?"

And he said, "I do well to be angry, even unto death."

Then said the Lord, "Thou hast had pity on the gourd, for the which thou hast not laboured, neither madest it grow; which came up in a night, and perished in a night: and should not I spare Nineveh, that great city, wherein are more than sixscore thousand persons that cannot discern between their right hand and their left hand; and also much cattle?"

RUTH

Now it came to pass in the days when the judges ruled, that there was a famine in the land. And a certain man of Beth-lehem-judah went to sojourn in the country of Moab,[1] he, and his wife, and his two sons. And the name of the man was Elimelech, and the name of his wife Naomi, and the name of his two sons Mahlon and Chilion, Ephrathites of Beth-lehem-judah. And they came into the country of Moab, and continued there. And Elimelech Naomi's husband died; and she was left, and her two sons. And they took them wives of the women of Moab; the name of the one was Orpah, and the name of the other Ruth: and they dwelled there about ten years. And Mahlon and Chilion died also both of them; and the woman was left of her two sons and her husband.

Then she arose with her daughters in law, that she might return from the country of Moab: for she had heard in the country of Moab how that the LORD had visited his people in giving them bread. Wherefore she went forth out of the place where she was, and her two daughters in law with her; and they went on the way to return unto the land of Judah.

And Naomi said unto her two daughters in law, "Go, return each to her mother's house: the LORD deal kindly with you, as ye have dealt with the dead, and with me. The LORD grant you that ye may find rest, each of you in the house of her husband." Then she kissed them; and they lifted up their voice, and wept.

[1] The fertile country east of the Dead Sea. The Moabites were not of Israel.

And they said unto her, "Surely we will return with thee unto thy people."

And Naomi said, "Turn again, my daughters: why will ye go with me? are there yet any more sons in my womb, that they may be your husbands? [2] Turn again, my daughters, go your way; for I am too old to have an husband. If I should say, 'I have hope,' if I should have an husband also to night, and should also bear sons; would ye tarry for them till they were grown? would ye stay for them from having husbands? nay, my daughters; for it grieveth me much for your sakes that the hand of the LORD is gone out against me."

And they lifted up their voice, and wept again: and Orpah kissed her mother in law; but Ruth clave unto her. And she said, "Behold, thy sister in law is gone back unto her people, and unto her gods: return thou after thy sister in law."

And Ruth said, "Intreat me not to leave thee, or to return from following after thee: for wither thou goest, I will go; and where thou lodgest, I will lodge: thy people shall be my people, and thy God my God: where thou diest, will I die, and there will I be buried: the LORD do so to me, and more also, if ought but death part thee and me." When she saw that she was stedfastly minded to go with her, then she left speaking unto her.

So they two went until they came to Beth-lehem. And it came to pass, when they were come to Beth-lehem, that all the city was moved about them, and they said, "Is this Naomi?" And she said unto them, "Call me not Naomi, call me Mara:[3] for the Almighty hath dealt very bitterly with me. I went out full, and the LORD hath brought me home again empty: why then call ye me Naomi, seeing the LORD hath testified against me, and the Almighty hath afflicted me?" So Naomi returned, and Ruth the Moabitess, her daughter in law, with her, which returned out of

---

[2] According to the Levirate Law (Deuteronomy 25), if a man died childless his brother must marry the widow. The first born son of the second marriage was the legal son and heir of the deceased.

[3] Bitter.

the country of Moab: and they came to Beth-lehem in the beginning of barley harvest.

And Naomi had a kinsman of her husband's, a mighty man of wealth, of the family of Elimelech; and his name was Boaz. And Ruth the Moabitess said unto Naomi, "Let me now go to the field, and glean ears of corn after him in whose sight I shall find grace." And she said unto her, "Go, my daughter." And she went, and came, and gleaned in the field after the reapers: and her hap was to light on a part of the field belonging unto Boaz, who was of the kindred of Elimelech.

And, behold, Boaz came from Beth-lehem, and said unto the reapers, "The LORD be with you." And they answered him, "The LORD bless thee."

Then said Boaz unto his servant that was set over the reapers, "Whose damsel is this?"

And the servant that was set over the reapers answered and said, "It is the Moabitish damsel that came back with Naomi out of the country of Moab: and she said, 'I pray you, let me glean and gather after the reapers among the sheaves': so she came, and hath continued even from the morning until now, that she tarried a little in the house."

Then said Boaz unto Ruth, "Hearest thou not, my daughter? Go not to glean in another field, neither go from hence, but abide here fast by my maidens: let thine eyes be on the field that they do reap, and go thou after them: have I not charged the young men that they shall not touch thee? and when thou art athirst, go unto the vessels, and drink of that which the young men have drawn."

Then she fell on her face, and bowed herself to the ground, and said unto him, "Why have I found grace in thine eyes, that thou shouldest take knowledge of me, seeing I am a stranger?"

And Boaz answered and said unto her, "It hath fully been shewed me, all that thou hast done unto thy mother in law since the death of thine husband: and how thou hast left thy father and thy mother, and the land of thy nativity, and art come unto a people which thou knewest not heretofore. The LORD recompense thy work, and a full reward be given thee of the LORD God of Israel, under whose wings thou art come to trust."

Then she said, "Let me find favour in thy sight, my lord; for that thou hast comforted me, and for that thou hast spoken friendly unto thine handmaid, though I be not like unto one of thine handmaidens."

And Boaz said unto her, "At mealtime come thou hither, and eat of the bread, and dip thy morsel in the vinegar." And she sat beside the reapers: and he reached her parched corn, and she did eat, and was sufficed, and left.

And when she was risen up to glean, Boaz commanded his young men, saying, "Let her glean even among the sheaves, and reproach her not: and let fall also some of the handfuls of purpose for her, and leave them, that she may glean them, and rebuke her not." So she gleaned in the field until even, and beat out that she had gleaned: and it was about an ephah of barley.

And she took it up, and went into the city: and her mother in law saw what she had gleaned: and she brought forth, and gave to her that she had reserved after she was sufficed. And her mother in law said unto her, "Where hast thou gleaned to day? and where wroughtest thou? blessed be he that did take knowledge of thee."

And she shewed her mother in law with whom she had wrought, and said, "The man's name with whom I wrought to day is Boaz."

And Naomi said unto her daughter in law, "Blessed be he of the LORD, who hath not left off his kindness to the living and to the dead." And Naomi said unto her, "The man is near of kin unto us, one of our next kinsmen."

And Ruth the Moabitess said, "He said unto me also, 'Thou shalt keep fast by my young men, until they have ended all my harvest.'"

And Naomi said unto Ruth her daughter in law, "It is good, my daughter, that thou go out with his maidens, that they meet thee not in any other field." So she kept fast by the maidens of Boaz to glean unto the end of barley harvest and of wheat harvest; and dwelt with her mother in law.

Then Naomi her mother in law said unto her, "My daughter, shall I not seek rest for thee, that it may be well with thee? And now is not Boaz of our kindred, with whose maidens thou wast? Behold, he winnoweth barley to night in the threshingfloor. Wash thyself therefore, and anoint thee, and put thy raiment upon thee, and get thee down to the floor: but make not thyself known unto the man, until he shall have done eating and drinking. And it shall be, when he lieth down, that thou shalt mark the place where he shall lie, and thou shalt go in, and uncover his feet, and lay thee down; and he will tell thee what thou shalt do."

And she said unto her, "All that thou sayest unto me I will do."

And she went down unto the floor, and did according to all that her mother in law bade her. And when Boaz had eaten and drunk, and his heart was merry, he went to lie down at the end of the heap of corn: and she came softly, and uncovered his feet, and laid her down.

And it came to pass at midnight, that the man was afraid, and turned himself: and, behold, a woman lay at his feet. And he said, "Who art thou?"

And she answered, "I am Ruth thine handmaid: spread therefore thy skirt over thine handmaid; for thou art a near kinsman." [4]

And he said, "Blessed be thou of the LORD, my daughter: for thou hast shewed more kindness in the latter end than at the beginning, inasmuch as thou followedst not young men, whether

[4] Since Naomi had no living sons, the duty of marrying Ruth might devolve upon the nearest kinsman of Mahlon.

poor or rich. And now, my daughter, fear not; I will do to thee all that thou requirest: for all the city of my people doth know that thou art a virtuous woman. And now it is true that I am thy near kinsman: howbeit there is a kinsman nearer than I. Tarry this night, and it shall be in the morning, that if he will perform unto thee the part of a kinsman, well; let him do the kinsman's part: but if he will not do the part of a kinsman to thee, then will I do the part of a kinsman to thee, as the LORD liveth: lie down until the morning."

And she lay at his feet until the morning: and she rose up before one could know another. And he said, "Let it not be known that a woman came into the floor." Also he said, "Bring the veil that thou hast upon thee, and hold it." And when she held it, he measured six measures of barley, and laid it on her: and she went into the city.

And when she came to her mother in law, she said, "Who art thou, my daughter?"

And she told her all that the man had done to her. And she said, "These six measures of barley gave he me; for he said to me, 'Go not empty unto thy mother in law.'"

Then said she, "Sit still, my daughter, until thou know how the matter will fall: for the man will not be in rest, until he have finished the thing this day."

Then went Boaz up to the gate, and sat him down there: and, behold, the kinsman of whom Boaz spake came by; unto whom he said, "Ho, such a one! turn aside, sit down here." And he turned aside, and sat down. And he took ten men of the elders of the city, and said, "Sit ye down here." And they sat down.

And he said unto the kinsman, "Naomi, that is come again out of the country of Moab, selleth a parcel of land, which was our brother Elimelech's: and I thought to advertise thee, saying, 'Buy it before the inhabitants, and before the elders of my people.' If thou wilt redeem it, redeem it: but if thou wilt not redeem it, then tell me, that I may know: for there is none to redeem it beside thee; and I am after thee."

And he said, "I will redeem it."

Then said Boaz, "What day thou buyest the field of the hand of Naomi, thou must buy it also of Ruth the Moabitess, the wife of the dead, to raise up the name of the dead upon his inheritance."

And the kinsman said, "I cannot redeem it for myself, lest I mar mine own inheritance: redeem thou my right to thyself; for I cannot redeem it."

Now this was the manner in former time in Israel concerning redeeming and concerning changing, for to confirm all things; a man plucked off his shoe, and gave it to his neighbour: and this was a testimony in Israel. Therefore the kinsman said unto Boaz, "Buy it for thee." So he drew off his shoe.

And Boaz said unto the elders, and unto all the people, "Ye are witnesses this day, that I have bought all that was Elimelech's, and all that was Chilion's and Mahlon's, of the hand of Naomi. Moreover Ruth the Moabitess, the wife of Mahlon, have I purchased to be my wife, to raise up the name of the dead upon his inheritance, that the name of the dead be not cut off from among his brethren, and from the gate of his place: ye are witnesses this day."

And all the people that were in the gate, and the elders, said, "We are witnesses. The LORD make the woman that is come into thine house like Rachel and like Leah, which two did build the house of Israel: and do thou worthily in Ephratah, and be famous in Beth-lehem: and let thy house be like the house of Pharez, whom Tamar bare unto Judah, of the seed which the LORD shall give thee of this young woman."

So Boaz took Ruth, and she was his wife: and when he went in unto her, the LORD gave her conception, and she bare a son. And the women said unto Naomi, "Blessed be the LORD, which hath not left thee this day without a kinsman, that his name may be famous in Israel. And he shall be unto thee a restorer of thy life, and a nourisher of thine old age: for thy daughter in law, which loveth thee, which is better to thee than seven sons, hath born him."

And Naomi took the child, and laid it in her bosom, and became nurse unto it. And the women her neighbours gave it a name, saying, "There is a son born to Naomi;" and they called his name Obed: he is the father of Jesse, the father of David.

From THE PSALMS

"Blessed is the man that walketh not in the counsel of the ungodly."

• PSALM 1 •

Blessed is the man that walketh not in the counsel of the
    ungodly.
Nor standeth in the way of sinners,
Nor sitteth in the seat of the scornful.
But his delight is in the law of the Lord;
And in his law doth he meditate day and night.
And he shall be like a tree planted by the rivers of water,
That bringeth forth his fruit in his season;
His leaf also shall not wither;
And whatsoever he doeth shall prosper.
The ungodly are not so:
But are like the chaff which the wind driveth away.
Therefore the ungodly shall not stand in the judgment.
Nor sinners in the congregation of the righteous.
For the Lord knoweth the way of the righteous:
But the way of the ungodly shall perish.

"O Lord our Lord, how excellent is thy name."

· PSALM 8 ·

O Lord our Lord,
How excellent is thy name in all the earth!
Who has set thy glory above the heavens.
Out of the mouth of babes and sucklings hast thou ordained
       strength because of thine enemies,
That thou mightest still the enemy and the avenger.
When I consider thy heavens, the work of thy fingers,
The moon and the stars, which thou hast ordained;
What is man, that thou art mindful of him?
And the son of man, that thou visitest him?
For thou hast made him a little lower than the angels,
And hast crowned him with glory and honour.
Thou madest him to have dominion over the works of thy hands;
Thou hast put all things under his feet:
All sheep and oxen,
Yea, and the beasts of the field;
The fowl of the air, and the fish of the sea,
And whatsoever passeth through the paths of the seas.
O Lord our Lord,
How excellent is thy name in all the earth!

"How long wilt thou forget me, O Lord?"

· PSALM 13 ·

How long will thou forget me, O Lord? for ever?
How long wilt thou hide thy face from me?
How long shall I take counsel in my soul,
Having sorrow in my heart daily?
How long shall mine enemy be exalted over me?

Consider and hear me, O Lord my God:
Lighten mine eyes, lest I sleep the sleep of death;
Lest mine enemy say, I have prevailed against him;
And those that trouble me rejoice when I am moved.
But I have trusted in thy mercy;
My heart shall rejoice in thy salvation.
I will sing unto the Lord,
Because he hath dealt bountifully with me.

"The heavens declare the glory of God."

• PSALM 19 •

The heavens declare the glory of God;
And the firmament sheweth his handywork.
Day unto day uttereth speech,
And night unto night sheweth knowledge.
There is no speech nor language,
Where their voice is not heard.
Their line is gone out through all the earth,
And their words to the end of the world.
In them hath he set a tabernacle for the sun,
Which is as a bridegroom coming out of his chamber,
And rejoiceth as a strong man to run a race.
His going forth is from the end of the heaven,
And his circuit unto the ends of it:
And there is nothing hid from the heat thereof.
The law of the Lord is perfect, converting the soul:
The testimony of the Lord is sure, making wise the simple.
The statutes of the Lord are right, rejoicing the heart:
The commandment of the Lord is pure, enlightening the eyes.
The fear of the Lord is clean, enduring for ever:
The judgments of the Lord are true and righteous altogether.
More to be desired are they than gold, yea, than much fine gold:

Sweeter also than honey and the honeycomb.
Moreover by them is thy servant warned:
And in keeping of them there is great reward.
Who can understand his errors?
Cleanse thou me from secret faults.
Keep back thy servant also from presumptuous sins;
Let them not have dominion over me: then shall I be upright,
And I shall be innocent from the great transgression.
Let the words of my mouth, and the meditation of my heart,
Be acceptable in thy sight,
O Lord, my strength, and my redeemer.

"The Lord is my shepherd."

• PSALM 23 •

The Lord is my shepherd; I shall not want.
He maketh me to lie down in green pastures:
He leadeth me beside the still waters.
He restoreth my soul:
He leadeth me in the paths of righteousness
For his name's sake.
Yea, though I walk through the valley of the shadow of death,
I will fear no evil: for thou art with me;
Thy rod and thy staff they comfort me.
Thou preparest a table before me
In the presence of mine enemies:
Thou anointest my head with oil;
My cup runneth over.
Surely goodness and mercy shall follow me
All the days of my life:
And I will dwell in the house of the Lord for ever.

"The earth is the Lord's, and the fulness thereof."

The earth is the Lord's, and the fulness thereof;
The world, and they that dwell therein.
For he hath founded it upon the seas,
And established it upon the floods.
Who shall ascend into the hill of the Lord?
Or who shall stand in his holy place?
He that hath clean hands, and a pure heart;
Who hath not lifted up his soul unto vanity,
Nor sworn deceitfully.
He shall receive the blessing from the Lord,
And righteousness from the God of his salvation.
This is the generation of them that seek him,
That seek thy face, O Jacob.
Lift up your heads, O ye gates;
And be ye lift up, ye everlasting doors;
And the King of glory shall come in.
Who is this King of glory?
The Lord strong and mighty,
The Lord mighty in battle.
Lift up your heads, O ye gates;
Even lift them up, ye everlasting doors;
And the King of glory shall come in.
Who is this King of glory?
The Lord of hosts, he is the King of glory.

"As the hart panteth after the water brooks."

As the hart panteth after the water brooks,
So panteth my soul after thee, O God.
My soul thirsteth for God, for the living God:
When shall I come and appear before God?
My tears have been my meat day and night,
While they continually say unto me, Where is thy God?
When I remember these things, I pour out my soul in me:
For I had gone with the multitude, I went with them to the
    House of God,
With the voice of joy and praise, with a multitude that kept
    holyday.
Why art thou cast down, O my soul?
And why art thou disquieted in me?
Hope thou in God: for I shall yet praise him
For the help of his countenance.
O my God, my soul is cast down within me:
Therefore will I remember thee from the land of Jordan,
And of the Hermonites, from the hill Mizar.
Deep calleth unto deep at the noise of thy waterspouts:
All thy waves and thy billows are gone over me.
Yet the Lord will command his lovingkindness in the daytime,
And in the night his song shall be with me,
And my prayer unto the God of my life.
I will say unto God my rock, Why hast thou forgotten me?
Why go I mourning because of the oppression of the enemy?
As with a sword in my bones, mine enemies reproach me;
While they say daily unto me, Where is thy God?
Why art thou cast down, O my soul?
And why art thou disquieted within me?
Hope thou in God: for I shall yet praise him,
Who is the health of my countenance, and my God.

"Judge me, O God, and plead my cause."

Judge me, O God, and plead my cause against an ungodly
     nation:
O deliver me from the deceitful and unjust man.
For thou art the God of my strength: why dost thou cast me
     off?
Why go I mourning because of the oppression of the enemy?
O send out thy light and thy truth: let them lead me;
Let them bring me unto thy holy hill,
And to thy tabernacles.
Then will I go unto the altar of God,
Unto God my exceeding joy:
Yea, upon the harp will I praise thee, O God my God.
Why art thou cast down, O my soul?
And why art thou disquieted within me?
Hope in God: for I shall yet praise him,
Who is the health of my countenance, and my God.

"God is our refuge and strength."

God is our refuge and strength,
A very present help in trouble.
Therefore will not we fear, though the earth be removed,
And though the mountains be carried into the midst of the sea;
Though the waters thereof roar and be troubled,
Though the mountains shake with the swelling thereof.
There is a river, the streams whereof shall make glad the city of
     God,
The holy place of the tabernacles of the most High.

God is in the midst of her; she shall not be moved:
God shall help her, and that right early.
The heathen raged, the kingdoms were moved:
He uttered his voice, the earth melted.
The Lord of hosts is with us;
The God of Jacob is our refuge.
Come, behold the works of the Lord,
What desolations he hath made in the earth.
He maketh wars to cease unto the end of the earth;
He breaketh the bow, and cutteth the spear in sunder;
He burneth the chariot in the fire.
Be still, and know that I am God:
I will be exalted among the heathen, I will be exalted in the
    earth.
The Lord of hosts is with us;
The God of Jacob is our refuge.

"Have mercy upon me, O God, according to thy lovingkindness."

• PSALM 51 •

Have mercy upon me, O God, according to thy lovingkindness:
According unto the multitude of thy tender mercies blot out my
    transgressions.
Wash me throughly from mine iniquity,
And cleanse me from my sin.
For I acknowledge my transgressions:
And my sin is ever before me.
Against thee, thee only, have I sinned, and done this evil in thy
    sight:
That thou mightest be justified when thou speakest, and be clear
    when thou judgest.
Behold, I was shapen in iniquity;

And in sin did my mother conceive me.
Behold, thou desirest truth in the inward parts:
And in the hidden part thou shalt make me to know wisdom.
Purge me with hyssop, and I shall be clean:
Wash me, and I shall be whiter than snow.
Make me to hear joy and gladness;
That the bones which thou hast broken may rejoice.
Hide thy face from my sins,
And blot out all mine iniquities.
Create in me a clean heart, O God;
And renew a right spirit within me.
Cast me not away from thy presence;
And take not thy holy spirit from me.
Restore unto me the joy of thy salvation;
And uphold me with thy free spirit.
Then will I teach transgressors thy ways;
And sinners shall be converted unto thee.
Deliver me from bloodguiltiness, O God, thou God of my
    salvation:
And my tongue shall sing aloud of thy righteousness.
O Lord, open thou my lips;
And my mouth shall shew forth thy praise.
For thou desirest not sacrifice; else would I give it:
Thou delightest not in burnt offering.
The sacrifices of God are a broken spirit:
A broken and a contrite heart, O God, thou wilt not despise.
Do good in thy good pleasure unto Zion:
Build thou the walls of Jerusalem.
Then shalt thou be pleased with the sacrifices of righteousness,
With burnt offering and whole burnt offering:
Then shall they offer bullocks upon thine altar.

"O God, thou art my God; early will I seek thee."

O God, thou art my God; early will I seek thee:
My soul thirsteth for thee, my flesh longeth for thee
In a dry and thirsty land, where no water is;
To see thy power and thy glory,
So as I have seen thee in the sanctuary.
Because thy lovingkindness is better than life,
My lips shall praise thee.
Thus will I bless thee while I live:
I will lift up my hands in thy name.
My soul shall be satisfied as with marrow and fatness;
And my mouth shall praise thee with joyful lips:
When I remember thee upon my bed,
And meditate on thee in the night watches.
Because thou hast been my help,
Therefore in the shadow of thy wings will I rejoice.
My soul followeth hard after thee:
Thy right hand upholdeth me.
But those that seek my soul, to destroy it,
Shall go into the lower parts of the earth.
They shall fall by the sword:
They shall be a portion for foxes.
But the king shall rejoice in God;
Every one that sweareth by him shall glory:
But the mouth of them that speak lies shall be stopped.

"How amiable are thy tabernacles, O Lord of hosts!"

How amiable are thy tabernacles, O Lord of hosts!
My soul longeth, yea, even fainteth for the courts of the Lord:
My heart and my flesh crieth out for the living God.
Yea, the sparrow hath found an house,
And the swallow a nest for herself, where she may lay her
      young,
Even thine altars, O Lord of hosts, my King, and my God.
Blessed are they that dwell in thy house:
They will be still praising thee.
Blessed is the man whose strength is in thee;
In whose heart are the ways of them.
Who passing through the valley of Baca make it a well;
The rain also filleth the pools.
They go from strength to strength,
Every one of them in Zion appeareth before God.
O Lord God of hosts, hear my prayer:
Give ear, O God of Jacob.
Behold, O God our shield,
And look upon the face of thine anointed.
For a day in thy courts is better than a thousand.
I had rather be a doorkeeper in the house of my God,
Than to dwell in the tents of wickedness.
For the Lord God is a sun and shield:
The Lord will give grace and glory:
No good thing will he withhold from them that walk uprightly.
O Lord of hosts, blessed is the man that trusteth in thee.

"Lord, thou hast been our dwelling place in all generations."

Lord, thou hast been our dwelling place
In all generations. Before the mountains were brought forth,
Or ever thou hadst formed the earth and the world,
Even from everlasting to everlasting, thou art God.
Thou turnest man to destruction;
And sayest, Return, ye children of men.
For a thousand years in thy sight
Are but as yesterday when it is past,
And as a watch in the night.
Thou carriest them away as with a flood; they are as a sleep:
In the morning they are like grass which groweth up.
In the morning it flourisheth, and groweth up;
In the evening it is cut down, and withereth.
For we are consumed by thine anger,
And by thy wrath are we troubled.
Thou hast set out iniquities before thee,
Our secret sins in the light of thy countenance.
For all our days are passed away in thy wrath:
We spend our years as a tale that is told.
The days of our years are threescore years and ten;
And if by reason of strength they be fourscore years,
Yet is their strength labour and sorrow;
For it is soon cut off, and we fly away.
Who knoweth the power of thine anger?
Even according to thy fear, so is thy wrath.
So teach us to number our days,
That we may apply our hearts unto wisdom.
Return, O Lord, how long?
And let it repent thee concerning thy servants.

O satisfy us early with thy mercy;
That we may rejoice and be glad all our days.
Make us glad according to the days wherein thou has afflicted us,
And the years wherein we have seen evil.
Let thy work appear unto thy servants,
And thy glory unto their children.
And let the beauty of the Lord our God be upon us:
And establish thou the work of our hands upon us;
Yea, the work of our hands establish thou it.

"He that dwelleth in the secret place of the most High."

• PSALM 91 •

He that dwelleth in the secret place of the most High
Shall abide under the shadow of the Almighty.
I will say of the Lord, He is my refuge and my fortress;
My God; in him will I trust.
Surely he shall deliver thee from the snare of the fowler,
And from the noisome pestilence.
He shall cover thee with his feathers,
And under his wings shalt thou trust:
His truth shall be thy shield and buckler.
Thou shalt not be afraid for the terror by night;
Nor for the arrow that flieth by day;
Nor for the pestilence that walketh in darkness;
Nor for the destruction that wasteth at noonday.
A thousand shall fall at thy side, and ten thousand at thy right
        hand;
But it shall not come nigh thee.
Only with thine eyes shalt thou behold
And see the reward of the wicked.
Because thou hast made the Lord, which is my refuge,
Even the most High, thy habitation;
There shall no evil befall thee,

Neither shall any plague come nigh thy dwelling.
For he shall give his angels charge over thee,
To keep thee in all thy ways.
They shall bear thee up in their hands,
Lest thou dash thy foot against a stone.
Thou shalt tread upon the lion and adder:
The young lion and the dragon shalt thou trample under feet.
Because he hath set his love upon me, therefore will I deliver
　　him:
I will set him on high, because he hath known my name.
He shall call upon me, and I will answer him:
I will be with him in trouble;
I will deliver him and honour him.
With long life will I satisfy him,
And shew him my salvation.

"O sing unto the Lord a new song."

· PSALM 98 ·

O sing unto the Lord a new song;
For he hath done marvellous things:
His right hand, and his holy arm,
Hath gotten him the victory.
The Lord hath made known his salvation:
His righteousness hath he openly shewed in the sight of the
　　heathen.
He hath remembered his mercy and his truth toward the house
　　of Israel:
All the ends of the earth have seen the salvation of our God.
Make a joyful noise unto the Lord, all the earth:
Make a loud noise, and rejoice, and sing praise.
Sing unto the Lord with the harp;
With the harp, and the voice of a psalm.

With trumpets and sound of cornet
Make a joyful noise before the Lord, the King.
Let the sea roar, and the fulness thereof;
The world, and they that dwell therein.
Let the floods clap their hands:
Let the hills be joyful together
Before the Lord; for he cometh to judge the earth:
With righteousness shall he judge the world,
And the people with equity.

"Bless the Lord, O my soul."

• PSALM 104 •

Bless the Lord, O my soul.
O Lord my God, thou art very great;
Thou art clothed with honour and majesty.
Who coverest thyself with light as with a garment:
Who stretchest out the heavens like a curtain:
Who layeth the beams of his chambers in the waters:
Who maketh the clouds his chariot:
Who walketh upon the wings of the wind:
Who maketh his angels spirits;
His ministers a flaming fire:
Who laid the foundations of the earth,
That it should not be removed for ever.
Thou coveredst it with the deep as with a garment:
The waters stood above the mountains.
At thy rebuke they fled;
At the voice of thy thunder they hasted away.
They go up by the mountains; they go down by the valleys
Unto the place which thou hast founded for them.
Thou hast set a bound that they may not pass over;
That they turn not again to cover the earth.

He sendeth the springs into the valleys,
Which run among the hills.
They give drink to every beast of the field:
The wild asses quench their thirst.
By them shall the fowls of the heaven have their habitation,
Which sing among the branches.
He watereth the hills from his chambers:
The earth is satisfied with the fruit of thy works.
He causeth the grass to grow for the cattle,
And herb for the service of man:
That he may bring forth food out of the earth;
And wine that maketh glad the heart of man,
And oil to make his face to shine,
And bread which strengtheneth man's heart.
The trees of the Lord are full of sap;
The cedars of Lebanon, which he hath planted;
Where the birds make their nests:
As for the stork, the fir trees are her house.
The high hills are a refuge for the wild goats;
And the rocks for the conies.
He appointed the moon for seasons:
The sun knoweth his going down.
Thou makest darkness, and it is night:
Wherein all the beasts of the forest do creep forth.
The young lions roar after their prey,
And seek their meat from God.
The sun ariseth, they gather themselves together
And lay them down in their dens.
Man goeth forth unto his work
And to his labour until the evening.
O Lord, how manifold are thy works!
In wisdom hast thou made them all:
The earth is full of thy riches.
So is this great and wide sea,
Wherein are things creeping innumerable,

Both small and great beasts.
There go the ships:
There is that leviathan, whom thou hast made to play therein.
These wait all upon thee;
That thou mayest give them their meat in due season.
That thou givest them they gather:
Thou openest thine hand, they are filled with good.
Thou hidest thy face, they are troubled:
Thou takest away their breath, they die,
And return to their dust.
Thou sendest forth thy spirit, they are created:
And thou renewest the face of the earth.
The glory of the Lord shall endure for ever:
The Lord shall rejoice in his works.
He looketh on the earth, and it trembleth:
He toucheth the hills, and they smoke.
I will sing unto the Lord as long as I live:
I will sing praise to my God while I have my being.
My meditation of him shall be sweet:
I will be glad in the Lord.
Let the sinners be consumed out of the earth,
And let the wicked be no more.
Bless thou the Lord, O my soul.
Praise ye the Lord.

"I will lift up mine eyes unto the hills."

• PSALM 121 •

I will lift up mine eyes unto the hills,
From whence cometh my help.
My help cometh from the Lord,
Which made heaven and earth.
He will not suffer thy foot to be moved:

He that keepeth thee will not slumber.
Behold, he that keepeth Israel
Shall neither slumber nor sleep.
The Lord is thy keeper:
The Lord is thy shade upon thy right hand.
The sun shall not smite thee by day,
Nor the moon by night.
The Lord shall preserve thee from all evil:
He shall preserve thy soul.
The Lord shall preserve thy going out and thy coming in
From this time forth, and even for evermore.

"I was glad when they said unto me, Let us go into the house of the Lord."

• PSALM 122 •

I was glad when they said unto me,
Let us go into the house of the Lord.
Our feet shall stand
Within thy gates, O Jerusalem.
Jerusalem is builded as a city
That is compact together:
Whither the tribes go up, the tribes of the Lord,
Unto the testimony of Israel,
To give thanks unto the name of the Lord.
For there are set thrones of judgment,
The thrones of the house of David.
Pray for the peace of Jerusalem:
They shall prosper that love thee.
Peace be within thy walls,
And prosperity within thy palaces.
For my brethren and companions' sakes,
I will now say, Peace be within thee.

Because of the house of the Lord our God
I will seek thy good.

"Out of the depths have I cried unto thee, O Lord."

· PSALM 130 ·

Out of the depths have I cried unto thee, O Lord.
Lord, hear my voice:
Let thine ears be attentive
To the voice of my supplications.
If thou, Lord, shouldest mark iniquities,
O Lord, who shall stand?
But there is forgiveness with thee,
That thou mayest be feared.
I wait for the Lord, my soul doth wait,
And in his word do I hope.
My soul waiteth for the Lord
More than they that watch for the morning:
I say, more than they that watch for the morning.
Let Israel hope in the Lord:
For with the Lord there is mercy,
And with him is plentous redemption.
And he shall redeem Israel
From all his iniquities.

"By the rivers of Babylon."

· PSALM 137 ·

By the rivers of Babylon, there we sat down,
Yea, we wept, when we remembered Zion.
We hanged our harps upon the willows

In the midst thereof.
For there they that carried us away captive required of us a
      song;
And they that wasted us required of us mirth, saying,
Sing us one of the songs of Zion.
How shall we sing the Lord's song
In a strange land?
If I forget thee, O Jerusalem,
Let my right hand forget her cunning.
If I do not remember thee,
Let my tongue cleave to the roof of my mouth,
If I prefer not Jerusalem
Above my chief joy.
Remember, O Lord, the children of Edom
In the day of Jerusalem;
Who said, Rase it, rase it,
Even to the foundation thereof.
O daughter of Babylon, who art to be destroyed;
Happy shall he be, that rewardeth thee as thou hast served us.
Happy shall he be, that taketh and dasheth thy little ones
Against the stones.

"O Lord, thou hast searched me, and known me."

• PSALM 139 •

O Lord, thou hast searched me, and known me.
Thou knowest my downsitting and mine uprising,
Thou understandest my thought afar off.
Thou compassest my path and my lying down,
And art acquainted with all my ways.
For there is not a word in my tongue,
But, lo, O Lord, thou knowest it altogether.
Thou hast beset me behind and before,

And laid thine hand upon me.
Such knowledge is too wonderful for me;
It is high, I cannot attain unto it.
Whither shall I go from thy spirit?
Or whither shall I flee from thy presence?
If I ascend up into heaven, thou art there:
If I make my bed in hell, behold, thou art there.
If I take the wings of the morning,
And dwell in the uttermost parts of the sea;
Even there shall thy hand lead me,
And thy right hand shall hold me.
If I say, Surely the darkness shall cover me;
Even the night shall be light about me.
Yea, the darkness hideth not from thee;
But the night shineth as the day:
The darkness and the light are both alike to thee.
For thou hast possessed my reins:
Thou hast covered me in my mother's womb.
I will praise thee; for I am fearfully and wonderfully made:
Marvellous are thy works; and that my soul knoweth right well.
My substance was not hid from thee, when I was made in secret,
And curiously wrought in the lowest parts of the earth.
Thine eye did see my substance, yet being unperfect;
And in thy book all my members were written,
Which in continuance were fashioned,
When as yet there was none of them.
How precious also are thy thoughts unto me, O God!
How great is the sum of them!
If I should count them, they are more in number than the sand:
When I awake, I am still with thee.
Surely thou wilt slay the wicked, O God:
Depart from me therefore, ye bloody men.
For they speak against thee wickedly,
And thine enemies take thy name in vain.
Do not I hate them, O Lord, that hate thee?

And am not I grieved with those that rise up against thee?
I hate them with perfect hatred:
I count them mine enemies.
Search me, O God, and know my heart:
Try me, and know my thoughts:
And see if there be any wicked way in me,
And lead me in the way everlasting.

"I will extol thee, my God, O king."

• PSALM 145 •

I will extol thee, my God, O king;
And I will bless thy name for ever and ever.
Every day will I bless thee;
And I will praise thy name for ever and ever.
Great is the Lord, and greatly to be praised;
And his greatness is unsearchable.
One generation shall praise thy works to another,
And shall declare thy mighty acts.
I will speak of the glorious honour of thy majesty,
And of thy wondrous works.
And men shall speak of the might of thy terrible acts:
And I will declare thy greatness.
They shall abundantly utter the memory of thy great goodness,
And shall sing of thy righteousness.
The Lord is gracious, and full of compassion;
Slow to anger, and of great mercy.
The Lord is good to all:
And his tender mercies are over all his works.
All thy works shall praise thee, O Lord;
And thy saints shall bless thee.
They shall speak of the glory of thy kingdom,
And talk of thy power;

To make known to the sons of men his mighty acts,
And the glorious majesty of his kingdom.
Thy kingdom is an everlasting kingdom,
And thy dominion endureth throughout all generations.
The Lord upholdeth all that fall,
And raiseth up all those that be bowed down.
The eyes of all wait upon thee;
And thou givest them their meat in due season.
Thou openest thine hand,
And satisfiest the desire of every living thing.
The Lord is righteous in all his ways,
And holy in all his works.
The Lord is nigh unto all them that call upon him,
To all that call upon him in truth.
He will fulfil the desire of them that fear him:
He also will hear their cry, and will save them.
The Lord preserveth all them that love him:
But all the wicked will he destroy.
My mouth shall speak the praise of the Lord:
And let all flesh bless his holy name for ever and ever.

"Praise ye the Lord. Praise God in his sanctuary."

• PSALM 150 •

Praise ye the Lord. Praise God in his sanctuary:
Praise him in the firmament of his power.
Praise him for his mighty acts:
Praise him according to his excellent greatness.
Praise him with the sound of the trumpet:
Praise him with the psaltery and harp.
Praise him with the timbrel and dance:
Praise him with stringed instruments and organs.

Praise him upon the loud cymbals:
Praise him upon the high sounding cymbals.
Let every thing that hath breath praise the Lord.
Praise ye the Lord.

From THE SONG OF SOLOMON

The Maiden's Description of Her Lover

• SONG OF SOLOMON 2: 3–17 •

As the apple tree among the trees of the wood,
So is my beloved among the sons.
I sat down under his shadow with great delight,
And his fruit was sweet to my taste.
He brought me to the banqueting house,
And his banner over me was love.
Stay me with flagons, comfort me with apples:
For I am sick of love.
His left hand is under my head,
And his right hand doth embrace me.
I charge you, O ye daughters of Jerusalem,
By the roes, and by the hinds of the field,
That ye stir not up, nor awake my love,
Till he please.
The voice of my beloved: behold, he cometh
Leaping upon the mountains,
Skipping upon the hills.
My beloved is like a roe or a young hart:
Behold, he standeth behind our wall,

He looketh forth at the windows,
Shewing himself through the lattice.
My beloved spake, and said unto me,
Rise up, my love, my fair one, and come away.
For, lo, the winter is past,
The rain is over and gone;
The flowers appear on the earth;
The time of the singing of birds is come,
And the voice of the turtle is heard in our land;
The fig tree putteth forth her green figs,
And the vines with the tender grape
Give a good smell.
Arise, my love, my fair one, and come away.
O my dove, that art in the clefts of the rock,
In the secret places of the stairs,
Let me see thy countenance,
Let me hear thy voice;
For sweet is thy voice, and thy countenance is comely.
Take us the foxes, the little foxes,
That spoil the vines:
For our vines have tender grapes.
My beloved is mine, and I am his:
He feedeth among the lilies.
Until the day break, and the shadows flee away,
Turn, my beloved, and be thou a roe or a young hart
Upon the mountains of Bether.

The King's Description of His Beloved

· SONG OF SOLOMON 4: 1–7 ·

Behold, thou art fair, my love; behold, thou art fair;
Thou hast doves' eyes within thy locks:
Thy hair is as a flock of goats,

That appear from mount Gilead.
Thy teeth are like a flock of sheep that are even shorn,
Which came up from the washing;
Whereof every one bear twins,
And none is barren among them.
Thy lips are like a thread of scarlet,
And thy speech is comely:
Thy temples are like a piece of a pomegranate
Within thy locks.
Thy neck is like the tower of David
Builded for an armoury,
Whereon there hang a thousand bucklers,
All shields of mighty men.
Thy two breasts are like two young roes that are twins,
Which feed among the lilies.
Until the day break, and the shadows flee away,
I will get me to the mountain of myrrh,
And to the hill of frankincense.
Thou art all fair, my love;
There is no spot in thee.

The Rewards of Wisdom

• PROVERBS 3: 13–26 •

Happy is the man that findeth wisdom,
And the man that getteth understanding.
For the merchandise of it is better than the merchandise of
  silver,
And the gain thereof than fine gold.
She is more precious than rubies:
And all the things thou canst desire are not to be compared unto
  her.
Length of days is in her right hand;
And in her left hand riches and honour.
Her ways are ways of pleasantness,
And all her paths are peace.
She is a tree of life to them that lay hold upon her:
And happy is every one that retaineth her.
The Lord by wisdom hath founded the earth;
By understanding hath he established the heavens.
By his knowledge the depths are broken up,
And the clouds drop down the dew.
My son, let not them depart from thine eyes:
Keep sound wisdom and discretion:
So shall they be life unto thy soul,
And grace to thy neck.
Then shalt thou walk in thy way safely,
And thy foot shall not stumble.
When thou liest down, thou shalt not be afraid:

Yea, thou shalt lie down, and thy sleep shall be sweet.
Be not afraid of sudden fear,
Neither of the desolation of the wicked, when it cometh.
For the Lord shall be thy confidence,
And shall keep thy foot from being taken.

The Call of Wisdom

• PROVERBS 8 •

Doth not wisdom cry?
And understanding put forth her voice?
She standeth in the top of high places,
By the way in the places of the paths.
She crieth at the gates, at the entry of the city,
At the coming in at the doors.
Unto you, O men, I call;
And my voice is to the sons of man.
O ye simple, understand wisdom:
And, ye fools, be ye of an understanding heart.
Hear; for I will speak of excellent things;
And the opening of my lips shall be right things.
For my mouth shall speak truth;
And wickedness is an abomination to my lips.
All the words of my mouth are in righteousness;
There is nothing froward or perverse in them.
They are all plain to him that understandeth,
And right to them that find knowledge.
Receive my instruction, and not silver;
And knowledge rather than choice gold.
For wisdom is better than rubies;
And all the things that may be desired are not to be compared
    to it.
I wisdom dwell with prudence,

And find out knowledge of witty inventions.
The fear of the Lord is to hate evil:
Pride, and arrogancy, and the evil way,
And the froward mouth, do I hate.
Counsel is mine, and sound wisdom:
I am understanding; I have strength.
By me kings reign,
And princes decree justice.
By me princes rule,
And nobles, even all the judges of the earth.
I love them that love me;
And those that seek me early shall find me.
Riches and honour are with me;
Yea, durable riches and righteousness.
My fruit is better than gold,
Yea, than fine gold;
And my revenue than choice silver.
I lead in the way of righteousness,
In the midst of the paths of judgment:
That I may cause those that love me to inherit substance;
And I will fill their treasures.
The Lord possessed me in the beginning of his way,
Before his works of old.
I was set up from everlasting, from the beginning,
Or ever the earth was.
When there were no depths, I was brought forth;
When there were no fountains abounding with water.
Before the mountains were settled,
Before the hills was I brought forth:
While as yet he had not made the earth, nor the fields,
Nor the highest part of the dust of the world.
When he prepared the heavens, I was there:
When he set a compass upon the face of the depth:
When he established the clouds above:
When he strengthened the fountains of the deep:

When he gave to the sea his decree,
That the waters should not pass his commandment:
When he appointed the foundations of the earth:
Then I was by him, as one brought up with him:
And I was daily his delight,
Rejoicing always before him;
Rejoicing in the habitable part of his earth;
And my delights were with the sons of men.
Now therefore hearken unto me, O ye children:
For blessed are they that keep my ways.
Hear instruction, and be wise,
And refuse it not.
Blessed is the man that heareth me,
Watching daily at my gates,
Waiting at the posts of my doors.
For whoso findeth me findeth life,
And shall obtain favour of the Lord.
But he that sinneth against me wrongeth his own soul:
All they that hate me love death.

The Strange Woman

• PROVERBS 7 •

My son, keep my words,
And lay up my commandments with thee.
Keep my commandments, and live;
And my law as the apple of thine eye.
Bind them upon thy fingers,
Write them upon the table of thine heart.
Say unto wisdom, Thou art my sister;
And call understanding thy kinswoman:
That they may keep thee from the strange woman,
From the stranger which flattereth with her words.

For at the window of my house
I looked through my casement,
And beheld among the simple ones,
I discerned among the youths,
A young man void of understanding,
Passing through the street near her corner;
And he went the way to her house,
In the twilight, in the evening,
In the black and dark night:
And, behold, there met him a woman
With the attire of an harlot, and subtil of heart.
(She is loud and stubborn;
Her feet abide not in her house:
Now is she without, now in the streets,
And lieth in wait at every corner.)
So she caught him, and kissed him,
And with an impudent face said unto him,
I have peace offerings with me;
This day have I payed my vows.
Therefore came I forth to meet thee,
Diligently to seek thy face, and I have found thee.
I have decked my bed with coverings of tapestry,
With carved works, with fine linen of Egypt.
I have perfumed my bed
With myrrh, aloes, and cinnamon.
Come, let us take our fill of love until the morning:
Let us solace ourselves with loves.
For the goodman is not at home,
He is gone a long journey:
He hath taken a bag of money with him,
And will come home at the day appointed.
With her much fair speech she caused him to yield,
With the flattering of her lips she forced him.
He goeth after her straightway,
As an ox goeth to the slaughter,

Or as a fool to the correction of the stocks;
Till a dart strike through his liver;
As a bird hasteth to the snare,
And knoweth not that it is for his life.
Hearken unto me now therefore, O ye children,
And attend to the words of my mouth.
Let not thine heart decline to her ways,
Go not astray in her paths.
For she hath cast down many wounded:
Yea, many strong men have been slain by her.
Her house is the way to hell,
Going down to the chambers of death.

The Worthy Woman

• PROVERBS 31:10–31 •

Who can find a virtuous woman?
For her price is far above rubies.
The heart of her husband doth safely trust in her,
So that he shall have no need of spoil.
She will do him good and not evil
All the days of her life.
She seeketh wool, and flax,
And worketh willingly with her hands.
She is like the merchants' ships;
She bringeth her food from afar.
She riseth also while it is yet night,
And giveth meat to her household,
And a portion to her maidens.
She considereth a field, and buyeth it:
With the fruit of her hands she planteth a vineyard.
She girdeth her loins with strength,
And strengtheneth her arms.

The Worthy Woman

She perceiveth that her merchandise is good:
Her candle goeth not out by night.
She layeth her hands to the spindle,
And her hands hold the distaff.
She stretcheth out her hand to the poor;
Yea, she reacheth forth her hands to the needy.
She is not afraid of the snow for her household:
For all her household are clothed with scarlet.
She maketh herself coverings of tapestry;
Her clothing is silk and purple.
Her husband is known in the gates,
When he sitteth among the elders of the land.
She maketh fine linen, and selleth it;
And delivereth girdles unto the merchant.
Strength and honour are her clothing;
And she shall rejoice in time to come.
She openeth her mouth with wisdom;
And in her tongue is the law of kindness.
She looketh well to the ways of her household,
And eateth not the bread of idleness.
Her children arise up, and call her blessed;
Her husband also, and he praiseth her.
Many daughters have done virtuously,
But thou excellest them all.
Favour is deceitful, and beauty is vain:
But a woman that feareth the Lord, she shall be praised.
Give her of the fruit of her hands;
And let her own works praise her in the gates.

The Vanity of Things

• ECCLESIASTES 1 •

The words of the Preacher, the son of David, king in Jerusalem.

Vanity of vanities, saith the Preacher, vanity of vanities; all is vanity. What profit hath a man of all his labour which he taketh under the sun? One generation passeth away, and another generation cometh: but the earth abideth for ever. The sun also ariseth, and the sun goeth down, and hasteth to his place where he arose. The wind goeth toward the south, and turneth about unto the north; it whirleth about continually, and the wind returneth again according to his circuits. All the rivers run into the sea; yet the sea is not full; unto the place from whence the rivers come, thither they return again. All things are full of labour; man cannot utter it: the eye is not satisfied with seeing, nor the ear filled with hearing. The thing that hath been, it is that which shall be; and that which is done is that which shall be done: and there is no new thing under the sun. Is there any thing whereof it may be said, "See, this is new"? It hath been already of old time, which was before us. There is no remembrance of former things; neither shall there be any remembrance of things that are to come with those that shall come after.

I the Preacher was king over Israel in Jerusalem. And I gave my heart to seek and search out by wisdom concerning all things that are done under heaven: this sore travail hath God given to the sons of man to be exercised therewith. I have seen all the works that are done under the sun; and, behold, all is vanity and vexation of spirit. That which is crooked cannot be made straight: and that which is wanting cannot be numbered. I communed with mine own heart, saying, "Lo, I am come to great estate, and have gotten more wisdom than all they that have been before me in Jerusalem": yea, my heart had great experience of wisdom and knowledge. And I gave my heart to know wisdom, and to know madness and folly: I perceived that this also is vexation of spirit. For in much wisdom is much grief: and he that increaseth knowledge increaseth sorrow.

Of Times and Seasons

• ECCLESIASTES 3: 1–15 •

To every thing there is a season, and a time to every purpose under the heaven: a time to be born, and a time to die; a time to plant, and a time to pluck up that which is planted: a time to kill, and a time to heal; a time to break down, and a time to build up; a time to weep, and a time to laugh; a time to mourn, and a time to dance; a time to cast away stones, and a time to gather stones together; a time to embrace, and a time to refrain from embracing; a time to get, and a time to lose; a time to keep, and a time to cast away; a time to rend, and a time to sew; a time to keep silence, and a time to speak; a time to love, and a time to hate; a time of war, and a time of peace.

What profit hath he that worketh in that wherein he laboureth? I have seen the travail, which God hath given to the sons of men to be exercised in it. He hath made every thing beautiful in his time: also he hath set the world in their heart, so that no man can find out the work that God maketh from the beginning to the end. I know that there is no good in them, but for a man to rejoice, and to do good in his life. And also that every man should eat and drink, and enjoy the good of all his labour, it is the gift of God. I know that, whatsoever God doeth, it shall be for ever: nothing can be put to it, nor any thing taken from it: and God doeth it, that men should fear before him. That which hath been is now; and that which is to be hath already been; and God requireth that which is past.

"Remember now thy Creator"

• ECCLESIASTES 12:1–7 •

Remember now thy Creator in the days of thy youth, while the evil days come not, nor the years draw nigh, when thou shalt say, I have no pleasure in them; while the sun, or the light, or the moon, or the stars, be not darkened, nor the clouds return after the rain: in the day when the keepers of the house shall tremble, and the strong men shall bow themselves, and the grinders cease because they are few, and those that look out of the windows be darkened, and the doors shall be shut in the streets, when the sound of the grinding is low, and he shall rise up at the voice of the bird, and all the daughters of music shall be brought low; also when they shall be afraid of that which is high, and fears shall be in the way, and the almond tree shall flourish, and the grasshopper shall be a burden, and desire shall fail: because man goeth to his long home, and the mourners go about the streets; or ever the silver cord be loosed, or the golden bowl be broken, or the pitcher be broken at the fountain, or the wheel broken at the cistern. Then shall the dust return to the earth as it was: and the spirit shall return unto God who gave it.

The Prologue

• JOB 1 AND 2 •

There was a man in the land of Uz,[1] whose name was Job; and that man was perfect and upright, and one that feared God, and eschewed evil. And there were born unto him seven sons and three daughters. His substance also was seven thousand sheep, and three thousand camels, and five hundred yoke of oxen, and five hundred she asses, and a very great household; so that this man was the greatest of all the men of the east. And his sons went and feasted in their houses, every one his day; and sent and called for their three sisters to eat and to drink with them. And it was so, when the days of their feasting were gone about, that Job sent and sanctified them, and rose up early in the morning, and offered burnt offerings according to the number of them all: for Job said, "It may be that my sons have sinned, and cursed God in their hearts." Thus did Job continually.

Now there was a day when the sons of God came to present themselves before the LORD, and Satan came also among them. And the LORD said unto Satan, "Whence comest thou?"

Then Satan answered the LORD, and said, "From going to and fro in the earth, and from walking up and down in it."

And the LORD said unto Satan, "Hast thou considered my servant Job, that there is none like him in the earth, a perfect and an upright man, one that feareth God, and escheweth evil?"

[1] Location unknown. It was probably to the east of Palestine, near the Arabian desert.

Then Satan answered the LORD, and said, "Doth Job fear God for nought? Hast not thou made an hedge about him, and about his house, and about all that he hath on every side? thou hast blessed the work of his hands, and his substance is increased in the land. But put forth thine hand now, and touch all that he hath, and he will curse thee to thy face."

And the LORD said unto Satan, "Behold, all that he hath is in thy power; only upon himself put not forth thine hand." So Satan went forth from the presence of the LORD.

And there was a day when his sons and his daughters were eating and drinking wine in their eldest brother's house: and there came a messenger unto Job, and said, "The oxen were plowing, and the asses feeding beside them: and the Sabeans fell upon them, and took them away; yea, they have slain the servants with the edge of the sword; and I only am escaped alone to tell thee."

While he was yet speaking, there came also another, and said, "The fire of God is fallen from heaven, and hath burned up the sheep, and the servants, and consumed them; and I only am escaped alone to tell thee."

While he was yet speaking, there came also another, and said, "The Chaldeans made out three bands, and fell upon the camels, and have carried them away, yea, and slain the servants with the edge of the sword; and I only am escaped alone to tell thee."

While he was yet speaking, there came also another, and said, "Thy sons and thy daughters were eating and drinking wine in their eldest brother's house: and, behold, there came a great wind from the wilderness, and smote the four corners of the house, and it fell upon the young men, and they are dead and I only am escaped alone to tell thee."

Then Job arose, and rent his mantle, and shaved his head, and fell down upon the ground, and worshipped, and said, "Naked came I out of my mother's womb and naked shall I return thither: the LORD gave, and the LORD hath taken away;

blessed be the name of the LORD." In all this Job sinned not, nor charged God foolishly.

Again there was a day when the sons of God came to present themselves before the LORD, and Satan came also among them to present himself before the LORD. And the LORD said unto Satan, "From whence comest thou?"

And Satan answered the LORD, and said, "From going to and fro in the earth, and from walking up and down in it."

And the LORD said unto Satan, "Hast thou considered my servant Job, that there is none like him in the earth, a perfect and an upright man, one that feareth God, and escheweth evil? and still he holdeth fast his integrity, although thou movedst me against him, to destroy him without cause."

And Satan answered the LORD, and said, "Skin for skin, yea, all that a man hath will he give for his life. But put forth thine hand now, and touch his bone and his flesh, and he will curse thee to thy face."

And the LORD said unto Satan, "Behold, he is in thine hand; but save his life."

So went Satan forth from the presence of the LORD, and smote Job with sore boils from the sole of his foot unto his crown. And he took him a potsherd to scrape himself withal; and he sat down among the ashes.

Then said his wife unto him, "Dost thou still retain thine integrity? curse God, and die."

But he said unto her, "Thou speakest as one of the foolish women speaketh. What? shall we receive good at the hand of God, and shall we not receive evil?" In all this did not Job sin with his lips.

Now when Job's three friends heard of all this evil that was come upon him, they came every one from his own place; Eliphaz the Temanite, and Bildad the Shuhite, and Zophar the Naamathite: for they had made an appointment together to come to mourn with him and to comfort him. And when they lifted up their eyes afar off, and knew him not, they lifted up their voice, and wept; and they rent every one his mantle, and sprinkled dust upon their heads toward heaven. So they sat down with him upon the ground seven days and seven nights, and none spake a word unto him: for they saw that his grief was very great.

Job's First Lament

• JOB 3 •

After this opened Job his mouth, and cursed his day. And Job
      spake, and said,
"Let the day perish wherein I was born,
And the night in which it was said, There is a man child
      conceived.
Let that day be darkness;
Let not God regard it from above,
Neither let the light shine upon it.
Let darkness and the shadow of death stain it;
Let a cloud dwell upon it;
Let the blackness of the day terrify it.
As for that night, let darkness seize upon it;
Let it not be joined unto the days of the year,
Let it not come into the number of the months.
Lo, let that night be solitary,
Let no joyful voice come therein.
Let them curse it that curse the day,
Who are ready to raise up their mourning.
Let the stars of the twilight thereof be dark;
Let it look for light, but have none;
Neither let it see the dawning of the day:
Because it shut not up the doors of my mother's womb,
Nor hid sorrow from mine eyes.
Why died I not from the womb?

Why did I not give up the ghost when I came out of the belly?
Why did the knees prevent me?
Or why the breasts that I should suck?
For now should I have lain still and been quiet,
I should have slept: then had I been at rest,
With kings and counsellors of the earth,
Which built desolate places for themselves;
Or with princes that had gold,
Who filled their houses with silver:
Or as an hidden untimely birth I had not been;
As infants which never saw light.
There the wicked cease from troubling;
And there the weary be at rest.
There the prisoners rest together;
They hear not the voice of the oppressor.
The small and great are there;
And the servant is free from his master.
Wherefore is light given to him that is in misery,
And life unto the bitter in soul;
Which long for death, but it cometh not;
And dig for it more than for hid treasures;
Which rejoice exceedingly,
And are glad, when they can find the grave?
Why is light given to a man whose way is hid,
And whom God hath hedged in?
For my sighing cometh before I eat,
And my roarings are poured out like the waters.
For the thing which I greatly feared is come upon me,
And that which I was afraid of is come unto me.
I was not in safety, neither had I rest,
Neither was I quiet; yet trouble came."

Bildad and Job

Then answered Bildad the Shuhite, and said, "How long wilt
    thou speak these things?
And how long shall the words of thy mouth be like a strong
    wind?
Doth God pervert judgment?
Or doth the Almighty pervert justice?
If thy children have sinned against him,
And he have cast them away for their transgression;
If thou wouldest seek unto God betimes,
And make thy supplication to the Almighty;
If thou wert pure and upright;
Surely now he would awake for thee,
And make the habitation of thy righteousness prosperous.
Though thy beginning was small,
Yet thy latter end should greatly increase.
For enquire, I pray thee, of the former age,
And prepare thyself to the search of their fathers:
(For we are but of yesterday, and know nothing,
Because our days upon earth are a shadow:)
Shall not they teach thee, and tell thee,
And utter words out of their heart?
Can the rush grow up without mire?
Can the flag grow without water?
Whilst it is yet in his greenness, and not cut down,
It withereth before any other herb.
So are the paths of all that forget God;
And the hypocrite's hope shall perish:
Whose hope shall be cut off,
And whose trust shall be a spider's web.
He shall lean upon his house, but it shall not stand:
He shall hold it fast, but it shall not endure.

He is green before the sun,
And his branch shooteth forth in his garden.
His roots are wrapped about the heap,
And seeth the place of stones.
If he destroy him from his place,
Then it shall deny him, saying, I have not seen thee.
Behold, this is the joy of his way,
And out of the earth shall others grow.
Behold God will not cast away a perfect man,
Neither will he help the evil doers:
Till he fill thy mouth with laughing,
And thy lips with rejoicing.
They that hate thee shall be clothed with shame;
And the dwelling place of the wicked shall come to nought."

Then Job answered and said,
"I know it is so of a truth:
But how should man be just with God?
If he will contend with him,
He cannot answer him one of a thousand.
He is wise in heart, and mighty in strength:
Who hath hardened himself against him, and hath prospered?
Which removeth the mountains, and they know not:
Which overturneth them in his anger.
Which shaketh the earth out of her place,
And the pillars thereof tremble.
Which commandeth the sun, and it riseth not;
And sealeth up the stars.
Which alone spreadeth out the heavens,
And treadeth upon the waves of the sea.
Which maketh Arcturus, Orion, and Pleiades,
And the chambers of the south.
Which doeth great things past finding out;
Yea, and wonders without number.
Lo, he goeth by me, and I see him not:

He passeth on also, but I perceive him not.
Behold, he taketh away, who can hinder him?
Who will say unto him, What doest thou?
If God will not withdraw his anger,
The proud helpers do stoop under him.
How much less shall I answer him,
And choose out my words to reason with him?
Whom, though I were righteous, yet would I not answer,
But I would make supplication to my judge.
If I had called, and he had answered me;
Yet would I not believe that he had hearkened unto my voice.
For he breaketh me with a tempest,
And multiplieth my wounds without cause.
He will not suffer me to take my breath,
But filleth me with bitterness.
If I speak of strength, lo, he is strong:
And if of judgment, who shall set me a time to plead?
If I justify myself, mine own mouth shall condemn me:
If I say, I am perfect, it shall also prove me perverse.
Though I were perfect, yet would I not know my soul:
I would despise my life.
This is one thing, therefore I said it,
He destroyeth the perfect and the wicked.
If the scourge slay suddenly,
He will laugh at the trial of the innocent.
The earth is given into the hand of the wicked:
He covereth the faces of the judges thereof;
If not, where, and who is he?
Now my days are swifter than a post:
They flee away, they see no good.
They are passed away as the swift ships:
As the eagle that hasteth to the prey.
If I say, I will forget my complaint,
I will leave off my heaviness, and comfort myself:
I am afraid of all my sorrows.

I know that thou wilt not hold me innocent.
If I be wicked,
Why then labour I in vain?
If I wash myself with snow water,
And make my hands never so clean;
Yet shalt thou plunge me in the ditch,
And mine own clothes shall abhor me.
For he is not a man, as I am, that I should answer him,
And we should come together in judgment.
Neither is there any daysman betwixt us,
That might lay his hand upon us both.
Let him take his rod away from me,
And let not his fear terrify me:
Then would I speak, and not fear him;
But it is not so with me.

My soul is weary of my life;
I will leave my complaint upon myself;
I will speak in the bitterness of my soul.
I will say unto God, Do not condemn me;
Shew me wherefore thou contendest with me.
Is it good unto thee that thou shouldest oppress,
That thou shouldest despise the work of thine hands,
And shine upon the counsel of the wicked?
Hast thou eyes of flesh?
Or seest thou as man seeth?
Are thy days as the days of men?
Are thy years as man's days,
That thou enquirest after mine iniquity,
And searchest after my sin?
Thou knowest that I am not wicked;
And there is none that can deliver out of thine hand.
Thine hands have made me and fashioned me
Together round about; yet thou dost destroy me.
Remember, I beseech thee, that thou hast made me as the clay;

And wilt thou bring me into dust again?
Hast thou not poured me out as milk,
And curdled me like cheese?
Thou hast clothed me with skin and flesh,
And hast fenced me with bones and sinews.
Thou hast granted me life and favour,
And thy visitation hath preserved my spirit.
And these things hast thou hid in thine heart:
I know that this is with thee.
If I sin, then thou markest me,
And thou wilt not acquit me from mine iniquity.
If I be wicked, woe unto me;
And if I be righteous, yet will I not lift up my head.
I am full of confusion;
Therefore see thou mine affliction;
For it increaseth. Thou huntest me as a fierce lion:
And again thou shewest thyself marvellous upon me.
Thou renewest thy witnesses against me,
And increasest thine indignation upon me;
Changes and war are against me.
Wherefore then hast thou brought me forth out of the womb?
Oh that I had given up the ghost, and no eye had seen me!
I should have been as though I had not been;
I should have been carried from the womb to the grave.
Are not my days few? Cease then,
And let me alone, that I may take comfort a little,
Before I go whence I shall not return,
Even to the land of darkness and the shadow of death;
A land of darkness, as darkness itself;
And of the shadow of death, without any order,
And where the light is as darkness."

Job on Man's Frailty

Man that is born of a woman
Is of few days, and full of trouble.
He cometh forth like a flower, and is cut down:
He fleeth also as a shadow, and continueth not.
And dost thou open thine eyes upon such an one,
And bringest me into judgment with thee?
Who can bring a clean thing out of an unclean? not one.
Seeing his days are determined,
The number of his months are with thee,
Thou hast appointed his bounds that he cannot pass;
Turn from him, that he may rest,
Till he shall accomplish, as an hireling, his day.
For there is hope of a tree,
If it be cut down, that it will sprout again,
And that the tender branch thereof will not cease.
Though the root thereof wax old in the earth,
And the stock thereof die in the ground;
Yet through the scent of water it will bud,
And bring forth boughs like a plant.
But man dieth, and wasteth away:
Yea, man giveth up the ghost, and where is he?
As the waters fail from the sea,
And the flood decayeth and drieth up:
So man lieth down, and riseth not:
Till the heavens be no more, they shall not awake,
Nor be raised out of their sleep.
O that thou wouldest hide me in the grave,
That thou wouldest keep me secret, until thy wrath be past,
That thou wouldest appoint me a set time, and remember me!
If a man die, shall he live again?
All the days of my appointed time will I wait,

Till my change come.
Thou shalt call, and I will answer thee:
Thou wilt have a desire to the work of thine hands.
For now thou numberest my steps:
Dost thou not watch over my sin?
My transgression is sealed up in a bag,
And thou sewest up mine iniquity.
And surely the mountain falling cometh to nought,
And the rock is removed out of his place.
The waters wear the stones:
Thou washest away the things which grow out of the dust of the
    earth;
And thou destroyest the hope of man.
Thou prevailest for ever against him, and he passeth:
Thou changest his countenance, and sendest him away.
His sons come to honour, and he knoweth it not;
And they are brought low, but he perceiveth it not of them.
But his flesh upon him shall have pain,
And his soul within him shall mourn.

God Speaks to Job out of the Whirlwind

• JOB 38, 39, 42: 1–6 •

Then the Lord answered Job out of the whirlwind, and said,
"Who is this that darkeneth counsel
By words without knowledge?
Gird up now thy loins like a man;
For I will demand of thee, and answer thou me.
Where wast thou when I laid the foundations of the earth?
Declare, if thou hast understanding.
Who hath laid the measures thereof, if thou knowest?
Or who hath stretched the line upon it?
Whereupon are the foundations thereof fastened?

Or who laid the corner stone thereof;
When the morning stars sang together,
And all the sons of God shouted for joy?
Or who shut up the sea with doors,
When it brake forth, as if it had issued out of the womb?
When I made the cloud the garment thereof,
And thick darkness a swaddlingband for it,
And brake up for it my decreed place,
And set bars and doors,
And said, Hitherto shalt thou come, but no further:
And here shall thy proud waves be stayed?
Hast thou commanded the morning since thy days;
And caused the dayspring to know his place;
That it might take hold of the ends of the earth,
That the wicked might be shaken out of it?
It is turned as clay to the seal;
And they stand as a garment.
And from the wicked their light is withholden,
And the high arm shall be broken.
Hast thou entered into the springs of the sea?
Or hast thou walked in the search of the depth?
Have the gates of death been opened unto thee?
Or hast thou seen the doors of the shadow of death?
Hast thou perceived the breadth of the earth?
Declare if thou knowest it all.
Where is the way where light dwelleth?
And as for darkness, where is the place thereof,
That thou shouldest take it to the bound thereof,
And that thou shouldest know the paths to the house thereof?
Knowest thou it, because thou wast then born?
Or because the number of thy days is great?
Hast thou entered into the treasures of the snow?
Or hast thou seen the treasures of the hail,
Which I have reserved against the time of trouble,
Against the day of battle and war?

By what way is the light parted,
Which scattereth the east wind upon the earth?
Who hath divided a watercourse for the overflowing of waters,
Or a way for the lightning of thunder;
To cause it to rain on the earth, where no man is;
On the wilderness, wherein there is no man;
To satisfy the desolate and waste ground;
And to cause the bud of the tender herb to spring forth?
Hath the rain a father?
Or who hath begotten the drops of dew?
Out of whose womb came the ice?
And the hoary frost of heaven, who hath gendered it?
The waters are hid as with a stone,
And the face of the deep is frozen.
Canst thou bind the sweet influences of Pleiades,
Or loose the bands of Orion?
Canst thou bring forth Mazzaroth in his season?
Or canst thou guide Arcturus with his sons?
Knowest thou the ordinances of heaven?
Canst thou set the dominion thereof in the earth?
Canst thou lift up thy voice to the clouds,
That abundance of waters may cover thee?
Canst thou send lightnings, that they may go,
And say unto thee, Here we are?
Who hath put wisdom in the inward parts?
Or who hath given understanding to the heart?
Who can number the clouds in wisdom?
Or who can stay the bottles of heaven,
When the dust groweth into hardness,
And the clods cleave fast together?
Wilt thou hunt the prey for the lion?
Or fill the appetite of the young lions,
When they couch in their dens,
And abide in the covert to lie in wait?
Who provideth for the raven his food?

When his young ones cry unto God,
They wander for lack of meat.

Knowest thou the time when the wild goats of the rock bring
      forth?
Or canst thou mark when the hinds do calve?
Canst thou number the months that they fulfil?
Or knowest thou the time when they bring forth?
They bow themselves, they bring forth their young ones,
They cast out their sorrows.
Their young ones are in good liking, they grow up with corn;
They go forth, and return not unto them.
Who hath sent out the wild ass free?
Or who hath loosed the bands of the wild ass?
Whose house I have made the wilderness,
And the barren land his dwellings.
He scorneth the multitude of the city,
Neither regardeth he the crying of the driver.
The range of the mountains is his pasture,
And he searcheth after every green thing.
Will the unicorn be willing to serve thee,
Or abide by thy crib?
Canst thou bind the unicorn with his band in the furrow?
Or will he harrow the valleys after thee?
Wilt thou trust him, because his strength is great?
Or wilt thou leave thy labour to him?
Wilt thou believe him, that he will bring home thy seed,
And gather it into thy barn?
Gavest thou the goodly wings unto the peacocks?
Or wings and feathers unto the ostrich?
Which leaveth her eggs in the earth,
And warmeth them in dust,
And forgetteth that the foot may crush them,
Or that the wild beast may break them.

She is hardened against her young ones, as though they were not
     hers:
Her labour is in vain without fear;
Because God hath deprived her of wisdom,
Neither hath he imparted to her understanding.
What time she lifteth up herself on high,
She scorneth the horse and his rider.
Hast thou given the horse strength?
Hast thou clothed his neck with thunder?
Canst thou make him afraid as a grasshopper?
The glory of his nostrils is terrible.
He paweth in the valley, and rejoiceth in his strength:
He goeth on to meet the armed men.
He mocketh at fear, and is not affrighted;
Neither turneth he back from the sword.
The quiver rattleth against him,
The glittering spear and the shield.
He swalloweth the ground with fierceness and rage:
Neither believeth he that it is the sound of the trumpet.
He saith among the trumpets, Ha, ha;
And he smelleth the battle afar off,
The thunder of the captains, and the shouting.
Doth the hawk fly by thy wisdom,
And stretch her wings toward the south?
Doth the eagle mount up at thy command,
And make her nest on high?
She dwelleth and abideth on the rock,
Upon the crag of the rock, and the strong place.
From thence she seeketh the prey,
And her eyes behold afar off.
Her young ones also suck up blood:
And where the slain are, there is she."

Then Job answered the Lord and said, "I know that thou canst
     do every thing,

And that no thought can be withholden from thee.
Who is he that hideth counsel without knowledge?
Therefore have I uttered that I understood not;
Things too wonderful for me, which I knew not.
Hear, I beseech thee, and I will speak:
I will demand of thee, and declare thou unto me.
I have heard of thee by the hearing of the ear:
But now mine eye seeth thee.
Wherefore I abhor myself,
And repent in dust and ashes."

The Epilogue

• JOB 42:7–17 •

And it was so, that after the LORD had spoken these words unto Job, the LORD said to Eliphaz the Temanite, "My wrath is kindled against thee, and against thy two friends: for ye have not spoken of me the thing that is right, as my servant Job hath. Therefore take unto you now seven bullocks and seven rams, and go to my servant Job, and offer up for yourselves a burnt offering; and my servant Job shall pray for you: for him will I accept: lest I deal with you after your folly, in that ye have not spoken of me the thing which is right, like my servant Job."

So Eliphaz the Temanite and Bildad the Shuhite and Zophar the Naamathite went, and did according as the LORD commanded them: the LORD also accepted Job.

And the LORD turned the captivity of Job, when he prayed for his friends: also the LORD gave Job twice as much as he had before. Then came there unto him all his brethren, and all his sisters, and all they that had been of his acquaintance before, and did eat bread with him in his house: and they bemoaned him, and comforted him over all the evil that the LORD had brought upon him: every man also gave him a piece of money, and every one an earring of gold. So the LORD blessed the latter end of Job more than his beginning: for he had fourteen thousand sheep, and six thousand camels, and a thousand yoke of oxen, and a thousand she asses. He had also seven sons and three daughters. And he called the name of the first, Jemima; and the name of the second, Kezia; and the name of the third, Keren-happuch. And in all the land were no women found so fair as the daughters of Job: and their father gave them inheritance among their brethren.

After this lived Job an hundred and forty years, and saw his sons, and his sons' sons, even four generations. So Job died, being old and full of days.

From DANIEL

The Fiery Furnace

• DANIEL 3 •

Nebuchadnezzar[1] the king made an image of gold, whose height was threescore cubits, and the breadth thereof six cubits: he set it up in the plain of Dura, in the province of Babylon. Then Nebuchadnezzar the king sent to gather together the princes, the governors, and the captains, the judges, the treasurers, the counsellors, the sheriffs, and all the rulers of the provinces, to come to the dedication of the image which Nebuchadnezzar the king had set up. Then the princes, the governors, and captains, the judges, the treasurers, the counsellors, the sheriffs, and all the rulers of the provinces, were gathered

[1] King of Babylon, 604-561 B.C.

together unto the dedication of the image that Nebuchadnezzar the king had set up; and they stood before the image that Nebuchadnezzar had set up.

Then an herald cried aloud, "To you it is commanded, O people, nations, and languages, that at what time ye hear the sound of the cornet, flute, harp, sackbut, psaltery, dulcimer, and all kinds of music, ye fall down and worship the golden image that Nebuchadnezzar the king hath set up: and whoso falleth not down and worshippeth shall the same hour be cast into the midst of a burning fiery furnace."

Therefore at that time, when all the people heard the sound of the cornet, flute, harp, sackbut, psaltery, and all kinds of music, all the people, the nations, and the languages, fell down and worshipped the golden image that Nebuchadnezzar the king had set up.

Wherefore at that time certain Chaldeans came near, and accused the Jews. They spake and said to the king Nebuchadnezzar, "O king, live for ever. Thou, O king, hast made a decree, that every man that shall hear the sound of the cornet, flute, harp, sackbut, psaltery, and dulcimer, and all kinds of music, shall fall down and worship the golden image: and whoso falleth not down and worshippeth, that he should be cast into the midst of a burning fiery furnace. There are certain Jews whom thou hast set over the affairs of the province of Babylon, Shadrach, Meshach, and Abed-nego; these men, O king, have not regarded thee: they serve not thy gods, nor worship the golden image which thou hast set up."

Then Nebuchadnezzar in his rage and fury commanded to bring Shadrach, Meshach, and Abed-nego. Then they brought these men before the king. Nebuchadnezzar spake and said unto them, "Is it true, O Shadrach, Meshach, and Abed-nego, do not ye serve my gods, nor worship the golden image which I have set up? Now if ye be ready that at what time ye hear the sound of the cornet, flute, harp, sackbut, psaltery, and dulcimer, and all kinds of music, ye fall down and worship the image which I have made; well: but if ye worship not, ye shall be cast the same hour into the midst of a burning fiery furnace; and who is that God that shall deliver you out of my hands?"

Shadrach, Meshach, and Abed-nego, answered and said to the king, "O Nebuchadnezzar, we are not careful to answer thee in this matter. If it be so, our God whom we serve is able to deliver us from the burning fiery furnace, and he will deliver us out of thine hand, O king. But if not, be it known unto thee, O king, that we will not serve thy gods, nor worship the golden image which thou hast set up."

Then was Nebuchadnezzar full of fury, and the form of his visage was changed against Shadrach, Meshach, and Abed-nego: therefore he spake, and commanded that they should heat the furnace one seven times more than it was wont to be heated. And he commanded the most mighty men that were in his army to bind Shadrach, Meshach, and Abed-nego, and to cast them into the burning fiery furnace.

Then these men were bound in their coats, their hosen, and their hats, and their other garments, and were cast into the midst of the burning fiery furnace. Therefore because the king's commandment was urgent, and the furnace exceeding hot, the flame of the fire slew those men that took up Shadrach, Meshach, and Abed-nego. And these three men, Shadrach, Meshach, and Abed-nego, fell down bound into the midst of the burning fiery furnace.

Then Nebuchadnezzar the king was astonied, and rose up in haste, and spake, and said unto his counsellors, "Did not we cast three men bound into the midst of the fire?"

They answered and said unto the king, "True, O king."

He answered and said, "Lo, I see four men loose, walking in the midst of the fire, and they have no hurt; and the form of the fourth is like the Son of God."

Then Nebuchadnezzar came near to the mouth of the burning fiery furnace, and spake, and said, "Shadrach, Meshach, and Abed-nego, ye servants of the most high God, come forth, and come hither."

Then Shadrach, Meshach, and Abed-nego, came forth of the midst of the fire. And the princes, governors, and captains, and the king's counsellors, being gathered together, saw these men, upon whose bodies the fire had no power, nor was an hair of their head singed, neither were their coats changed, nor the smell of fire had passed on them.

Then Nebuchadnezzar spake, and said, "Blessed be the God of Shadrach, Meshach, and Abed-nego, who hath sent his angel, and delivered his servants that trusted in him, and have changed the king's word, and yielded their bodies, that they might not serve nor worship any god, except their own God. Therefore I make a decree, that every people, nation, and language, which speak any thing amiss against the God of Shadrach, Meshach, and Abed-nego, shall be cut in pieces, and their houses shall be made a dunghill: because there is no other God that can deliver after this sort."

Then the king promoted Shadrach, Meshach, and Abed-nego, in the province of Babylon.

Belshazzar's Feast

· DANIEL 5 ·

Belshazzar[2] the king made a great feast to a thousand of his lords, and drank wine before the thousand. Belshazzar, whiles he tasted the wine, commanded to bring the golden and silver vessels which his father Nebuchadnezzar had taken out of the temple which was in Jerusalem; that the king, and his princes,

[2] A son of Nebuchadnezzar. He was not actually king, the family of Nebuchadnezzar having been deposed, but he served in Babylon as administrator during the reign of Nabonidus.

his wives, and his concubines, might drink therein. Then they brought the golden vessels that were taken out of the temple of the house of God which was at Jerusalem; and the king, and his princes, his wives, and his concubines, drank in them. They drank wine, and praised the gods of gold, and of silver, of brass, of iron, of wood, and of stone.

In the same hour came forth fingers of a man's hand, and wrote over against the candlestick upon the plaister of the wall of the king's palace: and the king saw the part of the hand that wrote. Then the king's countenance was changed, and his thoughts troubled him, so that the joints of his loins were loosed, and his knees smote one against another.

The king cried aloud to bring in the astrologers, the Chaldeans, and the soothsayers. And the king spake, and said to the wise men of Babylon, "Whosoever shall read this writing, and shew me the interpretation thereof, shall be clothed with scarlet, and have a chain of gold about his neck, and shall be the third ruler in the kingdom."

Then came in all the king's wise men: but they could not read the writing, nor make known to the king the interpretation thereof. Then was king Belshazzar greatly troubled, and his countenance was changed in him, and his lords were astonied.

Now the queen by reason of the words of the king and his lords came into the banquet house: and the queen spake and said, "O king, live for ever: let not thy thoughts trouble thee, nor let thy countenance be changed: there is a man in thy kingdom, in whom is the spirit of the holy gods; and in the days of thy father light and understanding and wisdom, like the wisdom of the gods, was found in him; whom the king Nebuchadnezzar thy father, the king, I say, thy father, made master of the magicians, astrologers, Chaldeans, and soothsayers; forasmuch as an excellent spirit, and knowledge, and understanding, interpreting of dreams, and shewing of hard sentences, and dissolving of doubts, were found in the same Daniel, whom the king named

Belteshazzar: now let Daniel be called, and he will shew the interpretation."

Then was Daniel brought in before the king. And the king spake and said unto Daniel, "Art thou that Daniel, which art of the children of the captivity of Judah, whom the king my father brought out of Jewry? I have even heard of thee, that the spirit of the gods is in thee, and that light and understanding and excellent wisdom is found in thee. And now the wise men, the astrologers, have been brought in before me, that they shall read this writing, and make known unto me the interpretation thereof: but they could not shew the interpretation of the thing. And I have heard of thee, that thou canst make interpretations, and dissolve doubts: now if thou canst read the writing, and make known to me the interpretation thereof, thou shalt be clothed with scarlet, and have a chain of gold about thy neck, and shalt be the third ruler in the kingdom."

Then Daniel answered and said before the king, "Let thy gifts be to thyself, and give thy rewards to another; yet I will read the writing unto the king, and make known to him the interpretation. O thou king, the most high God gave Nebuchadnezzar thy father a kingdom, and majesty, and glory, and honour: and for the majesty that he gave him, all people, nations, and languages, trembled and feared before him: whom he would he slew; and whom he would he kept alive; and whom he would he set up; and whom he would he put down. But when his heart was lifted up, and his mind hardened in pride, he was deposed from his kingly throne, and they took his glory from him: and he was driven from the sons of men; and his heart was made like the beasts, and his dwelling was with the wild asses: they fed him with grass like oxen, and his body was wet with the dew of heaven; till he knew that the most high God ruled in the kingdom of men, and that he appointeth over it whomsoever he will. And thou his son, O Belshazzar, hast not humbled thine heart, though thou knewest all this; but hast lifted up thyself against the Lord of heaven; and they have brought the vessels of his house before thee, and thou, and thy lords, thy wives, and thy concubines, have drunk wine in them; and thou hast praised the gods of silver, and gold, of brass, iron, wood, and stone, which see not, nor hear, nor know: and the God in whose hand thy breath is, and whose are all thy ways, hast thou not glorified. Then was the part of the hand sent from him; and this writing that was written.

"And this is the writing that was written, MENE, MENE, TEKEL, UPHARSIN. This is the interpretation of the thing: MENE; God hath numbered thy kingdom, and finished it. TEKEL; Thou art weighed in the balances, and art found wanting. PERES,[3] Thy kingdom is divided, and given to the Medes and Persians."

Then commanded Belshazzar, and they clothed Daniel with scarlet, and put a chain of gold about his neck, and made a proclamation concerning him, that he should be the third ruler in the kingdom.

In that night was Belshazzar the king of the Chaldeans slain. And Darius the Median took the kingdom, being about threescore and two years old.

The Den of Lions

• DANIEL 6 •

It pleased Darius to set over the kingdom an hundred and twenty princes, which should be over the whole kingdom; and over these three presidents; of whom Daniel was first: that the princes might give accounts unto them, and the king should have no damage. Then this Daniel was preferred above the presidents and princes, because an excellent spirit was in him; and the king thought to set him over the whole realm. Then the presidents and princes sought to find occasion against Daniel concerning

[3] The singular of [u]*pharsin*.

the kingdom; but they could find none occasion nor fault; forasmuch as he was faithful, neither was there any error or fault found in him. Then said these men, "We shall not find any occasion against this Daniel, except we find it against him concerning the law of his God."

Then these presidents and princes assembled together to the king, and said thus unto him, "King Darius, live for ever. All the presidents of the kingdom, the governors, and the princes, the counsellors, and the captains, have consulted together to establish a royal statute, and to make a firm decree, that whosoever shall ask a petition of any God or man for thirty days, save of thee, O king, he shall be cast into the den of lions. Now, O king, establish the decree, and sign the writing that it be not changed, according to the law of the Medes and Persians, which altereth not." Wherefore king Darius signed the writing and the decree.

Now when Daniel knew that the writing was signed, he went into his house; and his windows being open in his chamber toward Jerusalem, he kneeled upon his knees three times a day, and prayed, and gave thanks before his God, as he did aforetime. Then these men assembled, and found Daniel praying and making supplication before his God.

Then they came near, and spake before the king concerning the king's decree; "Hast thou not signed a decree, that every man that shall ask a petition of any God or man within thirty days, save of thee, O king, shall be cast into the den of lions?"

The king answered and said, "The thing is true, according to the law of the Medes and Persians, which altereth not."

Then answered they and said before the king, "That Daniel, which is of the children of the captivity of Judah, regardeth not thee, O king, nor the decree that thou hast signed, but maketh his petition three times a day."

Then the king, when he heard these words, was sore displeased with himself, and set his heart on Daniel to deliver him: and he laboured till the going down of the sun to deliver him.

Then these men assembled unto the king, and said unto the king, "Know, O king, that the law of the Medes and Persians is, that no decree nor statute which the king establisheth may be changed."

Then the king commanded, and they brought Daniel, and cast him into the den of lions. Now the king spake and said unto Daniel, "Thy God whom thou servest continually, he will deliver thee." And a stone was brought, and laid upon the mouth of the den; and the king sealed it with his own signet, and with the signet of his lords; that the purpose might not be changed concerning Daniel.

Then the king went to his palace, and passed the night fasting: neither were instruments of music brought before him: and his sleep went from him.

Then the king arose very early in the morning, and went in haste unto the den of lions. And when he came to the den, he cried with a lamentable voice unto Daniel: and the king spake and said to Daniel, "O Daniel, servant of the living God, is thy God, whom thou servest continually, able to deliver thee from the lions?"

Then said Daniel unto the king, "O king, live for ever. My God hath sent his angel, and hath shut the lions' mouths, that they have not hurt me: forasmuch as before him innocency was found in me; and also before thee, O king, have I done no hurt."

Then was the king exceeding glad for him, and commanded that they should take Daniel up out of the den. So Daniel was taken up out of the den, and no manner of hurt was found upon him, because he believed in his God. And the king commanded, and they brought those men which had accused Daniel, and they cast them into the den of lions, them, their children, and their wives; and the lions had the mastery of them, and brake all their bones in pieces or ever they came at the bottom of the den.

Then king Darius wrote unto all people, nations, and languages, that dwell in all the earth; "Peace be multiplied unto you. I make a decree, that in every dominion of my kingdom men tremble and fear before the God of Daniel: for he is the living God, and stedfast for ever, and his kingdom that which shall not be destroyed, and his dominion shall be even unto the end. He delivereth and rescueth, and he worketh signs and wonders in heaven and in earth, who hath delivered Daniel from the power of the lions."

So this Daniel prospered in the reign of Darius, and in the reign of Cyrus the Persian.

creases, that dwell in all the earth. *None be multiplied unto you. I make a decree, that in every dominion of my kingdom men tremble and fear before the God of Daniel: for he is the living God, and stedfast forever, and his kingdom that which shall not be destroyed, and his dominion shall be even unto the end. He delivereth and rescueth, and he worketh signs and wonders in heaven and in earth, who hath delivered Daniel from the power of the lions.*

So this Daniel prospered in the reign of Darius, and in the reign of Cyrus the Persian.

SELECTIONS FROM

THE NEW TESTAMENT

The Ministry of Jesus before the Transfiguration

The beginning of the gospel of Jesus Christ, the Son of God; as it is written in the prophets, "Behold, I send my messenger before thy face, which shall prepare thy way before thee. The voice of one crying in the wilderness, Prepare ye the way of the Lord, make his paths straight."

John did baptize in the wilderness, and preach the baptism of repentance for the remission of sins. And there went out unto him all the land of Judæa, and they of Jerusalem, and were all baptized of him in the river of Jordan, confessing their sins. And John was clothed with camel's hair, and with a girdle of a skin about his loins; and he did eat locusts and wild honey; and preached, saying, "There cometh one mightier than I after me, the latchet[1] of whose shoes I am not worthy to stoop down and unloose. I indeed have baptized you with water: but he shall baptize you with the Holy Ghost."

And it came to pass in those days, that Jesus came from Nazareth of Galilee, and was baptized of John in Jordan. And straightway coming up out of the water, he saw the heavens opened, and the Spirit like a dove descending upon him: and there came a voice from heaven, saying, "Thou art my beloved Son, in whom I am well pleased."

And immediately the spirit driveth him into the wilderness. And he was there in the wilderness forty days, tempted of Satan; and was with the wild beasts; and the angels ministered unto him.

Now after that John was put in prison, Jesus came into Galilee, preaching the gospel of the kingdom of God, and saying,

[1] Thong or strap.

"The time is fulfilled, and the kingdom of God is at hand: repent ye, and believe the gospel."

Now as he walked by the sea of Galilee, he saw Simon and Andrew his brother casting a net into the sea: for they were fishers. And Jesus said unto them, "Come ye after me, and I will make you to become fishers of men." And straightway they forsook their nets, and followed him. And when he had gone a little farther thence, he saw James the son of Zebedee, and John his brother, who also were in the ship mending their nets. And straightway he called them: and they left their father Zebedee in the ship with the hired servants, and went after him.

And they went into Capernaum;[2] and straightway on the sabbath day he entered into the synagogue, and taught. And they were astonished at his doctrine: for he taught them as one that had authority,[3] and not as the scribes. And there was in their synagogue a man with an unclean spirit; and he cried out, saying, "Let us alone; what have we to do with thee, thou Jesus of Nazareth? art thou come to destroy us? I know thee who thou art, the Holy One of God."

And Jesus rebuked him, saying, "Hold thy peace, and come out of him." And when the unclean spirit had torn him, and cried with a loud voice, he came out of him. And they were all amazed, insomuch that they questioned among themselves, saying, "What thing is this? what new doctrine is this? for with authority commandeth he even the unclean spirits, and they do obey him." And immediately his fame spread abroad throughout all the region round about Galilee.

And forthwith, when they were come out of the synagogue, they entered into the house of Simon and Andrew, with James and John. But Simon's wife's mother lay sick of a fever, and anon they tell him of her. And he came and took her by the hand, and lifted her up; and immediately the fever left her, and she ministered unto them.

[2] A town on the Sea of Galilee. The center of Jesus' ministry in Galilee.
[3] i.e., as a rabbi.

And at even, when the sun did set, they brought unto him all that were diseased, and them that were possessed with devils. And all the city was gathered together at the door. And he healed many that were sick of divers diseases, and cast out many devils; and suffered not the devils to speak, because they knew him.

And in the morning, rising up a great while before day, he went out, and departed into a solitary place, and there prayed. And Simon and they that were with him followed after him. And when they had found him, they said unto him, "All men seek for thee."

And he said unto them, "Let us go into the next towns, that I may preach there also: for therefore came I forth." And he preached in their synagogues throughout all Galilee, and cast out devils.

And there came a leper to him, beseeching him, and kneeling down to him, and saying unto him, "If thou wilt, thou canst make me clean."

And Jesus, moved with compassion, put forth his hand, and touched him, and saith unto him, "I will; be thou clean." And as soon as he had spoken, immediately the leprosy departed from him, and he was cleansed. And he straitly charged him, and forthwith sent him away; and saith unto him, "See thou say nothing to any man: but go thy way, shew thyself to the priest, and offer for thy cleansing those things which Moses commanded, for a testimony unto them." But he went out, and began to publish it much, and to blaze abroad the matter, insomuch that Jesus could no more openly enter into the city, but was without in desert places: and they came to him from every quarter.

And again he entered into Capernaum after some days; and it was noised that he was in the house. And straightway many were gathered together, insomuch that there was no room to receive them, no, not so much as about the door: and he preached the word unto them. And they come unto him, bringing one sick of the palsy, which was borne of four. And when they could not come nigh unto him for the press, they uncovered the roof where he was: and when they had broken it up, they let down the bed wherein the sick of the palsy lay. When Jesus saw their faith, he said unto the sick of the palsy, "Son, thy sins be forgiven thee."

But there were certain of the scribes sitting there, and reasoning in their hearts, "Why doth this man thus speak blasphemies? who can forgive sins but God only?"

And immediately when Jesus perceived in his spirit that they so reasoned within themselves, he said unto them, "Why reason ye these things in your hearts? Whether is it easier to say to the sick of the palsy, 'Thy sins be forgiven thee'; or to say 'Arise, and take up thy bed, and walk'? But that ye may know that the Son of man hath power on earth to forgive sins," (he saith to the sick of the palsy,) "I say unto thee, Arise, and take up thy bed, and go thy way into thine house."

And immediately he arose, took up the bed, and went forth before them all; insomuch that they were all amazed, and glorified God, saying, "We never saw it on this fashion."

And he went forth again by the sea side; and all the multitude resorted unto him, and he taught them. And as he passed by, he saw Levi the son of Alphæus sitting at the receipt of custom,[4] and said unto him, "Follow me." And he arose and followed him. And it came to pass, that, as Jesus sat at meat in his house, many publicans[5] and sinners sat also together with Jesus and his disciples: for there were many, and they followed him.

And when the scribes and Pharisees saw him eat with publicans and sinners, they said unto his disciples, "How is it that he eateth and drinketh with publicans and sinners?"

When Jesus heard it, he saith unto them, "They that are whole have no need of the physician, but they that are sick: I came not to call the righteous, but sinners to repentance."

And the disciples of John and of the Pharisees used to fast: and they come and say unto him, "Why do the disciples of John and of the Pharisees fast, but thy disciples fast not?"

[4] In the tax office.
[5] Tax gatherers for the Roman Empire.

And Jesus said unto them, "Can the children of the bride-chamber fast, while the bridegroom is with them? as long as they have the bridegroom with them, they cannot fast. But the days will come, when the bridegroom shall be taken away from them, and then shall they fast in those days. No man also seweth a piece of new cloth on an old garment: else the new piece that filled it up taketh away from the old, and the rent is made worse. And no man putteth new wine into old bottles:[6] else the new wine doth burst the bottles, and the wine is spilled, and the bottles will be marred: but new wine must be put into new bottles."

And it came to pass, that he went through the corn[7] fields on the sabbath day; and his disciples began, as they went, to pluck the ears of corn. And the Pharisees said unto him, "Behold, why do they on the sabbath day that which is not lawful?"

And he said unto them, "Have ye never read what David did, when he had need, and was an hungred, he, and they that were with him? How he went into the house of God in the days of Abiathar the high priest, and did eat the shewbread, which is not lawful to eat but for the priests, and gave also to them which were with him?" And he said unto them, "The sabbath was made for man, and not man for the sabbath: therefore the Son of man is Lord also of the sabbath."

And he entered again into the synagogue; and there was a man there which had a withered hand. And they watched him, whether he would heal him on the sabbath day; that they might accuse him. And he saith unto the man which had the withered hand, "Stand forth." And he saith unto them, "Is it lawful to do good on the sabbath days, or to do evil? to save life, or to kill?" But they held their peace. And when he had looked round about on them with anger, being grieved for the hardness of their hearts, he saith unto the man, "Stretch forth thine hand." And he stretched it out: and his hand was restored whole as the other.

[6] Wineskins.
[7] Grain.

And the Pharisees went forth, and straightway took counsel with the Herodians against him, how they might destroy him.

But Jesus withdrew himself with his disciples to the sea: and a great multitude from Galilee followed him, and from Judæa, and from Jerusalem, and from Idumæa, and from beyond Jordan; and they about Tyre and Sidon,[8] a great multitude, when they had heard what great things he did, came unto him. And he spake to his disciples, that a small ship should wait on him because of the multitude, lest they should throng him. For he had healed many; insomuch that they pressed upon him for to touch him, as many as had plagues. And unclean spirits, when they saw him, fell down before him, and cried, saying, "Thou art the Son of God." And he straitly charged them that they should not make him known.

And he goeth up into a mountain, and calleth unto him whom he would: and they came unto him. And he ordained twelve, that they should be with him, and that he might send them forth to preach, and to have power to heal sicknesses, and to cast out devils. And Simon he surnamed Peter; and James the son of Zebedee, and John the brother of James; and he surnamed them Boanerges, which is, the sons of thunder: and Andrew, and Philip, and Bartholomew, and Matthew, and Thomas, and James the son of Alphæus, and Thaddæus, and Simon the Canaanite, and Judas Iscariot, which also betrayed him.

And they went into an house. And the multitude cometh together again, so that they could not so much as eat bread. And when his friends heard of it, they went out to lay hold on him: for they said, "He is beside himself."

And the scribes which came down from Jerusalem said, "He hath Beelzebub, and by the prince of the devils casteth he out devils."

And he called them unto him, and said unto them in parables, "How can Satan cast out Satan? And if a kingdom be divided against itself, that kingdom cannot stand. And if a house

[8] Where the population was mainly Gentile.

be divided against itself, that house cannot stand. And if Satan rise up against himself, and be divided, he cannot stand, but hath an end. No man can enter into a strong man's house, and spoil his goods, except he will first bind the strong man; and then he will spoil his house. Verily I say unto you, all sins shall be forgiven unto the sons of men, and blasphemies wherewith soever they shall blaspheme: but he that shall blaspheme against the Holy Ghost hath never forgiveness, but is in danger of eternal damnation": because they said, "He hath an unclean spirit."

There came then his brethren and his mother, and, standing without, sent unto him, calling him. And the multitudes sat about him, and they said unto him, "Behold, thy mother and thy brethren without seek for thee."

And he answered them, saying, "Who is my mother, or my brethren?" And he looked round about on them which sat about him, and said, "Behold my mother and my brethren! For whosoever shall do the will of God, the same is my brother, and my sister, and mother."

And he began again to teach by the sea side: and there was gathered unto him a great multitude, so that he entered into a ship, and sat in the sea; and the whole multitude was by the sea on the land. And he taught them many things by parables, and said unto them in his doctrine, "Hearken; behold, there went out a sower to sow: and it came to pass, as he sowed, some fell by the way side, and the fowls of the air came and devoured it up. And some fell on stony ground, where it had not much earth; and immediately it sprang up, because it had no depth of earth: but when the sun was up, it was scorched; and because it had no root, it withered away. And some fell among thorns, and the thorns grew up, and choked it, and it yielded no fruit. And other fell on good ground, and did yield fruit that sprang up and increased; and brought forth, some thirty, and some sixty, and some an hundred." And he said unto them, "He that hath ears to hear, let him hear."

And when he was alone, they that were about him with the

twelve asked of him the parable. And he said unto them, "Unto you it is given to know the mystery of the kingdom of God: but unto them that are without, all these things are done in parables: that seeing they may see, and not perceive; and hearing they may hear, and not understand; lest at any time they should be converted, and their sins should be forgiven them."

And he said unto them, "Know ye not this parable? and how then will ye know all parables? The sower soweth the word. And these are they by the way side, where the word is sown; but when they have heard, Satan cometh immediately, and taketh away the word that was sown in their hearts. And these are they likewise which are sown on stony ground; who, when they have heard the word, immediately receive it with gladness; and have no root in themselves, and so endure but for a time: afterward, when affliction or persecution ariseth for the word's sake, immediately they are offended. And these are they which are sown among thorns; such as hear the word, and the cares of this world, and the deceitfulness of riches, and the lusts of other things entering in, choke the word, and it becometh unfruitful. And these are they which are sown on good ground; such as hear the word, and receive it, and bring forth fruit, some thirtyfold, some sixty, and some an hundred."

And he said unto them, "Is a candle brought to be put under a bushel, or under a bed? and not to be set on a candlestick? For there is nothing hid, which shall not be manifested; neither was any thing kept secret, but that it should come abroad. If any man have ears to hear, let him hear." And he said unto them, "Take heed what ye hear: with what measure ye mete, it shall be measured to you: and unto you that hear shall more be given. For he that hath, to him shall be given: and he that hath not, from him shall be taken even that which he hath."

And he said, "So is the kingdom of God, as if a man should cast seed into the ground; and should sleep, and rise night and day, and the seed should spring and grow up, he knoweth not how. For the earth bringeth forth fruit of herself, first the blade, then the ear, after that the full corn in the ear. But when the fruit is brought forth, immediately he putteth in the sickle, because the harvest is come."

And he said, "Whereunto shall we liken the kingdom of God? or with what comparison shall we compare it? It is like a grain of mustard seed, which, when it is sown in the earth, is less than all the seeds that be in the earth: but when it is sown, it groweth up, and becometh greater than all herbs, and shooteth out great branches; so that the fowls of the air may lodge under the shadow of it."

And with many such parables spake he the word unto them, as they were able to hear it. But without a parable spake he not unto them: and when they were alone, he expounded all things to his disciples.

And the same day, when the even was come, he saith unto them, "Let us pass over unto the other side." And when they had sent away the multitude, they took him even as he was in the ship. And there were also with him other little ships. And there arose a great storm of wind, and the waves beat into the ship, so that it was now full. And he was in the hinder part of the ship, asleep on a pillow: and they awake him, and say unto him, "Master, carest thou not that we perish?"

And he arose, and rebuked the wind, and said unto the sea, "Peace, be still." And the wind ceased, and there was a great calm. And he said unto them, "Why are ye so fearful? how is it that ye have no faith?"

And they feared exceedingly, and said one to another, "What manner of man is this, that even the wind and the sea obey him?"

And they came over unto the other side of the sea, into the country of the Gadarenes. And when he was come out of the ship, immediately there met him out of the tombs a man with an unclean spirit, who had his dwelling among the tombs; and no man could bind him, no, not with chains: because that he had been often bound with fetters and chains, and the chains had been plucked asunder by him, and the fetters broken in pieces: neither could any man tame him. And always, night and day, he was in the mountains, and in the tombs, crying, and cutting himself with stones. But when he saw Jesus afar off, he ran and worshipped him, and cried with a loud voice, and said, "What have I to do with thee, Jesus, thou Son of the most high God? I adjure thee by God, that thou torment me not."

For he said unto him, "Come out of the man, thou unclean spirit." And he asked him, "What is thy name?"

And he answered, saying, "My name is Legion: for we are many." And he besought him much that he would not send them away out of the country.

Now there was there nigh unto the mountains a great herd of swine feeding. And all the devils besought him, saying, "Send us into the swine, that we may enter into them." And forthwith Jesus gave them leave. And the unclean spirits went out, and entered into the swine: and the herd ran violently down a steep place into the sea, (they were about two thousand;) and were choked in the sea.

And they that fed the swine fled, and told it in the city, and in the country. And they went out to see what it was that was done. And they come to Jesus, and see him that was possessed with the devil, and had the legion, sitting, and clothed and in his right mind: and they were afraid. And they that saw it told them how it befell to him that was possessed with the devil, and also concerning the swine. And they began to pray him to depart out of their coasts.[9] And when he was come into the ship, he that had been possessed with the devil prayed him that he might be with him. Howbeit Jesus suffered him not, but saith unto him, "Go home to thy friends, and tell them how great things the Lord hath done for thee, and hath had compassion on thee." And he departed, and began to publish in Decapolis how great things Jesus had done for him: and all men did marvel.

And when Jesus was passed over again by ship unto the other

* Neighborhood.

side, much people gathered unto him: and he was nigh unto the sea. And, behold, there cometh one of the rulers of the synagogue, Jairus by name; and when he saw him, he fell at his feet, and besought him greatly, saying, "My little daughter lieth at the point of death: I pray thee, come and lay thy hands on her, that she may be healed; and she shall live." And Jesus went with him; and much people followed him, and thronged him.

And a certain woman, which had an issue of blood twelve years, and had suffered many things of many physicians, and had spent all that she had, and was nothing bettered, but rather grew worse, when she had heard of Jesus, came in the press behind, and touched his garment. For she said, "If I may touch but his clothes, I shall be whole." And straightway the fountain of her blood was dried up; and she felt in her body that she was healed of that plague.

And Jesus, immediately knowing in himself that virtue[10] had gone out of him, turned him about in the press, and said, "Who touched my clothes?"

And his disciples said unto him, "Thou seest the multitude thronging thee, and sayest thou, 'Who touched me?'" And he looked round about to see her that had done this thing. But the woman fearing and trembling, knowing what was done in her, came and fell down before him, and told him all the truth.

And he said unto her, "Daughter, thy faith hath made thee whole; go in peace, and be whole of thy plague."

While he yet spake, there came from the ruler of the synagogue's house certain which said, "Thy daughter is dead: why troublest thou the Master any further?"

As soon as Jesus heard the word that was spoken, he saith unto the ruler of the synagogue, "Be not afraid, only believe." And he suffered no man to follow him, save Peter, and James, and John the brother of James. And he cometh to the house of the ruler of the synagogue, and seeth the tumult, and them that wept and wailed greatly. And when he was come in, he saith

[10] Power.

unto them, "Why make ye this ado, and weep? the damsel is not dead, but sleepeth." And they laughed him to scorn. But when he had put them all out, he taketh the father and the mother of the damsel, and them that were with him, and entereth in where the damsel was lying. And he took the damsel by the hand, and said unto her, "Talitha cumi;" which is, being interpreted, "Damsel, I say unto thee, arise." And straightway the damsel arose, and walked; for she was of the age of twelve years. And they were astonished with a great astonishment. And he charged them strait that no man should know it; and commanded that something should be given her to eat.

And he went out from thence, and came into his own country;[11] and his disciples follow him. And when the sabbath day was come, he began to teach in the synagogue: and many hearing him were astonished, saying, "From whence hath this man these things? and what wisdom is this which is given unto him, that even such mighty works are wrought by his hands? Is not this the carpenter, the son of Mary, the brother of James, and Joses, and of Juda, and Simon? and are not his sisters here with us?" And they were offended at him.

But Jesus said unto them, "A prophet is not without honour, but in his own country, and among his own kin, and in his own house." And he could there do no mighty work, save that he laid his hands upon a few sick folk, and healed them. And he marvelled because of their unbelief. And he went round about the villages, teaching.

And he called unto him the twelve, and began to send them forth by two and two; and gave them power over unclean spirits; and commanded them that they should take nothing for their journey, save a staff only; no scrip,[12] no bread, no money in their purse: but be shod with sandals; and not put on two coats. And he said unto them, "In what place soever ye enter into an house, there abide till ye depart from that place. And

[11] i.e., to Nazareth.
[12] Bag.

whosoever shall not receive you, nor hear you, when ye depart thence, shake off the dust under your feet for a testimony against them. Verily I say unto you, it shall be more tolerable for Sodom and Gomorrha in the day of judgment, than for that city." And they went out, and preached that men should repent. And they cast out many devils, and anointed with oil many that were sick, and healed them.

And king Herod[18] heard of him; (for his name was spread abroad:) and he said, "That John the Baptist was risen from the dead, and therefore mighty works do shew forth themselves in him." Others said, "That it is Elias." And others said, "That it is a prophet, or as one of the prophets." But when Herod heard thereof, he said, "It is John, whom I beheaded: he is risen from the dead."

For Herod himself had sent forth and laid hold upon John, and bound him in prison for Herodias' sake, his brother Philip's wife: for he had married her. For John had said unto Herod, "It is not lawful for thee to have thy brother's wife." Therefore Herodias had a quarrel against him, and would have killed him; but she could not: for Herod feared John, knowing that he was a just man and an holy, and observed him; and when he heard him, he did many things, and heard him gladly. And when a convenient day was come, that Herod on his birthday made a supper to his lords, high captains, and chief estates of Galilee; and when the daughter of the said Herodias came in, and danced, and pleased Herod and them that sat with him, the king said unto the damsel, "Ask of me whatsoever thou wilt, and I will give it thee." And he sware unto her, "Whatsoever thou shalt ask of me, I will give it thee, unto the half of my kingdom."

And she went forth, and said unto her mother, "What shall I ask?" And she said, "The head of John the Baptist." And she came in straightway with haste unto the king, and asked, saying, "I will that thou give me by and by in a charger the head of

[18] The Roman-controlled King of Judaea.

John the Baptist." And the king was exceeding sorry; yet for his oath's sake, and for their sakes which sat with him, he would not reject her. And immediately the king sent an executioner, and commanded his head to be brought: and he went and beheaded him in the prison, and brought his head in a charger, and gave it to the damsel: and the damsel gave it to her mother. And when his disciples heard of it, they came and took up his corpse, and laid it in a tomb.

And the apostles gathered themselves together unto Jesus, and told him all things, both what they had done, and what they had taught. And he said unto them, "Come ye yourselves apart into a desert place, and rest a while": for there were many coming and going, and they had no leisure so much as to eat. And they departed into a desert place by ship privately. And the people saw them departing, and many knew him, and ran afoot thither out of all cities, and outwent them, and came together unto him. And Jesus, when he came out, saw much people, and was moved with compassion toward them, because they were as sheep not having a shepherd: and he began to teach them many things.

And when the day was now far spent, his disciples came unto him, and said, "This is a desert place, and now the time is far passed: send them away, that they may go into the country round about, and into the villages, and buy themselves bread: for they have nothing to eat."

He answered and said unto them, "Give ye them to eat."

And they say unto him, "Shall we go and buy two hundred pennyworth of bread, and give them to eat?"

He saith unto them, "How many loaves have ye? go and see."

And when they knew, they say, "Five, and two fishes."

And he commanded them to make all sit down by companies upon the green grass. And they sat down in ranks, by hundreds, and by fifties. And when he had taken the five loaves and the two fishes, he looked up to heaven, and blessed, and brake the loaves, and gave them to his disciples to set before them; and the two fishes divided he among them all. And they did all eat, and were filled. And they took up twelve baskets full of the fragments, and of the fishes. And they that did eat of the loaves were about five thousand men.

And straightway he constrained his disciples to get into the ship, and to go to the other side before unto Bethsaida, while he sent away the people. And when he had sent them away, he departed into a mountain to pray. And when even was come, the ship was in the midst of the sea, and he alone on the land. And he saw them toiling in rowing; for the wind was contrary unto them: and about the fourth watch of the night he cometh unto them, walking upon the sea, and would have passed by them. But when they saw him walking upon the sea, they supposed it had been a spirit, and cried out: for they all saw him, and were troubled. And immediately he talked with them, and saith unto them, "Be of good cheer: it is I; be not afraid." And he went up unto them into the ship; and the wind ceased: and they were sore amazed in themselves beyond measure, and wondered. For they considered not the miracle of the loaves: for their heart was hardened.

And when they had passed over, they came into the land of Gennesaret,[14] and drew to the shore. And when they were come out of the ship, straightway they knew him, and ran through that whole region round about, and began to carry about in beds those that were sick, where they heard he was. And whithersoever he entered, into villages, or cities, or country, they laid the sick in the streets, and besought him that they might touch if it were but the border of his garment: and as many as touched him were made whole.

Then came together unto him the Pharisees, and certain of the scribes, which came from Jerusalem. And when they saw some of his disciples eat bread with defiled, that is to say, with un-

[14] The area bordering the northern parts of the western shore of the Sea of Galilee.

washen, hands, they found fault. For the Pharisees, and all the Jews, except they wash their hands oft, eat not, holding the tradition of the elders. And when they come from the market, except they wash, they eat not. And many other things there be, which they have received to hold, as the washing of cups, and pots, brasen vessels, and of tables. Then the Pharisees and scribes asked him, "Why walk not thy disciples according to the tradition of the elders, but eat bread with unwashen hands?"

He answered and said unto them, "Well hath Esaias prophesied of you hypocrites, as it is written, 'This people honoureth me with their lips, but their heart is far from me. Howbeit in vain do they worship me, teaching for doctrines the commandments of men.' For laying aside the commandment of God, ye hold the tradition of men, as the washing of pots and cups: and many other such like things ye do." And he said unto them, "Full well ye reject the commandment of God, that ye may keep your own tradition. For Moses said, 'Honour thy father and thy mother'; and, 'Whoso curseth father or mother, let him die the death': But ye say, 'If a man shall say to his father or mother, It is Corban, (that is to say, a gift) by whatsoever thou mightest be profited by me, he shall be free.' [15] And ye suffer him no more to do ought for his father or his mother; making the word of God of none effect through your tradition, which ye have delivered: and many such like things do ye."

And when he had called all the people unto him, he said unto them, "Hearken unto me every one of you, and understand: there is nothing from without a man, that entering into him can defile him: but the things which come out of him, those are they that defile the man. If any man have ears to hear, let him hear." And when he was entered into the house from the people, his disciples asked him concerning the parable. And he saith unto them, "Are ye so without understanding also? Do ye not perceive, that whatsoever thing from without entereth into the man, it can-

[15] The sense of the passage is that by merely taking a vow a man might be freed from the obligation to assist his parents.

not defile him; because it entereth not into his heart, but into the belly, and goeth out into the draught, purging all meats?" And he said, "That which cometh out of the man, that defileth the man. For from within, out of the heart of men, proceed evil thoughts, adulteries, fornications, murders, thefts, covetousness, wickedness, deceit, lasciviousness, an evil eye, blasphemy, pride, foolishness: all these evil things come from within, and defile the man."

And from thence he arose, and went into the borders of Tyre and Sidon, and entered into an house, and would have no man know it: but he could not be hid. For a certain woman, whose young daughter had an unclean spirit, heard of him, and came and fell at his feet: the woman was a Greek, a Syrophenician by nation; and she besought him that he would cast forth the devil out of her daughter. But Jesus said unto her, "Let the children first be filled: for it is not meet to take the children's bread, and to cast it unto the dogs."

And she answered and said unto him, "Yes, Lord: yet the dogs under the table eat of the children's crumbs."

And he said unto her, "For this saying go thy way; the devil is gone out of thy daughter." And when she was come to her house, she found the devil gone out, and her daughter laid upon the bed.

And again, departing from the coasts of Tyre and Sidon, he came unto the sea of Galilee, through the midst of the coasts of Decapolis. And they bring unto him one that was deaf, and had an impediment in his speech; and they beseech him to put his hand upon him. And he took him aside from the multitude, and put his fingers into his ears, and he spit, and touched his tongue; And looking up to heaven, he sighed, and saith unto him, "Ephphatha," that is, "Be opened." And straightway his ears were opened, and the string of his tongue was loosed, and he spake plain.

And he charged them that they should tell no man: but the more he charged them, so much the more a great deal they pub-fished it; and were beyond measure astonished, saying, "He hath done all things well: he maketh both the deaf to hear, and the dumb to speak."

In those days the multitude being very great, and having nothing to eat, Jesus called his disciples unto him, and saith unto them, "I have compassion on the multitude, because they have now been with me three days, and have nothing to eat: and if I send them away fasting to their own houses, they will faint by the way: for divers of them came from far."

And his disciples answered him, "From whence can a man satisfy these men with bread here in the wilderness?"

And he asked them, "How many loaves have ye?" And they said, "Seven." And he commanded the people to sit down on the ground: and he took the seven loaves, and gave thanks, and brake and gave to his disciples to set before them; and they did set them before the people. And they had a few small fishes: and he blessed, and commanded to set them also before them. So they did eat, and were filled: and they took up of the broken meat that was left seven baskets. And they that had eaten were about four thousand: and he sent them away. And straightway, he entered into a ship with his disciples, and came into the parts of Dalmanutha.

And the Pharisees came forth, and began to question with him, seeking of him a sign from heaven, tempting him. And he sighed deeply in his spirit, and saith, "Why doth this generation seek after a sign? verily I say unto you, There shall no sign be given unto this generation." And he left them, and entering into the ship again departed to the other side.

Now the disciples had forgotten to take bread, neither had they in the ship with them more than one loaf. And he charged them, saying, "Take heed, beware of the leaven of the Pharisees, and of the leaven of Herod."

And they reasoned among themselves, saying, "It is because we have no bread."

And when Jesus knew it, he saith unto them, "Why reason

ye, because ye have no bread? perceive ye not yet, neither understand? have ye your heart yet hardened? Having eyes, see ye not? and having ears, hear ye not? and do ye not remember? When I brake the five loaves among five thousand, how many baskets full of fragments took ye up?"

They say unto him, "Twelve."

"And when the seven among four thousand, how many baskets full of fragments took ye up?"

And they said, "Seven."

And he said unto them, "How is it that ye do not understand?"

And he cometh to Bethsaida; and they bring a blind man unto him, and besought him to touch him. And he took the blind man by the hand, and led him out of the town; and when he had spit on his eyes, and put his hands upon him, he asked him if he saw ought. And he looked up, and said, "I see men as trees, walking." After that he put his hands again upon his eyes, and made him look up: and he was restored, and saw every man clearly. And he sent him away to his house, saying, "Neither go into the town, nor tell it to any in the town."

From the Transfiguration to the Entry into Jerusalem

And Jesus went out, and his disciples, into the towns of Cæsarea Philippi: [16] and by the way he asked his disciples, saying unto them, "Whom do men say that I am?"

And they answered, "John the Baptist: but some say, Elias; and others, one of the prophets."

And he saith unto them, "But whom say ye that I am?"

And Peter answereth and saith unto him, "Thou art the Christ."

And he charged them that they should tell no man of him.

[16] A Roman town on the southern slopes of Mt. Hermon, about 30 miles north of the Sea of Galilee.

And he began to teach them, that the Son of man must suffer many things, and be rejected of the elders, and of the chief priests, and scribes, and be killed, and after three days rise again. And he spake that saying openly. And Peter took him, and began to rebuke him. But when he had turned about and looked on his disciples, he rebuked Peter, saying, "Get thee behind me, Satan: for thou savourest not the things that be of God, but the things that be of men."

And when he had called the people unto him with his disciples also, he said unto them, "Whosoever will come after me, let him deny himself, and take up his cross, and follow me. For whosoever will save his life shall lose it; but whosoever shall lose his life for my sake and the gospel's, the same shall save it. For what shall it profit a man, if he shall gain the whole world, and lose his own soul? Or what shall a man give in exchange for his soul? Whosoever therefore shall be ashamed of me and of my words in this adulterous and sinful generation; of him also shall the Son of man be ashamed, when he cometh in the glory of his Father with the holy angels." And he said unto them, "Verily I say unto you, that there be some of them that stand here, which shall not taste of death, till they have seen the kingdom of God come with power."

And after six days Jesus taketh with him Peter, and James, and John, and leadeth them up into an high mountain[17] apart by themselves: and he was transfigured before them. And his raiment became shining, exceeding white as snow; so as no fuller[18] on earth can white them. And there appeared unto them Elias with Moses: and they were talking with Jesus. And Peter answered and said to Jesus, "Master, it is good for us to be here: and let us make three tabernacles; one for thee, and one for Moses, and one for Elias." For he wist not what to say; for they were sore afraid. And there was a cloud that overshadowed them: and a voice came out of the cloud, saying, "This is my beloved Son:

[17] Probably Mt. Hermon.
[18] One who cleanses cloth.

hear him." And suddenly, when they had looked round about, they saw no man any more, save Jesus only with themselves.

And as they came down from the mountain, he charged them that they should tell no man what things they had seen, till the Son of man were risen from the dead. And they kept that saying with themselves, questioning one with another what the rising from the dead should mean.

And they asked him, saying, "Why say the scribes that Elias must first come?"

And he answered and told them, "Elias verily cometh first, and restoreth all things; and how it is written of the Son of man, that he must suffer many things, and be set at nought. But I say unto you, that Elias is indeed come, and they have done unto him whatsoever they listed, as it is written of him."

And when he came to his disciples, he saw a great multitude about them, and the scribes questioning with them. And straightway all the people, when they beheld him, were greatly amazed, and running to him saluted him. And he asked the scribes, "What question ye with them?"

And one of the multitude answered and said, "Master, I have brought unto thee my son, which hath a dumb spirit; and wheresoever he taketh him, he teareth him: and he foameth, and gnasheth with his teeth, and pineth away: and I spake to thy disciples that they should cast him out; and they could not."

He answereth him, and saith, "O faithless generation, how long shall I be with you? how long shall I suffer you? bring him unto me." And they brought him unto him: and when he saw him, straightway the spirit tore him; and he fell on the ground, and wallowed foaming. And he asked his father, "How long is it ago since this came unto him?"

And he said, "Of a child. And ofttimes it hath cast him into the fire, and into the waters, to destroy him: but if thou canst do any thing, have compassion on us, and help us."

Jesus said unto him, "If thou canst believe, all things are possible to him that believeth."

And straightway the father of the child cried out, and said with tears, "Lord, I believe; help thou mine unbelief."

When Jesus saw that the people came running together, he rebuked the foul spirit, saying unto him, "Thou dumb and deaf spirit, I charge thee, come out of him, and enter no more into him." And the spirit cried, and rent him sore, and came out of him: and he was as one dead; insomuch that many said, "He is dead." But Jesus took him by the hand, and lifted him up; and he arose.

And when he was come into the house, his disciples asked him privately, "Why could not we cast him out?"

And he said unto them, "This kind can come forth by nothing, but by prayer and fasting."

And they departed thence, and passed through Galilee; and he would not that any man should know it. For he taught his disciples, and said unto them, "The Son of man is delivered into the hands of men, and they shall kill him; and after that he is killed, he shall rise the third day." But they understood not that saying, and were afraid to ask him.

And he came to Capernaum: and being in the house he asked them, "What was it that ye disputed among yourselves by the way?" But they held their peace: for by the way they had disputed among themselves, who should be the greatest. And he sat down, and called the twelve, and saith unto them, "If any man desire to be first, the same shall be last of all, and servant of all." And he took a child, and set him in the midst of them: and when he had taken him in his arms, he said unto them, "Whosoever shall receive one of such children in my name, receiveth me: and whosoever shall receive me, receiveth not me, but him that sent me."

And John answered him, saying, "Master, we saw one casting out devils in thy name, and he followeth not us: and we forbade him, because he followeth not us."

But Jesus said, "Forbid him not: for there is no man which shall do a miracle in my name, that can lightly speak evil of me.

For he that is not against us is on our part. For whosoever shall give you a cup of water to drink in my name, because ye belong to Christ, verily I say unto you, he shall not lose his reward.

"And whosoever shall offend one of these little ones that believe in me, it is better for him that a millstone were hanged about his neck, and he were cast into the sea. And if thy hand offend thee, cut it off: it is better for thee to enter into life maimed, than having two hands to go into hell, into the fire that never shall be quenched: where their worm dieth not, and the fire is not quenched. And if thy foot offend thee, cut it off: it is better for thee to enter halt into life, than having two feet to be cast into hell, into the fire that never shall be quenched; where their worm dieth not, and the fire is not quenched. And if thine eye offend thee, pluck it out: it is better for thee to enter into the kingdom of God with one eye, than having two eyes to be cast into hell fire: where their worm dieth not, and the fire is not quenched. For every one shall be salted with fire, and every sacrifice shall be salted with salt. Salt is good: but if the salt have lost his saltness, wherewith will ye season it? Have salt in yourselves, and have peace one with another."

And he arose from thence, and cometh into the coasts of Judæa by the farther side of Jordan: and the people resort unto him again; and, as he was wont, he taught them again.

And the Pharisees came to him, and asked him, "Is it lawful for a man to put away his wife?" tempting him.

And he answered and said unto them, "What did Moses command you?"

And they said, "Moses suffered to write a bill of divorcement, and to put her away."

And Jesus answered and said unto them, "For the hardness of your heart he wrote you this precept. But from the beginning of the creation God made them male and female. For this cause shall a man leave his father and mother, and cleave to his wife; and they twain shall be one flesh: so then they are no more twain, but one flesh. What therefore God hath joined together, let not man put asunder." And in the house his disciples asked him again of the same matter. And he saith unto them, "Whosoever shall put away his wife, and marry another, committeth adultery against her. And if a woman shall put away her husband, and be married to another, she committeth adultery."

And they brought young children to him, that he should touch them: and his disciples rebuked those that brought them. But when Jesus saw it, he was much displeased, and said unto them, "Suffer the little children to come unto me, and forbid them not: for of such is the kingdom of God. Verily I say unto you, whosoever shall not receive the kingdom of God as a little child, he shall not enter therein." And he took them up in his arms, put his hands upon them, and blessed them.

And when he was gone forth into the way, there came one running, and kneeled to him, and asked him, "Good Master, what shall I do that I may inherit eternal life?"

And Jesus said unto him, "Why callest thou me good? there is none good but one, that is, God. Thou knowest the commandments, 'Do not commit adultery, do not kill, do not steal, do not bear false witness, defraud not, honour thy father and mother.'"

And he answered and said unto him, "Master, all these have I observed from my youth."

Then Jesus beholding him loved him, and said unto him, "One thing thou lackest: go thy way, sell whatsoever thou hast, and give to the poor, and thou shalt have treasure in heaven: and come, take up the cross, and follow me." And he was sad at that saying, and went away grieved: for he had great possessions.

And Jesus looked round about, and saith unto his disciples, "How hardly shall they that have riches enter into the kingdom of God!" And the disciples were astonished at his words. But Jesus answereth again, and saith unto them, "Children, how hard is it for them that trust in riches to enter into the kingdom of

God! It is easier for a camel to go through the eye of a needle, than for a rich man to enter into the kingdom of God."

And they were astonished out of measure, saying among themselves, "Who then can be saved?"

And Jesus looking upon them saith, "With men it is impossible, but not with God: for with God all things are possible."

Then Peter began to say unto him, "Lo, we have left all, and have followed thee."

And Jesus answered and said, "Verily I say unto you, there is no man that hath left house, or brethren, or sisters, or father, or mother, or wife, or children, or lands, for my sake, and the gospel's, but he shall receive an hundredfold now in this time, houses, and brethren, and sisters, and mothers, and children, and lands, with persecutions; and in the world to come eternal life. But many that are first shall be last; and the last first."

And they were in the way going up to Jerusalem; and Jesus went before them: and they were amazed; and as they followed, they were afraid. And he took again the twelve, and began to tell them what things should happen unto him, saying, "Behold, we go up to Jerusalem; and the Son of man shall be delivered unto the chief priests, and unto the scribes; and they shall condemn him to death, and shall deliver him to the Gentiles: and they shall mock him, and shall scourge him, and shall spit upon him, and shall kill him: and the third day he shall rise again."

And James and John, the sons of Zebedee, come unto him, saying, "Master, we would that thou shouldest do for us whatsoever we shall desire."

And he said unto them, "What would ye that I should do for you?"

They said unto him, "Grant unto us that we may sit, one on thy right hand, and the other on thy left hand, in thy glory."

But Jesus said unto them, "Ye know not what ye ask: can ye drink of the cup that I drink of? and be baptized with the baptism that I am baptized with?"

And they said unto him, "We can."

And Jesus said unto them, "Ye shall indeed drink of the cup that I drink of; and with the baptism that I am baptized withal shall ye be baptized: but to sit on my right hand and on my left hand is not mine to give; but it shall be given to them for whom it is prepared."

And when the ten heard it, they began to be much displeased with James and John. But Jesus called them to him, and saith unto them, "Ye know that they which are accounted to rule over the Gentiles exercise lordship over them; and their great ones exercise authority upon them. But so shall it not be among you: but whosoever will be great among you, shall be your minister: and whosoever of you will be the chiefest, shall be servant of all. For even the Son of man came not to be ministered unto, but to minister, and to give his life a ransom for many."

And they came to Jericho: and as he went out of Jericho with his disciples and a great number of people, blind Bartimæus, the son of Timæus, sat by the highway side begging. And when he heard that it was Jesus of Nazareth, he began to cry out, and say, "Jesus, thou son of David, have mercy on me." And many charged him that he should hold his peace: but he cried the more a great deal, "Thou son of David, have mercy on me."

And Jesus stood still, and commanded him to be called. And they call the blind man, saying unto him, "Be of good comfort, rise; he calleth thee." And he, casting away his garment, rose, and came to Jesus.

And Jesus answered and said unto him, "What wilt thou that I should do unto thee?"

The blind man said unto him, "Lord, that I might receive my sight."

And Jesus said unto him, "Go thy way; thy faith hath made thee whole." And immediately he received his sight, and followed Jesus in the way.

And when they came nigh to Jerusalem, unto Bethphage and Bethany, at the mount of Olives, he sendeth forth two of his disciples, and saith unto them, "Go your way into the village over against you: and as soon as ye be entered into it, ye shall find a colt[19] tied, whereon never man sat; loose him, and bring him. And if any man say unto you, 'Why do ye this?' say ye that the Lord hath need of him; and straightway he will send him hither."

And they went their way, and found the colt tied by the door without in a place where two ways met; and they loose him. And certain of them that stood there said unto them, "What do ye, loosing the colt?" And they said unto them even as Jesus had commanded: and they let them go. And they brought the colt to Jesus, and cast their garments on him; and he sat upon him.

And many spread their garments in the way: and others cut down branches off the trees, and strawed them in the way. And they that went before, and they that followed, cried, saying, "Hosanna; Blessed is he that cometh in the name of the Lord: blessed be the kingdom of our father David, that cometh in the name of the Lord: Hosanna in the highest." And Jesus entered into Jerusalem, and into the temple: and when he had looked round about upon all things, and now the eventide was come, he went out unto Bethany with the twelve.

And on the morrow, when they were come from Bethany, he was hungry: and seeing a fig tree afar off having leaves, he came, if haply he might find any thing thereon: and when he came to it, he found nothing but leaves; for the time of figs was not yet. And Jesus answered and said unto it, "No man eat fruit of thee hereafter for ever." And his disciples heard it.

Jesus at Jerusalem. The Trial, the Crucifixion, and the Resurrection

And they come to Jerusalem: and Jesus went into the temple, and began to cast out them that sold and bought in the temple, and overthrew the tables of the moneychangers, and the seats of

[19] Of an ass.

them that sold doves: and would not suffer that any man should carry any vessel through the temple.[20] And he taught, saying unto them, "Is it not written, 'My house shall be called of all nations the house of prayer'? but ye have made it a den of thieves." And the scribes and chief priests heard it, and sought how they might destroy him: for they feared him, because all the people was astonished at his doctrine. And when even was come, he went out of the city.

And in the morning, as they passed by, they saw the fig tree dried up from the roots. And Peter calling to remembrance saith unto him, "Master, behold, the fig tree which thou cursedst is withered away."

And Jesus answering saith unto them, "Have faith in God. For verily I say unto you, that whosoever shall say unto this mountain, 'Be thou removed, and be thou cast into the sea,' and shall not doubt in his heart, but shall believe that those things which he saith shall come to pass; he shall have whatsoever he saith. Therefore I say unto you, what things soever ye desire, when ye pray, believe that ye receive them, and ye shall have them. And when ye stand praying, forgive, if ye have ought against any: that your Father also which is in heaven may forgive you your trespasses. But if ye do not forgive, neither will your Father which is in heaven forgive your trespasses."

And they come again to Jerusalem: and as he was walking in the temple, there come to him the chief priests, and the scribes, and the elders, and say unto him, "By what authority doest thou these things? and who gave thee this authority to do these things?"

And Jesus answered and said unto them, "I will also ask of you one question, and answer me, and I will tell you by what authority I do these things. The baptism of John, was it from heaven, or of men? answer me."

And they reasoned with themselves, saying, "If we shall say,

[20] Because many people used the Temple as a thoroughfare.

'From heaven'; he will say, 'Why then did ye not believe him?' But if we shall say, 'Of men' "—they feared the people: for all men counted John, that he was a prophet indeed. And they answered and said unto Jesus, "We cannot tell."

And Jesus answering saith unto them, "Neither do I tell you, by what authority I do these things."

And he began to speak unto them by parables. "A certain man planted a vineyard, and set an hedge about it, and digged a place for the winefat, and built a tower, and let it out to husbandmen, and went into a far country. And at the season he sent to the husbandmen a servant, that he might receive from the husbandmen of the fruit of the vineyard. And they caught him, and beat him, and sent him away empty. And again he sent unto them another servant; and at him they cast stones, and wounded him in the head, and sent him away shamefully handled. And again he sent another; and him they killed, and many others; beating some, and killing some. Having yet therefore one son, his wellbeloved, he sent him also last unto them, saying, 'They will reverence my son.' But those husbandmen said among themselves, 'This is the heir; come, let us kill him, and the inheritance shall be ours.' And they took him, and killed him, and cast him out of the vineyard. What shall therefore the lord of the vineyard do? he will come and destroy the husbandmen, and will give the vineyard unto others. And have ye not read this scripture; 'The stone which the builders rejected is become the head of the corner: this was the Lord's doing, and it is marvellous in our eyes'?"

And they sought to lay hold on him, but feared the people: for they knew that he had spoken the parable against them: and they left him, and went their way. And they send unto him certain of the Pharisees and of the Herodians,[21] to catch him in his words. And when they were come, they say unto him, "Master, we know that thou art true, and carest for no man: for thou re-

[21] The party of Herod.

gardest not the person of men, but teachest the way of God in truth. Is it lawful to give tribute to Cæsar, or not? Shall we give, or shall we not give?"

But he, knowing their hypocrisy, said unto them, "Why tempt ye me? bring me a penny, that I may see it." And they brought it. And he saith unto them, "Whose is this image and superscription?"

And they said unto him, "Cæsar's."

And Jesus answering said unto them, "Render to Cæsar the things that are Cæsar's, and to God the things that are God's." And they marvelled at him.

Then come unto him the Sadducees, which say there is no resurrection; and they asked him, saying, "Master, Moses wrote unto us, 'If a man's brother die, and leave his wife behind him, and leave no children, that his brother should take his wife, and raise up seed unto his brother.' Now there were seven brethren: and the first took a wife, and dying left no seed. And the second took her, and died, neither left he any seed: and the third likewise. And the seven had her, and left no seed: last of all the woman died also. In the resurrection therefore, when they shall rise, whose wife shall she be of them? for the seven had her to wife."

And Jesus answering said unto them, "Do ye not therefore err, because ye know not the scriptures, neither the power of God? For when they shall rise from the dead, they neither marry, nor are given in marriage; but are as the angels which are in heaven. And as touching the dead, that they rise: have ye not read in the book of Moses, how in the bush God spake unto him, saying, 'I am the God of Abraham, and the God of Isaac, and the God of Jacob?' He is not the God of the dead, but the God of the living: ye therefore do greatly err."

And one of the scribes came, and having heard them reasoning together, and perceiving that he had answered them well, asked him, "Which is the first commandment of all?"

And Jesus answered him, "The first of all the commandments is, 'Hear, O Israel; the Lord our God is one Lord: and thou shalt love the Lord thy God with all thy heart, and with all thy soul, and with all thy mind, and with all thy strength': this is the first commandment. And the second is like, namely this, 'Thou shalt love thy neighbour as thyself.' There is none other commandment greater than these."

And the scribe said unto him, "Well, Master, thou hast said the truth: for there is one God; and there is none other but he: and to love him with all the heart, and with all the understanding, and with all the soul, and with all the strength, and to love his neighbour as himself, is more than all whole burnt offerings and sacrifices."

And when Jesus saw that he answered discreetly, he said unto him, "Thou art not far from the kingdom of God." And no man after that durst ask him any question.

And Jesus answered and said, while he taught in the temple, "How say the scribes that Christ is the son of David? For David himself said by the Holy Ghost, 'The LORD said to my Lord, Sit thou on my right hand, till I make thine enemies thy footstool.' David therefore himself calleth him Lord; and whence is he then his son?" And the common people heard him gladly.

And he said unto them in his doctrine, "Beware of the scribes, which love to go in long clothing, and love salutations in the marketplaces, and the chief seats in the synagogues, and the uppermost rooms at feasts: which devour widows' houses, and for a pretence make long prayers: these shall receive greater damnation."

And Jesus sat over against the treasury, and beheld how the people cast money into the treasury: and many that were rich cast in much. And there came a certain poor widow, and she threw in two mites, which make a farthing. And he called unto him his disciples, and saith unto them, "Verily I say unto you, that this poor widow hath cast more in, than all they which have cast into the treasury: for all they did cast in of their abundance; but she of her want did cast in all that she had, even all her living."

And as he went out of the temple, one of his disciples saith unto him, "Master, see what manner of stones and what buildings are here!"

And Jesus answering said unto him, "Seest thou these great buildings? there shall not be left one stone upon another, that shall not be thrown down."

And as he sat upon the mount of Olives over against the temple, Peter and James and John and Andrew asked him privately, "Tell us, when shall these things be? and what shall be the sign when all these things shall be fulfilled?"

And Jesus answering them began to say, "Take heed lest any man deceive you: for many shall come in my name, saying, 'I am Christ'; and shall deceive many. And when ye shall hear of wars and rumours of wars, be ye not troubled: for such things must needs be; but the end shall not be yet. For nation shall rise against nation, and kingdom against kingdom: and there shall be earthquakes in divers places, and there shall be famines and troubles: these are the beginnings of sorrows.

"But take heed to yourselves: for they shall deliver you up to councils; and in the synagogues ye shall be beaten: and ye shall be brought before rulers and kings for my sake, for a testimony against them. And the gospel must first be published among all nations. But when they shall lead you, and deliver you up, take no thought beforehand what ye shall speak, neither do ye premeditate: but whatsoever shall be given you in that hour, that speak ye: for it is not ye that speak, but the Holy Ghost. Now the brother shall betray the brother to death, and the father the son; and children shall rise up against their parents, and shall cause them to be put to death. And ye shall be hated of all men for my name's sake: but he that shall endure unto the end, the same shall be saved.

"But when ye shall see the abomination of desolation, spoken of by Daniel the prophet, standing where it ought not, (let him that readeth understand,) then let them that be in Judæa flee to the mountains: and let him that is on the housetop not go down into the house, neither enter therein, to take any thing out of his house: and let him that is in the field not turn back again for to take up his garment. But woe to them that are with child, and to them that give suck in those days! And pray ye that your flight be not in the winter. For in those days shall be affliction, such as was not from the beginning of the creation which God created unto this time, neither shall be. And except that the Lord had shortened those days, no flesh should be saved: but for the elect's sake, whom he hath chosen, he hath shortened the days. And then if any man shall say to you, 'Lo, here is Christ'; or, 'lo, he is there'; believe him not: for false Christs and false prophets shall rise, and shall shew signs and wonders, to seduce, if it were possible, even the elect But take ye heed: behold, I have foretold you all things.

"But in those days, after that tribulation, the sun shall be darkened, and the moon shall not give her light, And the stars of heaven shall fall, and the powers that are in heaven shall be shaken. And then shall they see the Son of man coming in the clouds with great power and glory. And then shall he send his angels, and shall gather together his elect from the four winds, from the uttermost part of the earth to the uttermost part of heaven. Now learn a parable of the fig tree; when her branch is yet tender, and putteth forth leaves, ye know that summer is near: so ye in like manner, when ye shall see these things come to pass, know that it is nigh, even at the doors. Verily I say unto you, that this generation shall not pass, till all these things be done. Heaven and earth shall pass away: but my words shall not pass away.

"But of that day and that hour knoweth no man, no, not the angels which are in heaven, neither the Son, but the Father. Take ye heed, watch and pray: for ye know not when the time is. For the Son of man is as a man taking a far journey, who left his house, and gave authority to his servants, and to every man his work, and commanded the porter to watch. Watch ye therefore: for ye know not when the master of the house cometh, at even, or at midnight, or at the cockcrowing, or in the morning: lest coming suddenly he find you sleeping. And what I say unto you I say unto all, Watch."

After two days was the feast of the passover, and of unleavened bread: and the chief priests and the scribes sought how they might take him by craft, and put him to death. But they said, "Not on the feast day, lest there be an uproar of the people."

And being in Bethany in the house of Simon the leper, as he sat at meat, there came a woman having an alabaster box of ointment of spikenard very precious; and she brake the box, and poured it on his head. And there were some that had indignation within themselves, and said, "Why was this waste of the ointment made? For it might have been sold for more than three hundred pence, and have been given to the poor." And they murmured against her.

And Jesus said, "Let her alone; why trouble ye her? she hath wrought a good work on me. For ye have the poor with you always, and whensoever ye will ye may do them good: but me ye have not always. She hath done what she could: she is come aforehand to anoint my body to the burying. Verily I say unto you, wheresoever this gospel shall be preached throughout the whole world, this also that she hath done shall be spoken of for a memorial of her."

And Judas Iscariot, one of the twelve, went unto the chief priests, to betray him unto them. And when they heard it, they were glad, and promised to give him money. And he sought how he might conveniently betray him.

And the first day of unleavened bread, when they killed the passover, his disciples said unto him, "Where wilt thou that we go and prepare that thou mayest eat the passover?"

And he sendeth forth two of his disciples, and saith unto them, "Go ye into the city, and there shall meet you a man bearing a pitcher of water: follow him. And wheresoever he shall go in, say ye to the goodman of the house, 'The Master saith, Where is the guestchamber, where I shall eat the passover with my disciples?' And he will shew you a large upper room furnished and prepared: there make ready for us." And his disciples went forth, and came into the city, and found as he had said unto them: and they made ready the passover.

And in the evening he cometh with the twelve. And as they sat and did eat, Jesus said, "Verily I say unto you, one of you which eateth with me shall betray me."

And they began to be sorrowful, and to say unto him one by one, "Is it I?" and another said, "Is it I?"

And he answered and said unto them, "It is one of the twelve, that dippeth with me in the dish. The Son of man indeed goeth, as it is written of him: but woe to that man by whom the Son of man is betrayed! good were it for that man if he had never been born."

And as they did eat, Jesus took bread, and blessed, and brake it, and gave to them, and said, "Take, eat: this is my body." And he took the cup, and when he had given thanks, he gave it to them: and they all drank of it. And he said unto them, "This is my blood of the new testament, which is shed for many. Verily I say unto you, I will drink no more of the fruit of the vine, until that day that I drink it new in the kingdom of God."

And when they had sung an hymn, they went out into the mount of Olives. And Jesus saith unto them, "All ye shall be offended because of me this night: for it is written, 'I will smite the shepherd, and the sheep shall be scattered.' But after that I am risen, I will go before you into Galilee."

But Peter said unto him, "Although all shall be offended, yet will not I."

And Jesus saith unto him, "Verily I say unto thee, that this day, even in this night, before the cock crow twice, thou shalt deny me thrice."

But he spake the more vehemently, "If I should die with thee, I will not deny thee in any wise." Likewise also said they all.

And they came to a place which was named Gethsemane: and he saith to his disciples, "Sit ye here, while I shall pray." And he taketh with him Peter and James and John, and began to be sore amazed, and to be very heavy; and saith unto them, "My soul is exceeding sorrowful unto death: tarry ye here, and watch."

And he went forward a little, and fell on the ground, and prayed that, if it were possible, the hour might pass from him. And he said, "Abba, Father, all things are possible unto thee; take away this cup from me: nevertheless not what I will, but what thou wilt." And he cometh, and findeth them sleeping, and saith unto Peter, "Simon, sleepest thou? couldest not thou watch one hour? Watch ye and pray, lest ye enter into temptation. The spirit truly is ready, but the flesh is weak." And again he went away, and prayed, and spake the same words. And when he returned, he found them asleep again, (for their eyes were heavy,) neither wist they what to answer him. And he cometh the third time, and saith unto them, "Sleep on now, and take your rest:[22] it is enough, the hour is come; behold, the Son of man is betrayed into the hands of sinners. Rise up, let us go; lo, he that betrayeth me is at hand."

And immediately, while he yet spake, cometh Judas, one of the twelve, and with him a great multitude with swords and staves, from the chief priests and the scribes and the elders. And he that betrayed him had given them a token, saying, "Whomsoever I shall kiss, that same is he; take him, and lead him away safely." And as soon as he was come, he goeth straightway to him, and saith, "Master, master;" and kissed him.

And they laid their hands on him, and took him. And one of them that stood by[23] drew a sword, and smote a servant of the high priest, and cut off his ear. And Jesus answered and said unto them, "Are ye come out, as against a thief, with swords and with staves to take me? I was daily with you in the temple teach-

[22] Spoken reproachfully.
[23] In St. John's Gospel, Peter is named.

ing, and ye took me not: but the scriptures must be fulfilled." And they all forsook him, and fled.

And there followed him a certain young man,[24] having a linen cloth cast about his naked body; and the young men laid hold on him: and he left the linen cloth, and fled from them naked.

And they led Jesus away to the high priest: and with him were assembled all the chief priests and the elders and the scribes. And Peter followed him afar off, even into the palace of the high priest: and he sat with the servants, and warmed himself at the fire. And the chief priests and all the council sought for witness against Jesus to put him to death; and found none. For many bare false witness against him, but their witness agreed not together. And there arose certain, and bare false witness against him, saying, "We heard him say, 'I will destroy this temple that is made with hands, and within three days I will build another made without hands.' " But neither so did their witness agree together.

And the high priest stood up in the midst, and asked Jesus, saying, "Answerest thou nothing? what is it which these witness against thee?" But he held his peace, and answered nothing. Again the high priest asked him, and said unto him, "Art thou the Christ, the Son of the Blessed?"

And Jesus said, "I am: and ye shall see the Son of man sitting on the right hand of power, and coming in the clouds of heaven."

Then the high priest rent his clothes, and saith, "What need we any further witnesses? Ye have heard the blasphemy: what think ye?" And they all condemned him to be guilty of death. And some began to spit on him, and to cover his face, and to buffet him, and to say unto him, "Prophesy," and the servants did strike him with the palms of their hands.

And as Peter was beneath in the palace, there cometh one of the maids of the high priest: and when she saw Peter warm-

[24] According to many commentators, this was Mark himself.

ing himself, she looked upon him, and said, "And thou also wast with Jesus of Nazareth."

But he denied, saying, "I know not, neither understand I what thou sayest." And he went out into the porch; and the cock crew.

And a maid saw him again, and began to say to them that stood by, "This is one of them." And he denied it again. And a little after, they that stood by said again to Peter, "Surely thou art one of them: for thou art a Galilæan, and thy speech agreeth thereto."

But he began to curse and to swear, saying, "I know not this man of whom ye speak." And the second time the cock crew. And Peter called to mind the word that Jesus said unto him, "Before the cock crow twice, thou shalt deny me thrice." And when he thought thereon, he wept.

And straightway in the morning the chief priests held a consultation with the elders and scribes and the whole council, and bound Jesus, and carried him away, and delivered him to Pilate.[25] And Pilate asked him, "Art thou the King of the Jews?"

And he answering said unto him, "Thou sayest it." And the chief priests accused him of many things: but he answered nothing.

And Pilate asked him again, saying, "Answerest thou nothing? behold how many things they witness against thee." But Jesus yet answered nothing; so that Pilate marvelled.

Now at that feast he released unto them one prisoner, whomsoever they desired. And there was one named Barabbas, which lay bound with them that had made insurrection with him, who had committed murder in the insurrection. And the multitude crying aloud began to desire him to do as he had ever done unto them. But Pilate answered them, saying, "Will ye that I release unto you the King of the Jews?" For he knew that the chief priests had delivered him for envy. But the chief priests moved

[25] Pontius Pilate, the Roman governor of Judaea.

the people, that he should rather release Barabbas unto them. And Pilate answered and said again unto them, "What will ye then that I shall do unto him whom ye call the King of the Jews?"

And they cried out again, "Crucify him."

Then Pilate said unto them, "Why, what evil hath he done?"

And they cried out the more exceedingly, "Crucify him."

And so Pilate, willing to content the people, released Barabbas unto them, and delivered Jesus, when he had scourged him, to be crucified. And the soldiers led him away into the hall, called Prætorium; and they call together the whole band. And they clothed him with purple, and platted a crown of thorns, and put it about his head, and began to salute him, "Hail, King of the Jews!" And they smote him on the head with a reed, and did spit upon him, and bowing their knees worshipped him. And when they had mocked him, they took off the purple from him, and put his own clothes on him, and led him out to crucify him.

And they compel one Simon a Cyrenian, who passed by, coming out of the country, the father of Alexander and Rufus, to bear his cross. And they bring him unto the place Golgotha, which is, being interpreted, the place of a skull. And they gave him to drink wine mingled with myrrh: but he received it not. And when they had crucified him, they parted his garments, casting lots upon them, what every man should take. And it was the third hour, and they crucified him. And the superscription of his accusation was written over, THE KING OF THE JEWS. And with him they crucify two thieves; the one on his right hand, and the other on his left. And the scripture was fulfilled, which saith; "And he was numbered with the transgressors." And they that passed by railed on him, wagging their heads, and saying, "Ah, thou that destroyest the temple, and buildest it in three days, save thyself, and come down from the cross." Likewise also the chief priests mocking said among themselves with the scribes,

"He saved others; himself he cannot save. Let Christ the King of Israel descend now from the cross, that we may see and believe." And they that were crucified with him reviled him.

And when the sixth hour was come, there was darkness over the whole land until the ninth hour. And at the ninth hour Jesus cried with a loud voice, saying, "Eloi, Eloi, lama sabachthani?" which is, being interpreted, "My God, my God, why hast thou forsaken me?" And some of them that stood by, when they heard it, said, "Behold, he calleth Elias." And one ran and filled a sponge full of vinegar, and put it on a reed, and gave him to drink, saying, "Let alone; let us see whether Elias will come to take him down." And Jesus cried with a loud voice, and gave up the ghost. And the veil of the temple was rent in twain from the top to the bottom.

And when the centurion, which stood over against him, saw that he so cried out, and gave up the ghost, he said, "Truly this man was the Son of God." There were also women looking on afar off: among whom was Mary Magdalene, and Mary the mother of James the less and of Joses, and Salome; (who also, when he was in Galilee, followed him, and ministered unto him;) and many other women which came up with him unto Jerusalem.

And now when the even was come, because it was the preparation, that is, the day before the sabbath, Joseph of Arimathæa, an honourable counsellor, which also waited for the kingdom of God, came, and went in boldly unto Pilate, and craved the body of Jesus. And Pilate marvelled if he were already dead: and calling unto him the centurion, he asked him whether he had been any while dead. And when he knew it of the centurion, he gave the body to Joseph. And he bought fine linen, and took him down, and wrapped him in the linen, and laid him in a sepulchre which was hewn out of a rock, and rolled a stone unto the door of the sepulchre. And Mary Magdalene and Mary the mother of Joses beheld where he was laid.

And when the sabbath was past, Mary Magdalene, and Mary

the mother of James, and Salome, had bought sweet spices, that they might come and anoint him. And very early in the morning the first day of the week, they came unto the sepulchre at the rising of the sun. And they said among themselves, "Who shall roll us away the stone from the door of the sepulchre?" And when they looked, they saw that the stone was rolled away: for it was very great. And entering into the sepulchre, they saw a young man sitting on the right side, clothed in a long white garment; and they were affrighted. And he saith unto them, "Be not affrighted: ye seek Jesus of Nazareth, which was crucified: he is risen; he is not here: behold the place where they laid him. But go your way, tell his disciples and Peter that he goeth before you into Galilee: there shall ye see him, as he said unto you." And they went out quickly, and fled from the sepulchre; for they trembled and were amazed: neither said they any thing to any man; for they were afraid.

[26]Now when Jesus was risen early the first day of the week, he appeared first to Mary Magdalene, out of whom he had cast seven devils. And she went and told them that had been with him, as they mourned and wept. And they, when they had heard that he was alive, and had been seen of her, believed not. After that he appeared in another form unto two of them, as they walked, and went into the country. And they went and told it unto the residue: neither believed they them.

Afterward he appeared unto the eleven as they sat at meat, and upbraided them with their unbelief and hardness of heart, because they believed not them which had seen him after he was risen. And he said unto them, "Go ye into all the world, and preach the gospel to every creature. He that believeth and is baptized shall be saved; but he that believeth not shall be damned. And these signs shall follow them that believe; in my name shall they cast out devils; they shall speak with new tongues; they shall take up serpents; and if they drink any deadly thing, it shall not

[26] Many authorities believe that the passage from this point to the end of this Gospel was not written by Mark himself.

hurt them; they shall lay hands on the sick, and they shall recover."

So then after the Lord had spoken unto them, he was received up into heaven, and sat on the right hand of God. And they went forth, and preached every where, the Lord working with them, and confirming the word with signs following. Amen.

From MATTHEW

The Wise Men. The Flight into Egypt

• MATTHEW 2 •

Now when Jesus was born in Bethlehem of Judæa in the days of Herod the king, behold, there came wise men from the east to Jerusalem, saying, "Where is he that is born King of the Jews? for we have seen his star in the east, and are come to worship him."

When Herod the king had heard these things, he was troubled, and all Jerusalem with him. And when he had gathered all the chief priests and scribes of the people together, he demanded of them where Christ should be born. And they said unto him, "In Bethlehem of Judæa: for thus it is written by the prophet, 'And thou Bethlehem, in the land of Juda, art not the least among the princes of Juda: for out of thee shall come a Governor, that shall rule my people Israel.'"

Then Herod, when he had privily called the wise men, enquired of them diligently what time the star appeared. And he sent them to Bethlehem, and said, "Go and search diligently for the young child; and when ye have found him, bring me word again, that I may come and worship him also." When they had heard the king, they departed; and, lo, the star, which they saw in the east, went before them, till it came and stood over where the young child was. When they saw the star, they rejoiced with exceeding great joy.

And when they were come into the house, they saw the young child with Mary his mother, and fell down, and worshipped him: and when they had opened their treasures, they presented unto him gifts; gold, and frankincense, and myrrh. And being warned of God in a dream that they should not return to Herod, they departed into their own country another way.

And when they were departed, behold, the angel of the Lord appeareth to Joseph in a dream, saying, "Arise, and take the young child and his mother, and flee into Egypt, and be thou there until I bring thee word: for Herod will seek the young child to destroy him." When he arose, he took the young child and his mother by night, and departed into Egypt: and was there until the death of Herod: that it might be fulfilled which was spoken of the Lord by the prophet, saying, "Out of Egypt have I called my son."

Then Herod, when he saw that he was mocked of the wise men, was exceeding wroth, and sent forth, and slew all the children that were in Bethlehem, and in all the coasts thereof, from two years old and under, according to the time which he had diligently enquired of the wise men. Then was fulfilled that which was spoken by Jeremy the prophet, saying, "In Rama was there a voice heard, lamentation, and weeping, and great mourning, Rachel weeping for her children, and would not be comforted, because they are not."

But when Herod was dead, behold, an angel of the Lord appeareth in a dream to Joseph in Egypt, saying, "Arise, and take the young child and his mother, and go into the land of Israel: for they are dead which sought the young child's life." And he arose, and took the young child and his mother, and came into the land of Israel. But when he heard that Archelaus did reign in Judæa in the room of his father Herod, he was afraid to go thither: notwithstanding, being warned of God in a dream, he turned aside into the parts of Galilee: And he came and dwelt in a city called Nazareth: that it might be fulfilled which was spoken by the prophets, "He shall be called a Nazarene."

The Temptation

• MATTHEW 4: 1–11 •

Then was Jesus led up of the spirit into the wilderness to be tempted of the devil. And when he had fasted forty days and forty nights, he was afterward an hungred. And when the tempter came to him, he said, "If thou be the Son of God, command that these stones be made bread."

But he answered and said, "It is written, 'Man shall not live by bread alone, but by every word that proceedeth out of the mouth of God.'"

Then the devil taketh him up into the holy city, and setteth him on a pinnacle of the temple, and saith unto him, "If thou be the Son of God, cast thyself down: for it is written, 'He shall give his angels charge concerning thee: and in their hands they shall bear thee up, lest at any time thou dash thy foot against a stone.'"

Jesus said unto him, "It is written again, 'Thou shalt not tempt the Lord thy God.'"

Again, the devil taketh him up into an exceeding high mountain, and sheweth him all the kingdoms of the world, and the glory of them; and saith unto him, "All these things will I give thee, if thou wilt fall down and worship me."

Then saith Jesus unto him, "Get thee hence, Satan: for it is written, 'Thou shalt worship the Lord thy God, and him only shalt thou serve.'"

Then the devil leaveth him, and, behold, angels came and ministered unto him.

The Sermon on the Mount

And seeing the multitudes, he went up into a mountain: and when he was set, his disciples came unto him: and he opened his mouth, and taught them, saying, "Blessed are the poor in spirit: for theirs is the kingdom of heaven. Blessed are they that mourn: for they shall be comforted. Blessed are the meek: for they shall inherit the earth. Blessed are they which do hunger and thirst after righteousness: for they shall be filled. Blessed are the merciful: for they shall obtain mercy. Blessed are the pure in heart: for they shall see God. Blessed are the peace-makers: for they shall be called the children of God. Blessed are they which are persecuted for righteousness' sake: for theirs is the kingdom of heaven. Blessed are ye, when men shall revile you, and persecute you, and shall say all manner of evil against you falsely, for my sake. Rejoice, and be exceeding glad: for great is your reward in heaven: for so persecuted they the prophets which were before you.

"Ye are the salt of the earth: but if the salt have lost his savour, wherewith shall it be salted? it is thenceforth good for nothing, but to be cast out, and to be trodden under foot of men. Ye are the light of the world. A city that is set on an hill cannot be hid. Neither do men light a candle, and put it under a bushel, but on a candlestick; and it giveth light unto all that are in the house. Let your light so shine before men, that they may see your good works, and glorify your Father which is in heaven.

"Think not that I am come to destroy the law, or the prophets: I am not come to destroy, but to fulfil. For verily I say unto you, till heaven and earth pass, one jot[1] or one tittle[2] shall in

[1] *Yod*, the smallest letter in the Hebrew alphabet.
[2] A minute stroke used to distinguish two similar letters in the Hebrew alphabet.

no wise pass from the law, till all be fulfilled. Whosoever therefore shall break one of these least commandments, and shall teach
men so, he shall be called the least in the kingdom of heaven:
but whosoever shall do and teach them, the same shall be called
great in the kingdom of heaven. For I say unto you, that except
your righteousness shall exceed the righteousness of the scribes
and Pharisees, ye shall in no case enter into the kingdom of
heaven.

"Ye have heard that it was said by them of old time, 'Thou
shalt not kill; and whosoever shall kill shall be in danger of the
judgment.' But I say unto you, that whosoever is angry with his
brother without a cause shall be in danger of the judgment:[3] and
whosoever shall say to his brother, 'Raca,' [4] shall be in danger of
the council;[5] but whosoever shall say, 'Thou fool,' shall be in
danger of hell fire. Therefore if thou bring thy gift to the altar,
and there rememberest that thy brother hath ought against thee;
leave there thy gift before the altar, and go thy way; first be
reconciled to thy brother, and then come and offer thy gift.
Agree with thine adversary[6] quickly, whiles thou art in the way
with him; lest at any time the adversary deliver thee to
the judge, and the judge deliver thee to the officer, and thou be
cast into prison. Verily I say unto thee, thou shalt by no means
come out thence, till thou hast paid the uttermost farthing.

"Ye have heard that it was said by them of old time, 'Thou
shalt not commit adultery.' But I say unto you, that whosoever
looketh on a woman to lust after her hath committed adultery
with her already in his heart. And if thy right eye offend thee,
pluck it out, and cast it from thee: for it is profitable for thee
that one of thy members should perish, and not that thy whole
body should be cast into hell. And if thy right hand offend
thee, cut it off, and cast it from thee: for it is profitable for thee

[3] The local tribunal.
[4] "Worthless, empty-headed."
[5] The Sanhedrin.
[6] i.e., the injured brother mentioned above.

that one of thy members should perish, and not that thy whole body should be cast into hell. It hath been said. 'Whosoever shall put away his wife, let him give her a writing of divorcement.' But I say unto you, that whosoever shall put away his wife, saving for the cause of fornication, causeth her to commit adultery: and whosoever shall marry her that is divorced committeth adultery.

"Again, ye have heard that it hath been said by them of old time, 'Thou shalt not forswear thyself, but shalt perform unto the Lord thine oaths.' But I say unto you, swear not at all; neither by heaven; for it is God's throne: nor by the earth; for it is his footstool: neither by Jerusalem; for it is the city of the great King. Neither shalt thou swear by thy head, because thou canst not make one hair white or black. But let your communication be, 'Yea, yea; Nay, nay,' for whatsoever is more than these cometh of evil.

"Ye have heard that it hath been said, 'An eye for an eye, and a tooth for a tooth.' But I say unto you, that ye resist not evil: but whosoever shall smite thee on thy right cheek, turn to him the other also. And if any man will sue thee at the law, and take away thy coat, let him have thy cloak also. And whosoever shall compel thee to go a mile,[7] go with him twain. Give to him that asketh thee, and from him that would borrow of thee turn not thou away.

"Ye have heard that it hath been said, 'Thou shalt love thy neighbour, and hate thine enemy.' But I say unto you, love your enemies, bless them that curse you, do good to them that hate you, and pray for them which despitefully use you, and persecute you; that ye may be the children of your Father which is in heaven: for he maketh his sun to rise on the evil and on the good, and sendeth rain on the just and on the unjust. For if ye love them which love you, what reward have ye? do not even the publicans the same? And if ye salute your brethren only, what do ye more than others? do not even the publicans so? Be ye

[7] Roman soldiers might compel the natives of a subject country to carry their baggage.

therefore perfect, even as your Father which is in heaven is perfect.

"Take heed that ye do not your alms before men, to be seen of them: otherwise ye have no reward of your Father which is in heaven. Therefore when thou doest thine alms, do not sound a trumpet before thee, as the hypocrites do in the synagogues and in the streets, that they may have glory of men. Verily I say unto you, they have their reward. But when thou doest alms, let not thy left hand know what thy right hand doeth: that thine alms may be in secret: and thy Father which seeth in secret himself shall reward thee openly.

"And when thou prayest, thou shalt not be as the hypocrites are: for they love to pray standing in the synagogues and in the corners of the streets, that they may be seen of men. Verily I say unto you, they have their reward. But thou, when thou prayest, enter into thy closet, and when thou hast shut thy door, pray to thy Father which is in secret; and thy Father which seeth in secret shall reward thee openly. But when ye pray, use not vain repetitions, as the heathen do: for they think that they shall be heard for their much speaking. Be not ye therefore like unto them: for your Father knoweth what things ye have need of, before ye ask him. After this manner therefore pray ye: 'Our Father which art in heaven, Hallowed be thy name. Thy kingdom come. Thy will be done in earth, as it is in heaven. Give us this day our daily bread. And forgive us our debts, as we forgive our debtors. And lead us not into temptation, but deliver us from evil: for thine is the kingdom, and the power, and the glory, for ever. Amen.' For if ye forgive men their trespasses, your heavenly Father will also forgive you: but if ye forgive not men their trespasses, neither will your Father forgive your trespasses.

"Moreover when ye fast, be not, as the hypocrites, of a sad countenance: for they disfigure their faces, that they may appear unto men to fast. Verily I say unto you, they have their reward. But thou, when thou fastest, anoint thine head, and wash thy face; that thou appear not unto men to fast, but unto thy Father which is in secret: and thy Father, which seeth in secret, shall reward thee openly.

"Lay not up for yourselves treasures upon earth, where moth and rust doth corrupt, and where thieves break through and steal: but lay up for yourselves treasures in heaven, where neither moth nor rust doth corrupt, and where thieves do not break through nor steal: for where your treasure is, there will your heart be also. The light of the body is the eye: if therefore thine eye be single, thy whole body shall be full of light. But if thine eye be evil, thy whole body shall be full of darkness. If therefore the light that is in thee be darkness, how great is that darkness!

"No man can serve two masters: for either he will hate the one, and love the other; or else he will hold to the one, and despise the other. Ye cannot serve God and mammon. Therefore I say unto you, take no thought for your life, what ye shall eat, or what ye shall drink; nor yet for your body, what ye shall put on. Is not the life more than meat, and the body than raiment? Behold the fowls of the air: for they sow not, neither do they reap, nor gather into barns; yet your heavenly Father feedeth them. Are ye not much better than they? Which of you by taking thought can add one cubit unto his stature? And why take ye thought for raiment? Consider the lilies of the field, how they grow; they toil not, neither do they spin: and yet I say unto you, that even Solomon in all his glory was not arrayed like one of these. Wherefore, if God so clothe the grass of the field, which to day is, and to morrow is cast into the oven, shall he not much more clothe you, O ye of little faith? Therefore take no thought,[8] saying, 'What shall we eat?' or, 'What shall we drink?' or, 'Wherewithal shall we be clothed?' (for after all these things do the Gentiles seek:) for your heavenly Father knoweth that ye have need of all these things. But seek ye first the kingdom of God, and his righteousness; and all these things shall be

[8] i.e.. do not be anxious.

added unto you. Take therefore no thought for the morrow: for the morrow shall take thought for the things of itself. Sufficient unto the day is the evil thereof.

"Judge not, that ye be not judged. For with what judgment ye judge, ye shall be judged: and with what measure ye mete, it shall be measured to you again. And why beholdest thou the mote that is in thy brother's eye, but considerest not the beam[9] that is in thine own eye? Or how wilt thou say to thy brother, 'Let me pull out the mote out of thine eye,' and, behold, a beam is in thine own eye? Thou hypocrite, first cast out the beam out of thine own eye; and then shalt thou see clearly to cast out the mote out of thy brother's eye.

"Give not that which is holy unto the dogs, neither cast ye your pearls before swine, lest they trample them under their feet, and turn again and rend you.

"Ask, and it shall be given you; seek, and ye shall find; knock, and it shall be opened unto you: for every one that asketh receiveth; and he that seeketh findeth; and to him that knocketh it shall be opened. Or what man is there of you, whom if his son ask bread, will be give him a stone? Or if he ask a fish, will he give him a serpent? If ye then, being evil, know how to give good gifts unto your children, how much more shall your Father which is in heaven give good things to them that ask him? Therefore all things whatsoever ye would that men should do to you, do ye even so to them: for this is the law and the prophets.

"Enter ye in at the strait gate: for wide is the gate, and broad is the way, that leadeth to destruction, and many there be which go in thereat: because strait is the gate, and narrow is the way, which leadeth unto life, and few there be that find it.

"Beware of false prophets, which come to you in sheep's clothing, but inwardly they are ravening wolves. Ye shall know them by their fruits. Do men gather grapes of thorns, or figs of thistles? Even so every good tree bringeth forth good fruit; but a corrupt tree bringeth forth evil fruit. A good tree cannot bring

[9] Roof-beam—that is, something vastly larger than the infinitesimal mote.

forth evil fruit, neither can a corrupt tree bring forth good fruit. Every tree that bringeth not forth good fruit is hewn down, and cast into the fire. Wherefore by their fruits ye shall know them.

"Not every one that saith unto me, 'Lord, Lord,' shall enter into the kingdom of heaven; but he that doeth the will of my Father which is in heaven. Many will say to me in that day, 'Lord, Lord, have we not prophesied in thy name? and in thy name have cast out devils? and in thy name done many wonderful works?' And then will I profess unto them, 'I never knew you: depart from me, ye that work iniquity.'

"Therefore whosoever heareth these sayings of mine, and doeth them, I will liken him unto a wise man, which built his house upon a rock: and the rain descended, and the floods came, and the winds blew, and beat upon that house; and it fell not: for it was founded upon a rock. And every one that heareth these sayings of mine, and doeth them not, shall be likened unto a foolish man, which built his house upon the sand: and the rain descended, and the floods came, and the winds blew, and beat upon that house; and it fell: and great was the fall of it."

And it came to pass, when Jesus had ended these sayings, the people were astonished at his doctrine: for he taught them as one having authority, and not as the scribes.

The Parable of the Unmerciful Servant

• MATTHEW 18: 23–35 •

"Therefore is the kingdom of heaven likened unto a certain king, which would take account of his servants. And when he had begun to reckon, one was brought unto him, which owed him ten thousand talents. But forasmuch as he had not to pay, his lord commanded him to be sold, and his wife, and children, and all that he had, and payment to be made. The servant therefore fell down, and worshipped him, saying, 'Lord, have patience with me, and I will pay thee all.' Then the lord of that servant was moved with compassion, and loosed him, and forgave him the debt.

"But the same servant went out, and found one of his fellow-servants, which owed him an hundred pence: and he laid hands on him, and took him by the throat, saying, 'Pay me that thou owest.' And his fellow-servant fell down at his feet, and besought him, saying, 'Have patience with me, and I will pay thee all.' And he would not: but went and cast him into prison, till he should pay the debt.

"So when his fellow-servants saw what was done, they were very sorry, and came and told unto their lord all that was done. Then his lord, after that he had called him, said unto him, 'O thou wicked servant, I forgave thee all that debt, because thou desiredst me: shouldest not thou also have had compassion on thy fellow-servant, even as I had pity on thee?' And his lord was wroth, and delivered him to the tormentors, till he should pay all that was due unto him.

"So likewise shall my heavenly Father do also unto you, if ye from your hearts forgive not every one his brother their trespasses."

The Parable of the Laborers in the Vineyard

• MATTHEW 20: 1–16 •

"For the kingdom of heaven is like unto a man that is an householder, which went out early in the morning to hire labourers into his vineyard. And when he had agreed with the labourers for a penny a day, he sent them into his vineyard.

"And he went out about the third hour, and saw others standing idle in the marketplace, and said unto them; 'Go ye also into the vineyard, and whatsoever is right I will give you.' And they went their way.

"Again he went out about the sixth and ninth hour, and did likewise. And about the eleventh hour he went out, and found others standing idle, and saith unto them, 'Why stand ye here all the day idle?' They say unto him, 'Because no man hath hired us.' He saith unto them, 'Go ye also into the vineyard; and whatsoever is right, that shall ye receive.'

"So when even was come, the lord of the vineyard saith unto his steward, 'Call the labourers, and give them their hire, beginning from the last unto the first.' And when they came that were hired about the eleventh hour, they received every man a penny. But when the first came, they supposed that they should have received more; and they likewise received every man a penny. And when they had received it, they murmured against the goodman of the house, saying, 'These last have wrought but one hour, and thou hast made them equal unto us, which have borne the burden and heat of the day.'

"But he answered one of them, and said, 'Friend, I do thee no wrong: didst not thou agree with me for a penny? Take that thine is, and go thy way: I will give unto this last, even as unto thee. Is it not lawful for me to do what I will with mine own? Is thine eye evil, because I am good?' [10]

"So the last shall be first, and the first last: for many be called, but few chosen."

The Parable of the Marriage Feast

• MATTHEW 22:1–14 •

And Jesus answered and spake unto them again by parables, and said, "The kingdom of heaven is like unto a certain king, which made a marriage for his son, and sent forth his serv-

[10] Are you jealous because of my generosity?

ants to call them that were bidden to the wedding: and they would not come. Again, he sent forth other servants, saying, 'Tell them which are bidden, Behold, I have prepared my dinner: my oxen and my fatlings are killed, and all things are ready: come unto the marriage.' But they made light of it, and went their ways, one to his farm, another to his merchandise: and the remnant took his servants, and entreated them spitefully, and slew them.

"But when the king heard thereof, he was wroth: and he sent forth his armies, and destroyed those murderers, and burned up their city. Then saith he to his servants, 'The wedding is ready, but they which were bidden were not worthy. Go ye therefore into the highways, and as many as ye shall find, bid to the marriage.' So those servants went out into the highways, and gathered together all as many as they found, both bad and good: and the wedding was furnished with guests.

"And when the king came in to see the guests, he saw there a man which had not on a wedding garment: and he saith unto him, 'Friend, how camest thou in hither not having a wedding garment?' [11] And he was speechless. Then said the king to the servants, 'Bind him hand and foot, and take him away, and cast him into outer darkness; there shall be weeping and gnashing of teeth.'

"For many are called, but few are chosen."

Parables of the Coming

• MATTHEW 24:44 TO 25:46 •

"Therefore be ye also ready: for in such an hour as ye think not the Son of man cometh. Who then is a faithful and wise servant, whom his lord hath made ruler over his household,

[11] In terms of Oriental etiquette, a festive garment was obligatory at a wedding.

to give them meat in due season? Blessed is that servant, whom his lord when he cometh shall find so doing. Verily I say unto you, that he shall make him ruler over all his goods. But and if that evil servant shall say in his heart, 'My lord delayeth his coming': and shall begin to smite his fellow-servants, and to eat and drink with the drunken; the lord of that servant shall come in a day when he looketh not for him, and in an hour that he is not aware of, and shall cut him asunder, and appoint him his portion with the hypocrites: there shall be weeping and gnashing of teeth.

"Then shall the kingdom of heaven be likened unto ten virgins, which took their lamps, and went forth to meet the bridegroom. And five of them were wise, and five were foolish. They that were foolish took their lamps, and took no oil with them: but the wise took oil in their vessels with their lamps. While the bridegroom tarried, they all slumbered and slept. And at midnight there was a cry made, 'Behold, the bridegroom cometh; go ye out to meet him.' Then all those virgins arose, and trimmed their lamps. And the foolish said unto the wise, 'Give us of your oil; for our lamps are gone out.' But the wise answered, saying, 'Not so; lest there be not enough for us and you: but go ye rather to them that sell, and buy for yourselves.' And while they went to buy, the bridegroom came; and they that were ready went in with him to the marriage: and the door was shut. Afterward came also the other virgins, saying, 'Lord, Lord, open to us.' But he answered and said, 'Verily I say unto you, I know you not.' Watch therefore, for ye know neither the day nor the hour wherein the Son of man cometh.

"For the kingdom of heaven is as a man travelling into a far country, who called his own servants, and delivered unto them his goods. And unto one he gave five talents, to another two, and to another one; to every man according to his several ability; and straightway took his journey. Then he that had received the five talents went and traded with the same, and made them other five talents. And likewise he that had received two, he also gained other two. But he that had received one went and digged in the earth, and hid his lord's money. After a long time the lord of those servants cometh, and reckoneth with them. And so he that had received five talents came and brought other five talents, saying, 'Lord, thou deliveredst unto me five talents: behold, I have gained beside them five talents more.' His lord said unto him, 'Well done, thou good and faithful servant: thou hast been faithful over a few things, I will make thee ruler over many things: enter thou into the joy of thy lord.' He also that had received two talents came and said, 'Lord, thou deliveredst unto me two talents: behold, I have gained two other talents beside them.' His lord said unto him, 'Well done, good and faithful servant; thou hast been faithful over a few things, I will make thee ruler over many things: enter thou into the joy of thy lord.' Then he which had received the one talent came and said, 'Lord, I knew thee that thou art an hard man, reaping where thou hast not sown, and gathering where thou hast not strawed: and I was afraid, and went and hid thy talent in the earth: lo, there thou hast that is thine.' His lord answered and said unto him, 'Thou wicked and slothful servant, thou knewest that I reap where I sowed not, and gather where I have not strawed. Thou oughtest therefore to have put my money to the exchangers, and then at my coming I should have received mine own with usury. Take therefore the talent from him, and give it unto him which hath ten talents. For unto every one that hath shall be given, and he shall have abundance: but from him that hath not shall be taken away even that which he hath. And cast ye the unprofitable servant into outer darkness: there shall be weeping and gnashing of teeth.'

"When the Son of man shall come in his glory, and all the holy angels with him, then shall he sit upon the throne of his glory: and before him shall be gathered all nations: and he shall separate them one from another, as a shepherd divideth his sheep from the goats: and he shall set the sheep on his right hand, but the goats on the left. Then shall the King say unto them on his right hand, 'Come, ye blessed of my Father, inherit the kingdom prepared for you from the foundation of the world: for I was an hungred, and ye gave me meat: I was thirsty, and ye gave me drink: I was a stranger, and ye took me in: naked, and ye clothed me: I was sick, and ye visited me: I was in prison, and ye came unto me.' Then shall the righteous answer him, saying, 'Lord, when saw we thee an hungred, and fed thee? or thirsty, and gave thee drink? When saw we thee a stranger, and took thee in? or naked, and clothed thee? Or when saw we thee sick, or in prison, and came unto thee?' And the King shall answer and say unto them, 'Verily I say unto you, inasmuch as ye have done it unto one of the least of these my brethren, ye have done it unto me.' Then shall he say also unto them on the left hand, 'Depart from me, ye cursed, into everlasting fire, prepared for the devil and his angels: for I was an hungred, and ye gave me no meat: I was thirsty, and ye gave me no drink: I was a stranger, and ye took me not in: naked, and ye clothed me not: sick, and in prison, and ye visited me not.' Then shall they also answer him, saying, 'Lord, when saw we thee an hungred, or athirst, or a stranger, or naked, or sick, or in prison, and did not minister unto thee?' Then shall he answer them, saying, 'Verily I say unto you, inasmuch as ye did it not to one of the least of these, ye did it not to me.' And these shall go away into everlasting punishment: but the righteous into life eternal."

The Birth of John the Baptist. The Nativity and Infancy of Jesus

• LUKE 1 AND 2 •

Forasmuch as many have taken in hand to set forth in order a declaration of those things which are most surely believed among us, even as they delivered them unto us, which from the beginning were eyewitnesses, and ministers of the word; it seemed good to me also, having had perfect understanding of all things from the very first, to write unto thee in order, most excellent Theophilus, that thou mightest know the certainty of those things wherein thou hast been instructed.

There was in the days of Herod, the king of Judæa, a certain priest named Zacharias, of the course of Abia[1]: and his wife was of the daughters of Aaron, and her name was Elisabeth. And they were both righteous before God, walking in all the commandments and ordinances of the Lord blameless. And they had no child, because that Elisabeth was barren, and they both were now well stricken in years. And it came to pass, that while he executed the priest's office before God in the order of his course, according to the custom of the priest's office, his lot was to burn incense when he went into the temple of the Lord. And the whole multitude of the people were praying without at the time of incense.

And there appeared unto him an angel of the Lord standing on the right side of the altar of incense. And when Zacharias

[1] The priests were grouped in "courses" or divisions. Each division served in the Temple for two weeks of each year.

saw him, he was troubled, and fear fell upon him. But the angel said unto him, "Fear not, Zacharias: for thy prayer is heard; and thy wife Elisabeth shall bear thee a son, and thou shalt call his name John. And thou shalt have joy and gladness; and many shall rejoice at his birth. For he shall be great in the sight of the Lord, and shall drink neither wine nor strong drink; and he shall be filled with the Holy Ghost, even from his mother's womb. And many of the children of Israel shall he turn to the Lord their God. And he shall go before him in the spirit and power of Elias, to turn the hearts of the fathers to the children, and the disobedient to the wisdom of the just; to make ready a people prepared for the Lord."

And Zacharias said unto the angel, "Whereby shall I know this? for I am an old man, and my wife well stricken in years."

And the angel answering said unto him, "I am Gabriel, that stand in the presence of God; and am sent to speak unto thee, and to shew thee these glad tidings. And, behold, thou shalt be dumb, and not able to speak, until the day that these things shall be performed, because thou believest not my words, which shall be fulfilled in their season."

And the people waited for Zacharias, and marvelled that he tarried so long in the temple. And when he came out, he could not speak unto them: and they perceived that he had seen a vision in the temple: for he beckoned unto them, and remained speechless. And it came to pass, that, as soon as the days of his ministration were accomplished, he departed to his own house. And after those days his wife Elisabeth conceived, and hid herself five months, saying, "Thus hath the Lord dealt with me in the days wherein he looked on me, to take away my reproach among men."

And in the sixth month the angel Gabriel was sent from God unto a city of Galilee, named Nazareth, to a virgin espoused to a man whose name was Joseph, of the house of David; and the virgin's name was Mary. And the angel came in unto her, and said, "Hail, thou that art highly favoured, the Lord is with thee: blessed art thou among women." And when

Mary

she saw him, she was troubled at his saying, and cast in her mind what manner of salutation this should be.

And the angel said unto her, "Fear not, Mary: for thou hast found favour with God. And, behold, thou shalt conceive in thy womb, and bring forth a son, and shalt call his name JESUS. He shall be great, and shall be called the Son of the Highest: and the Lord God shall give unto him the throne of his father David: and he shall reign over the house of Jacob for ever; and of his kingdom there shall be no end."

Then said Mary unto the angel, "How shall this be, seeing I know not a man?"

And the angel answered and said unto her, "The Holy Ghost shall come upon thee, and the power of the Highest shall overshadow thee: therefore also that holy thing which shall be born of thee shall be called the Son of God. And, behold, thy cousin Elisabeth, she hath also conceived a son in her old age: and this is the sixth month with her, who was called barren. For with God nothing shall be impossible."

And Mary said, "Behold the handmaid of the Lord; be it unto me according to thy word." And the angel departed from her.

And Mary arose in those days, and went into the hill country with haste, into a city of Juda; and entered into the house of Zacharias, and saluted Elisabeth. And it came to pass, that, when Elisabeth heard the salutation of Mary, the babe leaped in her womb; and Elisabeth was filled with the Holy Ghost: and she spake out with a loud voice, and said, "Blessed art thou among women, and blessed is the fruit of thy womb. And whence is this to me, that the mother of my Lord should come to me? For, lo, as soon as the voice of thy salutation sounded in mine ears, the babe leaped in my womb for joy. And blessed is she that believed: for there shall be a performance of those things which were told her from the Lord."

And Mary said, "My soul doth magnify the Lord, and my spirit hath rejoiced in God my Saviour. For he hath regarded the low estate of his handmaiden: for, behold, from henceforth all generations shall call me blessed. For he that is mighty hath done to me great things; and holy is his name. And his mercy is on them that fear him from generation to generation. He hath shewed strength with his arm; he hath scattered the proud in the imagination of their hearts. He hath put down the mighty from their seats, and exalted them of low degree. He hath filled the hungry with good things; and the rich he hath sent empty away. He hath holpen his servant Israel, in remembrance of his mercy; as he spake to our fathers, to Abraham, and to his seed for ever." And Mary abode with her about three months, and returned to her own house.

Now Elisabeth's full time came that she should be delivered; and she brought forth a son. And her neighbours and her cousins heard how the Lord had shewed great mercy upon her; and they rejoiced with her. And it came to pass, that on the eighth day they came to circumcise the child; and they called him Zacharias, after the name of his father. And his mother answered and said, "Not so; but he shall be called John."

And they said unto her, "There is none of thy kindred that is called by this name."

And they made signs to his father, how he would have him called. And he asked for a writing table, and wrote, saying, "His name is John." And they marvelled all. And his mouth was opened immediately, and his tongue loosed, and he spake, and praised God. And fear came on all that dwelt round about them: and all these sayings were noised abroad throughout all the hill country of Judæa. And all they that heard them laid them up in their hearts, saying, "What manner of child shall this be!" And the hand of the Lord was with him.

And his father Zacharias was filled with the Holy Ghost, and prophesied, saying, "Blessed be the Lord God of Israel; for he hath visited and redeemed his people, and hath raised up an horn of salvation for us in the house of his servant David; as he spake by the mouth of his holy prophets, which have been since the world began: that we should be saved from our enemies, and from the hand of all that hate us; to perform the mercy promised to our fathers, and to remember his holy covenant; the oath which he sware to our father Abraham, that he would grant unto us, that we being delivered out of the hand of our enemies might serve him without fear, in holiness and righteousness before him, all the days of our life. And thou, child, shalt be called the prophet of the Highest: for thou shalt go before the face of the Lord to prepare his ways; to give knowledge of salvation unto his people by the remission of their sins, through the tender mercy of our God; whereby the dayspring from on high hath visited us, to give light to them that sit in darkness and in the shadow of death, to guide our feet into the way of peace." And the child grew, and waxed strong in spirit, and was in the deserts till the day of his shewing unto Israel.

And it came to pass in those days, that there went out a decree from Cæsar Augustus, that all the world should be taxed.[2] (And this taxing was first made when Cyrenius was governor of Syria.) And all went to be taxed, every one into his own city. And Joseph also went up from Galilee, out of the city of Nazareth, into Judæa, unto the city of David, which is called Bethlehem; (because he was of the house and lineage of David:) to be taxed with Mary his espoused wife, being great with child. And so it was, that, while they were there, the days were accomplished that she should be delivered. And she brought forth her firstborn son, and wrapped him in swaddling clothes, and laid him in a manger; because there was no room for them in the inn.

And there were in the same country shepherds abiding in the field, keeping watch over their flock by night. And, lo, the angel of the Lord came upon them, and the glory of the Lord shone round about them: and they were sore afraid. And the angel said unto them, "Fear not: for, behold, I bring you good tidings of great joy, which shall be to all people. For unto you is

[2] Enrolled, as for a census.

born this day in the city of David a Saviour, which is Christ the Lord. And this shall be a sign unto you; ye shall find the babe wrapped in swaddling clothes, lying in a manger." And suddenly there was with the angel a multitude of the heavenly host praising God, and saying, "Glory to God in the highest, and on earth peace, good will toward men."

And it came to pass, as the angels were gone away from them into heaven, the shepherds said one to another, "Let us now go even unto Bethlehem, and see this thing which is come to pass, which the Lord hath made known unto us." And they came with haste, and found Mary, and Joseph, and the babe lying in a manger. And when they had seen it, they made known abroad the saying which was told them concerning this child. And all they that heard it wondered at those things which were told them by the shepherds. But Mary kept all these things, and pondered them in her heart. And the shepherds returned, glorifying and praising God for all the things that they had heard and seen, as it was told unto them.

And when eight days were accomplished for the circumcising of the child, his name was called JESUS, which was so named of the angel before he was conceived in the womb. And when the days of her purification according to the law of Moses were accomplished, they brought him to Jerusalem, to present him to the Lord (as it is written in the law of the Lord, "Every male that openeth the womb shall be called holy to the lord") and to offer a sacrifice according to that which is said in the law of the Lord, "A pair of turtledoves, or two young pigeons." And, behold, there was a man in Jerusalem, whose name was Simeon; and the same man was just and devout, waiting for the consolation of Israel: and the Holy Ghost was upon him. And it was revealed unto him by the Holy Ghost, that he should not see death, before he had seen the Lord's Christ. And he came by the Spirit into the temple: and when the parents brought in the child Jesus, to do for him after the custom of the law, then took he him up in his arms, and blessed God, and said, "Lord, now lettest thou thy servant depart in peace, according to thy word: for mine eyes have seen thy salvation, which thou hast prepared before the face of all people; a light to lighten the Gentiles, and the glory of thy people Israel." And Joseph and his mother marvelled at those things which were spoken of him. And Simeon blessed them, and said unto Mary his mother, "Behold, this child is set for the fall and rising again of many in Israel; and for a sign which shall be spoken against; (yea, a sword shall pierce through thy own soul also,) that the thoughts of many hearts may be revealed."

And there was one Anna, a prophetess, the daughter of Phanuel, of the tribe of Aser: she was of a great age, and had lived with an husband seven years from her virginity; and she was a widow of about fourscore and four years, which departed not from the temple, but served God with fastings and prayers night and day. And she coming in that instant gave thanks likewise unto the Lord, and spake of him to all them that looked for redemption in Jerusalem.

And when they had performed all things according to the law of the Lord, they returned into Galilee, to their own city Nazareth. And the child grew, and waxed strong in spirit, filled with wisdom: and the grace of God was upon him.

Now his parents went to Jerusalem every year at the feast of the passover. And when he was twelve years old, they went up to Jerusalem after the custom of the feast. And when they had fulfilled the days, as they returned, the child Jesus tarried behind in Jerusalem; and Joseph and his mother knew not of it. But they, supposing him to have been in the company, went a day's journey; and they sought him among their kinsfolk and acquaintance. And when they found him not, they turned back again to Jerusalem, seeking him. And it came to pass, that after three days they found him in the temple, sitting in the midst of the doctors, both hearing them, and asking them questions. And all that heard him were astonished at his understanding and answers. And when they saw him, they were amazed: and his mother said unto him, "Son, why hast thou thus dealt with us? behold, thy father and I have sought thee sorrowing."

And he said unto them, "How is it that ye sought me? wist ye not that I must be about my Father's business?" And they understood not the saying which he spake unto them. And he went down with them, and came to Nazareth, and was subject unto them: but his mother kept all these sayings in her heart. And Jesus increased in wisdom and stature, and in favour with God and man.

The Good Samaritan

• LUKE 10:25–42 •

And, behold, a certain lawyer stood up, and tempted him, saying, "Master, what shall I do to inherit eternal life?"

He said unto him, "What is written in the law? how readest thou?"

And he answering said, "Thou shalt love the Lord thy God with all thy heart, and with all thy soul, and with all they strength, and with all thy mind; and thy neighbour as thyself."

And he said unto him, "Thou hast answered right: this do, and thou shalt live."

But he, willing to justify himself, said unto Jesus, "And who is my neighbour?"

And Jesus answering said, "A certain man went down from Jerusalem to Jericho, and fell among thieves, which stripped him of his raiment, and wounded him, and departed, leaving him half dead. And by chance there came down a certain priest that way: and when he saw him, he passed by on the other side. And likewise a Levite, when he was at the place, came and looked on him, and passed by on the other side. But a certain Samaritan,[3] as he journeyed, came where he was: and when he

[3] The Samaritans were looked upon by the Jews with intense antagonism.

saw him, he had compassion on him, and went to him, and bound up his wounds, pouring in oil and wine, and set him on his own beast, and brought him to an inn, and took care of him. And on the morrow when he departed, he took out two pence, and gave them to the host, and said unto him, 'Take care of him; and whatsoever thou spendest more, when I come again, I will repay thee.' Which now of these three, thinkest thou, was neighbour unto him that fell among the thieves?"

And he said, "He that shewed mercy on him."

Then said Jesus unto him, "Go, and do thou likewise."

Now it came to pass, as they went, that he entered into a certain village[4]: and a certain woman named Martha received him into her house. And she had a sister called Mary, which also sat at Jesus' feet, and heard his word. But Martha was cumbered about much serving, and came to him, and said, "Lord, dost thou not care that my sister hath left me to serve alone? bid her therefore that she help me."

And Jesus answered and said unto her, "Martha, Martha, thou art careful and troubled about many things: but one thing is needful: and Mary hath chosen that good part, which shall not be taken away from her."

The Prodigal Son

• LUKE 15:11–32 •

And he said, "A certain man had two sons: and the younger of them said to his father, 'Father, give me the portion of goods that falleth to me.' And he divided unto them his living. And not many days after the younger son gathered all together, and took his journey into a far country, and there wasted his substance with riotous living. And when he had spent all, there

[4] Bethany.

arose a mighty famine in that land; and he began to be in want. And he went and joined himself to a citizen of that country; and he sent him into his fields to feed swine. And he would fain have filled his belly with the husks that the swine did eat: and no man gave unto him.

"And when he came to himself, he said, 'How many hired servants of my father's have bread enough and to spare, and I perish with hunger! I will arise and go to my father, and will say unto him, Father, I have sinned against heaven, and before thee, and am no more worthy to be called thy son: make me as one of thy hired servants.'

"And he arose, and came to his father. But when he was yet a great way off, his father saw him, and had compassion, and ran, and fell on his neck, and kissed him. And the son said unto him, 'Father, I have sinned against heaven, and in thy sight, and am no more worthy to be called thy son.'

"But the father said to his servants, 'Bring forth the best robe, and put it on him; and put a ring on his hand, and shoes on his feet: and bring hither the fatted calf, and kill it; and let us eat, and be merry: for this my son was dead, and is alive again; he was lost, and is found.' And they began to be merry.

"Now his elder son was in the field: and as he came and drew nigh to the house, he heard music and dancing. And he called one of the servants, and asked what these things meant. And he said unto him, 'Thy brother is come; and thy father hath killed the fatted calf, because he hath received him safe and sound.' And he was angry, and would not go in: therefore came his father out, and intreated him. And he answering said to his father, 'Lo, these many years do I serve thee, neither transgressed I at any time thy commandment: and yet thou never gavest me a kid, that I might make merry with my friends: but as soon as this thy son was come, which hath devoured thy living with harlots, thou hast killed for him the fatted calf.'

"And he said unto him, 'Son, thou art ever with me, and all that I have is thine. It was meet that we should make merry, and be glad: for this thy brother was dead, and is alive again; and was lost, and is found.' "

The Trial, the Crucifixion, and the Resurrection

• LUKE 23 AND 24 •

And the whole multitude of them arose, and led him unto Pilate. And they began to accuse him, saying, "We found this fellow perverting the nation, and forbidding to give tribute to Cæsar, saying that he himself is Christ a King."

And Pilate asked him, saying, "Art thou the King of the Jews?"

And he answered him and said, "Thou sayest it."

Then said Pilate to the chief priests and to the people, "I find no fault in this man."

And they were the more fierce, saying, "He stirreth up the people, teaching throughout all Jewry, beginning from Galilee to this place." When Pilate heard of Galilee, he asked whether the man were a Galilæan. And as soon as he knew that he belonged unto Herod's jurisdiction, he sent him to Herod, who himself also was at Jerusalem at that time.

And when Herod saw Jesus, he was exceeding glad: for he was desirous to see him of a long season, because he had heard many things of him; and he hoped to have seen some miracle done by him. Then he questioned with him in many words; but he answered him nothing. And the chief priests and scribes stood and vehemently accused him. And Herod with his men of war set him at nought, and mocked him, and arrayed him in a gorgeous robe, and sent him again to Pilate. And the same day Pilate and Herod were made friends together: for before they were at enmity between themselves. And Pilate, when he had called together the chief priests and the rulers and the people, said unto them,

"Ye have brought this man unto me, as one that perverteth the people: and, behold, I, having examined him before you, have found no fault in this man touching those things whereof ye accuse him: no, nor yet Herod: for I sent you to him; and, lo, nothing worthy of death is done unto him. I will therefore chastise him, and release him." (For of necessity he must release one unto them at the feast.)

And they cried out all at once, saying, "Away with this man, and release unto us Barabbas." (Who for a certain sedition made in the city, and for murder, was cast into prison.) Pilate therefore, willing to release Jesus, spake again to them. But they cried, saying, "Crucify him, crucify him."

And he said unto them the third time, "Why, what evil hath he done? I have found no cause of death in him: I will therefore chastise him, and let him go." And they were instant with loud voices, requiring that he might be crucified. And the voices of them and of the chief priests prevailed.

And Pilate gave sentence that it should be as they required. And he released unto them him that for sedition and murder was cast into prison, whom they had desired; but he delivered Jesus to their will. And as they led him away, they laid hold upon one Simon, a Cyrenian, coming out of the country, and on him they laid the cross, that he might bear it after Jesus.

And there followed him a great company of people, and of women, which also bewailed and lamented him. But Jesus turning unto them said, "Daughters of Jerusalem, weep not for me, but weep for yourselves, and for your children. For, behold, the days are coming, in the which they shall say, 'Blessed are the barren, and the wombs that never bare, and the paps which never gave suck.' Then shall they begin to say to the mountains, 'Fall on us'; and to the hills, 'Cover us.' For if they do these things in a green tree, what shall be done in the dry?"

And there were also two other, malefactors, led with him to be put to death. And when they were come to the place, which is called Calvary,[5] there they crucified him, and the malefactors, one on the right hand, and the other on the left.

Then said Jesus, "Father, forgive them; for they know not what they do."

And they parted his raiment, and cast losts. And the people stood beholding. And the rulers also with them derided him, saying, "He saved others; let him save himself, if he be Christ, the chosen of God." And the soldiers also mocked him, coming to him, and offering him vinegar, and saying, "If thou be the king of the Jews, save thyself." And a superscription also was written over him in letters of Greek, and Latin, and Hebrew, THIS IS THE KING OF THE JEWS.

And one of the malefactors which were hanged railed on him, saying, "If thou be Christ, save thyself and us."

But the other answering rebuked him, saying, "Dost not thou fear God, seeing thou art in the same condemnation? And we indeed justly; for we receive the due reward of our deeds: but this man hath done nothing amiss." And he said unto Jesus, "Lord, remember me when thou comest into thy kingdom."

And Jesus said unto him, "Verily I say unto thee, to day shalt thou be with me in paradise."

And it was about the sixth hour, and there was a darkness over all the earth until the ninth hour. And the sun was darkened, and the veil of the temple was rent in the midst. And when Jesus had cried with a loud voice, he said, "Father, into thy hands I commend my spirit," and having said thus, he gave up the ghost.

Now when the centurion saw what was done, he glorified God, saying, "Certainly this was a righteous man." And all the people that came together to that sight, beholding the things which were done, smote their breasts, and returned. And all his acquaintance, and the women that followed him from Galilee, stood afar off, beholding these things.

And, behold, there was a man named Joseph, a counsellor;

[5] Latin *Calvarium*, the equivalent of *Golgotha*.

and he was a good man, and a just: (the same had not consented to the counsel and deed of them;) he was of Arimathæa, a city of the Jews: who also himself waited for the kingdom of God. This man went unto Pilate, and begged the body of Jesus. And he took it down, and wrapped it in linen, and laid it in a sepulchre that was hewn in stone, wherein never man before was laid. And that day was the preparation,[6] and the sabbath drew on. And the women also, which came with him from Galilee, followed after, and beheld the sepulchre, and how his body was laid. And they returned, and prepared spices and ointments; and rested the sabbath day according to the commandment.

Now upon the first day of the week, very early in the morning, they came unto the sepulchre, bringing the spices which they had prepared, and certain others with them. And they found the stone rolled away from the sepulchre. And they entered in, and found not the body of the Lord Jesus. And it came to pass, as they were much perplexed thereabout, behold, two men stood by them in shining garments: and as they were afraid, and bowed down their faces to the earth, they said unto them, "Why seek ye the living among the dead? He is not here, but is risen: remember how he spake unto you when he was yet in Galilee, saying, 'The Son of man must be delivered into the hands of sinful men, and be crucified, and the third day rise again.'"

And they remembered his words, and returned from the sepulchre, and told all these things unto the eleven, and to all the rest. It was Mary Magdalen, and Joanna, and Mary the mother of James, and other women that were with them, which told these things unto the apostles. And their words seemed to them idle tales, and they believed them not. Then arose Peter, and ran unto the sepulchre; and stooping down, he beheld the linen clothes laid by themselves, and departed, wondering in himself at that which was come to pass.

And, behold, two of them went that same day to a village called Emmaus, which was from Jerusalem about threescore fur-

The day preceding the sabbath.

longs. And they talked together of all these things which had happened. And it came to pass, that, while they communed together and reasoned, Jesus himself drew near, and went with them. But their eyes were holden that they should not know him.

And he said unto them, "What manner of communications are these that ye have one to another, as ye walk, and are sad?"

And the one of them, whose name was Cleopas, answering said unto him, "Art thou only a stranger in Jerusalem, and hast not known the things which are come to pass there in these days?"

And he said unto them, "What things?"

And they said unto him, "Concerning Jesus of Nazareth, which was a prophet mighty in deed and word before God and all the people: and how the chief priests and our rulers delivered him to be condemned to death, and have crucified him. But we trusted that it had been he which should have redeemed Israel: and beside all this, to day is the third day since these things were done. Yea, and certain women also of our company made us astonished, which were early at the sepulchre; and when they found not his body, they came, saying, that they had also seen a vision of angels, which said that he was alive. And certain of them which were with us went to the sepulchre, and found it even so as the women had said: but him they saw not."

Then he said unto them, "O fools, and slow of heart to believe all that the prophets have spoken: ought not Christ to have suffered these things, and to enter into his glory?" And beginning at Moses and all the prophets, he expounded unto them in all the scriptures the things concerning himself.

And they drew nigh unto the village, whither they went: and he made as though he would have gone further. But they constrained him, saying, "Abide with us: for it is toward evening, and the day is far spent." And he went in to tarry with them. And it came to pass, as he sat at meat with them, he took bread, and blessed it, and brake, and gave to them. And their eyes were opened, and they knew him; and he vanished out of their sight.

And they said one to another, "Did not our heart burn within us, while he talked with us by the way, and while he opened to us the scriptures?" And they rose up the same hour, and returned to Jerusalem, and found the eleven gathered together, and them that were with them, saying, "The Lord is risen indeed, and hath appeared to Simon." And they told what things were done in the way, and how he was known of them in breaking of bread.

And as they thus spake, Jesus himself stood in the midst of them, and saith unto them, "Peace be unto you." But they were terrified and affrighted, and supposed that they had seen a spirit. And he said unto them, "Why are ye troubled? and why do thoughts arise in your hearts? Behold my hands and my feet, that it is I myself: handle me, and see; for a spirit hath not flesh and bones, as ye see me have." And when he had thus spoken, he shewed them his hands and his feet.

And while they yet believed not for joy, and wondered, he said unto them, "Have ye here any meat?" And they gave him a piece of a broiled fish, and of an honeycomb. And he took it, and did eat before them. And he said unto them, "These are the words which I spake unto you, while I was yet with you, that all things must be fulfilled, which were written in the law of Moses, and in the prophets, and in the psalms, concerning me."

Then opened he their understanding, that they might understand the scriptures, and said unto them, "Thus it is written, and thus it behoved Christ to suffer, and to rise from the dead the third day: and that repentance and remission of sins should be preached in his name among all nations, beginning at Jerusalem. And ye are witnesses of these things. And, behold, I send the promise of my Father upon you: but tarry ye in the city of Jerusalem, until ye be endued with power from on high."

And he led them out as far as to Bethany, and he lifted up his hands, and blessed them. And it came to pass, while he blessed them, he was parted from them, and carried up into heaven. And they worshipped him, and returned to Jerusalem with great joy: and were continually in the temple, praising and blessing God. Amen.

From JOHN

~~~~~

The Incarnate Word

• JOHN 1:1–18 •

In the beginning was the Word,[1] and the Word was with God, and the Word was God. The same was in the beginning with God. All things were made by him; and without him was not any thing made that was made. In him was life; and the life was the light of men. And the light shineth in darkness; and the darkness comprehended it not.

There was a man sent from God, whose name was John.[2] The same came for a witness, to bear witness of the Light, that all men through him might believe. He was not that Light, but was sent to bear witness of that Light. That was the true Light, which lighteth every man that cometh into the world. He was in the world, and the world was made by him, and the world knew him not. He came unto his own, and his own received him not. But as many as received him, to them gave he power to become the sons of God, even to them that believe on his name: which were born, not of blood, nor of the will of the flesh, nor of the will of man, but of God. And the Word was made flesh, and dwelt among us, (and we beheld his glory, the glory as of the only begotten of the Father,) full of grace and truth.

[1] Greek *logos*—reason, intelligence.
[2] The Baptist, not the Evangelist.

John bare witness of him, and cried, saying, "This was he of whom I spake, 'He that cometh after me is preferred before me: for he was before me'." And of his fulness have all we received, and grace for grace. For the law was given by Moses, but grace and truth came by Jesus Christ. No man hath seen God at any time; the only begotten Son, which is in the bosom of the Father, he hath declared him.

The Story of Nicodemus

• JOHN 3: 1–21 •

There was a man of the Pharisees, named Nicodemus, a ruler of the Jews: the same came to Jesus by night, and said unto him, "Rabbi, we know that thou art a teacher come from God: for no man can do these miracles that thou doest, except God be with him."

Jesus answered and said unto him, "Verily, verily, I say unto thee, except a man be born again, he cannot see the kingdom of God."

Nicodemus saith unto him, "How can a man be born when he is old? can he enter the second time into his mother's womb, and be born?"

Jesus answered, "Verily, verily, I say unto thee, except a man be born of water and of the Spirit, he cannot enter into the kingdom of God. That which is born of the flesh is flesh; and that which is born of the Spirit is spirit. Marvel not that I said unto thee, 'Ye must be born again.' The wind bloweth where it listeth, and thou hearest the sound thereof, but canst not tell whence it cometh, and whither it goeth: so is every one that is born of the Spirit."

Nicodemus answered and said unto him, "How can these things be?"

Jesus answered and said unto him, "Art thou a master of Israel, and knowest not these things? Verily, verily, I say unto thee, we speak that we do know, and testify that we have seen; and ye receive not our witness. If I have told you earthly things, and ye believe not, how shall ye believe, if I tell you of heavenly things? And no man hath ascended up to heaven, but he that came down from heaven, even the Son of man which is in heaven. And as Moses lifted up the serpent in the wilderness, even so must the Son of man be lifted up: that whosoever believeth in him should not perish, but have eternal life."

For God so loved the world, that he gave his only begotten Son, that whosoever believeth in him should not perish, but have everlasting life. For God sent not his Son into the world to condemn the world; but that the world through him might be saved. He that believeth on him is not condemned: but he that believeth not is condemned already, because he hath not believed in the name of the only begotten Son of God. And this is the condemnation, that light is come into the world, and men loved darkness rather than light, because their deeds were evil. For every one that doeth evil hateth the light, neither cometh to the light, lest his deeds should be reproved. But he that doeth truth cometh to the light, that his deeds may be made manifest, that they are wrought in God.

The Good Shepherd

• JOHN 10 •

"Verily, verily, I say unto you, he that entereth not by the door into the sheepfold, but climbeth up some other way, the same is a thief and a robber. But he that entereth in by the door is the shepherd of the sheep. To him the porter openeth; and the sheep hear his voice: and he calleth his own sheep by name, and leadeth them out. And when he putteth forth his own sheep, he goeth before them, and the sheep follow him: for they know his voice. And a stranger will they not follow, but will flee from him: for they know not the voice of strangers." This parable spake Jesus unto them: but they understood not what things they were which he spake unto them.

Then said Jesus unto them again, "Verily, verily, I say unto you, I am the door of the sheep. All that ever came before me are thieves and robbers: but the sheep did not hear them. I am the door: by me if any man enter in, he shall be saved, and shall go in and out, and find pasture. The thief cometh not, but for to steal, and to kill, and to destroy: I am come that they might have life, and that they might have it more abundantly. I am the good shepherd: the good shepherd giveth his life for the sheep. But he that is an hireling, and not the shepherd, whose own the sheep are not, seeth the wolf coming, and leaveth the sheep, and fleeth: and the wolf catcheth them, and scattereth the sheep. The hireling fleeth, because he is an hireling, and careth not for the sheep. I am the good shepherd, and know my sheep, and am known of mine. As the Father knoweth me, even so know I the Father: and I lay down my life for the sheep. And other sheep I have, which are not of this fold: them also I must bring, and they shall hear my voice; and there shall be one fold, and one shepherd. Therefore doth my Father love me, because I lay down my life, that I might take it again. No man taketh it from me, but I lay it down of myself. I have power to lay it down, and I have power to take it again. This commandment have I received of my Father."

There was a division therefore again among the Jews for these sayings. And many of them said, "He hath a devil, and is mad; why hear ye him?" Others said, "These are not the words of him that hath a devil. Can a devil open the eyes of the blind?" And it was at Jerusalem the feast of the dedication,[3] and it was winter. And Jesus walked in the temple in Solomon's

[3] About the middle of December. Sometimes called the Feast of Lights.

porch. Then came the Jews round about him, and said unto him, "How long dost thou make us to doubt? If thou be the Christ, tell us plainly."

Jesus answered them, "I told you, and ye believed not: the works that I do in my Father's name, they bear witness of me But ye believe not, because ye are not of my sheep, as I said unto you. My sheep hear my voice, and I know them, and they follow me: and I give unto them eternal life; and they shall never perish, neither shall any man pluck them out of my hand. My Father, which gave them me, is greater than all; and no man is able to pluck them out of my Father's hand. I and my Father are one."

Then the Jews took up stones again to stone him. Jesus answered them, "Many good works have I shewed you from my Father; for which of those works do ye stone me?"

The Jews answered him, saying, "For a good work we stone thee not; but for blasphemy; and because that thou, being a man, makest thyself God."

Jesus answered them, "Is it not written in your law, 'I said, Ye are gods'? If he called them gods, unto whom the word of God came, and the scripture cannot be broken; say ye of him, whom the Father hath sanctified, and sent into the world, 'Thou blasphemest,' because I said, 'I am the Son of God'? If I do not the works of my Father, believe me not. But if I do, though ye believe not me, believe the works: that ye may know, and believe, that the Father is in me, and I in him."

Therefore they sought again to take him: but he escaped out of their hand, and went away again beyond Jordan into the place where John at first baptized; and there he abode. And many resorted unto him, and said, "John did no miracle: but all things that John spake of this man were true." And many believed on him there.

The Raising of Lazarus

Now a certain man was sick, named Lazarus, of Bethany, the town of Mary and her sister Martha. (It was that Mary which anointed the Lord with ointment, and wiped his feet with her hair, whose brother Lazarus was sick.) Therefore his sisters sent unto him, saying, "Lord, behold, he whom thou lovest is sick."

When Jesus heard that, he said, "This sickness is not unto death, but for the glory of God, that the Son of God might be glorified thereby."

Now Jesus loved Martha, and her sister, and Lazarus. When he had heard therefore that he was sick, he abode two days still in the same place where he was. Then after that saith he to his disciples, "Let us go into Judæa again."

His disciples say unto him, "Master, the Jews of late sought to stone thee; and goest thou thither again?"

Jesus answered, "Are there not twelve hours in the day? If any man walk in the day, he stumbleth not, because he seeth the light of this world. But if a man walk in the night, he stumbleth, because there is no light in him." These things said he: and after that he saith unto them, "Our friend Lazarus sleepeth; but I go, that I may awake him out of sleep."

Then said his disciples, "Lord, if he sleep, he shall do well."

Howbeit Jesus spake of his death: but they thought that he had spoken of taking of rest in sleep. Then said Jesus unto them plainly, "Lazarus is dead. And I am glad for your sakes that I was not there, to the intent ye may believe; nevertheless let us go unto him."

Then said Thomas, which is called Didymus, unto his fellow-disciples, "Let us also go, that we may die with him."

Then when Jesus came, he found that he had lain in the

grave four days already. Now Bethany was nigh unto Jerusalem, about fifteen furlongs off: and many of the Jews came to Martha and Mary, to comfort them concerning their brother. Then Martha, as soon as she heard that Jesus was coming, went and met him: but Mary sat still in the house. Then said Martha unto Jesus, "Lord, if thou hadst been here, my brother had not died. But I know, that even now, whatsoever thou wilt ask of God, God will give it thee."

Jesus saith unto her, "Thy brother shall rise again."

Martha saith unto him, "I know that he shall rise again in the resurrection at the last day."

Jesus said unto her, "I am the resurrection, and the life: he that believeth in me, though he were dead, yet shall he live: and whosoever liveth and believeth in me shall never die. Believest thou this?"

She saith unto him, "Yea, Lord: I believe that thou art the Christ, the Son of God, which should come into the world." And when she had so said, she went her way, and called Mary her sister secretly, saying, "The Master is come, and calleth for thee."

As soon as she heard that, she arose quickly, and came unto him. Now Jesus was not yet come into the town, but was in that place where Martha met him. The Jews then which were with her in the house, and comforted her, when they saw Mary, that she rose up hastily and went out, followed her, saying, "She goeth unto the grave to weep there."

Then when Mary was come where Jesus was, and saw him, she fell down at his feet, saying unto him, "Lord, if thou hadst been here, my brother had not died."

When Jesus therefore saw her weeping, and the Jews also weeping which came with her, he groaned in the spirit, and was troubled, and said, "Where have ye laid him?"

They said unto him, "Lord, come and see." Jesus wept.

Then said the Jews, "Behold how he loved him!" And some of them said, "Could not this man, which opened the eyes of the blind, have caused that even this man should not have died?"

Jesus therefore again groaning in himself cometh to the grave. It was a cave, and a stone lay upon it. Jesus said, "Take ye away the stone."

Martha, the sister of him that was dead, saith unto him, "Lord, by this time he stinketh: for he hath been dead four days."

Jesus saith unto her, "Said I not unto thee, that, if thou wouldest believe, thou shouldest see the glory of God?" Then they took away the stone from the place where the dead was laid. And Jesus lifted up his eyes, and said, "Father, I thank thee that thou hast heard me. And I knew that thou hearest me always: but because of the people which stand by I said it, that they may believe that thou hast sent me."

And when he thus had spoken, he cried with a loud voice, "Lazarus, come forth." And he that was dead came forth, bound hand and foot with graveclothes: and his face was bound about with a napkin. Jesus saith unto them, "Loose him, and let him go."

Then many of the Jews which came to Mary, and had seen the things which Jesus did, believed on him. But some of them went their ways to the Pharisees, and told them what things Jesus had done.

The Last Discourse

• JOHN 14 TO 17 •

"Let not your heart be troubled: ye believe in God, believe also in me. In my Father's house are many mansions: if it were not so, I would have told you. I go to prepare a place for you. And if I go and prepare a place for you, I will come again, and receive you unto myself; that where I am, there ye may be also. And whither I go ye know, and the way ye know."

Thomas saith unto him, "Lord, we know not whither thou goest; and how can we know the way?"

Jesus saith unto him, "I am the way, the truth, and the life: no man cometh unto the Father, but by me. If ye had known me, ye should have known my Father also: and from henceforth ye know him, and have seen him."

Philip saith unto him, "Lord, shew us the Father, and it sufficeth us."

Jesus saith unto him, "Have I been so long time with you, and yet hast thou not known me, Philip? he that hath seen me hath seen the Father; and how sayest thou then, 'Shew us the Father'? Believest thou not that I am in the Father, and the Father in me? the words that I speak unto you I speak not of myself: but the Father that dwelleth in me, he doeth the works. Believe me that I am in the Father, and the Father in me: or else believe me for the very works' sake.

"Verily, verily, I say unto you, he that believeth on me, the works that I do shall he do also; and greater works than these shall he do; because I go unto my Father. And whatsoever ye shall ask in my name, that will I do, that the Father may be glorified in the Son. If ye shall ask any thing in my name, I will do it.

"If ye love me, keep my commandments. And I will pray the Father, and he shall give you another Comforter, that he may abide with you for ever; even the Spirit of truth; whom the world cannot receive, because it seeth him not, neither knoweth him: but ye know him; for he dwelleth with you, and shall be in you.

"I will not leave you comfortless: I will come to you. Yet a little while, and the world seeth me no more; but ye see me: because I live, ye shall live also. At that day ye shall know that I am in my Father, and ye in me, and I in you. He that hath my commandments, and keepeth them, he it is that loveth me: and he that loveth me shall be loved of my Father, and I will love him, and will manifest myself to him."

Judas saith unto him, not Iscariot, "Lord, how is it that thou wilt manifest thyself unto us, and not unto the world?"

Jesus answered and said unto him, "If a man love me, he will keep my words: and my Father will love him, and we will come unto him, and make our abode with him. He that loveth me not keepeth not my sayings: and the word which ye hear is not mine, but the Father's which sent me.

"These things have I spoken unto you, being yet present with you. But the Comforter, which is the Holy Ghost, whom the Father will send in my name, he shall teach you all things, and bring all things to your remembrance, whatsoever I have said unto you. Peace I leave with you, my peace I give unto you: not as the world giveth, give I unto you. Let not your heart be troubled, neither let it be afraid. Ye have heard how I said unto you, 'I go away, and come again unto you.' If ye loved me, ye would rejoice, because I said, 'I go unto the Father': for my Father is greater than I. And now I have told you before it come to pass, that, when it is come to pass, ye might believe. Hereafter I will not talk much with you: for the prince of this world cometh, and hath nothing in me.[4] But that the world may know that I love the Father; and as the Father gave me commandment, even so I do. Arise, let us go hence.

"I am the true vine, and my Father is the husbandman. Every branch in me that beareth not fruit he taketh away: and every branch that beareth fruit, he purgeth it, that it may bring forth more fruit. Now ye are clean through the word which I have spoken unto you. Abide in me, and I in you. As the branch cannot bear fruit of itself, except it abide in the vine; no more can ye, except ye abide in me. I am the vine, ye are the branches: he that abideth in me, and I in him, the same bringeth forth much fruit: for without me ye can do nothing. If a man abide not in me, he is cast forth as a branch, and is withered; and men gather them, and cast them into the fire, and they are burned. If ye abide in me, and my words abide in you, ye shall

[4] i.e., has no power over me.

ask what ye will, and it shall be done unto you. Herein is my Father glorified, that ye bear much fruit; so shall ye be my disciples. As the Father hath loved me, so have I loved you: continue ye in my love. If ye keep my commandments, ye shall abide in my love; even as I have kept my Father's commandments, and abide in his love. These things have I spoken unto you, that my joy might remain in you, and that your joy might be full.

"This is my commandment, that ye love one another, as I have loved you. Greater love hath no man than this, that a man lay down his life for his friends. Ye are my friends, if ye do whatsoever I command you. Henceforth I call you not servants; for the servant knoweth not what his lord doeth: but I have called you friends; for all things that I have heard of my Father I have made known unto you. Ye have not chosen me, but I have chosen you, and ordained you, that ye should go and bring forth fruit, and that your fruit should remain: that whatsoever ye shall ask of the Father in my name, he may give it you. These things I command you, that ye love one another.

"If the world hate you, ye know that it hated me before it hated you. If ye were of the world, the world would love his own: but because ye are not of the world, but I have chosen you out of the world, therefore the world hateth you. Remember the word that I said unto you, 'The servant is not greater than his lord.' If they have persecuted me, they will also persecute you; if they have kept my saying, they will keep yours also. But all these things will they do unto you for my name's sake, because they know not him that sent me.

"If I had not come and spoken unto them, they had not had sin: but now they have no cloak for their sin. He that hateth me hateth my Father also. If I had not done among them the works which none other man did, they had not had sin: but now have they both seen and hated both me and my Father. But this cometh to pass, that the word might be fulfilled that is written in their law, 'They hated me without a cause.' But when the

Comforter is come, whom I will send unto you from the Father, even the Spirit of truth, which proceedeth from the Father, he shall testify of me: and ye also shall bear witness, because ye have been with me from the beginning.

"These things have I spoken unto you, that ye should not be offended. They shall put you out of the synagogues: yea, the time cometh, that whosoever killeth you will think that he doeth God service. And these things will they do unto you, because they have not known the Father, nor me. But these things have I told you, that when the time shall come, ye may remember that I told you of them.

"And these things I said not unto you at the beginning, because I was with you. But now I go my way to him that sent me; and none of you asketh me, 'Whither goest thou?' But because I have said these things unto you, sorrow hath filled your heart. Nevertheless I tell you the truth; it is expedient for you that I go away: for if I go not away, the Comforter will not come unto you; but if I depart, I will send him unto you. And when he is come, he will reprove the world of sin, and of righteousness, and of judgment: of sin, because they believe not on me; of righteousness, because I go to my Father, and ye see me no more; of judgment, because the prince of this world is judged.

"I have yet many things to say unto you, but ye cannot bear them now. Howbeit when he, the Spirit of truth, is come, he will guide you into all truth: for he shall not speak of himself; but whatsoever he shall hear, that shall he speak: and he will shew you things to come. He shall glorify me: for he shall receive of mine, and shall shew it unto you. All things that the Father hath are mine: therefore said I, that he shall take of mine, and shall shew it unto you. A little while, and ye shall not see me: and again, a little while, and ye shall see me, because I go to the Father."

Then said some of his disciples among themselves, "What is this that he saith unto us, 'A little while, and ye shall not see me': and again, 'A little while, and ye shall see me': and, 'Because I go to the Father'?" They said therefore, "What is this that he saith, 'A little while'? we cannot tell what he saith."

Now Jesus knew that they were desirous to ask him, and said unto them, "Do ye enquire among yourselves of that I said, 'A little while, and ye shall not see me': and again, 'A little while, and ye shall see me'? Verily, verily, I say unto you, that ye shall weep and lament, but the world shall rejoice: and ye shall be sorrowful, but your sorrow shall be turned into joy. A woman when she is in travail hath sorrow, because her hour is come: but as soon as she is delivered of the child, she remembereth no more the anguish, for joy that a man is born into the world. And ye now therefore have sorrow: but I will see you again, and your heart shall rejoice, and your joy no man taketh from you. And in that day ye shall ask me nothing. Verily, verily, I say unto you, whatsoever ye shall ask the Father in my name, he will give it you. Hitherto have ye asked nothing in my name: ask, and ye shall receive, that your joy may be full.

"These things have I spoken unto you in proverbs: but the time cometh, when I shall no more speak unto you in proverbs, but I shall shew you plainly of the Father. At that day ye shall ask in my name: and I say not unto you, that I will pray the Father for you: for the Father himself loveth you, because ye have loved me, and have believed that I came out from God. I came forth from the Father, and am come into the world: again, I leave the world, and go to the Father."

His disciples said unto him, "Lo, now speakest thou plainly, and speakest no proverb. Now are we sure that thou knowest all things, and needest not that any man should ask thee: by this we believe that thou camest forth from God."

Jesus answered them, "Do ye now believe? Behold, the hour cometh, yea, is now come, that ye shall be scattered, every man to his own, and shall leave me alone: and yet I am not alone, because the Father is with me. These things I have spoken unto you, that in me ye might have peace. In the world ye shall have tribulation: but be of good cheer; I have overcome the world."

These words spake Jesus, and lifted up his eyes to heaven, and said, "Father, the hour is come; glorify thy Son, that thy Son also may glorify thee: as thou hast given him power over all flesh, that he should give eternal life to as many as thou hast given him. And this is life eternal, that they might know thee the only true God, and Jesus Christ, whom thou hast sent. I have glorified thee on the earth: I have finished the work which thou gavest me to do. And now, O Father, glorify thou me with thine own self with the glory which I had with thee before the world was.

"I have manifested thy name unto the men which thou gavest me out of the world: thine they were, and thou gavest them me; and they have kept thy word. Now they have known that all things whatsoever thou hast given me are of thee. For I have given unto them the words which thou gavest me; and they have received them, and have known surely that I came out from thee, and they have believed that thou didst send me. I pray for them: I pray not for the world, but for them which thou hast given me; for they are thine. And all mine are thine, and thine are mine; and I am glorified in them. And now I am no more in the world, but these are in the world, and I come to thee. Holy Father, keep through thine own name those whom thou hast given me, that they may be one, as we are. While I was with them in the world, I kept them in thy name: those that thou gavest me I have kept, and none of them is lost, but the son of perdition; that the scripture might be fulfilled. And now come I to thee; and these things I speak in the world, that they might have my joy fulfilled in themselves. I have given them thy word; and the world hath hated them, because they are not of the world, even as I am not of the world. I pray not that thou shouldest take them out of the world, but that thou shouldest keep them from the evil. They are not of the world, even as I am not of the world. Sanctify them through thy truth: thy word is truth. As thou hast sent me into the world, even so have I also sent them into the world. And for their sakes I sanctify myself, that they also might be sanctified through the truth.

"Neither pray I for these alone, but for them also which shall believe on me through their word; that they all may be one; as thou, Father, art in me, and I in thee, that they also may be one in us: that the world may believe that thou hast sent me. And the glory which thou gavest me I have given them; that they may be one, even as we are one: I in them, and thou in me, that they may be made perfect in one; and that the world may know that thou hast sent me, and hast loved them, as thou hast loved me. Father, I will that they also, whom thou hast given me, be with me where I am; that they may behold my glory, which thou hast given me: for thou lovedst me before the foundation of the world. O righteous Father, the world hath not known thee: but I have known thee, and these have known that thou hast sent me. And I have declared unto them thy name, and will declare it: that the love wherewith thou hast loved me may be in them, and I in them."

The Ascension

• ACTS 1 •

The former treatise have I made, O Theophilus, of all that Jesus began both to do and teach, until the day in which he was taken up, after that he through the Holy Ghost had given commandments unto the apostles whom he had chosen: to whom also he shewed himself alive after his passion by many infallible proofs, being seen of them forty days, and speaking of the things pertaining to the kingdom of God: and, being assembled together with them, commanded them that they should not depart from Jerusalem, but wait for the promise of the Father, "which," saith he, "ye have heard of me. For John truly baptized with water; but ye shall be baptized with the Holy Ghost not many days hence."

When they therefore were come together, they asked of him, saying, "Lord, wilt thou at this time restore again the kingdom to Israel?"

And he said unto them, "It is not for you to know the times or the seasons, which the Father hath put in his own power. But ye shall receive power, after that the Holy Ghost is come upon you: and ye shall be witnesses unto me both in Jerusalem, and in all Judæa, and in Samaria, and unto the uttermost part of the earth."

And when he had spoken these things, while they beheld, he was taken up; and a cloud received him out of their sight. And while they looked stedfastly toward heaven as he went up, behold, two men stood by them in white apparel; which also said, "Ye men of Galilee, why stand ye gazing up into heaven? this same Jesus, which is taken up from you into heaven, shall so come in like manner as ye have seen him go into heaven."

Then returned they unto Jerusalem from the mount called Olivet, which is from Jerusalem a sabbath day's journey.[1] And when they were come in, they went up into an upper room, where abode both Peter, and James, and John, and Andrew, Philip, and Thomas, Bartholomew, and Matthew, James the son of Alphæus, and Simon Zelotes, and Judas the brother of James. These all continued with one accord in prayer and supplication, with the women, and Mary the mother of Jesus, and with his brethren.

And in those days Peter stood up in the midst of the disciples, and said, (the number of names together were about an hundred and twenty,) "Men and brethren, this scripture must needs have been fulfilled, which the Holy Ghost by the mouth of David spake before concerning Judas, which was guide to them that took Jesus. For he was numbered with us, and had obtained part of this ministry." (Now this man purchased a field with the reward of iniquity; and falling headlong, he burst asunder in the midst, and all his bowels gushed out. And it was known unto all the dwellers at Jerusalem; insomuch as that field is called in their proper tongue, Aceldama, that is to say, 'The field of blood.') "For it is written in the book of Psalms, 'Let his habitation be desolate, and let no man dwell therein: and his bishoprick let another take.' Wherefore of these men which have companied with us all the time that the Lord Jesus went in and out among us, beginning from the baptism of John, unto that same day that he was taken up from us, must one be ordained to be a witness with us of his resurrection."

And they appointed two, Joseph called Barsabas, who was surnamed Justus, and Matthias. And they prayed, and said, "Thou, Lord, which knowest the hearts of all men, shew whether of these two thou hast chosen, that he may take part of this

[1] Almost a mile.

ministry and apostleship, from which Judas by transgression fell, that he might go to his own place." And they gave forth their lots; and the lot fell upon Matthias; and he was numbered with the eleven apostles.

The Coming of the Holy Spirit

• ACTS 2 •

And when the day of Pentecost[2] was fully come, they were all with one accord in one place. And suddenly there came a sound from heaven as of a rushing mighty wind, and it filled all the house where they were sitting. And there appeared unto them cloven tongues like as of fire, and it sat upon each of them. And they were all filled with the Holy Ghost, and began to speak with other tongues, as the Spirit gave them utterance.

And there were dwelling at Jerusalem Jews, devout men, out of every nation under heaven. Now when this was noised abroad, the multitude came together, and were confounded, because that every man heard them speak in his own language. And they were all amazed and marvelled, saying one to another, "Behold, are not all these which speak Galilæans? And how hear we every man in our own tongue, wherein we were born? Parthians, and Medes, and Elamites, and the dwellers in Mesopotamia, and in Judæa, and Cappadocia, in Pontus, and Asia, Phrygia, and Pamphylia, in Egypt, and in the parts of Libya about Cyrene, and strangers of Rome, Jews and proseltyes, Cretes and Arabians, we do hear them speak in our tongues the wonderful works of God." And they were all amazed, and were in doubt, saying one to another, "What meaneth this?" Others mocking said, "These men are full of new wine."

But Peter, standing up with the eleven, lifted up his voice, and said unto them, "Ye men of Judæa, and all ye that dwell at

[2] The fiftieth day from the second day of the Passover.

Jerusalem, be this known unto you, and hearken to my words: for these are not drunken, as ye suppose, seeing it is but the third hour of the day. But this is that which was spoken by the prophet Joel; 'And it shall come to pass in the last days, saith God, I will pour out of my Spirit upon all flesh: and your sons and your daughters shall prophesy, and your young men shall see visions, and your old men shall dream dreams: and on my servants and on my handmaidens I will pour out in those days of my Spirit; and they shall prophesy: and I will shew wonders in heaven above, and signs in the earth beneath; blood, and fire, and vapour of smoke: the sun shall be turned into darkness, and the moon into blood, before that great and notable day of the Lord come: and it shall come to pass, that whosoever shall call on the name of the Lord shall be saved.'

"Ye men of Israel, hear these words; Jesus of Nazareth, a man approved of God among you by miracles and wonders and signs, which God did by him in the midst of you, as ye yourselves also know: Him, being delivered by the determinate counsel and foreknowledge of God, ye have taken, and by wicked hands have crucified and slain: whom God hath raised up, having loosed the pains of death: because it was not possible that he should be holden of it. For David speaketh concerning him, 'I foresaw the Lord always before my face, for he is on my right hand, that I should not be moved: therefore did my heart rejoice, and my tongue was glad; moreover also my flesh shall rest in hope: because thou wilt not leave my soul in hell, neither wilt thou suffer thine Holy One to see corruption. Thou hast made known to me the ways of life; thou shalt make me full of joy with thy countenance.'

"Men and brethren, let me freely speak unto you of the patriarch David, that he is both dead and buried, and his sepulchre is with us unto this day. Therefore being a prophet, and knowing that God had sworn with an oath to him, that of the fruit of his loins, according to the flesh, he would raise up Christ to sit on his throne; he seeing this before spake of the resurrection of Christ, that his soul was not left in hell, neither his flesh did see corruption. This Jesus hath God raised up, whereof we all are witnesses. Therefore being by the right hand of God exalted, and having received of the Father the promise of the Holy Ghost, he hath shed forth this, which ye now see and hear. For David is not ascended into the heavens: but he saith himself, 'The Lord said unto my Lord, Sit thou on my right hand, until I make thy foes thy footstool.' Therefore let all the house of Israel know assuredly, that God hath made that same Jesus, whom ye have crucified, both Lord and Christ."

Now when they heard this, they were pricked in their heart, and said unto Peter and to the rest of the apostles, "Men and brethren, what shall we do?"

Then Peter said unto them, "Repent, and be baptized every one of you in the name of Jesus Christ for the remission of sins, and ye shall receive the gift of the Holy Ghost. For the promise is unto you, and to your children, and to all that are afar off, even as many as the Lord our God shall call." And with many other words did he testify and exhort, saying, "Save yourselves from this untoward generation."

Then they that gladly received his word were baptized: and the same day there were added unto them about three thousand souls. And they continued stedfastly in the apostles' doctrine and fellowship, and in breaking of bread, and in prayers. And fear came upon every soul: and many wonders and signs were done by the apostles. And all that believed were together, and had all things common; and sold their possessions and goods, and parted them to all men, as every man had need. And they, continuing daily with one accord in the temple, and breaking bread from house to house, did eat their meat with gladness and singleness of heart, praising God, and having favour with all the people. And the Lord added to the church daily such as should be saved.

The First Martyr

• ACTS 6:8–15; 7:51 TO 8:2 •

And Stephen, full of faith and power, did great wonders and miracles among the people. Then there arose certain of the synagogue, which is called the synagogue of the Libertines, and Cyrenians, and Alexandrians, and of them of Cilicia and of Asia, disputing with Stephen. And they were not able to resist the wisdom and the spirit by which he spake. Then they suborned men, which said, "We have heard him speak blasphemous words against Moses, and against God." And they stirred up the people, and the elders, and the scribes, and came upon him, and caught him, and brought him to the council, and set up false witnesses, which said, "This man ceaseth not to speak blasphemous words against this holy place, and the law: for we have heard him say, that this Jesus of Nazareth shall destroy this place, and shall change the customs which Moses delivered us." And all that sat in the council, looking stedfastly on him, saw his face as it had been the face of an angel.

Then said the high priest, "Are these things so?"

And he said, "Ye stiffnecked and uncircumcised in heart and ears, ye do always resist the Holy Ghost: as your fathers did, so do ye. Which of the prophets have not your fathers persecuted? and they have slain them which shewed before of the coming of the Just One; of whom ye have been now the betrayers and murderers: who have received the law by the disposition of angels, and have not kept it."

When they heard these things, they were cut to the heart, and they gnashed on him with their teeth. But he, being full of the Holy Ghost, looked up stedfastly into heaven, and saw the glory of God, and Jesus standing on the right hand of God, and said, "Behold, I see the heavens opened, and the Son of man standing on the right hand of God."

Then they cried out with a loud voice, and stopped their ears, and ran upon him with one accord, and cast him out of the city, and stoned him: and the witnesses laid down their clothes at a young man's feet whose name was Saul.

And they stoned Stephen, calling upon God, and saying, "Lord Jesus, receive my spirit." And he kneeled down, and cried with a loud voice, "Lord, lay not this sin to their charge." And when he had said this, he fell asleep.

And Saul was consenting unto his death. And at that time there was a great persecution against the church which was at Jerusalem; and they were all scattered abroad throughout the regions of Judæa and Samaria, except the apostles. And devout men carried Stephen to his burial, and made great lamentation over him.

The Conversion of Paul

• ACTS 9: 1–22 •

And Saul, yet breathing out threatenings and slaughter against the disciples of the Lord, went unto the high priest, and desired of him letters to Damascus to the synagogues, that if he found any of this way, whether they were men or women, he might bring them bound unto Jerusalem.

And as he journeyed, he came near Damascus: and suddenly there shined round about him a light from heaven: and he fell to the earth, and heard a voice saying unto him, "Saul, Saul why persecutest thou me?"

And he said, "Who art thou, Lord?"

And the Lord said, "I am Jesus whom thou persecutest: it is hard for thee to kick against the pricks." [3]

And he trembling and astonished said, "Lord, what wilt thou have me to do?"

[3] Goads. The sense is that Saul (later Paul) cannot resist the will of Christ

And the Lord said unto him, "Arise, and go into the city, and it shall be told thee what thou must do."

And the men which journeyed with him stood speechless, hearing a voice, but seeing no man. And Saul arose from the earth; and when his eyes were opened, he saw no man: but they led him by the hand, and brought him into Damascus. And he was three days without sight, and neither did eat nor drink.

And there was a certain disciple at Damascus, named Ananias; and to him said the Lord in a vision, "Ananias." And he said, "Behold, I am here, Lord." And the Lord said unto him, "Arise, and go into the street which is called Straight, and enquire in the house of Judas for one called Saul, of Tarsus: for, behold, he prayeth, and hath seen in a vision a man named Ananias coming in, and putting his hand on him, that he might receive his sight."

Then Ananias answered, "Lord, I have heard by many of this man, how much evil he hath done to thy saints at Jerusalem: and here he hath authority from the chief priests to bind all that call on thy name."

But the Lord said unto him, "Go thy way: for he is a chosen vessel unto me, to bear my name before the Gentiles, and kings, and the children of Israel: for I will shew him how great things he must suffer for my name's sake."

And Ananias went his way, and entered into the house; and putting his hands on him said, "Brother Saul, the Lord, even Jesus, that appeared unto thee in the way as thou camest, hath sent me, that thou mightest receive thy sight, and be filled with the Holy Ghost." And immediately there fell from his eyes as it had been scales: and he received sight forthwith, and arose, and was baptized. And when he had received meat, he was strengthened.

Then was Saul certain days with the disciples which were at Damascus. And straightway he preached Christ in the synagogues, that he is the Son of God. But all that heard him were amazed, and said; "Is not this he that destroyed them which called on this name in Jerusalem, and came hither for that intent, that he might bring them bound into the chief priests?" But Saul increased the more in strength, and confounded the Jews which dwelt at Damascus, proving that this is very Christ.

Peter's Vision

• ACTS 10 •

There was a certain man in Cæsarea[4] called Cornelius, a centurion of the band called the Italian band, a devout man, and one that feared God with all his house, which gave much alms to the people, and prayed to God alway. He saw in a vision evidently about the ninth hour of the day an angel of God coming in to him, and saying unto him, "Cornelius." And when he looked on him, he was afraid, and said, "What is it, Lord?" And he said unto him, "Thy prayers and thine alms are come up for a memorial before God. And now send men to Joppa,[5] and call for one Simon, whose surname is Peter: he lodgeth with one Simon a tanner, whose house is by the sea side: he shall tell thee what thou oughtest to do." And when the angel which spake unto Cornelius was departed, he called two of his household servants, and a devout soldier of them that waited on him continually; and when he had declared all these things unto them, he sent them to Joppa.

On the morrow, as they went on their journey, and drew nigh unto the city, Peter went up upon the housetop to pray about the sixth hour: and he became very hungry, and would have eaten: but while they made ready, he fell into a trance, and saw heaven opened, and a certain vessel descending unto him, as it had been a great sheet knit at the four corners, and let down to the earth: wherein were all manner of fourfooted beasts of the earth,

[4] A city on the Mediterranean, 47 miles northwest of Jerusalem.
[5] 30 miles south of Caesarea.

and wild beasts, and creeping things, and fowls of the air. And there came a voice to him, "Rise, Peter; kill, and eat."

But Peter said, "Not so, Lord; for I have never eaten any thing that is common or unclean."

And the voice spake unto him again the second time, "What God hath cleansed, that call not thou common." This was done thrice: and the vessel was received up again into heaven.

Now while Peter doubted in himself what this vision which he had seen should mean, behold, the men which were sent from Cornelius had made enquiry for Simon's house, and stood before the gate, and called, and asked whether Simon, which was surnamed Peter, were lodged there.

While Peter thought on the vision, the Spirit said unto him, "Behold, three men seek thee: arise therefore, and get thee down, and go with them, doubting nothing: for I have sent them." Then Peter went down to the men which were sent unto him from Cornelius; and said, "Behold, I am he whom ye seek: what is the cause wherefore ye are come?"

And they said, "Cornelius the centurion, a just man, and one that feareth God, and of good report among all the nation of the Jews, was warned from God by an holy angel to send for thee into his house, and to hear words of thee."

Then called he them in, and lodged them.

And on the morrow Peter went away with them, and certain brethren from Joppa accompanied him. And the morrow after they entered into Cæsarea. And Cornelius waited for them, and had called together his kinsmen and near friends. And as Peter was coming in, Cornelius met him, and fell down at his feet, and worshipped him. But Peter took him up, saying, "Stand up; I myself also am a man." And as he talked with him, he went in, and found many that were come together.

And he said unto them, "Ye know how that it is an unlawful thing for a man that is a Jew to keep company, or come unto one of another nation; but God hath shewed me that I should not call any man common or unclean. Therefore came I unto you without gainsaying, as soon as I was sent for: I ask therefore for what intent ye have sent for me?"

And Cornelius said, "Four days ago I was fasting until this hour; and at the ninth hour I prayed in my house, and, behold, a man stood before me in bright clothing, and said, 'Cornelius, thy prayer is heard, and thine alms are had in remembrance in the sight of God. Send therefore to Joppa, and call hither Simon, whose surname is Peter; he is lodged in the house of one Simon a tanner by the sea side: who, when he cometh, shall speak unto thee.' Immediately therefore I sent to thee; and thou hast well done that thou art come. Now therefore are we all here present before God, to hear all things that are commanded thee of God."

Then Peter opened his mouth, and said, "Of a truth I perceive that God is no respecter of persons: but in every nation he that feareth him, and worketh righteousness, is accepted with him. The word which God sent unto the children of Israel, preaching peace by Jesus Christ: (he is Lord of all:) that word, I say, ye know, which was published throughout all Judæa, and began from Galilee, after the baptism which John preached; how God anointed Jesus of Nazareth with the Holy Ghost and with power: who went about doing good, and healing all that were oppressed of the devil; for God was with him. And we are witnesses of all things which he did both in the land of the Jews, and in Jerusalem; whom they slew and hanged on a tree: Him God raised up the third day, and shewed him openly; not to all the people, but unto witnesses chosen before of God, even to us, who did eat and drink with him after he rose from the dead. And he commanded us to preach unto the people, and to testify that it is he which was ordained of God to be the Judge of quick and dead. To him give all the prophets witness, that through his name whosoever believeth in him shall receive remission of sins."

While Peter yet spake these words, the Holy Ghost fell on all them which heard the word. And they of the circumcision which believed were astonished, as many as came with Peter, because that on the Gentiles also was poured out the gift of the Holy Ghost. For they heard them speak with tongues, and magnify God. Then answered Peter, "Can any man forbid water, that these should not be baptized, which have received the Holy Ghost as well as we?" And he commanded them to be baptized in the name of the Lord. Then prayed they him to tarry certain days.

Paul at Athens

• ACTS 17: 16–34 •

Now while Paul waited for them at Athens, his spirit was stirred in him, when he saw the city wholly given to idolatry. Therefore disputed he in the synagogue with the Jews, and with the devout persons, and in the market daily with them that met with him. Then certain philosophers of the Epicureans, and of the Stoics, encountered him. And some said, "What will this babbler say?" other some, "He seemeth to be a setter forth of strange gods," because he preached unto them Jesus, and the resurrection. And they took him, and brought him unto Areopagus,[6] saying, "May we know what this new doctrine, whereof thou speakest, is? For thou bringest certain strange things to our ears: we would know therefore what these things mean." For all the Athenians and strangers which were there spent their time in nothing else, but either to tell, or to hear some new thing.

Then Paul stood in the midst of Mars' hill, and said, "Ye men of Athens, I perceive that in all things ye are too superstitious. For as I passed by, and beheld your devotions, I found an altar with this inscription, TO THE UNKNOWN GOD[7] Whom therefore ye ignorantly worship, him declare I unto you.

[6] Mars' Hill, as in the next paragraph.
[7] Modern translations read, "To *an* unknown god."

God that made the world and all things therein, seeing that he is Lord of heaven and earth, dwelleth not in temples made with hands; neither is worshipped with men's hands, as though he needed any thing, seeing he giveth to all life, and breath, and all things; and hath made of one blood all nations of men for to dwell on all the face of the earth, and hath determined the times before appointed, and the bounds of their habitation; that they should seek the Lord, if haply they might feel after him, and find him, though he be not far from every one of us: for 'In him we live, and move, and have our being,' as certain also of your own poets have said, 'For we are also his offspring.'

"Forasmuch then as we are the offspring of God, we ought not to think that the Godhead is like unto gold, or silver, or stone, graven by art and man's device. And the times of this ignorance God winked at; but now commandeth all men every where to repent: because he hath appointed a day, in the which he will judge the world in righteousness by that man whom he hath ordained; whereof he hath given assurance unto all men, in that he hath raised him from the dead."

And when they heard of the resurrection of the dead, some mocked: and others said, "We will hear thee again of this matter." So Paul departed from among them. Howbeit certain men clave unto him, and believed: among the which was Dionysius the Areopagite, and a woman named Damaris, and others with them.

Paul and the Silversmiths of Ephesus

• ACTS 19:22–41 •

So [Paul] sent into Macedonia two of them that ministered unto him, Timotheus and Erastus; but he himself stayed in Asia for a season. And the same time there arose no small stir about that way. For a certain man named Demetrius, a silversmith, which made silver shrines for Diana, brought no small gain unto the craftsmen; whom he called together with the workmen of like occupation, and said, "Sirs, ye know that by this craft we have our wealth. Moreover ye see and hear, that not alone at Ephesus, but almost throughout all Asia, this Paul hath persuaded and turned away much people, saying that they be no gods, which are made with hands: so that not only this our craft is in danger to be set at nought; but also that the temple of the great goddess Diana should be despised, and her magnificence should be destroyed, whom all Asia and the world worshippeth."

And when they heard these sayings, they were full of wrath, and cried out, saying, "Great is Diana of the Ephesians." And the whole city was filled with confusion: and having caught Gaius and Aristarchus, men of Macedonia, Paul's companions in travel, they rushed with one accord into the theatre. And when Paul would have entered in unto the people, the disciples suffered him not. And certain of the chief of Asia, which were his friends, sent unto him, desiring him that he would not adventure himself into the theatre. Some therefore cried one thing, and some another: for the assembly was confused; and the more part knew not wherefore they were come together. And they drew Alexander out of the multitude, the Jews putting him forward. And Alexander beckoned with the hand, and would have made his defence unto the people. But when they knew that he was a Jew, all with one voice about the space of two hours cried out, "Great is Diana of the Ephesians."

And when the townclerk had appeased the people, he said, "Ye men of Ephesus, what man is there that knoweth not how that the city of the Ephesians is a worshipper of the great goddess Diana, and of the image which fell down from Jupiter? Seeing then that these things cannot be spoken against, ye ought to be quiet, and to do nothing rashly. For ye have brought hither these men, which are neither robbers of churches, nor yet blasphemers of your goddess. Wherefore if Demetrius, and the craftsmen which are with him, have a matter against any man, the law is open, and there are deputies: let them implead one another. But if ye enquire any thing concerning other matters, it shall be determined in a lawful assembly. For we are in danger to be called in question for this day's uproar, there being no cause whereby we may give an account of this concourse." And when he had thus spoken, he dismissed the assembly.

FROM THE EPISTLES

PAUL'S FIRST EPISTLE TO THE THESSALONIANS

Paul, and Silvanus, and Timotheus, unto the church of the Thessalonians which is in God the Father and in the Lord Jesus Christ: Grace be unto you, and peace, from God our Father, and the Lord Jesus Christ.

We give thanks to God always for you all, making mention of you in our prayers; remembering without ceasing your work of faith, and labour of love, and patience of hope in our Lord Jesus Christ, in the sight of God and our Father; knowing, brethren beloved, your election of God. For our gospel came not unto you in word only, but also in power, and in the Holy Ghost, and in much assurance; as ye know what manner of men we were among you for your sake. And ye became followers of us, and of the Lord, having received the word in much affliction, with joy of the Holy Ghost: so that ye were ensamples to all that believe in Macedonia and Achaia.[1] For from you sounded out the word of the Lord not only in Macedonia and Achaia, but also in every place your faith to God-ward is spread abroad; so that we need not to speak any thing. For they themselves shew of us what manner of entering in we had unto you, and how ye turned to God from idols to serve the living and true God; and to wait for his Son from heaven, whom he raised from the dead, even Jesus, which delivered us from the wrath to come.

For yourselves, brethren, know our entrance in unto you, that it was not in vain: but even after that we had suffered before, and were shamefully entreated, as ye know, at Philippi, we were

[1] Thessalonica was the capital city of Macedonia. Corinth, where this epistle was written, was the capital of Achaia.

bold in our God to speak unto you the gospel of God with much contention. For our exhortation was not of deceit, nor of uncleanness, nor in guile: but as we were allowed of God to be put in trust with the gospel, even so we speak; not as pleasing men, but God, which trieth our hearts. For neither at any time used we flattering words, as ye know, nor a cloak of covetousness; God is witness: nor of men sought we glory, neither of you, nor yet of others, when we might have been burdensome, as the apostles of Christ. But we were gentle among you, even as a nurse cherisheth her children: so being affectionately desirous of you, we were willing to have imparted unto you, not the gospel of God only, but also our own souls, because ye were dear unto us.

For ye remember, brethren, our labour and travail: for labouring night and day,[2] because we would not be chargeable unto any of you, we preached unto you the gospel of God. Ye are witnesses, and God also, how holily and justly and unblameably we behaved ourselves among you that believe: as ye know how we exhorted and comforted and charged every one of you, as a father doth his children, that ye would walk worthy of God, who hath called you unto his kingdom and glory.

For this cause also thank we God without ceasing, because, when ye received the word of God which ye heard of us, ye received it not as the word of men, but as it is in truth, the word of God, which effectually worketh also in you that believe. For ye, brethren, became followers of the churches of God which in Judæa are in Christ Jesus: for ye also have suffered like things of your own countrymen, even as they have of the Jews: who both killed the Lord Jesus, and their own prophets, and have persecuted us[3]; and they please not God, and are contrary to all men: forbidding us to speak to the Gentiles that they might be saved, to fill up their sins alway: for the wrath is come upon them to the uttermost. But we, brethren, being taken from you for a short time in presence, not in heart, endeavoured the more

[2] As a tent maker, so that he could be self-supporting.
[3] Paul had been driven out of Thessalonia by the leaders of the synagogue.

abundantly to see your face with great desire. Wherefore we would have come unto you, even I Paul, once and again; but Satan hindered us. For what is our hope, or joy, or crown of rejoicing? Are not even ye in the presence of our Lord Jesus Christ at his coming? For ye are our glory and joy.

Wherefore when we could no longer forbear, we thought it good to be left at Athens alone; and sent Timotheus, our brother, and minister of God, and our fellowlabourer in the gospel of Christ, to establish you, and to comfort you concerning your faith: that no man should be moved by these afflictions: for yourselves know that we are appointed thereunto. For verily, when we were with you, we told you before that we should suffer tribulation; even as it came to pass, and ye know. For this cause, when I could no longer forbear, I sent to know your faith, lest by some means the tempter have tempted you, and our labour be in vain.

But now when Timotheus came from you unto us, and brought us good tidings of your faith and charity, and that ye have good remembrance of us always, desiring greatly to see us, as we also to see you: therefore, brethren, we were comforted over you in all our affliction and distress by your faith; for now we live, if ye stand fast in the Lord. For what thanks can we render to God again for you, for all the joy wherewith we joy for your sakes before our God; night and day praying exceedingly that we might see your face, and might perfect that which is lacking in your faith? Now God himself and our Father, and our Lord Jesus Christ, direct our way unto you. And the Lord make you to increase and abound in love one toward another, and toward all men, even as we do toward you: to the end he may stablish your hearts unblameable in holiness before God, even our Father, at the coming of our Lord Jesus Christ with all his saints.

Furthermore then we beseech you, brethren, and exhort you by the Lord Jesus, that as ye have received of us how ye ought to walk and to please God, so ye would abound more and more.

For ye know what commandments we gave you by the Lord Jesus. For this is the will of God, even your sanctification, that ye should abstain from fornication: that every one of you should know how to possess his vessel[4] in sanctification and honour; not in the lust of concupiscence, even as the Gentiles which know not God: that no man go beyond and defraud his brother in any matter: because that the Lord is the avenger of all such, as we also have forewarned you and testified. For God hath not called us unto uncleanness, but unto holiness. He therefore that despiseth, despiseth not man, but God, who hath also given unto us his holy Spirit.

But as touching brotherly love ye need not that I write unto you: for ye yourselves are taught of God to love one another. And indeed ye do it toward all the brethren which are in all Macedonia: but we beseech you, brethren, that ye increase more and more; and that ye study to be quiet, and to do your own business, and to work with your own hands, as we commanded you; that ye may walk honestly toward them that are without, and that ye may have lack of nothing.

But I would not have you to be ignorant, brethren, concerning them which are asleep, that ye sorrow not, even as others which have no hope. For if we believe that Jesus died and rose again, even so them also which sleep in Jesus will God bring with him. For this we say unto you by the word of the Lord, that we which are alive and remain unto the coming of the Lord shall not prevent[5] them which are asleep. For the Lord himself shall descend from heaven with a shout, with the voice of the archangel, and with the trump of God: and the dead in Christ shall rise first: then we which are alive and remain shall be caught up together with them in the clouds, to meet the Lord in the air: and so shall we ever be with the Lord. Wherefore comfort one another with these words.

But of the times and the seasons, brethren, ye have no need

[4] Body. (Some authorities render the word as "wife".)
[5] Be before.

that I write unto you. For yourselves know perfectly that the day of the Lord so cometh as a thief in the night. For when they shall say, "Peace and safety;" then sudden destruction cometh upon them, as travail upon a woman with child; and they shall not escape. But ye, brethren, are not in darkness, that that day should overtake you as a thief. Ye are all the children of light, and the children of the day: we are not of the night, nor of darkness. Therefore let us not sleep, as do others; but let us watch and be sober. For they that sleep sleep in the night; and they that be drunken are drunken in the night. But let us, who are of the day, be sober, putting on the breastplate of faith and love; and for an helmet, the hope of salvation. For God hath not appointed us to wrath, but to obtain salvation by our Lord Jesus Christ, who died for us, that, whether we wake or sleep, we should live together with him. Wherefore comfort yourselves together, and edify one another, even as also ye do.

And we beseech you, brethren, to know them which labour among you, and are over you in the Lord, and admonish you; and to esteem them very highly in love for their work's sake. And be at peace among yourselves. Now we exhort you, brethren, warn them that are unruly, comfort the feebleminded, support the weak, be patient toward all men. See that none render evil for evil unto any man; but ever follow that which is good, both among yourselves, and to all men. Rejoice evermore. Pray without ceasing. In every thing give thanks: for this is the will of God in Christ Jesus concerning you. Quench not the Spirit. Despise not prophesyings. Prove all things; hold fast that which is good. Abstain from all appearance of evil.

And the very God of peace sanctify you wholly; and I pray God your whole spirit and soul and body be preserved blameless unto the coming of our Lord Jesus Christ. Faithful is he that calleth you, who also will do it.

Brethren, pray for us.

Greet all the brethren with an holy kiss.

I charge you by the Lord that this epistle be read unto all the holy brethren.

The grace of our Lord Jesus Christ be with you. Amen.

SELECTIONS FROM THE OTHER EPISTLES OF PAUL

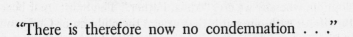

"There is therefore now no condemnation . . ."

• ROMANS 8 •

There is therefore now no condemnation to them which are in Christ Jesus, who walk not after the flesh, but after the Spirit. For the law of the Spirit of life in Christ Jesus hath made me free from the law of sin and death. For what the law could not do, in that it was weak through the flesh, God sending his own Son in the likeness of sinful flesh, and for sin, condemned sin in the flesh: that the righteousness of the law might be fulfilled in us, who walk not after the flesh, but after the Spirit. For they that are after the flesh do mind the things of the flesh; but they that are after the Spirit the things of the Spirit. For to be carnally minded is death; but to be spiritually minded is life and peace. Because the carnal mind is enmity against God: for it is not subject to the law of God, neither indeed can be. So then they that are in the flesh cannot please God.

But ye are not in the flesh, but in the Spirit, if so be that the Spirit of God dwell in you. Now if any man have not the Spirit of Christ, he is none of his. And if Christ be in you, the body is dead because of sin; but the Spirit is life because of righteousness. But if the Spirit of him that raised up Jesus from the dead dwell in you, he that raised up Christ from the dead shall also quicken your mortal bodies by his Spirit that dwelleth in you.

Therefore, brethren, we are debtors, not to the flesh, to live after the flesh. For if ye live after the flesh, ye shall die: but if ye through the Spirit do mortify the deeds of the body, ye shall live. For as many as are led by the Spirit of God, they are the sons of God. For ye have not received the spirit of bondage again to fear; but ye have received the Spirit of adoption, whereby we cry, "Abba, Father." The Spirit itself beareth witness with our spirit, that we are the children of God: and if children, then heirs; heirs of God, and joint-heirs with Christ; if so be that we suffer with him, that we may be also glorified together.

For I reckon that the sufferings of this present time are not worthy to be compared with the glory which shall be revealed in us. For the earnest expectation of the creature waiteth for the manifestation of the sons of God. For the creature was made subject to vanity, not willingly, but by reason of him who hath subjected the same in hope, because the creature itself also shall be delivered from the bondage of corruption into the glorious liberty of the children of God. For we know that the whole creation groaneth and travaileth in pain together until now. And not only they, but ourselves also, which have the firstfruits of the Spirit, even we ourselves groan within ourselves, waiting for the adoption, to wit, the redemption of our body. For we are saved by hope: but hope that is seen is not hope: for what a man seeth, why doth he yet hope for? But if we hope for that we see not, then do we with patience wait for it.

Likewise the Spirit also helpeth our infirmities: for we know not what we should pray for as we ought: but the Spirit itself maketh intercession for us with groanings which cannot be uttered. And he that searcheth the hearts knoweth what is the mind of the Spirit, because he maketh intercession for the saints according to the will of God. And we know that all things work together for good to them that love God, to them who are the

called according to his purpose. For whom he did foreknow, he
also did predestinate to be conformed to the image of his Son,
that he might be the firstborn among many brethren. Moreover
whom he did predestinate, them he also called: and whom he
called, them he also justified: and whom he justified, them he
also glorified.

What shall we then say to these things? If God be for us,
who can be against us? He that spared not his own Son, but
delivered him up for us all, how shall he not with him also
freely give us all things? Who shall lay any thing to the charge
of God's elect? It is God that justifieth. Who is he that con-
demneth? It is Christ that died, yea rather, that is risen again,
who is even at the right hand of God, who also maketh intercession for us. Who shall separate us from the love of Christ?
shall tribulation, or distress, or persecution, or famine, or nakedness, or peril, or sword? As it is written, "For thy sake we are
killed all the day long; we are accounted as sheep for the slaughter." Nay, in all these things we are more than conquerors through
him that loved us. For I am persuaded, that neither death,
nor life, nor angels, nor principalities, nor powers, nor things present, nor things to come, nor height, nor depth, nor any other
creature, shall be able to separate us from the love of God, which
is in Christ Jesus our Lord.

"I beseech you therefore, brethren, by the mercies of God . . ."

• ROMANS 12 •

I beseech you therefore, brethren, by the mercies of God,
that ye present your bodies a living sacrifice, holy, acceptable
unto God, which is your reasonable service. And be not conformed to this world: but be ye transformed by the renewing of

your mind, that ye may prove what is that good, and acceptable, and perfect, will of God.

For I say, through the grace given unto me, to every man that is among you, not to think of himself more highly than he ought to think; but to think soberly, according as God hath dealt to every man the measure of faith. For as we have many members in one body, and all members have not the same office: so we, being many, are one body in Christ, and every one members one of another. Having then gifts differing according to the grace that is given to us, whether prophecy, let us prophesy according to the proportion of faith, or ministry, let us wait on our ministering: or he that teacheth, on teaching; or he that exhorteth, on exhortation: he that giveth, let him do it with simplicity; he that ruleth, with diligence; he that sheweth mercy, with cheerfulness.

Let love be without dissimulation. Abhor that which is evil; cleave to that which is good. Be kindly affectioned one to another with brotherly love; in honour preferring one another; not slothful in business; fervent in spirit; serving the Lord; rejoicing in hope; patient in tribulation; continuing instant in prayer; distributing to the necessity of saints; given to hospitality.

Bless them which persecute you: bless, and curse not. Rejoice with them that do rejoice, and weep with them that weep. Be of the same mind one toward another. Mind not high things, but condescend to men of low estate. Be not wise in your own conceits. Recompense to no man evil for evil. Provide things honest in the sight of all men. If it be possible, as much as lieth in you, live peaceably with all men.

Dearly beloved, avenge not yourselves, but rather give place unto wrath: for it is written, "Vengeance is mine; I will repay, saith the Lord. Therefore if thine enemy hunger, feed him; if he thirst, give him drink: for in so doing thou shalt heap coals of fire on his head." Be not overcome of evil, but overcome evil with good.

"Let every soul be subject unto the higher powers."

Let every soul be subject unto the higher powers. For there is no power but of God: the powers that be are ordained of God. Whosoever therefore resisteth the power, resisteth the ordinance of God: and they that resist shall receive to themselves damnation. For rulers are not a terror to good works, but to the evil. Wilt thou then not be afraid of the power? do that which is good, and thou shalt have praise of the same: for he is the minister of God to thee for good. But if thou do that which is evil, be afraid; for he beareth not the sword in vain: for he is the minister of God, a revenger to execute wrath upon him that doeth evil. Wherefore ye must needs be subject, not only for wrath, but also for conscience sake.

For for this cause pay ye tribute[1] also: for they are God's ministers, attending continually upon this very thing. Render therefore to all their dues: tribute to whom tribute is due; custom to whom custom; fear to whom fear; honour to whom honour.

Owe no man any thing, but to love one another: for he that loveth another hath fulfilled the law. For this, "Thou shalt not commit adultery, Thou shalt not kill, Thou shalt not steal, Thou shalt not bear false witness, Thou shalt not covet," and if there be any other commandment, it is briefly comprehended in this saying, namely, "Thou shalt love thy neighbour as thyself." Love worketh no ill to his neighbour: therefore love is the fulfilling of the law.

And that, knowing the time, that now it is high time to awake out of sleep: for now is our salvation nearer than when we believed. The night is far spent, the day is at hand: let us therefore cast off the works of darkness, and let us put on the armour

[1] Taxes.

of light. Let us walk honestly, as in the day; not in rioting and drunkenness, not in chambering and wantonness, not in strife and envying. But put ye on the Lord Jesus Christ, and make not provision for the flesh, to fulfil the lusts thereof.

"Though I speak with the tongues of men and of angels . . ."

• 1 CORINTHIANS 13 •

Though I speak with the tongues of men and of angels, and have not charity,[2] I am become as sounding brass, or a tinkling cymbal. And though I have the gift of prophecy, and understand all mysteries, and all knowledge; and though I have all faith, so that I could remove mountains, and have not charity, I am nothing. And though I bestow all my goods to feed the poor, and though I give my body to be burned, and have not charity, it profiteth me nothing.

Charity suffereth long, and is kind; charity envieth not; charity vaunteth not itself, is not puffed up, doth not behave itself unseemly, seeketh not her own, is not easily provoked, thinketh no evil; rejoiceth not in iniquity, but rejoiceth in the truth; beareth all things, believeth all things, hopeth all things, endureth all things.

Charity never faileth: but whether there be prophecies, they shall fail; whether there be tongues, they shall cease; whether there be knowledge, it shall vanish away. For we know in part, and we prophesy in part. But when that which is perfect is come, then that which is in part shall be done away. When I was a child, I spake as a child, I understood as a child, I thought as a child: but when I became a man, I put away child-

[2] Many modern translations read *love* for *charity* throughout this passage. It is important to remember that *charity* in this context carries a broader meaning than it has today in ordinary, non-theological language.

ish things. For now we see through a glass, darkly[3]; but then face to face: now I know in part; but then shall I know even as also I am known. And now abideth faith, hope, charity, these three; but the greatest of these is charity.

"Moreover, brethren, I declare unto you the gospel . . ."

• 1 CORINTHIANS 15 •

Moreover, brethren, I declare unto you the gospel which I preached unto you, which also ye have received, and wherein ye stand; by which also ye are saved, if ye keep in memory what I preached unto you, unless ye have believed in vain.

For I delivered unto you first of all that which I also received, how that Christ died for our sins according to the scriptures; and that he was buried, and that he rose again the third day according to the scriptures: and that he was seen of Cephas, then of the twelve: after that, he was seen of above five hundred brethren at once; of whom the greater part remain unto this present, but some are fallen asleep. After that, he was seen of James; then of all the apostles. And last of all he was seen of me also, as of one born out of due time. For I am the least of the apostles, that am not meet to be called an apostle, because I persecuted the church of God. But by the grace of God I am what I am: and his grace which was bestowed upon me was not in vain; but I laboured more abundantly than they all: yet not I, but the grace of God which was with me. Therefore whether it were I or they, so we preach, and so ye believed.

Now if Christ be preached that he rose from the dead, how say some among you that there is no resurrection of the dead? But if there be no resurrection of the dead, then is Christ not risen: and if Christ be not risen, then is our preaching vain, and your faith is also vain. Yea, and we are found false witnesses of

[3] i.e., as in a mirror, imperfectly.

God; because we have testified of God that he raised up Christ: whom he raised not up, if so be that the dead rise not. For if the dead rise not, then is not Christ raised: and if Christ be not raised, your faith is vain; ye are yet in your sins. Then they also which are fallen asleep in Christ are perished. If in this life only we have hope in Christ, we are of all men most miserable.

But now is Christ risen from the dead, and become the firstfruits of them that slept. For since by man came death, by man came also the resurrection of the dead. For as in Adam all die, even so in Christ shall all be made alive. But every man in his own order: Christ the firstfruits; afterward they that are Christ's at his coming. Then cometh the end, when he shall have delivered up the kingdom to God, even the Father; when he shall have put down all rule and all authority and power. For he must reign, till he hath put all enemies under his feet. The last enemy that shall be destroyed is death. For he hath put all things under his feet. But when he saith all things are put under him, it is manifest that he is excepted, which did put all things under him. And when all things shall be subdued unto him, then shall the Son also himself be subject unto him that put all things under him, that God may be all in all.

Else what shall they do which are baptized for the dead, if the dead rise not at all? why are they then baptized for the dead? And why stand we in jeopardy every hour? I protest by your rejoicing[4] which I have in Christ Jesus our Lord, I die daily. If after the manner of men I have fought with beasts at Ephesus, what advantageth it me, if the dead rise not? let us eat and drink; for to morrow we die. Be not deceived: "evil communications corrupt good manners." [5] Awake to righteousness, and sin not; for some have not the knowledge of God: I speak this to your shame.

But some man will say, "How are the dead raised up? and

[4] i.e., by the pride I have in you.
[5] A quotation from Menander.

with what body do they come?" Thou fool, that which thou sowest is not quickened, except it die: and that which thou sowest,
thou sowest not that body that shall be, but bare grain, it may
chance of wheat, or of some other grain: but God giveth it a
body as it hath pleased him, and to every seed his own body.
All flesh is not the same flesh: but there is one kind of flesh of
men, another flesh of beasts, another of fishes, and another of
birds. There are also celestial bodies, and bodies terrestrial: but
the glory of the celestial is one, and the glory of the terrestrial
is another. There is one glory of the sun, and another glory of
the moon, and another glory of the stars: for one star differeth
from another star in glory.

So also is the resurrection of the dead. It is sown in corruption; it is raised in incorruption: it is sown in dishonour; it is
raised in glory: it is sown in weakness; it is raised in power: it
is sown a natural body; it is raised a spiritual body. There is a
natural body, and there is a spiritual body. And so it is written,
"The first man Adam was made a living soul; the last Adam was
made a quickening spirit." Howbeit that was not first which is
spiritual, but that which is natural; and afterward that which is
spiritual. The first man is of the earth, earthy: the second man
is the Lord from heaven. As is the earthy, such are they also
that are earthy: and as is the heavenly, such are they also that
are heavenly. And as we have borne the image of the earthy, we
shall also bear the image of the heavenly. Now this I say, brethren, that flesh and blood cannot inherit the kingdom of God;
neither doth corruption inherit incorruption.

Behold, I shew you a mystery; we shall not all sleep, but we
shall all be changed, In a moment, in the twinkling of an eye,
at the last trump: for the trumpet shall sound, and the dead
shall be raised incorruptible, and we shall be changed. For this
corruptible must put on incorruption, and this mortal must put
on immortality. So when this corruptible shall have put on incorruption, and this mortal shall have put on immortality, then shall
be brought to pass the saying that is written, "Death is swallowed

up in victory." O death, where is thy sting? O grave, where is thy victory? The sting of death is sin; and the strength of sin is the law. But thanks be to God, which giveth us the victory through our Lord Jesus Christ.

Therefore, my beloved brethren, be ye stedfast, unmoveable, always abounding in the work of the Lord, forasmuch as ye know that your labour is not in vain in the Lord.

"Children, obey your parents in the Lord . . ."

• EPHESIANS 6: 1–20 •

Children, obey your parents in the Lord: for this is right. "Honour thy father and mother;" which is the first commandment with promise; "that it may be well with thee, and thou mayest live long on the earth." And, ye fathers, provoke not your children to wrath: but bring them up in the nurture and admonition of the Lord.

Servants, be obedient to them that are your masters according to the flesh, with fear and trembling, in singleness of your heart, as unto Christ; not with eyeservice, as men pleasers; but as the servants of Christ, doing the will of God from the heart; with good will doing service, as to the Lord, and not to men: knowing that whatsoever good thing any man doeth, the same shall he receive of the Lord, whether he be bond or free.

And, ye masters, do the same things unto them, forbearing threatening: knowing that your Master also is in heaven; neither is there respect of persons with him.

Finally, my brethren, be strong in the Lord, and in the power of his might. Put on the whole armour of God, that ye may be able to stand against the wiles of the devil. For we wrestle not against flesh and blood, but against principalities, against powers, against the rulers of the darkness of this world, against spiritual wickedness in high places. Wherefore take unto you the

whole armour of God, that ye may be able to withstand in the
evil day, and having done all, to stand. Stand therefore, having
your loins girt about with truth, and having on the breastplate of
righteousness; and your feet shod with the preparation of the gospel of peace; above all, taking the shield of faith, wherewith ye
shall be able to quench all the fiery darts of the wicked. And
take the helmet of salvation, and the sword of the Spirit, which
is the word of God: praying always with all prayer and supplication in the Spirit, and watching thereunto with all perseverance
and supplication for all saints; and for me, that utterance may
be given unto me, that I may open my mouth boldly, to make
known the mystery of the gospel, for which I am an ambassa-
dor in bonds: that therein I may speak boldly, as I ought to
speak.

From THE EPISTLE TO THE HEBREWS

"Now faith is the substance of things hoped for . . ."

• HEBREWS 11: 1–16; 12: 1–2 •

Now faith is the substance[1] of things hoped for, the evi-
dence[2] of things not seen. For by it the elders obtained a good
report. Through faith we understand that the worlds were framed
by the word of God, so that things which are seen were not
made of things which do appear.

By faith Abel offered unto God a more excellent sacrifice
than Cain, by which he obtained witness that he was righteous,

[1] Assurance.
[2] Proving or conviction.

God testifying of his gifts: and by it he being dead yet speak-eth. By faith Enoch was translated that he should not see death; and was not found, because God had translated him: for before his translation he had this testimony, that he pleased God. But without faith it is impossible to please him: for he that cometh to God must believe that he is, and that he is a rewarder of them that diligently seek him. By faith Noah, being warned of God of things not seen as yet, moved with fear, prepared an ark to the saving of his house; by the which he condemned the world, and became heir of the righteousness which is by faith. By faith Abraham, when he was called to go out into a place which he should after receive for an inheritance, obeyed; and he went out, not knowing whither he went. By faith he sojourned in the land of promise, as in a strange country, dwelling in tabernacles with Isaac and Jacob, the heirs with him of the same promise: for he looked for a city which hath foundations, whose builder and maker is God. Through faith also Sara herself received strength to conceive seed, and was delivered of a child when she was past age, because she judged him faithful who had promised. Therefore sprang there even of one, and him as good as dead, so many as the stars of the sky in multitude, and as the sand which is by the sea shore innumerable.

These all died in faith, not having received the promises, but having seen them afar off, and were persuaded of them, and embraced them, and confessed that they were strang-ers and pilgrims on the earth. For they that say such things declare plainly that they seek a country. And truly, if they had been mindful of that country from whence they came out, they might have had opportunity to have returned. But now they desire a better country, that is, an heavenly: wherefore God is not ashamed to be called their God: for he hath prepared for them a city.

Wherefore seeing we also are compassed about with so great a cloud of witnesses, let us lay aside every weight, and the sin which doth so easily beset us, and let us run with patience the race that is set before us, looking unto Jesus the author and finisher of our faith; who for the joy that was set before him endured the cross, despising the shame, and is set down at the right hand of the throne of God.

From THE EPISTLES GENERAL

"My brethren, count it all joy . . ."

• JAMES 1 •

James, a servant of God and of the Lord Jesus Christ, to the twelve tribes which are scattered abroad, greeting.

My brethren, count it all joy when ye fall into divers temptations; knowing this, that the trying of your faith worketh patience. But let patience have her perfect work, that ye may be perfect and entire, wanting nothing.

If any of you lack wisdom, let him ask of God, that giveth to all men liberally, and upbraideth not; and it shall be given him. But let him ask in faith, nothing wavering. For he that wavereth is like a wave of the sea driven with the wind and tossed. For let not that man think that he shall receive any thing of the Lord. A double minded man is unstable in all his ways.

Let the brother of low degree rejoice in that he is exalted: but the rich, in that he is made low: because as the flower of the grass he shall pass away. For the sun is no sooner risen with a burning heat, but it withereth the grass, and the flower thereof falleth, and the grace of the fashion of it perisheth: so also shall the rich man fade away in his ways.

Blessed is the man that endureth temptation: for when he is tried, he shall receive the crown of life, which the Lord hath promised to them that love him. Let no man say when he is tempted, "I am tempted of God," for God cannot be tempted with evil, neither tempteth he any man: but every man is tempted, when he is drawn away of his own lust, and enticed. Then when lust hath conceived, it bringeth forth sin: and sin, when it is finished, bringeth forth death.

Do not err, my beloved brethren. Every good gift and every perfect gift is from above, and cometh down from the Father of lights, with whom is no variableness, neither shadow of turning. Of his own will begat he us with the word of truth, that we should be a kind of firstfruits of his creatures.

Wherefore, my beloved brethren, let every man be swift to hear, slow to speak, slow to wrath: for the wrath of man worketh not the righteousness of God. Wherefore lay apart all filthiness and superfluity of naughtiness, and receive with meekness the engrafted word, which is able to save your souls.

But be ye doers of the word, and not hearers only, deceiving your own selves. For if any be a hearer of the word, and not a doer, he is like unto a man beholding his natural face in a glass: for he beholdeth himself, and goeth his way, and straightway forgetteth what manner of man he was. But whoso looketh into the perfect law of liberty, and continueth therein, he being not a forgetful hearer, but a doer of the work, this man shall be blessed in his deed.

If any man among you seem to be religious, and bridleth not his tongue, but deceiveth his own heart, this man's religion is vain. Pure religion and undefiled before God and the Father is this, to visit the fatherless and widows in their affliction, and to keep himself unspotted from the world.

That which was from the beginning, which we have heard, which we have seen with our eyes, which we have looked upon, and our hands have handled, of the Word of life; (for the life was manifested, and we have seen it, and bear witness, and shew unto you that eternal life, which was with the Father, and was manifested unto us;) that which we have seen and heard declare we unto you, that ye also may have fellowship with us: and truly our fellowship is with the Father, and with his Son Jesus Christ. And these things write we unto you, that your joy may be full.

This then is the message which we have heard of him, and declare unto you, that God is light, and in him is no darkness at all. If we say that we have fellowship with him, and walk in darkness, we lie, and do not the truth: but if we walk in the light, as he is in the light, we have fellowship one with another, and the blood of Jesus Christ his Son cleanseth us from all sin. If we say that we have no sin, we deceive ourselves, and the truth is not in us. If we confess our sins, he is faithful and just to forgive us our sins, and to cleanse us from all unrighteousness. If we say that we have not sinned, we make him a liar, and his word is not in us.

My little children, these things write I unto you, that ye sin not. And if any man sin, we have an advocate with the Father, Jesus Christ the righteous: and he is the propitiation for our sins: and not for ours only, but also for the sins of the whole world. And hereby we do know that we know him, if we keep his commandments. He that saith, "I know him," and keepeth not his commandments, is a liar, and the truth is not in him. But whoso keepeth his word, in him verily is the love of God perfected: hereby know we that we are in him. He that saith he abideth in him, ought himself also so to walk, even as he walked.

Brethren, I write no new commandment unto you, but an old

commandment which ye had from the beginning. The old commandment is the word which ye have heard from the beginning. Again, a new commandment I write unto you, which thing is true in him and in you: because the darkness is past, and the true light now shineth. He that saith he is in the light, and hateth his brother, is in darkness even until now. He that loveth his brother abideth in the light, and there is none occasion of stumbling in him. But he that hateth his brother is in darkness, and walketh in darkness, and knoweth not whither he goeth, because that darkness hath blinded his eyes.

I write unto you, little children, because your sins are forgiven you for his name's sake. I write unto you, fathers, because ye have known him that is from the beginning. I write unto you, young men, because ye have overcome the wicked one. I write unto you, little children, because ye have known the Father. I have written unto you, fathers, because ye have known him that is from the beginning. I have written unto you, young men, because ye are strong, and the word of God abideth in you, and ye have overcome the wicked one.

Love not the world, neither the things that are in the world. If any man love the world, the love of the Father is not in him. For all that is in the world, the lust of the flesh, and the lust of the eyes, and the pride of life, is not of the Father, but is of the world. And the world passeth away, and the lust thereof: but he that doeth the will of God abideth for ever.

"Beloved, let us love one another . . ."

• 1 JOHN 4:7 TO 5:12 •

Beloved, let us love one another: for love is of God; and every one that loveth is born of God, and knoweth God. He that loveth not knoweth not God; for God is love. In this was manifested the love of God toward us, because that God sent his only begotten Son into the world, that we might live through him. Herein is love, not that we loved God, but that he loved us, and sent his Son to be the propitiation for our sins. Beloved, if God so loved us, we ought also to love one another.

No man hath seen God at any time. If we love one another, God dwelleth in us, and his love is perfected in us. Hereby know we that we dwell in him, and he in us, because he hath given us of his Spirit. And we have seen and do testify that the Father sent the Son to be the Saviour of the world. Whosoever shall confess that Jesus is the Son of God, God dwelleth in him, and he in God. And we have known and believed the love that God hath to us. God is love; and he that dwelleth in love dwelleth in God, and God in him. Herein is our love made perfect, that we may have boldness in the day of judgment: because as he is, so are we in this world. There is no fear in love; but perfect love casteth out fear: because fear hath torment. He that feareth is not made perfect in love. We love him, because he first loved us. If a man say, "I love God," and hateth his brother, he is a liar: for he that loveth not his brother whom he hath seen, how can he love God whom he hath not seen? And this commandment have we from him, that he who loveth God love his brother also.

Whosoever believeth that Jesus is the Christ is born of God: and every one that loveth him that begat loveth him also that is begotten of him. By this we know that we love the children of God, when we love God, and keep his commandments. For this is the love of God, that we keep his commandments: and his commandments are not grievous. For whatsoever is born of God overcometh the world: and this is the victory that overcometh the world, even our faith. Who is he that overcometh the world, but he that believeth that Jesus is the Son of God?

This is he that came by water and blood, even Jesus Christ; not by water only, but by water and blood. And it is the Spirit that beareth witness, because the Spirit is truth. For there are three that bear record in heaven, the Father, the Word, and the

Holy Ghost: and these three are one. And there are three that bear witness in earth, the spirit, and the water, and the blood: and these three agree in one. If we receive the witness of men, the witness of God is greater: for this is the witness of God which he hath testified of his Son. He that believeth on the Son of God hath the witness in himself: he that believeth not God hath made him a liar; because he believeth not the record that God gave of his Son. And this is the record, that God hath given to us eternal life, and this life is in his Son. He that hath the Son hath life; and he that hath not the Son of God hath not life.

FROM THE REVELATION OF ST. JOHN THE DIVINE

The Messages to the Seven Churches

• REVELATION 1 TO 3 •

The Revelation of Jesus Christ, which God gave unto him, to shew unto his servants things which must shortly come to pass; and he sent and signified it by his angel unto his servant John: who bare record of the word of God, and of the testimony of Jesus Christ, and of all things that he saw. Blessed is he that readeth, and they that hear the words of this prophecy, and keep those things which are written therein: for the time is at hand.

John to the seven churches which are in Asia: Grace be unto you, and peace, from him which is, and which was, and which is to come; and from the seven Spirits which are before his throne; and from Jesus Christ, who is the faithful witness, and the first begotten of the dead, and the prince of the kings of the earth. Unto him that loved us, and washed us from our sins in his own blood, and hath made us kings and priests unto God and his Father; to him be glory and dominion for ever and ever. Amen. Behold, he cometh with clouds; and every eye shall see him, and they also which pierced him: and all kindreds of the earth shall wail because of him. Even so, Amen.

"I am Alpha and Omega, the beginning and the ending," saith the Lord, which is, and which was, and which is to come, the Almighty.

I John, who also am your brother, and companion in tribulation, and in the kingdom and patience of Jesus Christ, was in the isle that is called Patmos,[1] for the word of God, and for the testimony of Jesus Christ. I was in the Spirit on the Lord's day, and heard behind me a great voice, as of a trumpet, saying, "I am Alpha and Omega, the first and the last," and, "What thou seest, write in a book, and send it unto the seven churches which are in Asia[2]; unto Ephesus, and unto Smyrna, and unto Pergamos, and unto Thyatira, and unto Sardis, and unto Philadelphia, and unto Laodicea."

And I turned to see the voice that spake with me. And being turned, I saw seven golden candlesticks; and in the midst of the seven candlesticks one like unto the Son of man, clothed with a garment down to the foot, and girt about the paps with a golden girdle. His head and his hairs were white like wool, as white as snow; and his eyes were as a flame of fire; and his feet like unto fine brass, as if they burned in a furnace; and his voice as the sound of many waters. And he had in his right hand seven stars: and out of his mouth went a sharp twoedged sword: and his countenance was as the sun shineth in his strength.

And when I saw him, I fell at his feet as dead. And he laid his right hand upon me, saying unto me, "Fear not; I am the first and the last: I am he that liveth, and was dead; and, behold, I am alive for evermore, Amen; and have the keys of hell and of death. Write the things which thou hast seen, and the things which are, and the things which shall be hereafter; the mystery of the seven stars which thou sawest in my right hand, and the seven golden candlesticks. The seven stars are the angels of the seven churches: and the seven candlesticks which thou sawest are the seven churches.

"Unto the angel of the church of Ephesus write; 'These things saith he that holdeth the seven stars in his right hand, who walketh in the midst of the seven golden candlesticks; I know thy works, and thy labour, and thy patience, and how thou

---

[1] A rocky island in the Aegean Sea to which John had been banished.
[2] Western Asia Minor.

canst not bear them which are evil: and thou hast tried them which say they are apostles, and are not, and hast found them liars: and hast borne, and hast patience, and for my name's sake hast laboured, and hast not fainted. Nevertheless I have somewhat against thee, because thou hast left thy first love. Remember therefore from whence thou art fallen, and repent, and do the first works; or else I will come unto thee quickly, and will remove thy candlestick out of his place, except thou repent. But this thou hast, that thou hatest the deeds of the Nicolaitanes,[3] which I also hate. He that hath an ear, let him hear what the Spirit saith unto the churches; to him that overcometh will I give to eat of the tree of life, which is in the midst of the paradise of God.'

"And unto the angel of the church in Smyrna write; 'These things saith the first and the last, which was dead, and is alive; I know thy works, and tribulation, and poverty, (but thou art rich) and I know the blasphemy of them which say they are Jews, and are not, but are the synagogue of Satan. Fear none of those things which thou shalt suffer: behold, the devil shall cast some of you into prison, that ye may be tried; and ye shall have tribulation ten days: be thou faithful unto death, and I will give thee a crown of life. He that hath an ear, let him hear what the Spirit saith unto the churches; He that overcometh shall not be hurt of the second death.' [4]

"And to the angel of the church in Pergamos write; 'These things saith he which hath the sharp sword with two edges; I know thy works, and where thou dwellest, even where Satan's seat is: and thou holdest fast my name, and hast not denied my faith, even in those days wherein Antipas was my faithful martyr, who was slain among you, where Satan dwelleth. But I have a few things against thee, because thou hast there them that hold the doctrine of Balaam, who taught Balac to cast a stumblingblock before the children of Israel, to eat things sacrificed unto idols, and to commit fornication. So hast thou also them that hold the

[3] An heretical sect at Ephesus.
[4] Final condemnation.

doctrine of the Nicolaitanes, which thing I hate. Repent; or else
I will come unto thee quickly, and will fight against them with
the sword of my mouth. He that hath an ear, let him hear what
the Spirit saith unto the churches; to him that overcometh will I
give to eat of the hidden manna, and will give him a white
stone, and in the stone a new name written, which no man
knoweth saving he that receiveth it.'

"And unto the angel of the church in Thyatira write; 'These
things saith the Son of God, who hath his eyes like unto a flame
of fire, and his feet are like fine brass; I know thy works, and
charity, and service, and faith, and thy patience, and thy works;
and the last to be more than the first. Notwithstanding I have a
few things against thee, because thou sufferest that woman
Jezebel,[5] which calleth herself a prophetess, to teach and to seduce my servants to commit fornication, and to eat things sacrificed unto idols. And I gave her space to repent of her fornication; and she repented not. Behold, I will cast her into a
bed, and them that commit adultery with her into great tribulation, except they repent of their deeds. And I will kill
her children with death; and all the churches shall know that
I am he which searcheth the reins and hearts: and I will give
unto every one of you according to your works. But unto you I
say, and unto the rest in Thyatira, as many as have not this doctrine, and which have not known the depths of Satan, as they
speak; I will put upon you none other burden. But that which ye
have already hold fast till I come. And he that overcometh, and
keepeth my works unto the end, to him will I give power over the
nations: and he shall rule them with a rod of iron; as the vessels
of a potter shall they be broken to shivers: even as I received of
my Father. And I will give him the morning star. He that hath
an ear, let him hear what the Spirit saith unto the churches.'

"And unto the angel of the church in Sardis write; 'These
things saith he that hath the seven Spirits of God, and the seven

[5] Probably the name is used figuratively, by way of comparison to Ahab's
wicked queen (see I Kings 16 ff.)

stars; I know thy works, that thou hast a name that thou livest, and art dead.[6] Be watchful, and strengthen the things which remain, that are ready to die: for I have not found thy works perfect before God. Remember therefore how thou hast received and heard, and hold fast, and repent. If therefore thou shalt not watch, I will come on thee as a thief, and thou shalt not know what hour I will come upon thee. Thou hast a few names even in Sardis which have not defiled their garments; and they shall walk with me in white: for they are worthy. He that overcometh, the same shall be clothed in white raiment; and I will not blot out his name out of the book of life, but I will confess his name before my Father, and before his angels. He that hath an ear, let him hear what the Spirit saith unto the churches.'

"And to the angel of the church in Philadelphia write; 'These things saith he that is holy, he that is true, he that hath the key of David, he that openeth, and no man shutteth; and shutteth, and no man openeth; I know thy works: behold, I have set before thee an open door, and no man can shut it: for thou hast a little strength, and hast kept my word, and hast not denied my name. Behold, I will make them of the synagogue of Satan, which say they are Jews, and are not, but do lie; behold, I will make them to come and worship before thy feet, and to know that I have loved thee. Because thou hast kept the word of my patience, I also will keep thee from the hour of temptation, which shall come upon all the world, to try them that dwell upon the earth. Behold, I come quickly: hold that fast which thou hast, that no man take thy crown. Him that overcometh will I make a pillar in the temple of my God, and he shall go no more out: and I will write upon him the name of my God, and the name of the city of my God, which is new Jerusalem, which cometh down out of heaven from my God: and I will write upon him my new name. He that hath an ear, let him hear what the Spirit saith unto the churches.'

"And unto the angel of the church of the Laodiceans write;

[6] i.e., you are Christians in name only.

'These things saith the Amen, the faithful and true witness, the beginning of the creation of God; I know thy works, that thou art neither cold nor hot: I would thou wert cold or hot. So then because thou art lukewarm, and neither cold nor hot, I will spew thee out of my mouth. Because thou sayest, "I am rich, and increased with goods, and have need of nothing;" and knowest not that thou art wretched, and miserable, and poor, and blind, and naked: I counsel thee to buy of me gold tried in the fire, that thou mayest be rich; and white raiment, that thou mayest be clothed, and that the shame of thy nakedness do not appear; and anoint thine eyes with eyesalve, that thou mayest see. As many as I love, I rebuke and chasten: be zealous therefore, and repent. Behold, I stand at the door, and knock: if any man hear my voice, and open the door, I will come in to him, and will sup with him, and he with me. To him that overcometh will I grant to sit with me in my throne, even as I also overcame, and am set down with my Father in his throne. He that hath an ear, let him hear what the Spirit saith unto the churches.' "

War in Heaven Renewed on Earth

• REVELATION 12 •

And there appeared a great wonder in heaven; a woman clothed with the sun, and the moon under her feet, and upon her head a crown of twelve stars: and she being with child cried, travailing in birth, and pained to be delivered. And there appeared another wonder in heaven; and behold a great red dragon, having seven heads and ten horns, and seven crowns upon his heads. And his tail drew the third part of the stars of heaven, and did cast them to the earth: and the dragon stood before the woman which was ready to be delivered, for to devour her child as soon as it was born. And she brought forth a man child, who was to rule all nations with a rod of iron: and her child was caught up unto God, and to his throne. And the woman fled into the wilderness, where she hath a place prepared of God, that they should feed her there a thousand two hundred and three-score days.

And there was war in heaven: Michael and his angels fought against the dragon; and the dragon fought and his angels, and prevailed not; neither was their place found any more in heaven. And the great dragon was cast out, that old serpent, called the Devil, and Satan, which deceiveth the whole world: he was cast out into the earth, and his angels were cast out with him. And I heard a loud voice saying in heaven, "Now is come salvation, and strength, and the kingdom of our God, and the power of his Christ: for the accuser of our brethren is cast down, which accused them before our God day and night. And they overcame him by the blood of the Lamb, and by the word of their testimony; and they loved not their lives unto the death. Therefore rejoice, ye heavens, and ye that dwell in them. Woe to the inhabiters of the earth and of the sea! for the devil is come down unto you, having great wrath, because he knoweth that he hath but a short time."

And when the dragon saw that he was cast unto the earth, he persecuted the woman which brought forth the man child. And to the woman were given two wings of a great eagle, that she might fly into the wilderness, into her place, where she is nourished for a time, and times, and half a time, from the face of the serpent. And the serpent cast out of his mouth water as a flood after the woman, that he might cause her to be carried away of the flood. And the earth helped the woman, and the earth opened her mouth, and swallowed up the flood which the dragon cast out of his mouth. And the dragon was wroth with the woman, and went to make war with the remnant of her seed, which keep the commandments of God, and have the testimony of Jesus Christ.

A New Heaven and a New Earth

And I saw a new heaven and a new earth: for the first heaven and the first earth were passed away; and there was no more sea. And I John saw the holy city, new Jerusalem, coming down from God out of heaven, prepared as a bride adorned for her husband. And I heard a great voice out of heaven saying, "Behold, the tabernacle of God is with men, and he will dwell with them, and they shall be his people, and God himself shall be with them, and be their God. And God shall wipe away all tears from their eyes; and there shall be no more death, neither sorrow, nor crying, neither shall there be any more pain: for the former things are passed away."

And he that sat upon the throne said, "Behold, I make all things new." And he said unto me, "Write: for these words are true and faithful." And he said unto me, "It is done. I am Alpha and Omega, the beginning and the end. I will give unto him that is athirst of the fountain of the water of life freely. He that overcometh shall inherit all things; and I will be his God, and he shall be my son. But the fearful, and unbelieving, and the abominable, and murderers, and whoremongers, and sorcerors, and idolaters, and all liars, shall have their part in the lake which burneth with fire and brimstone: which is the second death."

And there came unto me one of the seven angels which had the seven vials full of the seven last plagues, and talked with me, saying, "Come hither, I will shew thee the bride, the Lamb's wife." And he carried me away in the spirit to a great and high mountain, and shewed me that great city, the holy Jerusalem, descending out of heaven from God, having the glory of God: and her light was like unto a stone most precious, even like a jasper stone, clear as crystal; and had a wall great and high, and had twelve gates, and at the gates twelve angels, and names written thereon, which are the names of the twelve tribes of the children of Israel: on the east three gates; on the north three gates; on the south three gates; and on the west three gates. And the wall of the city had twelve foundations, and in them the names of the twelve apostles of the Lamb.

And he that talked with me had a golden reed to measure the city, and the gates thereof, and the wall thereof. And the city lieth foursquare, and the length is as large as the breadth: and he measured the city with the reed, twelve thousand furlongs. The length and the breadth and the height of it are equal. And he measured the wall thereof, an hundred and forty and four cubits, according to the measure of a man, that is, of the angel. And the building of the wall of it was of jasper: and the city was pure gold, like unto clear glass. And the foundations of the wall of the city were garnished with all manner of precious stones. The first foundation was jasper; the second, sapphire; the third, a chalcedony; the fourth, an emerald; the fifth, sardonyx; the sixth, sardius; the seventh, chrysolyte; the eighth, beryl; the ninth, a topaz; the tenth, a chrysophrasus; the eleventh, a jacinth; the twelfth, an amethyst. And the twelve gates were twelve pearls; every several gate was of one pearl: and the street of the city was pure gold, as it were transparent glass.

And I saw no temple therein: for the Lord God Almighty and the Lamb are the temple of it. And the city had no need of the sun, neither of the moon, to shine in it: for the glory of God did lighten it, and the Lamb is the light thereof. And the nations of them which are saved shall walk in the light of it: and the kings of the earth do bring their glory and honour into it. And the gates of it shall not be shut at all by day: for there shall be no night there. And they shall bring the glory and honour of the nations into it. And there shall in no wise enter into it any thing that defileth, neither whatsoever worketh abomination, or maketh a lie: but they which are written in the Lamb's book of life.

And he shewed me a pure river of water of life, clear as crystal, proceeding out of the throne of God and of the Lamb. In the midst of the street of it, and on either side of the river, was there the tree of life, which bare twelve manner of fruits, and yielded her fruit every month: and the leaves of the tree were for the healing of the nations. And there shall be no more curse: but the throne of God and of the Lamb shall be in it; and his servants shall serve him: and they shall see his face; and his name shall be in their foreheads. And there shall be no night there; and they need no candle, neither light of the sun; for the Lord God giveth them light: and they shall reign for ever and ever.

And he said unto me, "These sayings are faithful and true: and the Lord God of the holy prophets sent his angel to shew unto his servants the things which must shortly be done. Behold, I come quickly."

Blessed is he that keepeth the sayings of the prophecy of this book. And I John saw these things, and heard them. And when I had heard and seen, I fell down to worship before the feet of the angel which shewed me these things. Then saith he unto me, "See thou do it not,[7] for I am thy fellowservant, and of thy brethren the prophets, and of them which keep the sayings of this book: worship God." And he saith unto me, "Seal not the sayings of the prophecy of this book: for the time is at hand. He that is unjust, let him be unjust still: and he which is filthy, let him be filthy still: and he that is righteous, let him by righteous still: and he that is holy, let him be holy still."

"And, behold, I come quickly; and my reward is with me, to give every man according as his work shall be. I am Alpha and Omega, the beginning and the end, the first and the last."

Blessed are they that do his commandments, that they may have right to the tree of life, and may enter in through the gates into the city. For without are dogs, and sorcerers, and

[7] i.e., do not kneel to me.

whoremongers, and murderers, and idolaters, and whosoever loveth and maketh a lie.

"I Jesus have sent mine angel to testify unto you these things in the churches. I am the root and the offspring of David, and the bright and morning star."

And the Spirit and the bride say, "Come." And let him that heareth say, "Come." And let him that is athirst come. And whosoever will, let him take the water of life freely.

For I testify unto every man that heareth the words of the prophecy of this book, if any man shall add unto these things, God shall add unto him the plagues that are written in this book: and if any man shall take away the words of the book of this prophecy, God shall take away his part out of the book of life, and out of the holy city, and from the things which are written in this book.

He which testifieth these things saith, "Surely I come quickly." Amen. Even so, come, Lord Jesus.

The grace of our Lord Jesus Christ be with you all. Amen.

Whoremongers, and murderers, and idolaters, and whosoever loveth and maketh a lie.

I Jesus have sent mine angel to testify unto you these things in the churches. I am the root and the offspring of David, and the bright and morning star.

And the Spirit and the bride say, "Come." And let him that heareth say, "Come." And let him that is athirst come: and whosoever will, let him take the water of life freely.

For I testify unto every man that heareth the words of the prophecy of this book: If any man shall add unto these things, God shall add unto him the plagues that are written in this book: and if any man shall take away from the words of the book of this prophecy, God shall take away his part out of the book of life, and out of the holy city, and from these things which are written in this book.

He which testifieth these things saith, "Surely, I come quickly." Amen. Even so, come, Lord Jesus.

The grace of our Lord Jesus Christ be with you all. Amen.

Rinehart Editions

Addison and Steele, SEL. FROM THE TATLER & THE SPECTATOR 87

AMERICAN THOUGHT: CIVIL WAR TO WORLD WAR I 70

ANTHOLOGY OF ENGLISH DRAMA BEFORE SHAKESPEARE 45

ANTHOLOGY OF GREEK DRAMA: FIRST SERIES 29

ANTHOLOGY OF GREEK DRAMA: SECOND SERIES 68

ANTHOLOGY OF ROMAN DRAMA 101

Arnold, SELECTED POETRY AND PROSE 62

Austen, NORTHANGER ABBEY; Walpole, THE CASTLE OF OTRANTO; Radcliffe, THE MYSTERIES OF UDOLPHO (Abridged) 121

Austen, PRIDE AND PREJUDICE 22

Balzac, PÈRE GORIOT 18

Benét, S. V., SELECTED POETRY & PROSE 100

THE BIBLE: SEL. FROM OLD & NEW TESTAMENTS 56

Brontë, Charlotte, JANE EYRE 24

Brontë, Emily, WUTHERING HEIGHTS 23

Brown, C. B., ARTHUR MERVYN 112

Browning, Robert, SELECTED POETRY 71

Bunyan, THE PILGRIM'S PROGRESS 27

Burke, REFLECTIONS ON THE REVOLUTION IN FRANCE 84

Butler, THE WAY OF ALL FLESH 7

Byron, SELECTED POETRY AND LETTERS 54

Chaucer, THE CANTERBURY TALES 65

Chekhov, SIX PLAYS OF CHEKHOV 117

Coleridge, SELECTED POETRY AND PROSE 55

COLONIAL AMERICAN WRITING 43

Conrad, LORD JIM 85

Conrad, NOSTROMO 111

Cooper, THE PIONEERS 99

Cooper, THE PRAIRIE 26

Crane, RED BADGE OF COURAGE, SEL'D PROSE & POETRY 47

Dante, THE DIVINE COMEDY 72

Defoe, MOLL FLANDERS 25

De Forest, MISS RAVENEL'S CONVERSION 74

Dickens, GREAT EXPECTATIONS 20

Dickens, HARD TIMES 95

Dickens, OLIVER TWIST 115

Dostoevsky, THE FRIEND OF THE FAMILY and THE ETERNAL HUSBAND 119

Dreiser, SISTER CARRIE 86

Dryden, SELECTED WORKS 60

Eliot, ADAM BEDE 32

Eliot, SILAS MARNER 114

ELIZABETHAN FICTION 64

Emerson, SELECTED PROSE AND POETRY 30

ENGLISH PROSE AND POETRY 1660–1800: A SELECTION 110

Fielding, JOSEPH ANDREWS 15

FIFTEEN MODERN AMERICAN POETS 79

Flaubert, MADAME BOVARY 2

FOUR MODERN PLAYS: FIRST SERIES, Rev. Ibsen, Shaw, O'Neill, Chekhov 90

FOUR MODERN PLAYS: SECOND SERIES, Ibsen, Wilde, Rostand, Gorky 109

Franklin, AUTOBIOGRAPHY AND SELECTED WRITINGS 12

Frederic, THE DAMNATION OF THERON WARE 108

Frost, SELECTED POEMS OF ROBERT FROST 120

Garland, MAIN-TRAVELLED ROADS 66

Godwin, CALEB WILLIAMS 103

Goethe, FAUST: PART I 75

Goethe, SORROWS OF YOUNG WERTHER, NEW MELUSINA, NOVELLE 13

Gogol, DEAD SOULS 5

GREAT ENGLISH AND AMERICAN ESSAYS 34

Hardy, FAR FROM THE MADDING CROWD 98

Hardy, THE MAYOR OF CASTERBRIDGE 9

Hardy, THE RETURN OF THE NATIVE 39

Hauptmann, THREE PLAYS: The Weavers, Hannele, The Beaver Coat 52

Hawthorne, THE HOUSE OF THE SEVEN GABLES 89

Hawthorne, THE SCARLET LETTER 1

Hawthorne, SELECTED TALES AND SKETCHES 33

Hesse, STEPPENWOLF 122

Howe, E. W., THE STORY OF A COUNTRY TOWN 127

Howells, THE RISE OF SILAS LAPHAM 19

Ibsen, THREE PLAYS: Ghosts, Enemy of the People, Wild Duck 4

Irving, SELECTED PROSE 41

James, Henry, THE AMBASSADORS 104

James, Henry, THE AMERICAN 16

James, Henry, SELECTED SHORT STORIES 31

Johnson, RASSELAS, POEMS, & SELECTED PROSE 57

Keats, SELECTED POETRY AND LETTERS 50

Lincoln, SELECTED SPEECHES, MESSAGES, AND LETTERS 82

LITERATURE OF THE EARLY REPUBLIC 44

London, MARTIN EDEN 80

MASTERPIECES OF THE SPANISH GOLDEN AGE 93

Melville, MOBY DICK 6

Melville, SEL'D TALES AND POEMS 36

Melville, THE CONFIDENCE-MAN 126

Meredith, THE ORDEAL OF RICHARD FEVEREL 123

Milton, PARADISE LOST AND SELECTED POETRY AND PROSE 35

MODERN AMERICAN LITERATURE 53

Newman, THE IDEA OF A UNIVERSITY 102

Norris, Frank, MC TEAGUE 40

Parkman, THE DISCOVERY OF THE GREAT WEST: LA SALLE 77

PLUTARCH—EIGHT GREAT LIVES 105

Poe, SELECTED PROSE AND POETRY, Rev. 42

POETRY OF THE NEW ENGLAND RENAISSANCE, 1790–1890 38

Pope, SELECTED POETRY AND PROSE 46

RINEHART BOOK OF SHORT STORIES 59

RINEHART BOOK OF SHORT STORIES, Alt. Ed. 129

RINEHART BOOK OF VERSE 58

Robinson, E. A., SEL. EARLY POEMS AND LETTERS 107

Roosevelt, F. D., SPEECHES, MESSAGES, PRESS CONFERENCES, & LETTERS 83

Scott, THE HEART OF MIDLOTHIAN 14

SELECTED AMERICAN PROSE, 1841–1900 94

SELECTIONS FROM GREEK AND ROMAN HISTORIANS 88

SEVENTEENTH CENTURY POETRY 124

SEVENTEENTH CENTURY PROSE 125

Shakespeare, FIVE PLAYS: Hamlet; King Lear; Henry IV, Part I; Much Ado about Nothing; The Tempest 51

Shakespeare, AS YOU LIKE IT, JULIUS CAESAR, MACBETH 91

Shakespeare, TWELFTH NIGHT, OTHELLO 92

Shaw, SELECTED PLAYS AND OTHER WRITINGS 81

Shelley, SELECTED POETRY AND PROSE 49

SIR GAWAIN AND THE GREEN KNIGHT 97

Smollet, HUMPHREY CLINKER 48

SOUTHERN STORIES 106

Spenser, SELECTED POETRY 73

Sterne, TRISTRAM SHANDY 37

Stevenson, MASTER OF BALLANTRAE 67

Strindberg, SELECTED PLAYS AND PROSE 130

Swift, GULLIVER'S TRAVELS 10

Swift, SELECTED PROSE AND POETRY 78

Tennyson, SELECTED POETRY 69

Thackeray, HENRY ESMOND 116

Thackeray, VANITY FAIR 76

Thoreau, WALDEN, ON THE DUTY OF CIVIL DISOBEDIENCE 8

Thoreau, A WEEK ON THE CONCORD AND MERRIMACK RIVERS 118

Trollope, BARCHESTER TOWERS 21

Turgenev, FATHERS AND CHILDREN 17

Twain, THE ADVENTURES OF HUCKLEBERRY FINN 11

Twain, ROUGHING IT 61

Vergil, THE AENEID 63

VICTORIAN POETRY: Clough to Kipling 96

Wharton, HOUSE OF MIRTH 113

Whitman, LEAVES OF GRASS AND SELECTED PROSE 28

Wordsworth, THE PRELUDE, SEL'D SONNETS & MINOR POEMS, Rev. & Enl.